ACA
Advocacy
Competencies

A Social Justice
Framework for Counselors

Manivong J. Ratts
Rebecca L. Toporek
Judith A. Lewis

AMERICAN COUNSELING ASSOCIATION
2461 Eisenhower Avenue
Alexandria, VA 22331
www.counseling.org

ACA Advocacy Competencies
A Social Justice Framework for Counselors

American Counseling Association
2461 Eisenhower Avenue
Alexandria, VA 22331

Director of Publications
Carolyn C. Baker

Production Manager
Bonny E. Gaston

Copy Editor
Elaine Dunn

Editorial Assistant
Catherine A. Brumley

Text and cover design by Bonny E. Gaston

Library of Congress Cataloging-in-Publication Data

Ratts, Manivong J.
ACA advocacy competencies: a social justice framework for counselors / Manivong J. Ratts, Rebecca L. Toporek, and Judith A. Lewis
    p. cm.
  Includes bibliographical references and index.
  ISBN 978-1-55620-293-3 (alk. paper)
  1. Counseling psychology—Moral and ethical aspects. 2. Social advocacy. 3. Social justice. I. Toporek, Rebecca. II. Lewis, Judith A., 1939– III. American Counseling Association. IV. Title.
  BF636.67.R38 2010
  158'.3—dc22   2009029843

 # Dedication

This book is written in honor of the late *Dr. Mary Smith Arnold* (1946–2003) and *Dr. Reese M. House* (1938–2007), whose leadership, inspiration, and commitment to social justice have made everlasting contributions to the field of counseling and the American Counseling Association (ACA) Advocacy Competencies. Their unwavering commitment to social justice and advocacy is summarized below.

Dr. Mary Smith Arnold devoted her life to the struggle against oppression in all its forms. From the times she spent marching with Dr. Martin Luther King, Jr., to her latest efforts against the war in Iraq, Dr. Arnold was staunch in her convictions. In her personal life, she exemplified all that is meant by *advocacy competency*. In her professional life, she put this talent and wisdom to work in the counseling models she developed and in the inspiring mentorship she gave to the budding advocates who were her students. She also played a major role in awakening ACA and its divisions to the role of the counseling profession in antioppression work. Dr. Arnold originated her "Unlearning Oppression" workshop when she was still a doctoral student at the University of Iowa. Over the years she spent at Kent State University and then at Governors State University, she offered this training hundreds of times and taught scores of colleagues how to begin unlearning oppression themselves and teach others in a way that never engendered defensiveness. She understood how important it was to know all forms of oppression, to recognize that all of us are "sometimes in the shoes of the oppressor and sometimes in the shoes of the oppressed," and to be good allies across difference. As a scholar, she published widely on advocacy and diversity. As a leader, she joined in the effort to create Counselors for Social Justice (CSJ), a division of ACA; acted as CSJ's representative to the ACA Governing Council; and served as a valuable member of the Advocacy Competencies Task Force. The Mary Smith Arnold Anti-Oppression Award is given annually in her honor.

Reese M. House was one of the coauthors of the ACA Advocacy Competencies as a founding member of Counselors for Social Justice. A professor emeritus of school counselor education at Oregon State University (OSU), he left OSU to join the Education Trust in 1997 and was hired by Dr. Pat Martin to become program director of the National Center for Transforming School Counseling (NCTSC) from 2002 to 2006. In that time, over 100 school districts around the United States learned the new vision principles for transforming school counseling and over 40 counselor education/school counseling programs redid their curricula and practices based on Dr. Martin and Dr. House's work with the NCTSC. The focus on leadership and advocacy, including the importance of helping to close achievement and opportunity gaps for school counselors, became a part of the American School Counselor Association (ASCA) 2004 Ethical Standards for School Counselors, the ASCA National School Counseling Program Framework Model, and the 2009 Council for Accreditation of Counseling and Related Educational Programs' standards for all counselor education specialties.

In 2007, he received ACA's Arthur A. Hitchcock Distinguished Professional Service Award. In addition to transforming school counseling, Dr. House was a leader in focusing counselor education on issues of advocacy along with his OSU colleagues. During his time at OSU, he was founder and initial executive director of the Cascade AIDS Project in Portland, Oregon, and a board member with Oregon gay rights advocacy group Right to Privacy. His legacy of mentoring countless graduate students and school counselor educators and advocating for the academic, career, and college success of every K–12 student lives on with the annual Reese M. House Social Justice Advocacy award presented annually by Counselors for Social Justice.

Table of Contents

Section I
Transgressing Traditional Counseling Paradigms:
Connecting Social Justice and the ACA Advocacy Competencies

Section II
From Theory to Practice:
Application of the ACA Advocacy Competencies

Advocacy Across Populations

Section III
20/20: The Future of the Counseling Profession

 **Preface**

> *Getting a new idea adopted, even when it has obvious advantages,*
> *is difficult. Many innovations require a lengthy period of many years*
> *from the time when they become available to the time when they are*
> *widely adopted. Therefore, a common problem for many individuals and*
> *organizations is how to speed up the rate of diffusion of an innovation.*
>
> —Everett M. Rogers,
> *Diffusion of Innovations,* 2003, p. 1

This book is for the helping professional who seeks to eradicate society of the oppressive social, political, and economic conditions that impede human growth and development. Moreover, this book demonstrates how the American Counseling Association (ACA) Advocacy Competencies can be used as a framework for implementing microlevel and macrolevel advocacy strategies. The underlying premise behind the creation of the Advocacy Competencies is the belief that clients bring with them a complex set of problems that cannot be resolved simply through interventions that take place in the traditional office environment. Counselors need to also attend to the social milieu. In other words, counselors need to be adept at both individual counseling and community-based work if they wish to help clients achieve optimal psychological health and well-being. The Advocacy Competencies can help counselors achieve this goal.

The publication of this book is timely given the ACA Governing Council's endorsement of the Advocacy Competencies in 2003. This endorsement, coupled with the rise in the social justice counseling perspective, brings advocacy to the forefront of the profession. It has taken some time for the field as a whole to become familiar with the Advocacy Competencies. We attribute much of this to the fact that new ideas, no matter how beneficial they may be, take time for an organization to fully embrace. To help speed up the rate of adoption, and to diffuse any anxieties people may have about the Advocacy Competencies, we felt a book of this nature was needed.

Overview of the Book

This book is categorized into three sections. Section I is titled "Transgressing Traditional Counseling Paradigms: Connecting Social Justice and the ACA Advocacy Competencies." This section provides a foundation for understanding the place advocacy and social justice have in the field. The chapters in this section help to connect advocacy, social justice, and the Advocacy Competencies. An instrument is introduced in this section as a tool to help counselors determine their level of advocacy competence.

Section II is titled "From Theory to Practice: Application of the ACA Advocacy Competencies." The purpose of this section is to demonstrate the generalizability and applicability of the Advocacy Competencies. Chapters in this section offer examples of how the Advocacy Competencies can be used with diverse client populations (e.g., clients of color; clients with disabilities; lesbian, gay, bisexual, and transgender clients; etc.), across various counseling settings (e.g., K–12 schools, private practice, community colleges, etc.), and in specific specialty areas (e.g., group, career, drug and alcohol, etc.). Authors for this section were selected on the basis of their commitment to advancing social justice issues in their respective areas of expertise.

We titled Section III "20/20: The Future of the Counseling Profession" because we wanted to leave readers with an idea of what we hope the profession aspires to become. In this section we review and summarize the common factors and fresh ideas offered in Section II of the book. Strategies and suggestions for bringing these ideas into the mainstream of the counseling profession are also discussed.

To provide a consistent approach across all of the chapters, we asked each author to address the following questions in his or her chapter:

- What is the primary rationale for applying the Advocacy Competencies in your specific setting, specialty area, or population?
- Given the needs of the population you serve, how would you use the Advocacy Competencies to benefit your clients or students?
- How might issues of multiculturalism and diversity affect the advocacy program you describe in this chapter?
- What challenges might counselors face in implementing the Advocacy Competencies in your particular setting or specialty area?
- What are the expected benefits of carrying out the advocacy strategies that have been described in your chapter?

Whether you are a student, counselor, or counselor educator, we hope you will find this book useful. We believe the combination of theory and practical application offered in this book will provide readers with concrete strategies for how to operationalize the Advocacy Competencies. In addition, we hope the comprehensive nature of this book will help readers to see that the Advocacy Competencies are applicable across a variety of settings and specialty areas, and with various client populations. More important, we hope this book will help the clients and communities you serve to address the lethal impact oppression has on human growth and development.

—Manivong J. Ratts
Seattle University

—Rebecca L. Toporek
San Francisco State University

—Judith A. Lewis
Governors State University

Acknowledgments

The editors would like to thank Kari Aleshire and Bridgette Bethea, students at Seattle University, for their assistance with this book.

•

Manivong J. Ratts
I would like to thank my parents for their support and my father for instilling in me a sense of social justice.

•

Rebecca L. Toporek
I would like to thank Phil, Kaiya, and Dylan for their patience and support.

•

Judith A. Lewis
I would like to thank the faculty, staff, and students at Governors State University.

About the Editors

Manivong J. Ratts, PhD, NCC, is assistant professor and school counseling program director in the Department of Counseling and School Psychology at Seattle University. He received his PhD in counselor education and supervision from Oregon State University (OSU). He also holds a master's degree in school counseling from OSU, a bachelor's degree in psychology from Western Washington University, and an associate of arts and science degree from Yakima Valley Community College. He has published in the areas of social justice, multicultural and advocacy competence, and school counseling. His scholarship promotes social justice as a "fifth force" among counseling paradigms. He also serves on the editorial board of the *Journal of Counseling & Development* and the *Journal of Social Action*. He is the founder of Seattle University Counselors for Social Justice (www.sucsj.org) and is the recipient of the 2006 O'Hana Award from Counselors for Social Justice and the 2008 Professional Development Award from the Association for Multicultural Counseling and Development.

Rebecca L. Toporek, PhD, is a counselor educator, associate professor, and coordinator of the career counseling specialization at San Francisco State University. She was a member of the American Counseling Association Task Force that developed the Advocacy Competencies and has written numerous articles and chapters in the areas of advocacy, social justice, community engagement, multicultural competence and training, and career counseling. In addition, she coedited the *Handbook for Social Justice in Counseling and Psychology* and the *Handbook of Multicultural Competencies* and is coeditor of the *Journal for Social Action in Counseling and Psychology*. She worked for over 10 years as a career counselor and community college counselor and in 2001 received her PhD in counseling psychology from the University of Maryland, College Park.

Judith A. Lewis received her PhD in counseling from the University of Michigan. She is a retired professor in the College of Health Professions at Governors State University. She has served as president of the American Counseling Association (ACA) and the International Association of Marriage and Family Counselors. She has published a number of books, chapters, and articles related to counseling and advocacy and chaired the ACA Task Force that was charged with developing the Advocacy Competencies.

# About the Authors

Loretta J. Bradley, PhD, is a Paul Whitfield Horn professor and coordinator of counselor education at Texas Tech University. Prior to her affiliation at Texas Tech, Dr. Bradley held positions at Temple University and Peabody College of Vanderbilt University. Dr. Bradley was president of the American Counseling Association (ACA) from 1998 to 1999 and president of the Association for Counselor Education and Supervision (ACES) from 1995 to 1996. Her theme as president of ACA was "Advocacy: A Voice for Our Clients and Communities." Dr. Bradley has been the corecipient of research awards from the British Association for Counselling and Psychotherapy, ACA, and ACES. She is one of 25 counselors featured in the book *Legends and Legacies.* Dr. Bradley has been a frequent speaker and writer at counseling conferences and in journals.

Robert C. Chope, PhD, is professor in the Department of Counseling at San Francisco State University, where he founded the career counseling program. He is also the founder of the Career and Personal Development Institute in San Francisco, a practice that he has had for over 29 years. His is one of the oldest professional career development practices in the United States and is the source of much of the data featured in his consultation and scholarship. Dr. Chope has been licensed in California as a marriage and family therapist since 1971 and a psychologist since 1977 and has been listed in the National Registry of Health Care Providers in Psychology since 1980. He is the president (2008–2009) of the National Employment Counseling Association. In March 2008, Dr. Chope was honored as a fellow of the American Counseling Association. In June 2008, Dr. Chope was initiated into the H. B. McDaniel Hall of Fame at Stanford University for his "exemplary contributions to the field of counseling and guidance."

Hugh C. Crethar, PhD, is associate professor of counseling and counseling psychology in the School of Applied Health and Educational Psychology at Oklahoma State University. He has served in numerous positions within the American Counseling Association and was the 2007–2008 president of Counselors for Social Justice. His scholarly interests include the promotion of multicultural and advocacy competence in the field of counseling, school counseling, professional development of counselors, and counselors as academic leaders, change agents, and advocates.

Jerome V. D'Agostino, PhD, associate professor of education and human ecology at The Ohio State University, earned his doctorate in 1997 from the University of Chicago in measurement, evaluation, and statistical analysis. He specializes in applied measurement and assessment. Over the past 9 years, he has conducted several studies on the validity of standards-based assessments. He has served on numerous assessment advisory committees and presently is chair of the Arizona Technical Advisory Committee for AIMS (the state standards-based assessments). He has extensive experience in working with educators to develop formative assessments to monitor learning. He led a team that collaborated with science teachers in Tucson, Arizona, to develop online, formative assessments aligned with the districts' science curriculum, and he has conducted numerous workshop throughout the country on classroom grading and test score interpretation for teachers. Many of his over 30 publications have appeared in assessment journals such as *Applied Measurement in Education* and *Educational Assessment* and evaluation journals such as *Educational Evaluation and Policy Analysis.* In 2000, he was awarded a Spencer/National Academy of Education Postdoctoral Fellowship to study teacher tests, and he presently serves on the editorial board of the *Journal of Psychoeducational Assessment, Educational Assessment,* and *Reading Research Quarterly.* Dr. D'Agostino has been involved in research funded by over $3 million from organizations such as the National Science Foundation, U.S. Department of Education, and Spencer Foundation.

Matthew A. Diemer, PhD, is assistant professor in the Department of Counseling, Educational Psychology and Special Education at Michigan State University. His research interests include critical consciousness, youth sociopolitical development, vocational psychology, and structural equation modeling. His research examines factors that help marginalized youths negotiate social inequity and self-determine their lives within an inequitable opportunity structure. He serves on the editorial boards of the *Journal of Counseling Psychology* and the *Journal of Counseling & Development.*

Ryan D. Duffy, MA, is a doctoral candidate in counseling psychology at the University of Maryland, College Park, and is currently a predoctoral intern at the University of Delaware's Center for Counseling and Student Development. He received his bachelor's degree from Boston College and master's degree from the University of Maryland, College Park. His research interests are broadly in the area of vocational psychology, and he has published on topics related to work values, job satisfaction, research productivity, and the interface of spirituality and career development.

Judith C. Durham, APRN, PhD, LPC, is associate professor at Saint Joseph College, Connecticut, in the Department of Counseling and Family Therapy. Having begun professionally as a psychiatric nurse, she has maintained a psychotherapy/counseling/supervision practice for many years. She has been active in the Association for Counselor Education and Supervision (ACES) on national and regional levels, serving as North Atlantic Regional Association for Counselor Education and Supervision president (2004–2005) and ACES president (2007–2008). Her area of specialization is multicultural counseling, and her scholarly pursuits include using immersion experiences and reflective practice to enhance cultural competence and a social justice advocacy orientation in counseling.

Jacqueline Elder, PsyD, CADC, is assistant professor in the graduate program of addictions studies at Governors State University, University Park, Illinois. She has worked clinically in the fields of mental health, substance abuse (for 28 years), and harm reduction (for 5 years). She has been a full-time educator in substance abuse counseling education for 10 years. She is a member of the Motivational Interviewing Network of Trainers and has used motivational interviewing since 1991. She has presented and trained in motivational interviewing in the United States and internationally. She is also a graduate of the Family Institute at Northwestern University in Evanston, Illinois, and is trained as a family therapist. She is currently the chair of the Advisory Council of the Illinois Department of Drug and Alcohol Abuse.

Noel Estrada-Hernández, PhD, CRC, is assistant professor of rehabilitation counseling at the University of Iowa, College of Education, Departments of Counseling, Rehabilitation, and Student Development. His research interests and published work are in the areas of psychosocial aspects and attitudes toward persons with disabilities, especially those with albinism; multicultural issues and competencies in rehabilitation counseling; and assistive technology for persons with disabilities. Dr. Estrada-Hernández is an active member of various professional organizations and in 2007 received a research award from the American Rehabilitation Counseling Association.

Kathy M. Evans, PhD, is associate professor of counseling and program coordinator in the counselor education program at the University of South Carolina. Her research interests include multicultural counseling, supervision of multicultural counseling, racial identity, feminist identity, and career development. Her most recent book is titled *Gaining Cultural Competence in Career Counseling.* She is past president of the Southern Association for Counselor Education and Supervision.

Amy Ford, PhD, is the program advisor for the MA in community counseling program. She began her tenure at Northwest Christian University (NCU) in 2004, teaching courses in theories of counseling, counseling strategies and treatment, research methods, career development, and individual appraisal. She is one of the clinical supervisors in the community counseling program and provides counseling services to clients at the NCU Counseling Center.

Harriet L. Glosoff, PhD, LPC, NCC, ACS, is associate professor and coordinator of the doctoral program in counselor education and supervision at the University of Virginia. She has extensive experience in counseling supervision and in the provision of counseling services in diverse settings. She has served in numerous positions within the American Counseling Association (ACA) and its divisions. Most recently, she was president of the Association for Counselor Education and Supervision, chair of the ACA Ethics Committee, and secretary of the Virginia Counselors Association. Her scholarly interests include ethical and cultural issues in counseling, supervision, and counselor education; social justice and advocacy; and spirituality and counseling.

Jane Goodman, PhD, is professor emerita of counseling at Oakland University in Rochester, Michigan. She was the 2001–2002 president of the American Counseling Association (ACA), during which time she commissioned the ACA Advocacy Competencies. She is a past president and Eminent Career Awardee of the National Career Development Association (NCDA). She is also a founding member of Counselors for Social Justice. She is the author of many articles and book chapters, primarily in the area of transitions and the career development of adults, including the third edition of *Counseling Adults in Transition* (with Nancy Schlossberg and Mary Anderson) and the *NCDA Case Book* (with Drs. Spencer Niles and Mark Pope). She is the mother or stepmother of seven children and has eight grandchildren on whom she dotes.

Bret Hendricks, EdD, is associate professor of counselor education in the College of Education at Texas Tech University. He is a licensed professional counselor (Texas) and a licensed professional counselor supervisor (Texas). Dr. Hendricks has published research articles in national and international journals and is a frequent speaker at regional, national, and international conferences. His speaking experience includes presentations at numerous international, national, state, and regional conferences. He serves on the editorial boards of two national journals. Dr. Hendricks served as the president of the International Association of Marriage and Family Counselors (2006–2008) and is very active in professional counseling organizations.

A. Michael Hutchins, PhD, is a licensed professional counselor in private practice in Tucson, Arizona. He works primarily in individual and group settings with men who have histories of early childhood abuse and trauma, and he has been active in human rights and social justice advocacy endeavors throughout his career. He was the founding president of Counselors for Social Justice and is a past president and fellow of the Association for Specialists in Group Work. He currently serves on the City of Tucson Gay, Lesbian, Bisexual and Transgender Commission, which advises the mayor and city council. Dr. Hutchins has become an avid cyclist and can likely be found on one of the many bike paths in Tucson early in the morning.

Kelley R. Kenney, EdD, NCC, LPC, is a licensed professional counselor and a full professor in the Department of Counseling and Human Services at Kutztown University, Kutztown, Pennsylvania, where she coordinates the student affairs administration and college counseling graduate programs. Dr. Kenney is a coauthor of *Counseling Multiracial Families,* published by Sage, and *Counseling the Multiracial Population: Couples, Individuals, and Families,* training video, distributed by Insight Media and Micro-training Associates, as well as an author and coauthor of numerous articles, monographs, and book chapters regarding the multiracial population. She is a cochair of the American Counseling Association's (ACA's) Multiracial/Multiethnic Counseling Concerns Interest Network, a board member of the Association of Multiethnic Americans, and the Governing Council representative for ACA's North Atlantic region.

Mark E. Kenney, MEd, NCC, LPC, is a licensed professional counselor, coordinator of the Diakon Family Life Services (Topton, Pennsylvania), Pride Bridge-Builders LGBT (Lesbian, Gay, Bisexual, Transgender) Grant, and an adjunct professor at Chestnut Hill College/DeSales University campus in the Department of Counseling Psychology and Human Services, Center Valley, Pennsylvania, and Albright College Department of Interdisciplinary Studies, Reading, Pennsylvania. He is a coauthor of *Counseling Multiracial Families,* published by Sage, and *Counseling the Multiracial Population: Couples, Individuals, and Families,* training video, distributed by Insight Media and Micro-training Associates, as well as coauthor of several book chapters addressing the multiracial population. He is cochair of the American Counseling Association's Multiracial/Multiethnic Counseling Concerns Interest Network and board member of the Association of Multiethnic Americans.

William Ming Liu, PhD, is associate professor and program coordinator of counseling psychology at the University of Iowa. He received his doctorate in counseling psychology from the University of Maryland, College Park. His research interests are in social class and classism, men and masculinity, and multicultural competencies. He has been given the Emerging Leader Award in 2008 from the Committee on Socioeconomic Status (American Psychological Association [APA]), the Emerging Young Professional Award (Division 45, APA), and the Researcher of the Year Award (Division 51, APA). He is the associate editor for *Psychology of Men and Masculinity* and has served on the editorial boards of *The Counseling Psychologists, Cultural Diversity and Ethnic Minority Psychology, Journal of Multicultural Counseling and Development,* and *Clinician's Research Digest.* He one of the editors of the *Handbook of Multicultural Competencies in Counseling and Psychology* (Sage, 2003), an editor of the forthcoming *Culturally Responsive Counseling With Asian American Men* (Routledge), the author of the forthcoming *Social Class and Classism in the Helping Professions: Research, Theory, and Practice* (Sage), and the editor of the forthcoming *Handbook of Social Class in Counseling* (Oxford University Press).

Renée A. Middleton, PhD, is the dean of the College of Education at Ohio University. Dr. Middleton holds a BS in speech and hearing, an MA in clinical audiology, and a PhD in rehabilitation administration. She advocates for issues concerning shared governance, multicultural diversity, and effective learning. Prior to being dean of education at Ohio University, Dr. Middleton served as director of the Office of Research, Human Resources and Outreach, College of Education, at Auburn University. Dr. Middleton's over 19 years of research experience include areas of expertise in disability policy issues, education and workforce diversity, aging and disability, White racial identity development, and multicultural counseling competencies. Her consultation years of experience include collaborative efforts with the Office of Special Education and Rehabilitation Services and the National Institute for Disability and Rehabilitation Research. She is dually proficient in both college- and universitywide outreach related efforts as well as the obtaining of multiple grant funding to enhance diverse areas of teaching and learning. Dr. Middleton's areas of professional service include but are not limited to the National Rehabilitation Association, National Rehabilitation Counseling Association, American Counseling Association, American Rehabilitation Counseling Association, National Council on Rehabilitation Education, Consortium on Native American Rehabilitation, past president of the National Association of Multicultural Rehabilitation Concerns, Association for Multicultural Counseling and Development, and the Association for Counselor Education and Supervision, all of which she has served in varying capacities including editorial board, editorial consultant, and committee chairs.

Ameena S. Mu'min, MSEd, is a doctoral candidate in the counseling and higher education program at Ohio University. Ms. Mu'min holds a BA in psychology from Kentucky State University and an MSEd in community counseling from the University of Dayton. She is a member of various counseling associations, including the National Rehabilitation Association, National Association for Multicultural Rehabilitation Concerns, Ohio Rehabilitation Association (board member), Central Ohio Rehabilitation Association, and Ohio Counseling Association. She is currently president of the Southeast Ohio Counseling Association; serves as the Awards Committee Chair for the Ohio Association for Spiritual, Ethical, and Religious Values in Counseling; and serves in other national and statewide counseling associations. In addition, she serves on the Ohio University Graduate Student Senate as the representative for the counseling and higher education department. Ms Mu'min's most notable activities within these organizations are her dedication to political awareness through advocacy and grassroots efforts in governmental policy as they affect counselors in Ohio.

Joseph S. Pangelinan, MS, NCC, LPC, is a doctoral student at the University of Missouri–Saint Louis (UMSL) and is from Micronesia. He has taught multicultural counseling, career counseling, and both practicum and field experience courses. He is the director of behavior studies at Logos School in Saint Louis, Missouri. He is the author of one book and six other articles and chapters in the professional literature and recipient of the UMSL Outstanding Doctoral Student Award. As a counselor for lower socioeconomic status people in Micronesia and now in Missouri, he has seen and sees the need for advocacy in counseling every day.

Jennifer Pepperell, PhD, NCC, LPC, is an assistant professor at Minnesota State University, Mankato. Prior to moving into a faculty position, her primary clinical focus had been with children and adolescents in both shelter and school settings. She completed her doctoral degree at Oregon State University in counselor education and supervision. Her areas of interest are related to girls, identity development, and other feminist issues, research all done primarily from a qualitative perspective.

Mark Pope, EdD, NCC, MCC, MAC, ACS, is professor and chair of the Division of Counseling and Family Therapy at the University of Missouri–Saint Louis. When he was American Counseling Association president in 2003–2004, the theme of his national convention was "The Professional Counselor: Practice, Science, and Client Advocacy." His undergraduate major in political science and his graduate degrees in counseling prepared him to be a tremendous advocate for his clients. His cultural context, growing up as a poor, gay Cherokee from rural southeast Missouri, impelled him toward such advocacy. He is the author of 6 books, 33 book chapters, 42 journal articles, and over 100 professional presentations at the international, national, and state levels. He was president of the National Career Development Association (NCDA) and Association for Lesbian, Gay, Bisexual, and Transgender Issues in Counseling, editor of *The Career Development Quarterly*, and recipient of the NCDA Eminent Career Award, the highest award in career counseling and development.

Mona C. Robinson, PhD, CRC, PC, LSW, is assistant professor of counselor education at Ohio University. Dr. Robinson holds a BS in psychology, MA in rehabilitation counseling, and PhD in rehabilitation services from The Ohio State University. Prior to her employment at Ohio University, Dr. Robinson served as a counselor and administrator of vocational rehabilitation counseling and employment services to persons with severe mental illness and other barriers to employment. She also served as a consultant and adjunct professor at Wilberforce University. Dr. Robinson teaches core counselor education courses for master's- and doctoral-level students. Her areas of expertise include rehabilitation counselor education, psychiatric rehabilitation, multicultural counseling, dual diagnosis, and clinical supervision with an emphasis on multicultural concerns. Dr. Robinson is the immediate past president of the Ohio Rehabilitation Association, board member of the National Association of Multicultural Rehabilitation Concerns, board member of the National Rehabilitation Association Great Lakes Region, and past president of the Ohio Rehabilitation Counseling Association. She is a member of several professional organizations, including the Ohio Counseling Association, National Counseling Association, National Council on Rehabilitation Education, and National Rehabilitation Counseling Association.

Deborah J. Rubel, PhD, has been an assistant professor of counselor education in the College of Education at Oregon State University since 2002. Raised in interior Alaska, she received her BS in food science from Utah State University. After a midlife career change, she received her master's degree in mental health counseling and doctorate in counselor education from Idaho State University. Her areas of specialization are group work, multicultural/social justice counseling, and qualitative research methodology.

Anneliese A. Singh, PhD, LPC, NCC, is assistant professor in the Department of Counseling and Human Development Services at the University of Georgia. She received her doctorate in counseling psychology from Georgia State University in 2007. Her clinical, research, and advocacy interests include lesbian, gay, bisexual, transgender, and queer (LGBTQ) youths; Asian American/Pacific Islander counseling and psychology; multicultural counseling and social justice training; qualitative methodology with historically marginalized groups (e.g., people of color, LGBTQ people, immigrants); feminist theory and practice; and empowerment interventions with survivors of trauma. Dr. Singh has been the president of the Association of Lesbian, Gay, Bisexual, and Transgender Issues. She is the recipient of the 2007 Ramesh and Vijaya Bakshi Community Change Award and the 2008 O'Hana Award from Counselors for Social Justice for her organizing work to end child sexual abuse in South Asian communities and to increase visibility of South Asian LGBTQ people.

Cirecie A. West-Olatunji, PhD, is assistant professor of counselor education at the University of Florida and is the immediate past president of the Association for Multicultural Counseling and Development. Her publications include coauthorship of three books, several book chapters, and numerous peer-reviewed journal articles. She has disseminated her research at national and international conferences and provided consultation in Brazil, Canada, China, Ghana, Japan, Malaysia, Singapore, and South Africa. She has also been involved as an educational consultant in a public television initiative to create a children's television show focusing on diversity through KCET-TV in Los Angeles, California ("Puzzle Place").

Marsha I. Wiggins, PhD, LPC, NCC, LMFT, is chair and professor in the Division of Counseling Psychology and Counselor Education at the University of Colorado, Denver. She received her master's of divinity from Emory University and her PhD in counselor education from the University of Florida. Dr. Wiggins has provided clinical counseling services to children, adults, and families. She is an ordained minister in the United Methodist Church and has served in several churches in Florida. Dr. Wiggins has specializations in spirituality, marriage and family, sexual abuse, family violence, parenting, and grief. She has written more than 30 journal articles and book chapters and has recently published the book *Integrating Religion and Spirituality in Counseling*. She has served on the editorial board of *Counseling and Values* and *The Family Journal*. She is a past president of the Colorado Association for Counselor Educators and the Colorado Association for Marriage and Family Counseling. Dr. Wiggins is a recipient of the University of Colorado, Denver, Teacher of the Year Award.

Chris Wood, PhD, NCC, NCSC, is a counselor educator at Seattle University. He has been a faculty member at The Ohio State University and the University of Arizona. He is the president-elect of the Western Association for Counselor Education and Supervision. Dr. Wood is on the editorial board of the *Professional School Counseling* journal and has published articles in *Professional School Counseling, Journal of College Counseling, Counselor Education and Supervision, The Elementary School Journal,* as well as numerous book chapters. He has previous experience as a high school counselor, a guidance department chair, a counselor/group leader at a residential youth facility for troubled teens, and a career counselor at an alternative school serving Grades 7–12. He was a career assessment coordinator and research assistant on a $1.3 million Community Employment Education Center grant from the Office of Adult and Vocational Education and a faculty research associate on a grant from the National Research Center for Career and Technical Education. Dr. Wood is one of the editors of the fifth edition of the National Career Development Association publication *A Counselor's Guide to Career Assessment Instruments*.

Section

I

Transgressing Traditional Counseling Paradigms

Connecting Social Justice and the ACA Advocacy Competencies

Chapter 1

Advocacy and Social Justice:
A Helping Paradigm for the 21st Century

Manivong J. Ratts, Judith A. Lewis, and Rebecca L. Toporek

Social justice counseling, also referred to as the "fifth force" in counseling (Ratts, 2009; Ratts, D'Andrea, & Arredondo, 2004), is an emerging paradigm that uses advocacy as a mechanism to address client problems. Counselors who integrate advocacy into their work with clients do so because they believe that human development issues cannot be resolved simply through interventions that occur in an office setting (Toporek, Gerstein, Fouad, Roysircar, & Israel, 2006). Counseling professionals need to also consider approaches that are geared toward altering oppressive environmental structures when situations call for such measures. The need for counselors to attend to the social milieu is based on the belief that client problems are often systemically based. If counselors are to operate from a social justice counseling perspective, they need to step outside of the rigid and often unyielding boundaries placed on them by professional organizations as well as certification and accreditation bodies.

Using advocacy as a mechanism to address oppressive social structures can be accomplished through the American Counseling Association (ACA) Advocacy Competencies developed by Lewis, Arnold, House, and Toporek (2002). The notion that the Advocacy Competencies can be used to improve conditions for those who have historically been disenfranchised in society shifts the helping paradigm, moving it from an intrapsychic-based model to a more social-justice-based model that requires counselors to balance microlevel and macrolevel advocacy strategies and interventions (Ratts, 2009).

There are many reasons behind the need for a social justice counseling perspective that is rooted in advocacy. One reason is related to the prevalence of oppression in society. Research continues to suggest that the "isms" such as racism, sexism, heterosexism, ableism, ageism, classism, and anti-Semitism have a debilitating effect on people's ability to achieve optimal mental health (Callahan, Brighton, & Hertberg-Davis, 2007). Despite what research suggests, counselors continue to use intrapsychic approaches that ignore the social milieu (Prilleltensky, 1994). Intrapsychic-based counseling approaches view client problems as an inner phenomenon and require that change resides within the client. Vera and Speight (2007) contended that ignoring the social milieu is problematic because it forces clients to "adapt to and cope with their environments, rather than change the social context, and in so doing, join the forces that perpetuate social injustice" (p. 373). Albee (1990) concurred, adding that systems interventions and community-based work are needed if problems are environmentally based.

Two, counselors have a moral and ethical obligation to advocate for clients because counselors are in a profession that is about helping people (Lee & Walz, 1998). Lee (2007) added that counselors need to do a more adequate job of determining when individual counseling is needed and when systems change interventions are necessary. This is a position that aligns with the *ACA Code of Ethics* (American Counseling Association, 2005), which states in Section A.6.a, "when appropriate, counselors advocate at the individual, group, institutional, and societal levels to examine potential barriers and obstacles that inhibit access and/or the growth and development of clients" (p. 5). This perspective is also reflected in the American School Counselor Association's (ASCA's, 2004) *Ethical Standards for School Counselors*, which states, "professional school counselors are advocates, leaders, collaborators and consultants who create opportunities for equity in access and success in educational opportunities by connecting their programs to the mission of schools" (p. 1).

Three, the United Nations' (1948) Universal Declaration of Human Rights also serves as a rationale behind the need for counselors to make advocacy and social justice a platform within the profession. Adopted by the United Nations General Assembly in 1948 and the ACA Governing Council in 2001, this document contains 30 articles that address various human rights issues. Developed by member countries, of which the United States is a part, the document serves as a guideline to ensuring that every individual is afforded the right to be treated with dignity and has the right to freedom, justice, and peace. As human service professionals concerned with the mental health of individuals, counselors may find themselves needing to enact social justice advocacy to ensure that clients' rights are not being violated. This may involve helping clients understand their rights as human beings and ensuring that counseling practices are not counter to these rights.

Four, the training that counselors receive also puts them in ideal positions to be change agents and advocates for social justice. According to Kiselica and Robinson (2001), counselors (a) have access to technology, (b) understand life span development issues, (c) possess cross-cultural communication skills, (d) understand how systems operate and their impact on human behavior and experience, and (e) possess research and assessment skills. These skills are foundational to being a successful agent of change. For example, counselors can use technology to develop websites to bring issues of equity to the public eye. In addition, understanding life span development issues and possessing cross-cultural communication skills allow counselors to determine whether client problems are biologically, psychologically, and/or sociologically based. This awareness and understanding will allow counselors opportunities to develop culturally appropriate advocacy strategies. Similarly, knowing how systems operate can help counselors determine whether client problems are a function of systemic barriers. Research and assessment can also be used to build a case for why advocacy with and on behalf of clients may be necessary with particular clients and populations.

It is critical that the profession consider the place social justice has in the field if it is to remain a viable resource to society. The world has changed and so too must the profession. The field can no longer remain static by relying on archaic practices and ways of thinking to solve 21st-century problems. If the profession is to remain a viable resource to society, it will need to make a shift in how counseling has traditionally been practiced. This can be achieved through the Advocacy Competencies. The generalizability of the Advocacy Competencies, as will be demonstrated in Section II of this book, makes it applicable across a variety of contexts and with various client populations. Moreover, we believe the Advocacy Competencies have the potential to transform the field in the same way the Multicultural Counseling Competencies developed by Sue, Arredondo, and McDavis (1992) revolutionized the profession. Specifically, the Advocacy Competencies have the potential to alter how client problems are conceptualized and the types of interventions used, and it can revolutionize the role of the professional counselor.

This chapter provides a foundation for understanding the connection between social justice, advocacy, and the Advocacy Competencies. A historical overview of social justice is provided along with a review of concepts related to social justice and their definitions in the literature. How the Advocacy Competencies can be used to help counseling professionals actualize social justice and advocacy in their work with clients, families, and communities will also be discussed.

Social Justice and Advocacy: A Historical Overview

Social justice and advocacy are intricately linked concepts that have been integral to the counseling profession since its inception in the early 1900s beginning with the work of Frank Parsons (Kiselica & Robinson, 2001). Parsons, also known as the father of vocational guidance, was a tireless social advocate for immigrants who sought better career opportunities. Clifford Beers continued Parsons's legacy of advocacy for oppressed communities by bringing issues of mental illness to the forefront. This helped change conditions for individuals with mental illness.

In the 1970s the social justice perspective gained momentum in the field with the social and political revolution occurring across America's landscape. This is perhaps best reflected in the 1971 special issue of the *Personnel and Guidance Journal* titled "Counseling and the Social Revolution" (Vol. 49, Issue 9). Articles published in this special issue addressed (a) the impact of social, political, and economic forces on client well-being; (b) the need for counselors to be change agents and advocates for social justice; and (c) the importance of adequately preparing counselors for social justice advocacy work in counselor education programs. This was also a period of time when terms such as *social advocacy* and *social action* began to appear with increasing frequency in the counseling literature (Ratts, 2006). In addition, the development of the Association for Non-White Concerns (ANWC), a division of the ACA, came to fruition in 1972 (Jackson, 1995). The creation of ANWC marked a significant milestone for addressing issues of racial inequality in the profession. It also reflected the beginning of the multicultural counseling movement. Similarly, in 1975, gay, lesbian, and bisexual issues became more prevalent in ACA with the creation of the Caucus for Gay and Lesbian Counselors (Rhode, 2009). In that same year, Hutchinson and Stadler (1975) published the book *Social Change Counseling: A Radical Approach*, arguing that counselors needed to adopt a social activist approach if issues of oppression were to be successfully addressed.

The 1980s saw a real shift away from advocacy for clients to advocacy for the profession (Fouad, Gerstein, & Toporek, 2006). The influence of managed care industries, psychiatry, and educational administrators on mental health and school counseling caused the profession to shift its focus to maintenance of the profession. The multicultural counseling perspective also became broader in scope during this time. In 1982, a historic call to the profession asserted the need for competence in multiculturalism across all counseling (Sue et al., 1982). Sue et al.'s article formed the foundation for later literature and standards for multicultural competence. In addition, helping professionals began to categorize variables such as gender, sexual orientation, social class, and religion under the "multicultural umbrella." This caused ANWC to change its name in 1985 to the Association for Multicultural Counseling and Development. The change in name better reflected its members and the complexities of human diversity. In 1987, ACA published a position paper on human rights. This paper signified the profession's commitment to advocating for the rights of those who are marginalized in society.

The 1990s saw a movement toward multicultural competence and a recommitment to advocacy for clients (Fouad et al., 2006). The notion that counselors needed to be multiculturally competent helping professionals led to the development of the Multicultural Counseling Competencies by Sue et al. (1992). Lewis and Arnold (1998) added that developing multicultural competence was limiting if it did not also include a focus on social justice and advocacy. The need for social justice and advocacy is perhaps best reflected in Lee and Walz's (1998) book, *Social Action: A Mandate for Counselors*. The authors argued that the role counselors play in society, coupled with the profession's ethical codes, required them to be change agents and advocates for social and political justice. The lesbian, gay, and bisexual movement also came to fruition in 1997 when ACA finally recognized the Association for Gay, Lesbian, and Bisexual Issues in Counseling as a division of ACA (Rhode, 2009). This recognition has been important in the development of the *Journal of Lesbian, Gay, Bisexual, and Transgender Issues in Counseling*.

Lewis and Bradley (2000) published an edited book titled *Advocacy in Counseling: Counselors, Clients, and Community* that conceptualized the place advocacy had in the counseling profession.

That same year, Jane Goodman, then president of ACA, commissioned a task force to make advocacy more prevalent in the field (Ratts, 2006). The work of the task force led to the creation of the Advocacy Competencies, which were then adopted by the ACA Governing Council in March 20–22, 2003. In an effort to facilitate implementation of the Advocacy Competencies, a special section was developed and published in the summer 2009 issue of the *Journal of Counseling & Development*. The social justice perspective also became more legitimized within the profession with the development of Counselors for Social Justice (CSJ). On September 27, 2002, the ACA Governing Council officially recognized CSJ as a division of the ACA. These developments led Ratts et al. (2004) to refer to the social justice perspective as a "fifth force" in counseling. In addition, Ratts (2009) argued that social justice is a paradigm unto itself, unique from the psychoanalytic, cognitive–behavioral, humanistic, and multicultural "forces" that currently exists in the field.

Overview of Social Justice Concepts

Comprehension of a social justice counseling perspective requires an understanding of concepts such as *social justice, advocacy,* and *change agent*. Adams, Bell, and Griffin (2007) described social justice as both a goal and a process. The goal of social justice is to ensure that all individuals have an opportunity to achieve their academic, career, and personal/social potential in society. However, helping clients achieve individual needs does not mean they can do whatever they want. As counselors, it is important that we help clients balance individual needs with the needs of the collective because we live in a democratic society. Bell (2007) added that the process of achieving social justice should be "democratic and participatory, inclusive and affirming of human agency and human capacities for working collaboratively to create change" (p. 2).

Advocacy can be viewed as the process of achieving social justice ideals. Specifically, advocacy involves taking social justice ideals and putting them into action. Toporek (2000) defined advocacy as "an action taken by a counseling professional to facilitate the removal of external and institutional barriers to clients' well-being" (p. 6). Lewis and Bradley (2000) described advocacy as an act of speaking out and advocating with and/or on behalf of an individual or a group.

Individuals who stand for social justice and incorporate advocacy in their practice are often referred to as change agents. Baker and Cramer (1972) defined a change agent as "someone who strives to move against the status quo when [she or he] feels that it is hurting those individuals whom [she or he] is trying to help" (p. 661). This description implies that a certain mindset or frame of mind is required to be a change agent. Nilsson and Schmidt's (2005) study suggested that change agents are socially and politically invested in their communities and possess a desire to create a just world.

Linking Oppression With Mental Health

Clients who live in oppressive conditions or experience oppression often face many obstacles in life. Adams et al. (2007) described oppression as a pervasive, restricting, hierarchical, and complex phenomenon that subjugates people to lesser roles in society. Harro (2000) added that living in a world in which oppression exists can lead those who are marginalized in society to develop psychosomatic symptoms such as depression and low self-esteem. Similarly, Jacobs (1994) argued that mental health issues are often externally based. Research seems to support this perspective. For example, a national study of K–12 public schools found that homophobia and heterosexism contributed to higher suicide rates, increased depression, and poor academic performance among lesbian, gay, bisexual, and transgender youths (Gay Lesbian Straight Education Network, 2007). Callahan et al. (2007) concluded in their study that youths of color and those in poverty tend to have more difficulty reaching their academic, career, and personal/social potential when compared with their European American and more affluent peers because of the barriers that racism and generational poverty placed on them.

The prevalence of oppression in society, coupled with the lethal impact it has on human growth and development, is a call to action of sorts for counselors to use advocacy to alter the social context. This seems especially important in light of Goodman et al.'s (2004) contention that intrapsychic-based helping models are not as effective as social justice–based helping paradigms that are grounded in advocacy because they do not address oppressive environmental structures. For this reason, counselors need to become adept at community-based interventions.

From Theory to Practice: A Rationale for the Advocacy Competencies

The negative impact oppression has on mental health, and the recent shift toward a social justice counseling perspective, can be met by using the Advocacy Competencies (Ratts, DeKruyf, & Chen-Hayes, 2007; Toporek, Lewis, & Crethar, 2009). The Advocacy Competencies provide counselors with a structure for addressing issues of oppression *with* and on *behalf* of clients. Moreover, the Advocacy Competencies, which will be explained in more detail in Chapter 2 of this book, offer a conceptual framework for implementing advocacy strategies (Lewis et al., 2002). Connecting social justice and advocacy with the Advocacy Competencies is timely given its adoption by the ACA Governing Council in March 2003 and the growing demand to make social justice advocacy more relevant in the field.

The ACA Governing Council's adoption of the Advocacy Competencies marks a significant moment in the profession. Moreover, it acknowledges that a shift needs to occur in how counseling services are delivered if the profession is to address systemic barriers that impede human growth and development. The shift toward use of the Advocacy Competencies has been considered so important that Washington State's Office of Superintendent of Public Instruction included the Advocacy Competencies as part of the state's professional certificate for school counselors seeking continuing licensure.

The framework of the Advocacy Competencies is also practical in that it helps counselors to determine whether clients are best served by using client/student, school/community, and/or public arena advocacy strategies. At the client/student level, counselors can use empowerment strategies such as narrative counseling to help clients/students externalize problems they may have initially internalized. Situations that call for school/community level advocacy may include collaborating with community leaders or consulting with teachers and building principals. Interventions at the public arena level can also be useful in certain situations and contexts. Lobbying legislators, attending community forums, creating websites to inform the general public, and writing grants are examples of public arena level advocacy strategies.

Implications for the Profession

We believe that the Advocacy Competencies are an important tool that can help counselors look at ways to assist clients from a broader perspective that goes beyond traditional helping roles and practices. Integrating the Advocacy Competencies into the profession will require an understanding of the change process, a willingness to try alternative approaches, and a period of self-reflection. As suggested by Ponzo (1974), developing patience and collaborating with others can go a long way to implementing social justice initiatives and programs. For this reason, counseling professionals would do well to familiarize themselves with the diffusion of innovation theory (Murray, 2008). The diffusion of innovation theory posits that a new idea, no matter how beneficial, takes time and can be difficult to implement (Rogers, 2003). Understanding when to take risks, how much information to give, the roles people play in an organization, and how an organization works can help to speed up the rate at which the Advocacy Competencies are infused into counselor training, accreditation bodies such as the Council for Accreditation of Counseling and Related Educational Programs, the ACA and ASCA ethical codes, certification and licensure policies, and, more important, counseling practices.

Being open to alternative helping approaches is also critical to embracing the Advocacy Competencies. Kiselica and Robinson (2001) argued that "rigid boundaries between the counselor and the client sometimes have the effect of shackling the humanity of the counselor, and consequently, impair the client–counselor relationship" (p. 395). This is important to note in light of the common misconception that advocacy is a skill set that belongs to the social work profession. Embracing alternative helping approaches requires moving outside of the rigid boundaries professional organizations such as ACA, the American Psychological Association, and the National Association of Social Workers tend to place on helping professionals. For this to occur, helping professionals need to stop being territorial with the services they purport to provide. There is no place for turf wars when it comes to helping human beings. As helping professionals, we can collaborate, learn from each other, and take the best from each other's profession to help clients achieve their academic, career, and personal/social goals.

Embracing the Advocacy Competencies also requires that counselors take the time to reflect on how being a social change agent fits with their personal and professional identity. This can be achieved by using the Advocacy Competencies Self-Assessment (ACSA) Survey© to understand one's level of advocacy competence as outlined in the Advocacy Competencies. (Note: The ACSA Survey© will be covered in Chapter 3.) More specifically, the ACSA Survey© can help counselors understand their level of competence as an advocate along the six domains of the Advocacy Competencies.

Conclusion

We conclude this chapter with a quote from Dr. Martin Luther King, Jr., in a speech he gave about the Vietnam War titled "Beyond Vietnam" at the Riverside Church in New York City on April 4, 1967:

> We are now faced with the fact, my friends, that tomorrow is today. We are confronted with the fierce urgency of now. In this unfolding conundrum of life and history, there is such a thing as being too late. Procrastination is still the thief of time. Life often leaves us standing bare, naked and dejected with a lost opportunity….Over the bleached bones and jumbled residues of numerous civilizations are written the pathetic words, "Too late." (King, 2001, p. 162)

As a counseling profession we all have a choice to make today. We can allow complacency to seep in and be passive observers of an oppressive status quo, or we can use this moment to change and revolutionize how counseling is practiced. The moment for change within the profession has never been more important than now. We must move past our complacency and act! We must not lose sight that we are a profession founded on social justice ideals. If as a profession we do not act we run the risk of losing our grip of being a crucial resource to society.

We can address, in Dr. King's words, the "fierce urgency of now" by integrating social justice into all facets of the profession. Our contention is that predominant counseling models and ways of helping are not adequately addressing the root of client problems. Counselors need to move beyond approaches that focus solely on helping clients gain insight. In other words, developing microskills, multicultural competence and helping clients understand that they live in poverty or that racism exists are not enough (Vera & Speight, 2003). While helpful, these types of approaches do not lead to sustainable changes. Instead, counselors need to adopt a social-justice-based helping model that is rooted in advocacy. We believe this can be achieved by using the Advocacy Competencies as a framework for conceptualizing client problems and interventions. The Advocacy Competencies ensure that clients, and the problems they present, will be examined through a lens that considers the individual and her or his environment. It is not too late.

References

Adams, M., Bell, L. A., & Griffin, P. (Eds.). (2007). *Teaching for diversity and social justice* (2nd ed.). New York: Routledge.

Albee, G. (1990). The futility of psychotherapy. *Journal of Mind and Behavior, 11,* 368–384.

American Counseling Association. (2005). *ACA code of ethics.* Alexandria, VA: Author.

American School Counselor Association. (2004). *Ethical standards for school counselors.* Retrieved May 14, 2007, from http://www.schoolcounselor.org/content.asp?contentid=173

Baker, S. B., & Cramer, S. H. (1972). Counselor or change agent: Support from the profession. *Personnel and Guidance Journal, 50,* 661–665.

Bell, L. A. (2007). Theoretical foundations for social justice education. In M. Adams, L. A. Bell, & P. Griffin (Eds.), *Teaching for diversity and social justice* (2nd ed., pp. 1–14). New York: Routledge.

Callahan, C. M., Brighton, C. M., & Hertberg-Davis, H. (2007). *Evaluation report: Accelerated progress program.* Retrieved September 1, 2009, from http://www.seattleschools.org/area/advlearning/APPEvaluationReportSeattle.pdf

Fouad, N. A., Gerstein, L. H., & Toporek, R. L. (2006). Social justice and counseling psychology in context. In R. L. Toporek, L. H. Gerstein, N. A. Fouad, G. Roysircar, & T. Israel (Eds.), *Handbook for social justice in counseling psychology: Leadership, vision, and action* (pp. 1–16). Thousand Oaks, CA: Sage.

Gay Lesbian Straight Education Network. (2007). *The 2007 National School Climate Survey: The experiences of lesbian, gay, bisexual, and transgender youth in our nation's schools.* Retrieved September 1, 2009, from http://www.glsen.org/cgi-bin/iowa/all/library/record/2340.html?state=research&type=research

Goodman, L. A., Liang, B., Helms, J. E., Latta, R. E., Sparks, E., & Weintrab, S. R. (2004). Training counseling psychologists as social justice agents: Feminist and multicultural principles in action. *The Counseling Psychologist, 32,* 793–837.

Harro, B. (2000). The cycle of socialization. In M. Adams, W. J. Blumenfeld, R. Castaneda, H. W. Hackman, M. L. Peters, & X. Zuniga (Eds.), *Readings for diversity and social justice* (pp. 15–21). New York: Routledge.

Hutchinson, M. A., & Stadler, H. A. (1975). *Social change counseling: A radical approach.* Boston: Houghton Mifflin.

Jackson, M. L. (1995). Multicultural counseling: Historical perspectives. In J. G. Ponterotto, J. M. Casas, L. Suzuki, & C. M. Alexander (Eds.), *Handbook of multicultural counseling* (pp. 3–16). Thousand Oaks, CA: Sage.

Jacobs, D. H. (1994). Environmental failure: Oppression is the only cause of psychopathology. *Journal of Mind and Behavior, 15,* 1–18.

King, M. L. K. (2001). Beyond Vietnam. In C. Carson & K. Shepard (Eds.), *A call to conscience: The landmark speeches of Dr. Martin Luther King, Jr.* (pp. 139–164). New York: Warner Books.

Kiselica, M. S., & Robinson, M. (2001). Bringing advocacy counseling to life: The history, issues, and human dramas of social justice work in counseling. *Journal of Counseling & Development, 79,* 387–398.

Lee, C. C. (Ed.). (2007). *Counseling for social justice* (2nd ed.). Alexandria, VA: American Counseling Association.

Lee, C. C., & Walz, G. R. (Eds.). (1998). *Social action: A mandate for counselors.* Alexandria, VA: American Counseling Association.

Lewis, J., & Arnold, M. S. (1998). From multiculturalism to social action. In C. C. Lee & G. R. Walz (Eds.), *Social action: A mandate for counselors* (pp. 51–65). Alexandria, VA: American Counseling Association and ERIC Counseling and Student Services Clearinghouse.

Lewis, J. A., Arnold, M. S., House, R., & Toporek, R. L. (2002). *ACA Advocacy Competencies.* Retrieved May 27, 2008, from http://www.counseling.org/Publications/

Lewis, J., & Bradley, L. (Eds.). (2000). *Advocacy in counseling: Counselors, clients, and community.* Greensboro, NC: ERIC Clearinghouse on Counseling and Student Services.

Murray, C. E. (2008). Diffusion of innovation theory: A bridge for the research–practice gap. *Journal of Counseling & Development, 87,* 108–116.

Nilsson, J. E., & Schmidt, C. K. (2005). Social justice advocacy among graduate students in counseling: An initial exploration. *Journal of College Student Development, 46,* 267–279.

Ponzo, Z. (1974). A counselor and change: Reminiscences and resolutions. *Personnel and Guidance Journal, 53,* 27–32.

Prilleltensky, I. (1994). *The morals and politics of psychology: Psychological discourse and the status quo.* New York: State University of New York Press.

Ratts, M. (2006). *Social justice counseling: A study of social justice counselor training in CACREP-accredited counselor preparation programs.* Unpublished doctoral dissertation, Oregon State University.

Ratts, M. J. (2009). Social justice counseling: Toward the development of a "fifth force" among counseling paradigms. *Journal of Humanistic Counseling, Education and Development, 48,* 160–172.

Ratts, M., D'Andrea, M., & Arredondo, P. (2004). Social justice counseling: Fifth "force" in field. *Counseling Today, 47,* 28–30.

Ratts, M. J., DeKruyf, L., & Chen-Hayes, S. F. (2007). The ACA Advocacy Competencies: A social justice advocacy framework for professional school counselors. *Professional School Counseling, 11,* 90–97.

Rhode, B. (2009). *ALGBTIC history.* Retrieved February 7, 2009, from http://www.algbtic.org/about/history.htm

Rogers, E. M. (2003). *Diffusion of innovations* (5th ed.). New York: Free Press.

Sue, D. W., Arredondo, P., & McDavis, R. J. (1992). Multicultural counseling competencies and standards: A call to the profession. *Journal of Multicultural Counseling and Development, 20,* 64–89.

Sue, D. W., Bernier, Y., Durran, A., Feinberg, L., Pederson, P. B., Smith, E. J., et al. (1982). Position paper: Cross-cultural counseling competencies. *The Counseling Psychologist, 10,* 45–52.

Toporek, R. L. (2000). Developing a common language and framework for understanding advocacy in counseling. In J. Lewis & L. Bradley (Eds.), *Advocacy in counseling: Counselors, clients, and community* (pp. 5–14). Greensboro, NC: CAPS Publications.

Toporek, R. L., Gerstein, L. H., Fouad, N. A., Roysircar, G., & Israel, T. (Eds.). (2006). *Handbook for social justice in counseling psychology: Leadership, vision, and action.* Thousand Oaks, CA: Sage.

Toporek, R., Lewis, J., & Crethar, H. (2009). Promoting systemic change through the Advocacy Competencies. *Journal of Counseling & Development, 87,* 260–268.

United Nations. (1948). *The universal declaration of human rights.* Retrieved February 7, 2009, from http://www.un.org/Overview/rights.html

Vera, E. M., & Speight, S. L. (2003). Multicultural competence, social justice, and counseling psychology: Expanding our roles. *The Counseling Psychologist, 31,* 253–272.

Vera, E. M., & Speight, S. L. (2007). Advocacy, outreach, and prevention: Integrating social action roles in professional training. In E. Aldarondo (Ed.), *Advancing social justice through clinical practice* (pp. 373–416). Mahwah, NJ: Erlbaum.

Chapter 2

The ACA Advocacy Competencies: An Overview

Rebecca L. Toporek, Judith A. Lewis, and Manivong J. Ratts

While the roots of the profession of counseling have acknowledged the significance of external forces in clients' lives, the extent to which counselors have focused attention on these external barriers has fluctuated and been influenced by the zeitgeist of the time. Until recently, there has been little guidance regarding appropriate use of advocacy in the context of counseling. The intent of this chapter is to introduce one milestone, the American Counseling Association (ACA) Advocacy Competencies (Lewis, Arnold, House, & Toporek, 2002), and describe the events leading to their development. We then provide an overview of the Advocacy Competencies model including its dimensions and domains. This introduction is intended to provide the reader with a basic structure and understanding of the Advocacy Competencies as well as facilitate application of the chapters that follow.

History and Development of the ACA Advocacy Competencies

In the past four decades, there has been a greater acknowledgment in the counseling field of the importance of cultural and sociopolitical factors on client, family, and community well-being. This acknowledgment did not occur spontaneously. Rather, it resulted from tremendous advocacy from counselors to bring issues of marginalized and historically underserved clients to the forefront (D'Andrea et al., 2001). In the process, the development of the Multicultural Counseling Competencies (Sue, Arredondo, & McDavis, 1992) established the need to acknowledge systemic and unjust conditions in clients' lives. Toporek, Lewis, and Crethar (2009) noted two important conditions created by the Multicultural Counseling Competencies:

> First, they showed that a well-thought-out and readily understandable set of competencies can play a key role in professional development. Second, they ensured the presence of a population of multiculturally competent counselors who could be in the vanguard of the social justice movement. (p. 261)

Simultaneously with the development of the multicultural movement, community counseling emphasized the need for counselors to be involved in client advocacy (e.g., Lewis & Lewis, 1977; Lewis, Lewis, Daniels, & D'Andrea, 1998).

In 1999, Loretta Bradley, then president of ACA, put forward a presidential theme of "Advocacy: A Voice for Our Clients and Communities." Reflecting this theme, authors were invited to contribute papers focused on advocacy with particular client groups and in particular settings. These papers shaped a special roundtable session at the ACA Convention and were subsequently published as an edited book (Lewis & Bradley, 2000). In 2000, Jane Goodman as president of ACA appointed an Advocacy Competencies Task Force charged with developing a set of competencies for counselors advocating for clients. These competencies were to focus on facilitating clients, schools, and communities in addressing and removing barriers to well-being and positive growth. In particular, the directive identified clients and communities that had limited access to resources and power. An important assumption of this charge was that counselors could play an important role in shifting the balance of inequity and injustice by directly and indirectly working with clients and communities to advocate for systemic change.

The task force created a model based on literature and practice in counseling and identified specific knowledge and skill areas to guide counselors in implementing advocacy in counseling practice (Lewis et al., 2002). The resulting Advocacy Competencies document was adopted by the ACA Governing Council in March 2003. The Advocacy Competencies document was made available to members through the ACA website, but a comprehensive description was not published until 6 years later (see Toporek et al., 2009).

In 2009, a special section in the *Journal of Counseling & Development (JCD)* was devoted to the Advocacy Competencies, featuring an introduction by Jane Goodman (2009) and a call to action by Gargi Roysircar (2009). The body of the section presented the first in-depth description of the competencies model (Toporek, Lewis, & Crethar, 2009) as well as three articles elaborating on each level of the Advocacy Competencies: individual (Ratts & Hutchins, 2009), community or school (Lopez-Baez & Paylo, 2009), and societal (Lee & Rodgers, 2009). While this special section of *JCD* provides a needed foundation for counselors, there is a need for further elaboration of the Advocacy Competencies across the various settings and populations with whom counselors work. This book endeavors to extend the discussion regarding applications of the Advocacy Competencies in just this way. First, however, an understanding of the Advocacy Competencies is needed.

As we will describe in this chapter, the Advocacy Competencies provide a framework for counselor practice and training toward addressing barriers faced by clients. In the following section, we provide an overview of the competencies beginning with a discussion of the two dimensions that shape the model followed by an elaboration of each of the six dimensions that make up the model.

Dimensions of the Advocacy Competencies

The Advocacy Competencies are organized around two intersecting dimensions, Extent of Client's Involvement and Level of Intervention, that create six domains: Empowerment, Client or Student Advocacy, Community Collaboration, Systems Advocacy, Public Information, and Social and Political Advocacy. These domains vary based on extent of client involvement and level of intervention (see Figure 2-1 and Appendix A).

Extent of Client's Involvement

This dimension of advocacy refers to the extent to which the client is involved in the advocacy efforts and includes *advocacy with* the client or community/school and *advocacy on behalf* of the client or community/school. The Advocacy Competencies model assumes that advocacy actions are always driven by a client's or community's needs. Yet, it also asserts that there are times when a client may be directly involved in the advocacy process and other times when the counselor may advocate on behalf of the client. When the client is directly involved in the advocacy process, the counselor and client collaborate on identifying the issues, discussing possible courses of action and consequences, and potentially acting

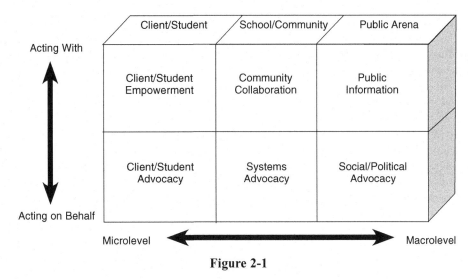

Figure 2-1

ACA Advocacy Competency/Domains

Note. The ACA (American Counseling Association) Advocacy Competencies were endorsed by the ACA Governing Council, March 20–22, 2003. From ACA Advocacy Competencies, by J. A. Lewis, M. S. Arnold, R. House, and R. L. Toporek, 2002. Available at http://www.counseling.org/Publications/. Copyright 2002 by the American Counseling Association. Reprinted with permission.

on the advocacy plan. For example, consider a counseling session in which a client reports to a counselor that her supervisor seems to always choose other employees for desirable work assignments, regardless of their superiority. Throughout the following sessions, the client shares that she is the only Latina in her office and that the employees who receive other assignments have not been there as long, have not been as well trained, and seem to have problems completing required tasks. She also reports that her supervisor has made comments about her family and her role in her family and has stated that she may not have what it takes because "with Mexican women, they always put family before work." She reports that the supervisor has said that employees who show commitment to the company get rewarded.

In the counseling process, the client and counselor explore possible ways of interpreting these experiences and consider possible discrimination based on gender and ethnicity. Further, they discuss what this experience means to the client in terms of her work there, her goals, and her well-being. Alternative courses of action may be considered, including client empowerment or a process by which the counselor and client work together to develop the client's sense of agency and self-advocacy skills. Within the dimension of Extent of Client Involvement, this approach would represent working with the client, identified in the model as Client Empowerment. If the client chooses not to pursue advocacy, the counselor and client may determine whether advocacy on behalf of the client would be appropriate. When advocating on behalf of the client, the counselor advocates directly in the system. In the case described above, it is most likely that the appropriate intervention would be empowerment rather than advocacy on behalf of the client.

There are other cases, however, in which advocacy on behalf of the client may be appropriate. For example, consider a case in which a client in a community counseling agency is reporting extreme depression due to an injury that required a change in occupation. He fears that he will lose rehabilitation benefits because he has not chosen a training program and is running out of time. For demonstration purposes, we assume that the counselor is unfamiliar with the particular rehabilitation program that the client is enrolled in and is having difficulty understanding the regulations the client is trying to describe to her. Even after several assignments to gather clearer information regarding the regulations, the client continues to seem befuddled. In addition to assessing the client's cognitive functioning and the impact of depression, the counselor may need to gain additional information directly from the client's rehabilitation case worker to understand the situation. With permission from the client to contact the case worker, the counselor may gather information that allows the client and counselor to clarify the realities of the situation and more accurately determine the extent to which advocacy may be important. Advocacy may take place when the counselor talks with the case worker to understand the regulations better and discuss possible avenues to facilitate the client's progress.

Level of Intervention

The second dimension of the competencies is referred to as Level of Intervention. This reflects the focus of the advocacy intervention ranging from the individual client/student to the community/school to the public or societal level. This dimension recognizes the ecological context in which the client(s) exist and the need to acknowledge and address change at these various levels. Depending on the issue and the goals identified in partnership with the client(s), advocacy may take place at one or all of these levels. In the examples provided above, the empowerment and client advocacy interventions take place at an individual level. Interventions at the community/school level reflect organizational or structural advocacy interventions, such as raising issues of discrimination or unfair promotion practices as organizational policy issues. At the macrolevel of intervention, counselors work with clients toward creating greater public awareness around an issue, work on public information, or work on behalf of clients in raising issues in public policy or legislative arenas. An example of advocacy in the public policy arena may be an extension of the case presented in the previous paragraph. It could be that the client and the counselor determine that the rehabilitation services training period allowed does not take into account experiences with mental illness (e.g., depression) and that policies should take that into consideration. In developing a sense of agency, the counselor and client together may identify potential legislation that could influence the rehabilitation services available to this client. Advocacy in the public arena tends to be relatively slow; thus, the counselor and client may also want to identify immediate individual advocacy actions. Social and political advocacy may not change the client's current situation; however, taking action on such issues may serve future clients and the public who face similar situations. If clients choose to get involved at this level, the reward for them may be an increased sense of agency as well as the sense that they are doing something that they believe in.

In the next section, each of the six advocacy domains is described to provide a foundation for the specific areas of advocacy held within the chapters of this book.

Domains of Advocacy Competence

Individual Level of Intervention

Empowerment

Empowerment reflects advocacy action taken in collaboration with the client/student. In the Advocacy Competencies model, empowerment involves assisting the client/student in recognizing the external forces that affect his or her development. In this process, the counselor and client may develop an action plan to address the issue at hand. The counselor may also assist the client in developing the skills needed for self-advocacy.

To work toward client empowerment, the Advocacy Competencies suggest that counselors must be able to help clients identify their strengths and resources as well as recognize when their behavior is in response to oppression. The counselor should be able to recognize social, political, economic, and cultural factors and, in a developmentally appropriate way, assist the client in understanding the impact of those factors.

Client or Student Advocacy

This domain refers to advocacy on behalf of an individual client or student. This type of advocacy is particularly relevant when the client or student lacks access to needed resources. The Advocacy Competencies indicate that in order to put this process into action, counselors should be able to effectively negotiate systems on behalf of clients and to facilitate clients in gaining access to resources. Counselors should be able to develop appropriate action plans, identify allies, and implement action plans.

One of the important aspects of client advocacy competence is being able to distinguish when empowerment, or facilitating greater agency in the client, is appropriate and when the most appropriate course of action is direct advocacy in the system on behalf of the client. As noted in the Advocacy Competencies, client advocacy may be an appropriate choice when the counselor has access to resources in ways that the client does not.

School and Community Level

Community Collaboration

The community/school level of advocacy acknowledges that counselors are often able to see patterns or themes across the experiences of the groups with whom they work. In community collaboration, the counselor works with individuals from a particular group, community, organization, or school to identify issues of oppression or systemic barriers faced within those entities. The role of the counselor in community collaboration is one of an ally as well as facilitator. At times, the counselor's role may involve alerting existing organizations to issues raised by the community or facilitating community members in locating such groups. The expertise that counselors develop in the areas of interpersonal relations, communications, training, and research may be especially suited to assist the community, school, or organization in identifying and defining the problem as well as designing a strategy for addressing the problem.

The Advocacy Competencies note that counselors should be able to help the community/school clarify and communicate concerns, identify strengths and resources, acknowledge and affirm those strengths, and share with the group the resources and skills the counselor may bring to the process. The Advocacy Competencies also emphasize that counselors should assess and examine their involvement with the community to determine the extent to which they are facilitating and maintaining the community's autonomy and goals.

Systems Advocacy

This domain refers to situations in which it is appropriate for the counselor to advocate on behalf of a group in the community or school. This may be the case when individuals in the group either do not have similar access to resources or are not in positions to make change. This may also be the case when a counselor advocates within his or her own organization. As with community collaboration, counselors are in a position to see a number of individuals who may be facing similar systemic barriers. When appropriate, the counselor can take this knowledge and raise awareness in the community, school, or the organization. The Advocacy Competencies state that "Change is a process that requires vision, persistence, leadership, collaboration, systems analysis, and strong data. In many situations, a counselor is the right person to take leadership" (Lewis et al., 2002, p. 2). The object of advocacy and change may be organizational policies or procedures or other systemic structures that create unjust barriers for client groups.

The competencies and skills identified as important for enacting systems advocacy include ability to recognize environmental and systemic barriers and to analyze sources of power within systems. In addition, counselors should be able to provide and interpret data and use that data to develop strategies and plans for advocacy, taking into consideration the possible responses to the advocacy and calls for change. In the process of advocating for change in the status quo, it is likely that the counselor will encounter resistance. Thus, planning for this event, providing data to support the need for change, and assessing the effect of advocacy on systems are important areas of competence.

Public Level

Public Information

This domain reflects the counselor advocating with the client or client communities to address external barriers on a macrolevel through raising the public's awareness of these circumstances. Beyond the competencies identified in the other domains, such as recognizing the influence of external and systemic barriers, to effectively implement public information as a form of advocacy, counselors should have skills in developing multimedia public information materials as well as understanding how these may be most effectively shared with the public. The Advocacy Competencies note that counselors should understand how to develop and disseminate these materials in ways that are ethical and appropriate for the population facing the barriers. It is most helpful if counselors work in concert with stakeholders who reflect the population that is most affected. In addition, collaborating with other professionals who are addressing similar problems is desirable.

Social and Political Advocacy

There are situations in which counselors have exposure and experience with an issue or population facing environmental constraints or injustices that are reflected in public policy and legislation. The social and political advocacy domain refers to actions that counselors take on behalf of populations for whom they serve. This domain is appropriate when the counselor sees a broad issue and also sees that public policy is interfering in healthy development or wellness, even if there may not be a particular client who is advocating for change. For example, counselors may recognize that public policy that does not address discrimination on the basis of sexual orientation is harmful to the well-being of their clients. Clients may choose not to participate in advocacy for fear of retribution; however, the counselor may choose to advocate on behalf of client populations, working toward change in public policy that would address discrimination.

Integrating Advocacy Competence and Multicultural Competence

Numerous authors within multicultural counseling have highlighted the need for comprehensive counselor roles to address institutional oppression and systemic barriers (e.g., Sue et al., 1998; Toporek & Pope-Davis, 2005). For example, Lewis and Arnold (1998) asserted,

> Multiculturalism and social action are highly complementary efforts. The lens of multiculturalism helps us as counselors to view our clients in a new light. We learn that all of us exist in a social, economic and political context. The reality of oppression is brought to the forefront of our perceptions, and our awakening to oppression leads us inexorably toward social action. We know that the most isolated and powerless among our clients need to be able to count on us to speak up on their behalf. (p. 87)

A critical component of multicultural training is developing an understanding of the power dynamics and sociopolitical and historical relationships between different cultural groups. Sometimes, an "aha" experience occurs when counselor trainees try to make connections between what they are learning in their multicultural counseling classes and what they are seeing in the real world of their internships or early career encounters. Consider the following:

> At the end of a multicultural counseling class session devoted to gay, lesbian, bisexual, and transgender issues, a student raised her hand. "This information is all very interesting but...I don't know what to do. I see students in my high school struggling with their sexual orientation and identity. Our school district has a strict policy prohibiting counselors from addressing these issues with students. The policy states that students who bring up these issues should be referred to their parents and that counseling should not address these issues. But, this doesn't make sense given that many of these students are afraid to talk to their parents about it. I can either disobey district policy and see these students, thereby risking my job, or follow district policy and know that the students will suffer and potentially face greater mental health problems. I watch these students become more depressed and I just feel powerless."

Sometimes, we can see that the forces working against our clients are beyond the capacity of individual counseling. By focusing on the individual and efforts toward helping the individual adjust and cope with oppressive environments, we are, in effect, supporting those oppressive environments.

Yet, many of us went into this profession to help people, not to oppress them. We feel ineffectual, we feel frustrated, and we feel helpless. Or, we accept the individual gains and ignore that the big picture has not gotten any better. This should not be the case.

Counselors have the capacity to intervene at levels broader than the individual. "When counselors become attuned to the oppression of gay, lesbian, bisexual, and transgendered individuals, they also begin to see the need for participation at a level that goes beyond their immediate school or community" (Lassiter & Barret, 2007, p. 47). In the illustration provided above, it is clear that individual counseling is limited in the context of an oppressive environment, whereas intervention at a community level may have a broader impact. For example, the policies of the school district create a situation in which counselors are limited in their ability to address serious mental health concerns of students. Including the external environment as a part of the case conceptualization allows counselors to more accurately discern the source of the problem and opens avenues for a broader range of interventions. While attending to client distress and risk is still a necessity, counselor involvement at the school board level to challenge policies that put clients at risk is also a necessity. According to the Advocacy Competencies, the counselor could engage in community collaboration to challenge the school board policy. It is possible that students may not feel safe speaking out, especially if homoprejudice and hate crimes are prevalent. In this case, it may be appropriate for the counselor to engage in community/ school advocacy, wherein the counselor speaks on behalf of the community or school. In the face of institutional barriers, counselor trainees may not realize that working to break down such barriers is, in fact, an important part of what professional counselors do. What begins with a counselor taking note of the effects of oppression on her own students or clients can lead that counselor to take her first, tentative steps on the road toward macrolevel interventions.

The movement toward advocacy as an integral part of the counselor's role built on the foundation of the multicultural competencies (Sue et al., 1992). Some work has been done to integrate the Multicultural Counseling Competencies with the Advocacy Competencies. For example, Toporek (2005) developed an integrative approach for applying the Multicultural Counseling Competencies (Sue et al., 1992), the Advocacy Competencies, and the Career Counseling Competencies (NCDA, 1997). The intent was that, in practice, counselors are expected to implement multiple models of competence, and this process could be simplified by acknowledging the interrelationship of those competencies. The model presented by Toporek provides a structure for counselors to consider competencies needed and appropriate actions to be taken. The starting point of the model is consideration of the client's stated needs through which relevant aspects are assessed, such as the circumstances (systemic variables, resources, setting, and counseling relationship); client variables (expectations, skills, identities, commitment to the process of counseling); and counselor competencies. The interplay of these three sets of variables is then used to determine the appropriate level of intervention and the competencies needed. Alternatively, Ratts (2008) proposed the Multicultural and Advocacy Dimensions Model, which describes the dynamic nature of the interaction between the Multicultural Counseling Competencies and Advocacy Competencies as they revolve around the working alliance, including the task, bond, and goals of counseling. Depending on the issue and a host of other variables, certain competencies may be more or less relevant at various times in counseling. The model also acknowledges that all counseling takes place within a sociopolitical context.

Ethical Practice and Advocacy

There are a number of considerations in implementing advocacy in counseling, such as ethics and training issues. In one respect, neglecting to address the social context may result in ethical problems and could be considered doing harm to the client. At the same time, ethical issues of consent, scope of practice, and scope of competence are areas that have also been discussed in reference to social justice advocacy in counseling (Toporek & Liu, 2001; Toporek & Williams, 2006). Client dependency, complexities of informed consent, politicization of counseling, and other cautions reflect valid concerns when advocacy competence and training is not integrated into practice and counselor education. Many counselors work with populations facing very difficult external circumstances, and the need for advocacy may seem clear. Yet, without appropriate training, individual counselors are left to their own experience to determine how to proceed ethically. The Advocacy Competencies endeavor to facilitate training and decision making so that counselors have assistance in this process. As noted in Chapter 1, social justice has historically been a part of counseling, and the *ACA Code of Ethics* (American Counseling Association, 2005) and the Council for the Accreditation of Counseling and Related Educational Programs (CACREP, 2008) Standards all support the role of advocate within counseling. Clearly, advocacy is within the scope of practice of counseling.

Scope of competence reflects the need for training. When counselors are providing services to clients, it is expected that they are adequately trained in the areas that are within the scope of practice and have gained some level of competence in these areas. Further, CACREP identifies advocacy as an area of necessary training. For example, in Section II, Professional Identity, under the section on Professional Orientation and Ethical Practice, the 2009 CACREP Standards note that curriculum should include "advocacy processes needed to address institutional and social barriers that impede access, equity, and success for clients" (p. 9). In the section that refers to required curriculum in the area of Social and Cultural Diversity, CACREP Standards note that training should include "counselors' roles in developing cultural self-awareness, promoting cultural social justice, advocacy and conflict resolution, and other culturally supported behaviors that promote optimal wellness and growth of the human spirit, mind, or body" (p. 10). In addition to the general standards that apply to all counseling specializations, diversity and advocacy are also identified in each of the counseling specializations. This highlights the need for comprehensive training regarding advocacy at all levels.

The literature regarding advocacy training in counseling has been relatively scarce. However, social justice literature has addressed some aspects of training relevant to advocacy (Constantine, Hage, Kindaichi, & Bryant, 2007; Nilsson & Schmidt, 2005; Pieterse, Evans, Risner-Butner, Collins, & Mason, 2009). Hage et al. (2007) proposed a set of best practices for prevention practice, research, training, and social advocacy for psychologists. Many of these principles can be useful for counseling training as well. Toporek, Dodge, Tripp, and Alarcón (2009) identified several areas of concern for counseling trainees addressing social justice issues in the community, including understanding the intricacies of facilitating empowerment while addressing a sense of powerlessness, learning how to promote change within systems, developing skills in program design and evaluation, and training students in investigative skills to assess community needs and evaluate effectiveness of advocacy and social action efforts.

There has been much less literature specifically focused on advocacy training for counselors. Toporek, Lewis, and Crethar (2009) noted that there is a need for training programs to help students develop an understanding of systems-level issues and interventions as well as ethical practice of advocacy. Further, they asserted the importance of integrating this training throughout the curriculum, including core theory and practicum courses, as well as ensuring that this role is included in the socialization of the counselor identity. Steele (2008) proposed a constructivist approach to curriculum infusion of advocacy training framed within a Liberation Model. This proposed approach is grounded in liberation psychology and the work of Paolo Friere and encompasses four phases: "(a) examining the explicit and implicit cultural and political ideology in the United States today; (b) examining the explicit and implicit cultural and political ideology of counseling; (c) interdisciplinary study of relevant issues; (d) applying the Liberation Model to the practice of counselor advocacy" (Steele, 2008, p. 77). In the area of school counseling, Ratts, DeKruyf, and Chen-Hayes (2007) discussed the application of the Advocacy Competencies in school counseling and provided recommendations for training of school counselors. Providing a concrete example of a training program that has social justice and advocacy at its core, Talleyrand, Chung, and Bemak (2006) described the counseling training program at George Mason University and the integration of both didactic and field experience in advocacy at policy, organizational, and individual levels.

Although there have been some advances in the area of training, particularly conceptually, there is clearly a need for more curricular development, training resources, and research regarding the advocacy training process. This is particularly important if we are serious about equipping emerging counselors for the realities of the profession.

Conclusion

The Advocacy Competencies provide a framework to assist counselors and counselor trainees in identifying appropriate levels of advocacy for a range of situations in which clients are facing injustice, inequity, or external barriers. In addition, specific skills and knowledge areas are outlined to facilitate the implementation of advocacy strategies. The overview provided in this chapter is intended to introduce the reader to the Advocacy Competencies and offers a foundation for a more meaningful reading of the specific applications of the Advocacy Competencies addressed in the following chapters. The reader is encouraged to explore the complete Advocacy Competencies document in Appendix A for a more comprehensive framework. In addition, Appendix B of the book provides the reader with a tool to assess his or her level of advocacy competence along the six domains outlined in the Advocacy Competencies. It is hoped that advocacy applied to specific settings, populations, and specializations within counseling will provide the reader with a complex exposure and inspire active use of the Advocacy Competencies toward positive social change for clients, communities, and society as a whole.

References

American Counseling Association. (2005). *ACA code of ethics*. Alexandria, VA: Author.

Constantine, M. G., Hage, S. M., Kindaichi, M. M., & Bryant, R. M. (2007). Social justice and multicultural issues: Implications for practice and training of counselors and counseling psychologists. *Journal of Counseling & Development, 85,* 24–29.

Council for Accreditation of Counseling and Related Educational Programs. (2008). *2009 Standards*. Alexandria, VA: Author. Retrieved March 1, 2009, from http://www.cacrep.org/2009standards.html

D'Andrea, M., Daniels, J., Arredondo, P., Ivey, A. E., Ivey, M. B., Locke, D. C., et al. (2001). Fostering organizational changes to realize the revolutionary potential of the multicultural movement: An updated case study. In J. G. Ponterotto, J. M. Casas, L. A. Suzuki, & C. M. Alexander (Eds.), *Handbook of multicultural counseling* (pp. 222–254). Thousand Oaks, CA: Sage.

Goodman, J. (2009). Starfish, salmon, and whales: An introduction to the special section [Special section on Advocacy Competence]. *Journal of Counseling & Development, 87,* 259.

Hage, S. M., Romano, J. L., Conyne, R. K., Kenny, M., Matthews, C., Schwartz, J. P., & Waldo, M. (2007). Best practice guidelines on prevention practice, research, training, and social advocacy for psychologists. *The Counseling Psychologist, 35,* 493–566.

Lassiter, P. S., & Barret, B. (2007). Gay and lesbian social justice: Strategies for social advocacy. In C. C. Lee (Ed.), *Counseling for social justice* (pp. 31–50). Alexandria, VA: American Counseling Association.

Lee, C. C., & Rodgers, R. A. (2009). Counselor advocacy: Affecting systemic change in the public arena [Special section on ACA Advocacy Competence]. *Journal of Counseling & Development, 87,* 284–287.

Lewis, J. A., & Arnold, M. S. (1998). From multiculturalism to social action. In C. C. Lee & G. R. Walz (Eds.), *Social action: A mandate for counselors* (pp. 1–66). Alexandria, VA: American Counseling Association.

Lewis, J. A., Arnold, M. S., House, R., & Toporek, R. L. (2002). *ACA Advocacy Competencies*. Retrieved September 13, 2008, from http://www.counseling.org/Publications/

Lewis, J., & Bradley, L. (Eds.). (2000). *Advocacy in counseling: Counselors, clients, and community*, Greensboro, NC: ERIC Counseling and Student Services Clearinghouse.

Lewis, J. A., & Lewis, M. (1977). *Community counseling: A human services approach*. New York: Wiley.

Lewis, J. A., Lewis, M., Daniels, J., & D'Andrea, M. (1998). *Community counseling* (2nd ed.) Pacific Grove, CA: Brooks/Cole.

Lopez-Baez, S. I., & Paylo, M. (2009). Social justice advocacy: Community collaboration and systems advocacy [Special section on ACA Advocacy Competencies]. *Journal of Counseling & Development, 87,* 276–283.

National Career Development Association. (1997). *Guidelines: Career counseling competencies.* Retrieved February 24, 2009, from http://associationdatabase.com/aws/NCDA/pt/sp/guidelines

Nilsson, J. E., & Schmidt, C. K. (2005). Social justice advocacy among graduate students in counseling: An initial exploration. *Journal of College Student Development, 46,* 267–279.

Pieterse, A. L., Evans, S. A., Risner-Butner, A., Collins, N. M., & Mason, L. B. (2009). Multicultural competence and social justice training in counseling psychology and counselor education: A review and analysis of a sample of multicultural course syllabi. *The Counseling Psychologist, 37,* 93–115.

Ratts, M. J. (2008, November). *Multicultural and advocacy dimensions model.* Paper presented at the Western Association of Counselor Education and Supervision Conference, Palm Springs, CA.

Ratts, M. J., DeKruyf, L., & Chen-Hayes, S. F. (2007). The ACA Advocacy Competencies: A social justice advocacy framework for professional school counselors. *Professional School Counseling, 11,* 90–97.

Ratts, M. J., & Hutchins, A. M. (2009). ACA Advocacy Competencies: Social justice advocacy at the client/student level [Special section on Advocacy Competence]. *Journal of Counseling & Development, 87,* 269–275.

Roysircar, G. (2009). The big picture of advocacy: Counselor, heal society and thyself [Special section on ACA Advocacy Competencies]. *Journal of Counseling & Development, 87,* 288–294.

Steele, J. M. (2008). Preparing counselors to advocate for social justice: A liberation model. *Counselor Education and Supervision, 48,* 74–85.

Sue, D. W., Arredondo, P., & McDavis, R. (1992). Multicultural counseling competencies and standards: A call to the profession. *Journal of Counseling & Development, 70,* 477–486.

Sue, D. W., Carter, R. T., Casas, J. M., Fouad, N. A., Ivey, E. A., Jensen, M., et al. (1998). *Multicultural counseling competencies: Individual and organizational development.* Thousand Oaks, CA: Sage.

Talleyrand, R. M., Chung, R. C. Y., & Bemak, F. (2006). Incorporating social justice in counselor training programs: A case study example. In R. L. Toporek, L. H. Gerstein, N. A. Fouad, G. S. Roysircar, & T. Israel (Eds.), *Handbook for social justice in counseling psychology: Leadership, vision, and action* (pp. 44–54). Thousand Oaks, CA: Sage.

Toporek, R. L. (2005). An integrative approach for competencies: Career counseling, social justice advocacy and the multicultural counseling competencies. *Career Planning and Adult Development Journal, 21,* 34–50.

Toporek, R. L., Dodge, D., Tripp, F., & Alarcón, L. (2009). Social justice and community engagement: Developing relationships beyond the university. In J. Ponterotto, J. M. Casas, L. A. Suzuki, & C. M. Alexander (Eds.), *Handbook of multicultural counseling* (3rd ed., pp. 603–617). Thousand Oaks, CA: Sage.

Toporek, R. L., Lewis, J. A., & Crethar, H. C. (2009). Promoting systemic change through the ACA Advocacy Competencies [Special section on ACA Advocacy Competencies]. *Journal of Counseling & Development, 87,* 260–268.

Toporek, R. L., & Liu, W. M. (2001). Advocacy in counseling: Addressing race, class, and gender oppression. In D. B. Pope-Davis & H. L. K. Coleman (Eds.), *The intersection of race, class and gender in multicultural counseling* (pp. 385–413). Thousand Oaks, CA: Sage.

Toporek, R. L., & Pope-Davis, D. B. (2005). Exploring the relationships between multicultural training, racial attitudes, and attributions of poverty among graduate counseling trainees. *Cultural Diversity and Ethnic Minority Psychology, 11,* 259–271.

Toporek, R. L., & Williams, R. A. (2006). Ethics and professional issues related to the practice of social justice in counseling psychology. In R. L. Toporek, L. H. Gerstein, N. A. Fouad, G. S. Roysircar, & T. Israel (Eds.), *Handbook for social justice in counseling psychology: Leadership, vision, and action* (pp. 17–34). Thousand Oaks, CA: Sage.

Chapter 3

Advocacy Competencies Self-Assessment Survey©: A Tool for Measuring Advocacy Competence

Manivong J. Ratts and Amy Ford

W ith the development of the American Counseling Association (ACA) Advocacy Competencies (Lewis, Arnold, House, & Toporek, 2002) comes a need for counselors to assess their level of advocacy competence. Our contention is that counselors will be better equipped to advocate for clients if they possess an understanding of themselves as advocates. Being able to assess one's competence as an advocate allows the helping professional to identify professional development opportunities. This also allows the social justice-oriented counselor to assess for potential barriers that may arise when doing advocacy work.

There are a variety of instruments that help counselors reflect and explore issues of privilege, oppression, and social justice. For example, Chen-Hayes (2001) developed a 188-item instrument called the Social Justice Advocacy Readiness Questionnaire that measures respondents' awareness, knowledge, and skills around diversity and social justice issues. Similarly, Hays, Chang, and Decker (2007) created an 82-item instrument, the Privilege and Oppression Inventory, which assesses counselors' awareness of privilege and oppression along the dimensions of race, sexual orientation, religion, and gender. Z. van Soest (1996) developed the Social Justice Advocacy Scale, a self-report instrument that measures respondents' advocacy behaviors on behalf of individuals from oppressed populations. However, there are no instruments to date that assess counselors' level of advocacy competence as outlined in the Advocacy Competencies. This is concerning in light of the ACA Governing Council's endorsement of the Advocacy Competencies. For this reason, the Advocacy Competencies Self-Assessment (ACSA) Survey© was created to help practitioners and educators determine their level of competence around the three levels and six domains of the Advocacy Competencies.

The need for an instrument that informs helping professionals' effectiveness as social justice advocates as articulated by the Advocacy Competencies is important for many reasons. One reason is related to professional competence. Section C.2.d of the *ACA Code of Ethics* states, "counselors continually monitor their effectiveness as professionals and take steps to improve when necessary" (American Counseling Association, 2005, p. 9). Adams, Bell, and Griffin (2007) noted that being a competent advocate requires an awareness and understanding of one's strengths and limitations as a social justice advocate. Understanding where areas of growth are needed can help counselors seek out appropriate professional development opportunities. In addition, it ensures that counselors are not practicing beyond the scope of their level of expertise.

The notion that counselors need to be advocacy-competent helping professionals also aligns with ACA's position on the importance of social advocacy. In March 2003, the ACA Governing Council endorsed the Advocacy Competencies. This endorsement represents a call to the profession of sorts and necessitates that all counselors need to be competent advocates. The need for helping professionals to be competent advocates has grown within the last few years because of an increase in the need for counselors to better address systemic factors that contribute to client stress (Fouad, Gerstein, & Toporek, 2006).

An advocacy instrument allows counselors opportunities to assess and reflect on how being a social change agent aligns with their personal and professional identity. Exploring the ways in which advocacy is integrated into one's personal and professional life allows the helping professional to determine whether these two aspects of identity are synergistic. That is, does one identify as a social justice advocate only in one's professional life, or is this also the case in one's personal life? Reflecting on one's level of advocacy competence seems especially important when one considers Sue and Sue's (2008) contention that many counselors lack social justice advocacy skills.

Given the need to prepare counselors to be social change agents and suggestions that this may be accomplished through the Advocacy Competencies, this chapter introduces readers to the Advocacy Competencies Self-Assessment (ACSA) Survey© (see Appendix B). The ACSA Survey© was developed as a tool to help social service and education professionals understand their level of advocacy competence. More specifically, helping professionals can use the survey to assess their comfort level with being a social change agent as it pertains to the framework articulated in the Advocacy Competencies. The following sections begin with an overview of what competencies entail and their relevance to the counseling profession. A description of the ACSA Survey© is also provided. Suggestions for using the ACSA Survey© in counseling and counselor education are also discussed.

Advocacy Competence: An Overview

Overview of Competence

The term *competence* infers that a certain degree of proficiency is required to complete an identified task or job. N. J. Rubin et al. (2007) described competencies as "complex and dynamically interactive clusters of integrated knowledge of concepts and procedures; skills and abilities; behaviors and strategies; attitudes, beliefs, and values; dispositions and personal characteristics; self-perceptions; and motivations that enable a person to execute a professional activity with myriad potential outcomes" (p. 453). Moreover, competencies are abstract constructs that are developed by experts in the field (N. J. Rubin et al., 2007). Competencies are critical to a profession because they help to determine best practice, standards of service, and professional qualifications.

The notion of having a set of competencies for the counseling profession is not new. Many divisions within ACA have developed sets of core competencies for working with specific client populations. For example, competencies have been developed for working with lesbian, gay, bisexual, and transgender (LGBT) clients (Association for Lesbian, Gay, Bisexual and Transgender Issues in Counseling, 2006), culturally diverse clients (Sue, Arredondo, & McDavis, 1992), and aging adults (Association for Adult Development and Aging, 1990). Competencies have also been developed for specific specialty areas, such as assessment competencies for school counselors (Association for Assessment in Counseling and Education, 1998), career counseling competencies (National Career Development Association, 1997), school counseling competencies (American School Counselor Association, 2004), spiritual competencies (Association for Spiritual, Ethical and Religious Values in Counseling, 1994), and group work competencies (Association for Specialists in Group Work, 1998). The widespread use of competencies in the field makes it reasonable that ACA also developed competencies for advocacy (Lewis et al., 2002).

Advocacy Competence

For purposes of this chapter, advocacy-competent counselors include helping professionals who are comfortable with individual and community-based forms of advocacy. More specifically, advocacy-competent counselors are aware, knowledgeable, and skilled with implementing the microlevel (client/student), mesolevel (school/community), and macrolevel (public arena) advocacy strategies outlined in the Advocacy Competencies (Lewis et al., 2002). Advocacy-competent counselors are aware of how sociopolitical factors contribute to client problems, they are knowledgeable of various types of advocacy interventions, and they are skilled with implementing culturally appropriate advocacy strategies. Advocacy competent counselors are also adept at assessing whether advocacy with or on behalf of clients is necessary.

Advocacy Competencies Self-Assessment Survey©

Overview

Practitioners and educators can use the ACSA Survey© as a tool for reflection and dialogue regarding competence with the Advocacy Competencies. The ACSA Survey© allows helping professionals to determine areas of strength and areas of growth as a social justice advocate. The ACSA Survey© also helps counselors determine where they tend to focus their energy in their advocacy work with clients. Educators can use results from the ACSA Survey© to determine where they need to focus their attention. Some students may require more help with the public arena levels of advocacy than others because this is not given as much attention in counselor training programs.

The ACSA Survey© consists of 30 items. The items were derived from the competency statements within the client/student, school/community, and public arena levels of the Advocacy Competencies. Each item also aligns with one of the six domains of the Advocacy Competencies. The ACSA Survey© was reviewed by Drs. Judy Lewis and Rebecca Toporek, two of the authors of the Advocacy Competencies, and piloted by two counselor education programs. Revisions to the survey were made on the basis of their feedback. The ACSA Survey© is in its infancy. Psychometric properties have yet to be conducted but are in development.

Survey Administration

Students should be familiar with the Advocacy Competencies before taking the ACSA Survey©. This introduction lays a foundation for understanding the framework behind the survey. The ACSA Survey© is a self-administered instrument that takes approximately 15–20 minutes to complete and score. Respondents should be instructed to address each item with the first answer that comes to mind. The options for each item are "almost never," "sometimes," and "almost always." Users should be allowed to ask questions to clarify items on the survey.

Scoring the ACSA Survey© is relatively simple. Respondents are instructed to score Items 1, 7, and 13 first. These 3 items are scored using the following scale: 4 = *almost never,* 2 = *sometimes,* and 0 = *almost always.* The remaining items are scored as follows: 0 = *almost never,* 2 = *sometimes,* and 4 = *almost always.* The range of scores for each of the six advocacy domains is from 0 to 20. Adding the total score for the six advocacy domains determines respondents' overall advocacy rating scale. The total range of scores possible is from 0 to 120. Scores of 69 and below indicate that respondents may need further training in a particular advocacy domain (e.g., client/student empowerment). Knowing where a student is lacking in a particular advocacy domain can help counselor educators develop meaningful curriculum. Scores ranging from 70 to 99 indicate that respondents have demonstrated competence with certain advocacy domains but may need to further develop competence in other advocacy areas. Scores ranging from 100 to 120 indicate a high level of competence in each of the six advocacy domains.

Implications

Inherent in the previous discussion and introduction of the ACSA Survey© is the idea that social justice advocacy must become an integral part of the work of counselors. While it may still be a seminal paradigm for contemporary counselors, social justice advocacy is necessary for holistic client intervention in an oppressive society (Constantine, Hage, Kindaichi, & Bryant, 2007). Counselors must be prepared to integrate these concepts, more specifically the Advocacy Competencies, into their professional work.

The ACSA Survey© can be an important tool in helping practitioners and educators develop as social change agents. First, it provides respondents with a quantifiable estimation of their knowledge of the Advocacy Competencies. Second, it gives respondents an idea of their level of commitment to social justice advocacy. This information can help counselors better understand their strengths and weaknesses as social justice change agents.

Engaging in social justice advocacy presents challenges to practitioners and educators alike. The first challenge is assisting counselors with developing their professional identities as social change agents along with the traditional individual counseling philosophy (Sue & Sue, 2008). Many counselors express that they have chosen the counseling profession because they prefer to help individuals change rather than help systems change, equating social justice counseling with other systemic helping professions such as social work. However, many counselors, as well as counselor educators themselves, do not realize that social justice advocacy is becoming a standard for all therapeutic professions, including psychologists (Goodman et al., 2004) and school counselors (House, 2004). Furthermore, if counselors were to reflect on the origins of the field, beginning with the social justice advocacy work of Frank Parsons, the "father of vocational guidance," they would discover that social justice has been a strong theme within the profession since its inception (Kiselica & Robinson, 2001). If helping professionals are aware of this history, they may have less difficulty bridging the gap between seeing themselves as "individual counselors" and seeing themselves as "social justice counselors."

Counselor educators could implement the ACSA Survey© early on in a program orientation, in a professional identity course, or in an ethics course to set the tone for the rest of the program. Another suggestion would be to implement the ACSA Survey© both at the beginning of the students' programs and at the end in an effort to compare how their scores may have changed during the program. The data would be useful in measuring student outcomes related to attitudes toward and the practice of the Advocacy Competencies, the program's success in assimilating the Advocacy Competencies, and relationship outcomes in the three main evaluation areas of counselor preparation: clinical skill, academic performance, and fit for the profession. Finally, students would solidify the idea that social justice and the Advocacy Competencies will not only be an expectation of their practice but also an integral part of developing their professional identities.

One of the challenges practitioners face has to do with developing practical techniques that can be integrated into practice. The ACSA Survey© is designed to assist counselors with this task. The survey helps respondents discover their areas of strength and areas that need further development. More specifically, the 30-item questionnaire yields an individual score for each of the six advocacy domains and gives a global score to assess the overall level of competencies. These individual scores can be corroborated with both therapeutic and advocacy techniques.

Conclusion

On a final note, it is not enough for counselors to receive social justice training in their programs, they must also make a commitment to promoting social change throughout their careers (Parra-Cardona, Holtrop, & Cordova, 2005). Being a competent social justice advocate requires honest self-reflection and continued professional development. Thus, obtaining continuing education is imperative. The ACSA Survey© is a practical tool that consultants, trainers, and workshop presenters can use as they accomplish this end. This practice is particularly important if helping professionals are to address the various forms of oppression that have a debilitating impact on clients' lives. More important, the ACSA Survey© allows helping professionals to identify their strengths and areas for growth as social justice change agents. Using the ACSA Survey© to develop the advocacy strategies outlined in the Advocacy Competencies not only will have a transformative impact on clients but also has the potential to revolutionize the counseling profession as we know it.

References

Adams, M., Bell, L. A., & Griffin, P. (Eds.). (2007). *Teaching for diversity and social justice* (2nd ed.). New York: Routledge.

American Counseling Association. (2005). *ACA code of ethics*. Alexandria, VA: Author.

American School Counselor Association. (2004). *ASCA national standards for students.* Retrieved February 24, 2009, from http://www.schoolcounselor.org/resources_list.asp?c=33&i=15

Association for Adult Development and Aging. (1990). *Gerontological competencies for counselors and human development specialists.* Retrieved February 24, 2009, from http://www.uncg.edu/~jemyers/jem_info/docs/competencies.htm

Association for Assessment in Counseling and Education. (1998). *Competencies in assessment and evaluation for school counselors.* Retrieved February 24, 2009, from http://www.theaaceonline.com/resources.htm

Association for Lesbian, Gay, Bisexual and Transgender Issues in Counseling. (2006). *Competencies for counseling gay, lesbian, bisexual and transgender (LGBT) clients.* Retrieved February 24, 2009, from http://www.algbtic.org/resources/competencies.html

Association for Specialists in Group Work. (1998). *Principles for diversity-competent group workers.* Retrieved February 24, 2009, from http://www.asgw.org/PDF/Group_Stds_Brochure.pdf

Association for Spiritual, Ethical and Religious Values in Counseling. (1994). *Spiritual competencies.* Retrieved February 24, 2009, from http://www.aservic.org/competencies.html

Chen-Hayes, S. (2001). Social justice advocacy readiness questionnaire. *Journal of Gay and Lesbian Social Services, 13,* 191–203.

Constantine, M. G., Hage, S. M., Kindaichi, M. M., & Bryant, R. M. (2007). Social justice and multicultural issues: Implications for practice and training of counselors and counseling psychologists. *Journal of Counseling & Development, 85,* 24–29.

Fouad, N. A., Gerstein, L. H., & Toporek, R. L. (2006). Social justice and counseling psychology in context. In R. L. Toporek, L. H. Gerstein, N. A. Fouad, G. Roysircar, & T. Israel (Eds.), *Handbook for social justice in counseling psychology: Leadership, vision, and action* (pp. 1–16). Thousand Oaks, CA: Sage.

Goodman, L. A., Liang, B., Helms, J. E., Latta, R. E., Sparks, E., & Weintrab, S. R. (2004). Training counseling psychologists as social justice agents: Feminist and multicultural principles in action. *The Counseling Psychologist, 32,* 793–837.

Hays, D. G., Chang, C. Y., & Decker, S. L. (2007). Initial development and psychometric data for the privilege and oppression inventory. *Measurement and Evaluation in Counseling and Development, 40,* 66–79.

House, R. (2004). School counselors working as social justice advocates. *Oregon Professional School Counselor Journal, 1,* 1–6.

Kiselica, M. S., & Robinson, M. (2001). Bringing advocacy counseling to life: The history, issues, and human dramas of social justice work in counseling. *Journal of Counseling & Development, 79,* 387–398.

Lewis, J. A., Arnold, M. S., House, R., & Toporek, R. L. (2002). *ACA Advocacy Competencies.* Retrieved May 27, 2008, from http://www.counseling.org/Publications/

National Career Development Association. (1997). *Guidelines: Career counseling competencies.* Retrieved February 24, 2009, from http://associationdatabase.com/aws/NCDA/pt/sp/guidelines

Parra-Cardona, J. R., Holtrop, K., & Cordova, D. (2005). We are clinicians committed to cultural diversity and social justice: Good intentions that can wane over time. *Guidance and Counseling, 21,* 36–46.

Rubin, N. J., Leigh, I. W., Nelson, P. D., Smith, I. L., Bebeau, M., Lichtenberg, J. W., et al. (2007). The competency movement within psychology: An historical perspective. *Professional Psychology: Research and Practice, 38,* 452–462.

Sue, D. W., Arredondo, P., & McDavis, R. J. (1992). Multicultural counseling competencies and standards: A call to the profession. *Journal of Counseling & Development, 70,* 477–486.

Sue, D. W., & Sue, D. (2008). *Counseling the culturally diverse: Theory and practice* (5th ed.). New York: Wiley.

van Soest, D. (1996). Impact of social work education on student attitudes and behavior concerning oppression. *Journal of Social Work Education, 32,* 191–202.

Section

II

From Theory to Practice

Application of the ACA Advocacy Competencies

Chapters 4–10
•
Advocacy Across Populations

Chapters 11–14
•
Advocacy Across Settings

Chapters 15–21
•
Advocacy Across Specialty Areas

Chapter 4

It Takes More Than a Rainbow Sticker!: Advocacy on Queer Issues in Counseling

Anneliese A. Singh

Matt is no longer with us today because the men who killed him learned to hate. Somehow and somewhere they received the message that the lives of gay people are not as worthy of respect, dignity and honor as the lives of other people. They were given the impression that society condoned or at least was indifferent to violence against gay and lesbian Americans. Today, we have it within our power to send a very different message than the one received by the people who killed my son.

—Judy Shepherd, in her testimony to
the Senate Judiciary Committee
supporting the passage of the
Hate Crimes Prevention Act
on May 11, 1999

The above quote reminds counselors that in order for queer people to feel safe and thrive in society, counselors must move beyond tolerance of queer people to actively building spaces where queer youths, adults, and communities may not only be safe but also thrive. For the purposes of this chapter, the word *queer* is used as an umbrella term to encompass individuals who identify as lesbian, gay, bisexual, transgender, and questioning (LGBTQ; Fish & Harvey, 2005). This word has been reclaimed more recently as a term of empowerment and pride, especially within queer youth communities. However, it is also important to be aware that this term was historically used as a pejorative for people whose sexual orientation or gender identity was nonheteronormative. A person's *sexual orientation* refers to the affectional and/or sexual attractions to same- or opposite-gender people, whereas the term *gender identity* encompasses a person's sense of internal experience of her or his gender as a woman, man, or another self-defined gender label (such as genderqueer) and is often related to a person's gender behavior and expression. The counselor advocate working for justice on queer issues in counseling should be well versed in important terms used in the queer community, as there are many words some clients will identify with and others may find offensive (see Fassinger & Arseneau, 2007).

The literature on queer issues in counseling has historically focused on the damaging consequences of heterosexism and homophobia for queer people (Goodman & Moradi, 2008; Human Rights Watch, 2001; Rosario, Schrimshaw, Hunter, & Gwadz, 2002). Identifying the devastating effects of heterosexism on queer people seems especially important when considering the 2008 murder of gender-variant adolescent Lawrence King by his 14-year-old classmate. In this tragic case, Lawrence King—who began expressing his gender and sexual identity in nonheteronormative ways in eighth grade—was shot in the back of the head at school for no apparent reason other than his peer's fear of who and what Lawrence King represented.

Unfortunately, there are many stories of hate and violence toward queer people. Hence, there is a vital need to understand the heterosexism queer people experience. In addition, there has been a call for counselors to focus on the resilience queer people have developed as a result of living in a predominantly heterosexist society (Russell, 2005; Singh, Dew, Hays, & Gailis, 2007). The rationale for this focus is not to ignore the deleterious effects of heterosexism but rather to recognize that queer people have long histories of creating innovative ways to buffer themselves against discrimination (e.g., community-building, the gay rights movement of the 1960s, reclaiming spirituality). In spite of this resilience, it is becoming increasingly apparent that direct counseling alone may not be enough or even appropriate for the types of changes that are needed to create safe and inclusive spaces for queer-identified and queer-perceived individuals (Chen-Hayes, 2001; Mahan, Varjas, Dew, Meyers, & Singh, 2007; Stone, 2003).

Counselors may take an active role in both addressing systemic discrimination and prejudice toward queer people and valuing the resilience of this community. Both perspectives are critical aspects of ending heterosexism, homophobia, biphobia, and transphobia. This can be achieved by using the American Counseling Association (ACA) Advocacy Competencies (Lewis, Arnold, House, & Toporek, 2002) as a framework for advocacy with, and on behalf of, those in the queer community. The premise is that the individual and systemic interventions promoted within the Advocacy Competencies can provide a more holistic approach to addressing issues of homophobia, biphobia, transphobia, and heterosexism in society. Specifically, this chapter addresses how counselors across various settings (e.g., school and community mental health) may use the three levels of the Advocacy Competencies (e.g., client/student, school/community, and public arena) to create a more just world for queer people.

Why End Heterosexism?
Addressing Heterosexual Privilege and Its Costs

An important preliminary step to using the Advocacy Competencies is to understand what heterosexism means and its harmful impact on both queer-identified and queer-perceived individuals. *Heterosexism* is a systemic force that works closely with other forms of oppression, such as racism and sexism, to strictly delineate norms of gender and sexual identity (Chernin & Johnson, 2002). Heterosexism uses the mechanisms of homophobia (i.e., the irrational fear of gay and lesbian people), biphobia (i.e., the irrational fear of bisexuals), and transphobia (i.e., the irrational fear of transgender people) to bolster its system of power and privilege for heterosexuals. This fear contributes to escalating hate crimes against queer people, with sexual orientation comprising a third of all reported hate crimes (Federal Bureau of Investigation, 2007). Logan (1996) discusses the importance of acknowledging that the behaviors of homophobia have an active component of discrimination and prejudice, and encourage counselors to use the word *homoprejudice* when describing these behaviors. Ultimately, heterosexism not only is a cost to queer people but also negatively affects heterosexual people. Heterosexism demands that all people operate their daily lives within traditionally defined roles and behaviors of a binary gender system of male and female.

Understanding heterosexism to its fullest and the mechanisms it uses to create discrimination and prejudice toward queer people also requires that counselors explore the concept of *heterosexual privilege*—the unearned advantages heterosexual and gender-conforming people have that are not always available to those in the queer community (Simoni & Walters, 2001). Heterosexual privileges are extensive in society, including the right to marry, have child and adoptive rights, and feel safe being with one's partner in public. Currently in the United States, 44 states have constitutional amendments or state laws restricting the definition of marriage to be "a man and a woman," with only Iowa, Massachusetts, Vermont, and Connecticut offering same-gender marriage rights and New

Jersey offering civil unions. New York and the District of Columbia now recognize legal same-sex marriages performed in other jurisdictions. The 2008 passage of Proposition 8 in California, which amended the state's constitution to define marriage to exclude same-gender unions, has reignited the debate about queer rights in the United States. This renewed debate is such that many state laws are in flux (including the states of New Hampshire and Maine as we go to press), meaning that the United States may see more states support same-gender marriages or civil unions. What may help to advance the issue of gay marriage is to repeal the Defense of Marriage Act (Pub. Law 106-199), which was signed into law by President Bill Clinton in 1996. President Barack Obama signed historic legislation in October 2009, which included sexual orientation and gender identity as hate crimes. This legislation was named after two men killed by hate crimes in 1998—Matthew Shepard murdered due to his sexual orientation and James Byrd Jr. murdered due to his race.

In addition to the right to get married, another important heterosexual privilege is the right to adopt children. Queer parents are prohibited from adoption rights in Florida, Mississippi, and Utah, and they may face challenges in fostering children as well (Human Rights Campaign, 2009). Other heterosexual privileges include being able to visit loved ones in the hospital in the event of a medical emergency and having legal and financial rights to property in the event of the death of a spouse. Heterosexual privilege exists everywhere, from being embedded in the media (e.g., valuing of heterosexual relationships as the norm, portraying queer people as either comic relief or danger) to being present throughout the workplace (e.g., water cooler discussions about events outside of work focusing on heterosexual families; Ji, 2007). Essentially, heterosexual privilege translates to being able to be in the company of other heterosexual people in most environments, and to not be questioned about the value of one's gender and/or sexual identity.

Although this chapter focuses on using the Advocacy Competencies with queer people, counselors can also look to the *ACA Code of Ethics* (American Counseling Association, 2005), the American School Counselor Association (ASCA, 2004) *Ethical Standards for School Counselors*, and the Competencies for Counseling Lesbian, Gay, Bisexual and Transgender (LGBT) Clients (Association for Gay, Lesbian, and Bisexual Issues in Counseling, 2005) for guidance on best practices with queer people. There are also specific counseling competencies for working with transgender people that are grounded in a strength-based wellness, feminist, and social justice perspective (Association for Lesbian, Gay, Bisexual, and Transgender Issues in Counseling, 2009). The *ACA Code of Ethics*, Standard A.4., establishes that counselors must do no harm to clients and must not impose personal values into work with clients; therefore, heterosexist practices would be prohibited by this standard. Also, there has been a large body of research indicating that attempts to "change" a client's sexual orientation and/or gender identity are harmful to clients (Bieschke, Paul, & Blasko, 2007). The ASCA *Ethical Standards* prohibits school counselors from discriminating against clients based on sexual orientation. The competencies for GLBT clients assert that counselors should not engage in antiqueer counseling approaches (e.g., conversion therapy) that attempt to change a person's gender identity and/or sexual orientation. The competencies also provide a roadmap for ethical and affirmative practice with queer and transgender clients in various counseling modalities (individual, group, career counseling) and across the developmental life span.

Nurturing the Resilience of Queer People: Empowerment and Advocacy at the Client/Student Level

This section addresses the client/student level of the Advocacy Competencies with queer people. The client/student level of the Advocacy Competencies directs counselors to act with clients/students to identify empowerment strategies and to act on behalf of clients/students by using advocacy as a means to address systemic barriers. Empowerment has been defined as the ability individuals and communities have to access resources needed to improve their lives (McWhirter, 1991). In the context of advocacy competence with queer people at the student and client level, empowerment is considered for this chapter to refer to (a) the removal of barriers from queer student and clients' lives and (b) supporting the resilience of queer student/clients.

Client/Student Empowerment Domain: Addressing Internalized Heterosexism

Many queer clients/students have questions about their own self-worth that are amplified by societal "debates" about the worth and value of queer people in general (Vaid, 1995). Oftentimes, these questions lead queer clients/students to negatively internalize heterosexist values, beliefs, and ideals. This is a process referred to as internalized heterosexism, and addressing internalized heterosexism is an empowering form of client/student advocacy. Internalized heterosexism is defined as negative attitudes queer people may hold about their own sexual and/or gender identity (Szymanski & Chung, 2001). Therefore, a significant counselor role is to act with clients/students to confront and deconstruct any negative attitudes they may have internalized (Goodman & Moradi, 2008; Stone, 2003). This can be accomplished by exploring how heterosexism may be affecting an individual's feelings about her or his own value as a human being (i.e., self-esteem). A useful tool to assess internalized heterosexism, and thereby empower clients, is the *Basic Human Rights* handout, which details the value and worth of all people, including those who are queer (Whitman & Boyd, 2003). The handout is also helpful in establishing a baseline of what types of negative attitudes queer people may hold about themselves. It can direct counselors where they may most effectively intervene. Counselors may also use formal, validated assessments of internalized heterosexism with queer students and clients, such as the Internalized Homonegativity Inventory (Mayfield, 2001) and the Lesbian Internalized Homophobia Scale (Szymanski & Chung, 2001).

Counselors can additionally act with queer students through conducting one-on-one role-plays where students may safely brainstorm how to address daily challenges they face. Examples of these role-plays include practicing how they may "come out" to families, friends, teachers, and other important people in their lives, as well as role-plays about how they may respond to an antiqueer epithet such as "you're so gay." In another example, if a student—whether queer or not—expresses that "being gay is not normal," there is a rich opportunity for a counselor to not only educate the student about heterosexism but also act with the student and explore from where these internalized heterosexist beliefs emerged (Whitman & Boyd, 2003).

Client/Student Advocacy Domain:
Affirming Gender and Sexual Identity Expression

Given that research studies have long cited queer youths as having higher suicidal ideation and suicide completion than their heterosexual peers (Espelage, Aragon, Birkett, & Koenig, 2008; McDaniel, Purcell, & D'Augelli, 2001; Russell, 2003; Savin-Williams & Ream, 2003), it is imperative that counselors advocate on behalf of queer students to create affirming school environments. When counselors are working with students in prekindergarten through college (P–16) settings, there will be a variety of gender and sexual identity behaviors expressed by youths whether or not they ultimately will identify as queer. Because counselors are in the position to notice negative attitudes and behaviors toward queer people, they may act on behalf of queer students by educating parents, teachers, students, and other community members about queer concerns. Essentially, the advocacy role for counselors within the client/student advocacy domain requires active affirmation of the development of gender identity and affectional and/or sexual attractions of students that challenge traditional gender and sexual identity norms. Especially because empirical studies across disciplines have suggested that sexual and gender identity development matures throughout the life span, with major milestones occurring through childhood and adolescence (DeLamater & Friedrich, 2002), counselors should use research on human development to support their queer student/client advocacy efforts.

Other counselor roles within this domain include having queer-positive resources and "coming-out" resources available from such organizations as the Human Rights Campaign (www.hrc.org) and the Gay, Lesbian, Straight, Education Network (GLSEN; www.glsen.org) displayed in the counseling department as one way to advocate on behalf of queer students. Often, school counselors express feeling "nervous" about providing these types of resources to queer students or students who are questioning their gender and/or sexual identity. In these cases, the Multicultural Counseling Competencies (Sue, Arredondo, & McDavis, 1992) guide the counselor to focus on increasing their awareness of queer issues. Indeed, developing multicultural competence is a precursor to effective social justice advocacy. Then, school counselors may move beyond their fear to advocate on behalf of queer youths, providing them with the necessary resources they need. Often, school counselors may feel isolated from resources and support for working with queer students. When this occurs, an advocacy role for school counselors is to actively seek the information they need to advocate on behalf of queer youths through attending local, state, and national professional development trainings. Because school counselors may be the only safe haven these students have, school counselors should proactively build their collection of queer-affirmative resources (e.g., websites, brochures, books) on behalf of these students.

Imagine a Place Where All Queer People Are Safe and Valued: Systems Advocacy and Community Collaboration at the School/Community Levels

Counselors may use the Advocacy Competencies' specific recommendations for the school and community levels to create safe environments where queer students and clients may thrive. This section explores a range of possibilities for engaging in community collaboration and systems advocacy at the school and community levels.

Systems Advocacy Domain: Schoolwide Advocacy for Queer Students

The Advocacy Competencies direct school counselors to become an ally of queer students and students who are perceived to be queer within a school setting. School counselors who are allies to queer-identified and -perceived youths actively challenge heterosexism in their schools and focus their efforts on building a queer-positive school climate (Ji, 2007; Russell & McGuire, 2008). The following three systems-level advocacy approaches are offered as ways school counselors may act on behalf of queer students and establish a positive school environment: (a) conducting campus climate surveys in schools, (b) establishing Gay–Straight Alliances (GSAs), and (c) creating a districtwide LGBTQ advocacy team (comprising teachers, administrators, parents, etc.) led by school counselors to make recommendations for training, advocacy, and best practices for working with queer students in schools.

Conducting campus climate surveys involves using informal and formal assessments of bullying and violence toward queer-identified and -perceived youths and is an important way to act on their behalf. Research suggests that school personnel (school counselors included) are not consistently addressing antiqueer bullying even when they hear antiqueer epithets (e.g., "that's so gay," "faggot," or "dyke") in the hallways and classrooms (GLSEN, 2007; Human Rights Watch, 2001). Other research seems to indicate that school personnel also actively participate in heterosexist statements and behaviors (Szalacha, 2003). This creates an unsafe learning environment for all students. Therefore, an important advocacy role for counselors is to conduct a safety audit of the degree to which a school is queer-positive. These assessments of bullying and violence toward those students who are or perceived as queer must include formal and informal assessments of students and school personnel (Singh, Orpinas, & Horne, in press). Although there is not a specific assessment tool to comprehensively measure levels of bullying based on sexual and/or gender identity, certain formal assessments, such as the Olweus Bully/Victim measure (Olweus, 1993), will allow school counselors to add items asking about this type of bullying. To collect qualitative data on queer bullying within the school, counselors may hold focus groups and individual interviews with students at different levels, as well as with teachers and parents. Qualitative data often provide particularly powerful information, as they document the narratives of those affected by queer bullying and may be used when directly advocating with school administrators. Another important advocacy role in this domain is to provide school administrators with information on queer students' needs. School counselors fulfill this role by using materials such as *Just the Facts* (Just the Facts Coalition, 2008), a guide endorsed by ACA outlining how to most effectively work on behalf of queer students with school administrators on safety issues and concerns.

Acting on behalf of queer students by helping establish GSAs or being an active participant by serving as an advisor to a GSA is also an important systemic approach at the school/community level of the Advocacy Competencies. This can be a significant role for counselors, as research on intervention efficacy data suggests that schools with active GSAs are safer for all students (Goodenow, Szalacha, & Westheimer, 2006). However, some states, such as Washington, prohibit school counselors from initiating such school clubs, so it is important for counselors to be aware of the guidelines in their state. Additionally, because there has been a long history of backlash against students who start GSAs in their school, counselors should be informed of the legalities surrounding GSAs in their state. For example, in the 2006 Georgia case of *Kerry Pacer v. White County School District*, high school student Kerry Pacer wanted to start a GSA called PRIDE (Peers Rising in Diverse Education) at her school. The White County School District went to great lengths to stop the GSA from meeting, including shutting down all school clubs so the GSA could not meet on campus. The American Civil Liberties Union (ACLU) represented Kerry Pacer in a lawsuit against the school district, resting on the claim that her rights (in addition to the rights of other students at the school) were violated under the federal Equal Access Act that requires equal treatment in schools of all noncurricular clubs. The ACLU won its case, with the court issuing a permanent injunction against the school in addition to fining the principal and school district (ACLU, 2006). Learning from this case and in anticipation of possible resistance, school counselors would do well to equip themselves with data (quantitative and qualitative) collected from the campus climate surveys to bolster the case for starting a GSA in their school. Counselors may also act on behalf of queer students by using their leadership skills to organize workshops on queer student concerns (e.g., safety, rates of suicide) to present to parents, teachers, and administrators.

A third approach school counselors make take with systems advocacy on behalf of queer students is to create a districtwide LGBTQ advocacy team of administrators, teachers, and parents, led by school counselors, that may make recommendations for advocacy and best practices for working with queer students in schools. To fulfill this advocacy role, school counselors may use monthly district meetings they are required to attend to organize a leadership team with the knowledge, awareness, and skills of best practices with queer youths to create a broader alliance working systemically on queer student issues. This type of initiative would meet the systems advocacy competencies to use strategic data collection methods, an understanding of organizational theory, and collaborative leadership as ways to address heterosexism.

Community Collaboration Domain: Creating Safer School Environments for LGBTQ Youth

School counselors can also act with queer people and their allies to access resources from, and build alliances with, community organizations such as Parents, Families, and Friends of Lesbians and Gays (PFLAG). An advocacy role in this domain would include collaborating with community organizations to identify strengths, competencies, and resources queer youths have to negotiate heterosexism in the schools. For instance, to fulfill this role, school counselors could work with PFLAG on a campaign to ensure that transgender students have safe access to unisex bathrooms in schools. Collective engagement around such issues can be more effective than a school counselor working in isolation. Counselors could also collaborate with community partners to establish a Safe Zone or Safe Space program similar to those created within universities (Finkel, Storaasli, Bandele, & Schaefer, 2003). Within these programs, a train-the-trainers model is used to educate others about queer issues. Program attendees receive rainbow stickers to display in their office that signify they are a "safe space" for queer people to seek support (Evans, 2002). However, it is important that counselors guard against complacency because such programs could become a "feel-good" project where Safe Zone emblems replace action and progress on queer issues in schools. To provide accountability, counselors can create student and participant surveys to collect data to assess the effectiveness of the program. They could use this survey data to demonstrate how students' academic, career, and personal/social development have improved and how this may have positively affected campus climate as a result of the program.

Systems Advocacy Domain:
Advocacy for Queer Clients in Community Organizations

In community settings, such as mental health agencies and nonprofit organizations, counselors have similar responsibilities as in school settings to act on behalf of queer people by advocating for systemic change and initiating community collaborations that address queer issues. This section focuses on four distinct strategies counselors may use to create change in community settings: (a) assessing the capacity of community organizations to address queer concerns, (b) exploring organizational barriers that affect queer resilience, (c) compiling a local resource directory of support networks for queer people, and (d) advocating for and supporting the development of new initiatives to address gaps in the access queer people have to necessary resources. These four suggestions build upon one another and are likely to be successful when counselors recognize that systems advocacy requires patience, a well-developed strategy, time, and alliance-building. These are highlighted under the framework of the systems advocacy and community collaboration domains of the Advocacy Competencies.

An important counselor role in this domain is to assess the capacity of the counselor's organization to address queer concerns. This is an important first step to acting on behalf of queer concerns. Similar to the campus climate surveys recommended for school counselors, organizational assessment will allow counselors to build a strong rationale for creating a more queer-positive environment. It is helpful to consider what the capacity of an organization is when engaging in queer advocacy. *Capacity* is defined as the shared responsibility, collective competence, and resilience of a community (Bowen, Martin, Mancini, & Nelson, 2000). As applied to queer advocacy, it is the degree to which the organization can respond to internal and external threats on queer issues while also attending to the strengths the organization has to respond. Counselors may assess the capacity of community organizations by (a) collecting quantitative and qualitative data on queer individuals and families using agency services; (b) holding focus groups with all staff (e.g., front-desk staff, counselors, psychiatrists) in the organization to take a pulse of the staff's awareness, knowledge, and skills on queer issues; and (c) identifying organizational resources that are queer-positive.

When counselors assess the capacity of their organization to make positive changes about queer issues, it allows them to better address organizational barriers to queer resilience. For instance, a mental health organization in a middle-class neighborhood that is racially and ethnically diverse may have held previous inservice trainings on how racism contributes to mental health issues. Counselors can build on the organization's capacity to discuss issues of race and mental health by incorporating queer issues into the training to further understand the complex intersections between racism and heterosexism. However, in other community settings, data may reveal that organizational capacity is low with respect to staff awareness, knowledge, and skills on queer concerns. In this case, counselors may decide to hold a more basic training dedicated solely to queer issues.

Community Collaboration Domain:
Acting With LGBTQ Leaders and Organizations

Oftentimes, work in the systems advocacy area of the Advocacy Competencies can lead a counselor to work within the community collaboration domain of the competencies. Exploring what staff and environmental barriers to queer resilience exist organizationally can be enhanced when counselors act with existing queer-positive resources in their community. For example, counselors can act with leaders in the queer community to develop a directory of queer community resources if such a resource does not exist. Some cities publish a queer directory that has local resources for counselors, lawyers, and financial assistance.

Counselors operating in the community collaboration domain of the Advocacy Competencies can also act with members of the community to initiate and support the development of new initiatives that ensure that queer people will have equal access to resources such as education, employment, legal, medical, and mental health services. The three steps previously discussed—assessing capacity, identifying barriers to queer resilience, and compiling local queer support resources—are important steps during which counselors will notice what queer community needs are not being met.

Making Change at the Public Arena Level on Queer Issues: Public Information and Social/Political Advocacy

Much of the work at the microlevel (client/student) and mesolevel (school/community) of the Advocacy Competencies can lay the groundwork for working at the public arena level (Ratts, DeKruyf, & Chen-Hayes, 2007). The public arena level of the Advocacy Competencies includes the public information domain where counselors act with queer people and issues, as well as the social/political advocacy domains where counselors work on behalf of queer concerns. Indeed, there is some overlap across these levels in the roles for counselors—most notably the counselor continues to work as an ally, build larger alliances, and build the case for systemic change on queer issues. The difference in the role for counselors advocating at the public arena level is that counselors engage in distributing public information as well as social and political advocacy.

With regard to public information, a major role for counselors is to use their knowledge of queer issues from their own school and community settings to ensure that this knowledge is shared with the general public. The desired outcome of this is not only increased information about queer issues but also potential positive solutions and strategies to address these concerns. For instance, school counselors may have worked individually with queer students and their families on coming-out issues. They may have also learned how to best intervene when bullying and violence toward queer students occurs. With these two examples, school counselors may identify both the common barriers and supports to the healthy development of queer youths in written and multimedia materials. In an effort to clearly delineate these factors, school counselors could also collaboratively work with a local queer community partner to ensure this knowledge is disseminated widely through various forms of media. Similarly, counselors working in community settings may use their knowledge of the impact of internalized homophobia on queer mental health and well-being, informing the public on ways to make work and community settings more queer-affirmative. With this example, counselors could also work collaboratively to create a public service announcement with positive images of queer individuals and families and their resilience to oppression.

Within the social and political advocacy domain, counselors may take action on behalf of the many pressing political concerns that affect queer individuals and families. In this domain, counselors should initially (and ideally in collaboration) work to determine the issues that are most relevant to the local, state, and/or national queer community. For instance, in an urban city where there are many queer youths of color who do not have safe spaces to gather, advocacy may focus on increasing community resources for all youths. In this situation, school counselors may partner with community organizations to create safe spaces or write to legislators about the dearth of school and community resources. In another example, there may be states with laws causing queer families to face significant barriers to adoption rights (e.g., Florida), providing counselors with the opportunity to advocate for adoptive rights for queer parents. In some areas of the United States, there may be extensive advocacy for same-sex marriage rights, but there may be little attention to transgender employment rights. In these situations, counselors may highlight the fact that queer people, including transgender people, do not currently have federal employment protection. School counselors engaging in social and political advocacy may partner with other queer allies within the school to discuss how to integrate these public arena issues in the school curriculum or possibly initiate a schoolwide statement of action on a specific queer issue. Counselors working in community settings may act at the public arena level by identifying how these issues affect clients at the individual level through mental health stressors and then seeking to communicate these challenges to legislators at a broader level.

Another counselor role within the social and political advocacy domain is to support and initiate queer grassroots movements. An important part of this advocacy is to be aware of the previous queer liberation movements in the United States (e.g., Stonewall, gay rights movement) and around the world (Vaid, 1995). For instance, India held its first Queer Pride march in 2007, and Spain recently legalized same-gender marriage. Again, counselors will want to consult closely with queer individuals and communities in determining which grassroots movements are most in need of support or need to be initiated. For instance, if there are high rates of bullying and violence toward queer students and those who are perceived to be queer, school counselors can initiate a movement of school counselors actively working collaboratively to make schools safer for queer youths. If counselors working in community settings identify a recent queer hate crime, they can organize together and contact local, state, and national safety authorities to demand change on hate crimes legislation and better police response and protection for queer people.

Finally, counselors can work on behalf of global queer issues within the public arena advocacy domain. Many people assume that the United States is more progressive on queer issues, and in some cases this is true. However, there are also other countries that may be leading the United States on certain queer issues; therefore, awareness about and action on global concerns are important. Examples of this include countries that have same-sex marriage or domestic partnership rights, such as the Netherlands, Belgium, Spain, and Canada (International Gay and Lesbian Human Rights Commission, 2008). Both school and community counselors may connect with community activists who worked on these queer issues globally, which is an important step of building the rationale for having queer rights in the United States, especially when data exist in these countries about declining hate crimes, increased safety of queer youths, and so on. In other examples, there are countries where being queer is not only considered wrong but is punishable by death (e.g., Iran, Nigeria). When queer-international events occur, school and community counselors can issue proactive statements that are queer-affirmative, or they can possibly organize with other queer allies to initiate letter-writing campaigns of support on queer-global concerns.

Throughout working in the public arena domain of advocacy, school and community counselors should remember that queer people come from a diversity of racial/ethnic, gender, ability levels, class levels, and geographic regions and that salient issues may differ across these communities. Therefore, counselors should seek to closely consult with queer communities to select issues that are most important to them and that are missing from advocacy initiatives.

Addressing the Backlash Against Queer Advocacy: Challenges and Opportunities for Using the Advocacy Competencies

Counselors who have previously engaged in advocacy on queer issues know there are both challenges and opportunities in doing this type of social justice work. Because societal discrimination toward queer people is still acceptable in many school and community settings, counselors may find themselves targeted by covert and/or overt heterosexist comments and behaviors when they engage in queer advocacy at the different levels of the Advocacy Competencies. For instance, a challenge to queer advocacy at the microlevel may be that a school or community organization overtly or subtly issues threats to counselors (e.g., being fired) if they advocate on behalf of queer clients or provide them with necessary queer resources (Mahan et al., 2007). Another challenge at the mesolevel may include confronting other personnel and staff when counselors witness verbal or physical antiqueer threats. Many school counselors share that they hear teachers, principals, and other school personnel actively participating in heterosexism, making negative comments about students being "fairies and sissies" or "acting too gay." When school counselors speak out against this type of prejudice as allies, they may find themselves targeted with similar heterosexist comments (Ji, 2007). These are legitimate and real concerns for queer allies to consider at the micro- and mesolevels. A significant challenge at the macrolevel may be antiqueer messages that are delivered via the media (e.g., television shows, websites). For instance, after the 2008 passage of Proposition 8 in California (which made same-sex marriages legally unrecognized), news media pundits fostered a comparison of queer issues with racial/ethnic issues, which furthered the erroneous idea that queer issues and people-of-color issues are separate entities.

Another common challenge to those engaging in queer advocacy is the conflict that may emerge when conversations occur surrounding religious beliefs and a person's sexuality and/or gender identity. These typically occur across the micro-, meso-, and macrolevels (for an in-depth discussion of religion and queer issues and resources see www.soulforce.org). While these issues are complex, all counselors need to be able to address them because many queer people have faith, religious, and spiritual traditions that are an important aspect of their identities. Building queer-positive relationships and coalitions, in addition to using resources (such as the Advocacy Competencies), can aid counselors when responding to these issues at the three levels of the Advocacy Competencies.

Just as there are challenges to using the Advocacy Competencies with queer people, there are several benefits that arise as well. At the microlevel, counselors have the opportunity to have a positive impact on queer youths and adults. This is a significant advantage considering the rates of depression, suicide, and anxiety resulting from internalized homophobia, biphobia, and transphobia. Also at the microlevel, counselors have the advantage to be able to reflect on their own socialization around gender identity and sexual orientation, which can bring a sense of personal liberation and freedom. Engaging in queer advocacy at the mesolevel gives counselors the opportunity to connect with a larger community of queer allies, and this sense of connection can be both personally and professionally rewarding. Finally, the benefits of queer advocacy at the macrolevel include the recognition that counselors are a vital part of a global effort to make the world a more just and safe place for queer people—an immeasurable reward in itself.

Diversity

A critical aspect of using the Advocacy Competencies on queer issues with sophistication is to be able to understand the importance of multiple identities for queer people. A full discussion of this is beyond the scope of this chapter, so a focus on race/ethnicity, gender, and religion/spirituality is provided. In terms of race/ethnicity, the literature with queer people of color suggests that "coming out" is a Western construct and may not be appropriate for people in many cultures (Singh, Chung, & Dean, 2006). Therefore, counselors will need to be cautious when using the Advocacy Competencies at the client/student level with people of color to ensure the counselor is acting with the individual and not on behalf of the individual when it involves coming-out issues. For many queer people of color, their families and communities of color may provide them with connection and support that they do not experience in queer communities, which may be predominantly White, may have Western values, and may potentially expose queer people of color to racism.

In terms of gender, there are a wide range of gender identities and expression within the queer community that are gender nonconforming. There are also differences between female-identified and male-identified spaces in queer communities. Counselors may act with clients and students to identify communities that feel comfortable to them, in addition to identifying challenges they may face in terms of their gender identity (e.g., using bathrooms, paperwork with only options of "male" and "female"). At the school/community level, counselors may identify barriers and opportunities for queer people to feel safe and supported in their gender identity and expression. In school and community settings, counselors can begin "gender chat" groups at the high school level where queer people can explore their gender identity. Within the public arena level, counselors may connect with helping professionals from other disciplines, such as social workers, psychologists, and psychiatrists, to form collaborations where they can share the challenges and opportunities their youth and adult clients experience in terms of discrimination based on gender identity, and where they can also identify needed services (e.g., counseling, support groups) that would improve the lives of queer people.

In terms of religion/spirituality, counselors should be prepared to address these issues because many queer people have faith, religious, and/or spiritual traditions that are an important aspect of their identities. At the microlevel, counselors can correct the myth that queer people do not subscribe to faith traditions. There are several books and online resources that have queer-positive approaches to religion and spirituality (e.g., Daniel Helminiak's *What the Bible Really Says About Homosexuality* and www.soulforce.org). There are also web resources (e.g., www.exgaywatch.com) that may help counselors to counter the backlash against queer people from the religious right and/or those who seek to "convert" the gender and sexual identities of queer people. At the mesolevel, counselors should be well versed in how to engage in an informed conversation about the history of religion and sexuality, including being prepared to speak out against those who practice unethical practices, such as conversion therapy. Counselors may access many resources to engage in these types of discussions online (e.g., www.thetaskforce.org/issues/faith). Within the public arena level, counselors may consider working with faith organizations to assess the resources provided for queer people.

Conclusion

This chapter discussed the opportunities for counselors across settings (e.g., school, mental health) to advocate on behalf of queer issues at the student/client, school/community, and public arena levels. Specific strategies at each level were provided, in addition to the benefits and challenges involved in working at each of these levels. Counselors are encouraged both to maintain a focus on how heterosexism imposes barriers to queer mental health and to identify opportunities to nurture the resilience of queer people to oppression. At all levels of advocacy, counselors should identify issues of diversity, multiple identities, and intersecting oppressions that affect the queer community.

References

American Civil Liberties Union. (2006). *PRIDE v. White County School District: Case profile.* Retrieved May 30, 2008, from www.aclu.org/lgbt/youth/25917res20060227.html

American Counseling Association. (2005). *ACA code of ethics.* Alexandria, VA: Author.

American School Counselor Association. (2004). *Ethical standards for school counselors* (4th ed.). Alexandria, VA: Author.

Association for Gay, Lesbian, and Bisexual Issues in Counseling. (2005). *Competencies for counseling gay, lesbian, bisexual, and transgender (GLBT) clients.* Retrieved May 15, 2008, from www.algbtic.org/resources/competencies

Association for Lesbian, Gay, Bisexual, and Transgender Issues in Counseling. (2009). *Competencies for counseling with transgender clients.* Retrieved November 10, 2009, from www.ALGBTIC.org.

Bieschke, K. J., Paul, P. L., & Blasko, K. A. (2007). Review of empirical research focused on the experiences of lesbian, gay, and bisexual clients in counseling and psychotherapy. In K. J. Bieschke, R. M. Perez, & DeBord, K. A. (Eds.), *Handbook of counseling and psychotherapy with lesbian, gay, bisexual, and transgender clients* (2nd ed., pp. 293–315). Washington, DC: American Psychological Association.

Bowen, G. L., Martin, J. A., Mancini, J. A., & Nelson, J. P. (2000). Community capacity: Antecedents and consequences. *Journal of Community Practice, 8*(2), 1–21.

Chen-Hayes, S. F. (2001). Counseling and advocacy with transgendered and gender-variant persons in schools and families. *Journal of Humanistic Counseling, Education and Development, 40,* 34–48.

Chernin, J. N., & Johnson, M. R. (2002). *Affirmative psychotherapy and counseling for lesbians and gay men.* Thousand Oaks, CA: Sage.

DeLamater, J., & Friedrich, W. N. (2002). Human sexual development. *Journal of Sex Research, 39,* 10–14.

Espelage, D. L., Aragon, S. R., Birkett, M., & Koenig, B. W. (2008). Homophobic teasing, psychological outcomes, and sexual orientation among high school students: What influence do parents and schools have? *School Psychology Review, 37,* 202–216.

Evans, N. J. (2002). The impact of an LGBT Safe Zone project on campus climate. *Qualitative Research, 43,* 522–539.

Fassinger, R. E., & Arseneau, J. R. (2007). "I'd rather get wet than be under that umbrella": Differentiating the experiences and identities of lesbian, gay, bisexual, and transgender people. In K. J.

Bieschke, R. M. Perez, & DeBord, K. A. (Eds.), *Handbook of counseling and psychotherapy with lesbian, gay, bisexual, and transgender clients* (2nd ed., pp. 19–49). Washington, DC: American Psychological Association.

Federal Bureau of Investigation. (2007). *A summary of hate crimes statistics*. Retrieved November 19, 2008, from http://fbi.gov/ucr/hc2007/index.html

Finkel, M. J., Storaasli, R. D., Bandele, A., & Schaefer, V. (2003). Diversity training in graduate school: An exploratory evaluation of the Safe Zone project. *Professional Psychology: Research and Practice, 34,* 555–561.

Fish, L. S., & Harvey, R. G. (2005). *Nurturing queer youth: Family therapy transformed*. New York: Norton.

Gay, Lesbian, and Straight Education Network. (2007). *The 2007 GLSEN National School Climate Survey: The experiences of lesbian, gay, bisexual, and transgender youth in our nation's schools*. Retrieved November 15, 2008, from http://www.glsen.org/binary-data/GLSEN_ATTACHMENTS/file/000/001/1290-1.pdf

Goodenow, C., Szalacha, L., & Westheimer, K. (2006). School support groups, other school factors, and the safety of sexual minority adolescents. *Psychology in the Schools, 43,* 573–589.

Goodman, M. B., & Moradi, B. (2008). Attitudes and behaviors toward lesbian and gay persons: Critical correlates and mediated relations. *Journal of Counseling Psychology, 55,* 371–384.

Human Rights Campaign. (2009). *Introduction*. Retrieved February 24, 2009, from http://www.hrc.org/issues/marriage.asp

Human Rights Watch. (2001). *Hatred in the hallways: Violence and discrimination against lesbian, gay, bisexual, and transgender students in U.S. schools*. New York: Human Rights Watch.

International Gay and Lesbian Human Rights Commission. (2008). *Urgent appeal re: arrests and persecution based on actual or presumed sexual orientation in Senegal*. Retrieved May 15, 2008, from www.iglhrc.org/site/iglhrc/section.php?id=66

Ji, P. (2007). Being a heterosexual ally to the lesbian, gay, bisexual, and transgendered community: Reflections and development. *Journal of Gay and Lesbian Psychotherapy, 11,* 173–185.

Just the Facts Coalition. (2008). *Just the facts about sexual orientation and youth: A primer for principals, educators, and school personnel*. Washington, DC: American Psychological Association. Retrieved May 15, 2008, from www.apa.org/pi/lgbc/publications/justthefacts.html

Lewis, J. A., Arnold, M. S., House, R., & Toporek, R. L. (2002). *ACA Advocacy Competencies*. Retrieved May 16, 2009, from http://www.counseling.org/Publications/

Logan, C. (1996). Homophobia? No, homoprejudice. *Journal of Homosexuality, 31(3),* 31–53.

Mahan, W., Varjas, K., Dew, B. J., Meyers, J., & Singh, A. A. (2007). School and community providers' perspectives on gay, lesbian, and questioning bullying. *Journal of LGBT Issues in Counseling, 2,* 45–66.

Mayfield, W. (2001). The development of an internalized homonegativity inventory for gay men. *Journal of Homosexuality, 41*(2), 53–76.

McDaniel, J. S., Purcell, D., & D'Augelli, A. R. (2001). The relationship between sexual orientation and risk for suicide: Research findings and future directions for research and prevention. *Suicide and Life-Threatening Behavior, 31,* 84–105.

McWhirter, E. H. (1991). Empowerment in counseling. *Journal of Counseling & Development, 69,* 222–227.

Olweus, D. (1993). *Bullying at school: What we know and what we can do*. Cambridge, MA: Blackwell.

Ratts, M. J., DeKruyf, L., & Chen-Hayes, S. F. (2007). The ACA Advocacy Competencies: A social justice advocacy framework for professional school counselors. *Professional School Counseling, 11,* 90–96.

Rosario, M., Schrimshaw, E. W., Hunter, J., & Gwadz, M. (2002). Gay-related stress and emotional distress among gay, lesbian, and bisexual youths: A longitudinal examination. *Journal of Consulting and Clinical Psychology, 70,* 967–975.

Russell, S. T. (2003). Sexual minority youth and suicide risk. *American Behavioral Scientist, 4,* 1241–1257.

Russell, S. T. (2005). Beyond risk: Resilience in the lives of sexual minority youth. *Journal of Gay and Lesbian Issues, 2*(3), 5–18.

Russell, S. T., & McGuire, J. (2008). The school climate for lesbian, gay, bisexual, and transgender (LGBT) students. In M. Shinn & H. Yoshikawa (Eds.), *Toward positive youth development: Transforming schools and community programs* (pp. 133–149). New York: Oxford University Press.

Savin-Williams, R. C., & Ream, G. L. (2003). Suicide attempts among sexual minority male youth. *Journal of Clinical Child and Adolescent Psychology, 32,* 509–522.

Simoni, J., & Walters, K. L. (2001). Heterosexual identity and heterosexism: Recognizing privilege to reduce prejudice. *Journal of Homosexuality, 41,* 157–172.

Singh, A. A., Chung, Y. B., & Dean, J. K. (2006). Acculturation and internalized homophobia of Asian American lesbian and bisexual women: An exploratory analysis. *Journal of LGBT Issues in Counseling, 2,* 3–19.

Singh, A. A., Dew, B. J., Hays, D. G., & Gailis, A. (2007). Stress coping resources of lesbian and bisexual women. *Journal of LGBT Issues in Counseling, 3,* 15–31.

Singh, A. A., Orpinas, P., & Horne, A. M. (in press). Empowering schools to reduce bullying: A holistic approach. In E. M. Vernberg & B. K. Biggs (Eds.), *Whole school intervention approaches for reducing bullying.* New York: Oxford University Press.

Stone, C. B. (2003). Counselors as advocates for gay, lesbian, and bisexual youth: A call for equity and action. *Multicultural Counseling and Development, 31,* 143–155.

Sue, D. W., Arredondo, P. A., & Davis, R. J. (1992). Multicultural counseling competencies and standards: A call to the profession. *Journal of Counseling & Development, 70,* 477–485.

Szalacha, L. A. (2003). Safer sexual diversity climates: Lessons learned from an evaluation of Massachusetts Safe Schools Program for gay and lesbian adolescents. *American Journal of Education, 110,* 58–88.

Szymanski, D. M., & Chung, Y. B. (2001). The Lesbian Internalized Homophobia Scale: A rational/theoretical approach. *Journal of Homosexuality, 41*(2), 37–52.

Vaid, U. (1995). *Virtual equality: The mainstreaming of gay and lesbian liberation.* New York: Anchor Books.

Whitman, J. S., & Boyd, C. J. (2003). *The therapist's notebook for lesbian, gay, and bisexual clients: Homework, hand-outs, and activities for use in psychotherapy.* Binghamton, NY: Hayworth Press.

Chapter 5

Counseling and Advocacy for Individuals Living in Poverty

William Ming Liu and Noel Estrada-Hernández

The United States, like many other industrialized and postindustrial societies around the world, is marked by economic inequality (Liu, in press). For the United States, this disparity puts a vast amount of wealth into the hands of a few (Drucker, 2008), while many other middle-class Americans toil under the myth of meritocracy (Duncan & Smeeding, 1992; Liu, 2001, 2006; Liu & Ali, 2008; Liu, Ali, et al., 2004; Liu, Soleck, Hopps, Dunston, & Pickett, 2004), and still others are encased in poor, impoverished, and economically unjust conditions (American Psychological Association, 2007). These individual who live in poor and near-poor conditions are likely the ones who receive the poorest mental and physical health care (Hopps & Liu, 2006), receive the lowest quality education (Liu, Fridman, & Hall, 2008; Liu & Hernandez, 2008), and are likely to have poor facility with public services (Lott, 2002; Smith, 2005, 2006; Smith, Foley, & Chaney, 2008). They are likely living in toxic environments, are exposed to neighborhood violence, and have limited access to supermarkets, recreation, or health care (American Psychological Association, 2007; Liu, in press; Liu & Ali, 2008). Living in poverty also means constant psychological distress, which has physical consequences such as obesity (Kuo et al., 2007; Lustig & Strauser, 2007), cardiovascular disease (Epel et al., 2006), and diabetes (Kumari, Head, & Marmot, 2004). Exacerbating these conditions are stressors caused by racism, sexism, ageism, and ableism, to name a few (Liu, 2002; Liu, Hernandez, Mahmood, & Stinson, 2006).

Given all these barriers, this community is always in desperate need. How do counselors advocate and empower clients in poverty? And just as important, how do counselors challenge and change social and economic system and these sociostructural forces that marginalize and oppress individuals at the lowest rungs of the social ladder (Liu & Ali, 2005)? These are some of the questions we address in this chapter. We also define poverty, social class, classism, and class consciousness. Finally, we provide examples of counselor advocacy among one group of individuals who are homeless.

Definitions

According to the U.S. Census Bureau (2007), 12.3% of the population fits in the nation's official poverty definition. Although the U.S. Census reported a slight decrease in the poverty rate from the one reported in 2005, for the year 2006 there were 36.5 million people living in poverty and 46 million living without health coverage, with African Americans, Hispanics, non-Hispanic Whites, and Native Americans, especially those living in reservations, composing the majority of this group (U.S. Census Bureau, 2007). In addition, families with one or more members with a disability had a poverty rate of 12.8%, compared with the 7.7% for families without members with a disability (U.S. Census Bureau, 2000). Although all these individuals have one common denominator (living in poverty), their experience and meaning of what is poverty will likely differ.

When counselors describe someone in poverty, it is unlikely they are referring to the guidelines set forth by the U.S. Census Bureau. The U.S. Census Bureau calculates an income number, graduated by the number of parents/guardians and children in the household, and puts those individuals at or below that number "in poverty." Given a particular poverty threshold, households who make close to or below that threshold are considered near poverty or in severe poverty, respectively (U.S. Census Bureau, 2003). This definition does not take into account other expenditures (i.e., real costs of living) by households, such as child care, health insurance, or gasoline and only addresses basic costs of food (Liu, 2006, in press). Moreover, the poverty threshold is national and does not consider geographic variability such as rural or urban locations (Liu, in press).

While these are definitional problems related to who is considered "in poverty," the threshold also does not account for other experiences with poverty that have lifelong consequences (Sapolsky, 2005). Falling into the category of poverty does not take into account episodic and chronic experiences of poverty, nor does it reflect the possible trauma associated with entry into poverty or struggles and challenges to exit poverty (Stern, 2008). The variability within which poverty is experienced and the trauma and challenges associated with poverty are areas counselors may address as they help, advocate, and empower clients in poverty.

Clients' Definition of Poverty

Counselors need to be aware that individuals living in poverty may have the conception or feeling that people look down on them and think they are lazy, dependent on social welfare, and are not able to make decisions for themselves (Lustig & Strauser, 2007). Other researchers suggest that this perceived lack of privilege, on behalf of the client, will indeed lead to low self-esteem and feelings of powerlessness (Liu, Pickett, & Ivey, 2007). This may present a challenge to counselors when initiating advocacy services. As in counseling, when working on advocacy strategies with individuals in poverty, counselors should pay particular attention to the clients' subjective interpretations of their world. This phenomenological approach to social class or poverty, as described by Liu et al. (2007), focuses on the experience of the individual rather than on the implied stereotypes of the individual based on his or her categorization into a social class group. The personal meaning clients give to their experience as individuals living in poverty will likely be integrated and displayed by their actions.

Liu and Arguello (2006) posited that individuals often perpetuate certain behaviors, such as incurring debt, to uphold their membership in certain groups or maintain a certain social position or appearance. Individuals who fail in their attempts to meet these economic demands may experience internalized classism (Liu & Arguello, 2006). Certainly, not being able to maintain assets and a place in a social group will result in emotional distress, anxiety, and feelings of social inadequacy. Advocacy-oriented counselors should pay attention to the client's understanding of the economic situation experienced and of the consequences and identify the sources of oppression that may affect the client's well-being. Emphasis is placed on the client's meaning of the situation and behavior; for instance, what is the client doing to "fit in" a certain social group (Liu & Arguello, 2006, p. 4). For example, Maria is a single parent who moved to the United States from Colombia. Her only source of income is her job as a clerk at the local grocery store. Even if that is the only income she has for herself and her son Juan, she buys him brand name clothes and shoes so Juan feels better during his high school years. For Maria this is the right thing to do because she wants Juan to be perceived as a successful young man. Exploring the client's rationale and developing awareness on these behaviors and on the client's personal and environmental factors are essential for the development of new and less harmful behaviors for the client (Liu & Arguello, 2006). Once the counselor and client have identified the potential causes or sources of the behavior, it is central to the advocacy process that the counselor identifies with the client key individual and environmental resources that will provide different types of support as needed as well as devises a plan to develop empowerment and assertiveness skills.

As suggested by Liu and his colleagues (Liu, 2001, 2006; Liu & Ali, 2008; Liu, Ali, et al., 2004; Liu & Arguello, 2006; Liu, Soleck, et al., 2004), understanding and integrating social class and classism into counseling is an important multicultural competency. But using social class and classism is a problem if sociological perspectives are used rather than a subjective and phenomenological approach. That is, counselors may understand and use the interpersonal and intrapsychic construction of race and racism, for instance, and frame their work with clients using theories such as racial identity and acculturation; that is, counselors do not focus specifically on race but the psychological construction and experiences of race (i.e., racial identity, acculturation). Building on this premise, Liu and his colleagues (Liu, Soleck, et al., 2004) developed the Social Class Worldview Model (SCWM), which shifts counseling work away from sociological indices such as income, education, and occupation to focus on the lenses through which people construct their social class selves and experiences. The SCWM also assumes that classism is an important coconstruct to social class, much like race is necessary for racism to exist. Liu has argued that a coherent theory must link these two constructs together.

The SCWM assumes that individuals live within economic cultures that place expectations on individuals to develop and use resources or capital in the areas of social networks, aesthetics (cultural capital), and human capital (physical or intellectual abilities). People make sense of these expectations through their worldview, which is divided into subcategories such as socialization messages around social class, the importance of materialism, the necessary social class behaviors, and lifestyle considerations. Liu assumes that individuals use and experience different levels of classism to maintain a social class position. These are upward classism (derogation against those perceived to be in a higher social class), downward classism (derogation against those perceived to be in a lower social class), lateral classism (derogation against those perceived to be in a similar social class), and internalized classism (self-derogation for not being able to maintain one's social class standing).

For counselors, working with clients means exploring these various aspects of their worldview, helping them gain insight into these experiences, and eventually leading them to action to change their environment or situation (Liu & Ali, 2008). But one assumption left unexplored by Liu was the way in which people come to see themselves as social classed beings (Liu, in press). Thus, Liu developed the Social Class and Classism Consciousness (SCCC) model. This model focuses on the ways in which people come to realize they live in an economic system that is unjust and unequal. This realization assists the individual to understand him- or herself as a social classed being that is active in his or her world and neighborhood. In the SCCC model, people may move between 10 stages. These stages are presented here in a hierarchical order, but Liu and colleagues acknowledge that individuals may inhabit and move between the stages in any order. For clarity and presentation, the stages are conceptualized as hierarchical, categorical, and orthogonal. The 10 stages are as follows: Unawareness (social class is not a salient part of the person's worldview), Status Position Saliency (the individual recognizes people in higher and lower social classes), Questioning (the individual questions the role of social class in his or her life), Exploration and Justification (the individual seeks answers to and support for previous beliefs), Despair (the individual may recognize there is no way to change his or her situation or the system), The World Is Just (the individual accepts inequality as a natural state), Intellectualized Anger and Frustration (the individual develops a superficial understanding of inequality and acts on this knowledge), Reinvestment (the individual reexplores the meaningfulness of social class to find different answers), Engagement (the individual engages inequality in his or her immediate surroundings), and Equilibration (the individual understands him- or herself as a social classed being and is active in his or her world and neighborhood). The SCCC model provides a foundation from which counselors are able to assess how individuals see themselves and others as social classed persons and relationships.

Advocacy Competencies With People in Poverty

Advocating and working with clients in poverty necessitates the counselor to be aware of his or her experiences, perspectives, and biases around poverty (Liu & Pope-Davis, 2003). For instance, counselors may need to be aware of their own upward mobility bias that favors people who want to be in a higher social class and denigrates those who do not subscribe to this ideology (Liu et al., 2007). Just as important, counselors need to be sensitive to their own social class–based traumas associated with social class transitions, experiences with trauma, or personal experiences with poverty. Taking account of these experiences means the counselor is aware, sensitive, and capable of using these experiences beneficially with the client and in session. From the American Counseling Association (ACA) Advocacy Competencies (Lewis, Arnold, House, & Toporek, 2002), we have selected three domains that we feel illustrate how counselors may best advocate for their clients in poverty. To illustrate each point, the first author (Liu) will use his experiences working with homeless individuals and supervising trainees in practicums at a homeless shelter.

Advocacy and Empowerment

Working with clients in poverty means that the client and counselor need to have an accurate assessment and understanding of the client's understanding and conceptualization of the current situation and an accurate accounting of objective resources (i.e., income, family support, Social Security Insurance, disabilities). Instilling hope, being empathic with the client, or collaborating with the client does not mean providing false hope or distorting the situation for the client. Instead, it is important to use the terminology of the situation and context. The clients do understand they are in poverty and are poor; using these terms in descriptive as opposed to negative terms may be a form of client empowerment. Finally, as the SCCC model suggests, clients may struggle as they come to realize themselves as social classed individuals within a system that marginalizes them. Helping clients to be aware of this variability and helping them understand their experiences more clearly may guide them to discriminate among individual, system, and cultural barriers.

Example

A Latino family of two parents and two young children came to the homeless shelter seeking services. The father was distraught at the prospect of being considered homeless and felt deep shame associated with being homeless. The mother was distressed and focused her attention on distracting and attending to the two small children. The counselor initially worked with the parents to account for the objective resources for the family. Because the family was only in the homeless shelter for a few days, the next important work for the family was to discuss and focus on their experiences of homelessness and the trauma of losing their apartment and living from their car for a few days. From an SCCC model perspective, working with this family to come to a full realization that they were now poor and homeless was imperative because using these terms to denigrate themselves was easy, and so it was critical that the counselor work with the parents to reframe being poor and homeless as a situational event rather than a dispositional character flaw. As the family came to see their poverty status as situational, they became more receptive to the idea of accessing community, church, and legal services. The acts of accessing resources, cognitively reframing their situation, and seeing themselves as having hope to overcome their current context became forms of personal empowerment.

Community Collaboration

People in poverty potentially have a great amount of services available to them. The problem is that many of these services may have large administrative structures (e.g., the Social Security Administration or a hospital), are stand-alone entities (e.g., a community mental health center), or provide unique services (e.g., rape crisis center). Thus, the agencies may serve one purpose, but for some clients, agencies serving a compendium of problems (e.g., comorbid problems) at a single session may be the most appropriate service. Additionally, some of these agencies may appear to be too monolithic and therefore impersonal, and clients may reject seeking services that do not recognize the individual. Yet for many people who are in poverty, their current situation may encompass a number of these agencies and in different capacities. In advocating for clients, counselors need to help clients develop their health, financial, and legal literacy. But even if clients become better versed, their knowledge, access, and capacity to navigate these services may still be limited. That is, just because clients know their rights and can understand how administrative structures function does not mean they have the facility to navigate these entities. Hence, advocacy-oriented counselors need to constantly think systemically how agencies and other help services may better work with clients in poverty. For instance, one way of collaborating with these agencies is to frame better coordination of services as an economical benefit. Sharing client information across agencies and departments not only eases case management but also facilitates communication and coordination between professionals. Additionally, having a client available for follow-up sessions and other evaluations could potentially reduce costs resulting from missed or late appointments. Because agencies often need training and education about the populations they serve, providing pro bono training and helping these agencies deliver services efficiently may help streamline or reduce costs. In these trainings, it may be helpful to discuss the work being done with impoverished clientele so agency expectations and client knowledge are congruent.

Example

The first author's work with clients at the homeless shelter regularly meant advocating for clients at the hospital, at the Veterans Administration, and at other public service venues (e.g., the city police). At an advocacy level, he was able to use his degree and affiliation with a university to establish credibility and leverage additional or unique services for his clients. The problem was that these types of client-level advocacy would need to be repeated for every individual client, and the organizations with which he interacted would have no institutional memory of these interactions. Community collaboration first meant that the institutional agents with whom contact would be repeated (e.g., psychiatry, sheriff, Veterans Administration psychologist) would need to become better acquainted with each other and the homeless shelter. To start this process, he invited them to attend a fundraising dinner for the homeless shelter. This was a communitywide event that was attended by prominent community and university officials and many donors. Along with the service providers, shelter residents were included in the event, some of whom were honored for their own educational, vocational, and life-changing accomplishments. During this event, these new collaborators saw that they would be a part of a larger network of help givers and that their services would be recognized. The dinner also provided the new collaborators an opportunity to interact with those in other agencies and with those to whom services were to be provided.

Social/Political Advocacy

The access and ability to influence larger systems of political power are likely truncated or completely diminished for individuals in poverty. Especially for those who are homeless, their ability to influence local politics is dramatically limited because of their transient situation in search of jobs or housing. For many city and municipal leaders, people who are homeless do not pay enough taxes or contribute positively to the conditions in the city. The burden of advocacy at this level often falls to the full-time staff, directors, and other ad hoc committee members of homeless shelters. Of course the problem is that many of these individuals have multiple commitments that limit their ability to engage in full-time advocacy.

Example

For the first author, social and political advocacy comes in two forms. First, he is actively engaged in providing public forums that present and discuss issues of poverty, being poor, and homelessness.

Participants are varied and often reflect the general population of the city. Always included in these discussions are residents from the shelter and other individuals who are homeless and from impoverished backgrounds. It is critical that these presentations and discussions not take place in intellectually sterile contexts but rather involve the voices and lives of those we want to better serve. For many shelter residents, these become important opportunities to speak publicly and to see themselves as change agents. This is an important form of social and political advocacy because the first author is able to use his privileges of being male, educated, and of an upper social class to allow audience members to understand these issues through someone with whom they may identify.

Second, the first author's research and clinical interests are in the areas of poverty and homelessness. As such, at a broader professional level, theoretical and research writings often infuse his clinical experiences. The result is that other programs are attempting to and are considering offering practicum experiences in their own local homeless shelters and poverty-focused agencies. These new practicum experiences may provide counselors and psychologists in training with additional experiences to become multiculturally competent with these communities and provide opportunities for these trainees to practice their own advocacy work. Social policy may also integrate this community-based research because the research reflects actual clients using these services. At a foundational level, the research is important in creating and refining current programs and services (e.g., science to practice and practice to science). At a policy level, the research offers data to policymakers as to how, when, and where resources and programs should be located and directed.

Challenges for Counselors When Advocating for Clients in Poverty

In this section, we discuss the potential challenges counselors might face when working on their advocacy efforts with individuals in poverty. These challenges include the counselor's biases and worldview, the integration of a phenomenological approach when advocating with and on behalf of individuals in poverty, the development of clients' self-advocacy skills, environmental barriers to advocacy, and the development of counselors' advocacy skills. This chapter concludes with a presentation of the benefits of implementing the Advocacy Competencies when working with individuals living in poverty.

Generalizing and Idealizing Poverty

Through their interactions with their clients, counselors may unintentionally develop profiles of their clients based on their characteristics or life situations. Counselors who provide support or advocacy services to individuals living in poverty may be challenged by their own assumption that all individuals living in poverty will have the same worldview (Liu & Arguello, 2006). Yet the possibilities are that individuals living in similar conditions and having similar education levels and occupations will have different experiences and views of their world, considering their individual environments. Counselors who do not attempt to understand their clients' world from a phenomenological perspective, that is, from the subjective interpretation of the client (Corey, 2008), will likely be imposing personal values, perspectives, and even potential options to the client. This *clinical judgment bias* (Rosenthal & Kosciulek, 1996) uses a single attribute of the person (i.e., poverty) and deemphasizes other characteristics while the counselor is processing information and planning for services. As a result, the client is not empowered, has not developed an awareness of resources and assets, and lacks assertiveness skills necessary to cope. Not being able to recognize personal bias will result in the counselor being emotionally absent from his or her counseling or advocacy interventions (Robinson, 2009). Liu and Arguello (2006) suggested that counselors should take a contextualized approach when counseling individuals in poverty. In other words, counselors should pay attention to the wide range of personal, psychological, and social/economical effects of poverty on a person's life (Robinson, 2009). This will become particularly important in the practice of advocacy, as clients should take an active role with the counselor in identifying barriers to well-being needs and the services needed to satisfy those needs. In addition, counselors may be challenged by their idealization of their clients (Liu et al., 2007). When a counselor idealizes a client, attitudes of a dominant position are manifested; the counselor may hold beliefs that the client is novel, a victim, without agency, and deserving of constant help. In contrast, counselors should view their clients as individuals, different from others, who are living within economic cultures that place demands on them to develop social connections, cultural tastes, and human abilities (Liu & Arguello, 2006).

Development of Self-Advocacy Skills

Lustig and Strauser (2007) suggested that individuals living in poverty, especially those with disabilities, have difficulties acting in an empowered manner, feel that change in the environment will not have positive outcomes, and are likely to be surrounded by disempowered role models that reduce any positive social learning. For the advocacy-oriented counselor, this may prove a difficult challenge. Through advocacy-oriented counseling, a client's sense of empowerment can be increased. Advocacy counseling stresses the role of the counselor in helping clients to identify and confront oppression and other forms of sociopolitical policies that limit or hamper their success (Toporek, 2000, cited in Astramovich & Harris, 2007). Advocacy counseling, which is based on multiculturalism, helps clients develop self-worth, efficacy, and empowerment to deal with these discriminatory behaviors (Liu & Toporek, 2004). When working with individuals in poverty, counselors face a major challenge of developing the client's self-advocacy skills. Self-advocacy involves the process of identifying and meeting personal needs "without compromising or affecting one's or others' dignity" (Skinner, 1998, cited in Astramovich & Harris, 2007, p. 271). The development of self-advocacy skills focuses on personal rights and responsibilities. The goal is to enhance the client's self-agency skills in a way that personal needs and the help necessary from the environment are articulated (Astramovich & Harris, 2007; Liu & Toporek, 2004). Clients may need to be coached in how to be situationally assertive and how to develop self-agency skills to confront oppressive behaviors. Ultimately, individuals will be responsible for the satisfaction of their needs and their success. To develop the individual success advocacy skills, counselors should work on assisting the client in becoming aware of the importance of self-advocacy, increasing their knowledge of advocacy, and helping them develop communication, negotiation, and assertiveness skills to successfully access and navigate through environmental systems (Astramovich & Harris, 2007).

Environmental Barriers to Advocacy

Literature suggests that for individuals who live in poverty, and likely those with disabilities (Lustig & Strauser, 2007), in addition to having difficulties being situationally assertive, making career selections, or maintaining employment, one of the biggest obstacles is navigating through social service systems (Liu & Toporek, 2004; Lustig & Strauser, 2007). It is through advocacy that counselors working with individuals in poverty can confront environmental oppressive behaviors that are limiting clients' access to resources, services, and overall participation in the community. Counselors advocating in the community may be challenged by the existing perception or stereotypes toward individuals living in poverty or the lack of social services or adequate policies to guide available services. Counselors entering a community initially may use their status as a professional (Toporek, Lewis, & Crethar, 2009) to provide information on ways that the community or the involved organizations are perpetuating behaviors that lead to oppression and marginalization of this population. Also, counselors can gain access to a community through organizations or groups. Communities often have different organizations (i.e., neighborhood associations/boards) or specific groups addressing certain social issues (e.g., religion, race/ethnicity, sports, etc.; Hopps & Liu, 2006). Counselors may consider working as allies with these groups to overcome resistance to exploring oppressive behaviors or to obtain access to the community. At the same time, the counselor should be identifying social resources and developing networks to collaborate in an advocacy plan (Liu & Toporek, 2004; Toporek et al., 2009).

This imparting of information and community involvement likely will lead to lowered resistance and increased insight on privilege and ways to facilitate access to resources and social participation of individuals living in poverty in their communities.

Counselor Preparation Programs

Counselor education programs have included multicultural counseling training following the model presented by Sue, Arredondo, and McDavis (1992), which states that counselors should have awareness, knowledge, and skills in the domains of understanding personal beliefs and biases, clients' worldviews, and the development of culturally sensitive interventions. Considering the fit of advocacy as a social justice practice, it is important that the issue of training as an advocate be addressed. Many researchers have described the positive impact of advocacy efforts on behalf of the client (Astramovich & Harris, 2007; Liu & Toporek, 2004; Meyers & Sweeney, 2004) and on behalf of the profession itself (Meyers & Sweeney, 2004; O'Connell & Shupe, 2007; Toporek et al., 2009). However, even with the reported positive impact on clients and social organizations, research suggests that advocacy training is a contemporary need of professional counselors and an area of high importance in the counseling practice (Meyers & Sweeney, 2004). Such a statement has also been supported by other researchers (Liu & Arguello, 2006). It is clear that lack of advocacy training will limit the range of efforts and services a counselor can provide to clients. Thus it is important that counselor preparation programs consider the inclusion in their curriculum of contemporary advocacy literature and research, development of advocacy skills (e.g., communication, negotiation, empowerment skills), and, whenever possible, practicums and supervision.

In relation to the practicum side, Liu et al. (2007) suggested that counselors need to be aware of how their views and applications of their counseling theories and techniques may affect their conceptualization of poverty given the fact that these models and theories have been mainly developed by White, Western middle-class individuals. Without the identification of personal attitudes, counselors are at risk of perpetuating behaviors and attitudes that will enable classism. Also, not addressing these issues in counseling and advocacy practice may hinder the development of a healthy working relationship between the counselor and a client. Counselors in training should seek professional experience in advocacy in a supportive environment that will challenge their beliefs and knowledge of social class, poverty, and classism (Liu & Ali, 2008). In doing so, they can implement the SCWM as presented by Liu, Soleck, et al. (2004). This model focuses on explaining the individual's personal experience with social class and how socialization messages and personal relationships come together to make personal meaning of social class and membership into desired social groups. However, if a practicum experience in advocacy cannot be facilitated by the counselor preparation program, counselors in training are encouraged to explore other alternatives to document their advocacy development, for instance, preparing a professional portfolio (Liu & Toporek, 2004). In this portfolio the student can record any volunteer activities or workshops attended that relate to advocacy at the individual or social levels, include any class papers or personal research conducted in this area, and include personal developmental reflections as they relate to the development of advocacy skills. As suggested by Liu and Toporek, this will allow the student to obtain more comprehensive training materials and will provide program faculty with evaluative information on the student's advocacy development.

Benefits of Interventions Based on the Advocacy Competencies

To more comprehensively address the needs of individuals who are not only living in poverty but also facing other social threats to their well-being, counselors have been called upon to maximize their interventions out of the counseling office (Toporek et al., 2009). Certainly the implementation of the Advocacy Competencies to the situation of individuals living in poverty has its challenges, but it also has potential benefits for all the parties involved in these efforts. As helping professionals, counselors will benefit from their continued self-exploration and development of specialized skills as required by the Multicultural Counseling Competencies (Sue et al., 1992). Considering the fact that most of multicultural efforts in counseling have been traditionally focused on race and gender issues (Liu & Toporek, 2004), it is beneficial for counselors to bring the issues experienced by individuals living in poverty to the forefront. This allows counselors to keep a constant exploration of self-beliefs and biases and constant documentation of their multicultural development.

Individuals living in poverty will benefit the greatest from advocacy interventions. First, they will gain awareness of how the experience of living in poverty is affecting life in terms of behavior, health, or psychosocial aspects. Second, they will increase their awareness of how issues of power and access relate to their socioeconomic status and thus their presenting problems. Third, because the counseling literature stresses the fact that awareness brings choice and responsibility (Corey, 2008), through these advocacy efforts clients will be able to develop more self-agency and empowerment skills. These skills, in the form of assertiveness, communication, and decision making, will allow the client to better articulate and negotiate pressing needs caused by oppressive behavior in the community.

At the systems, public, or community levels, advocacy strategies can strengthen an individual's investment in community efforts (Hopps & Liu, 2006). This likely will result in the identification of social needs for change in policies and service delivery for individuals living in poverty. Community involvement in these efforts speaks to the eradication or abandonment of oppressive ideologies that affect individuals based not only on their socioeconomic status but also on their race, ethnicity, ability, or sexual orientation.

Conclusion

In this chapter we explored the application of the ACA Advocacy Competencies to individuals living in poverty. Emphasis was made on the need to approach poverty from a phenomenological standpoint as described by Liu's SCWM (Liu, Soleck, et al., 2004). In doing so, counselors have the opportunity to empower their clients and teach them self-agency skills. In relation to training, we recommend that counselors seek experience in the delivery of advocacy services and that they keep constant documentation of their advocacy skills. Counselor preparation programs should include this content in their curriculum to satisfy this contemporary need within our profession and our clients.

References

American Psychological Association. (2007). *Taskforce report on socioeconomic status.* Retrieved January 31, 2007, from www.apa.org/pi/SES_task_force_report.pdf

Astramovich, R. L., & Harris, K. R. (2007). Promoting self-advocacy among minority students in school counseling. *Journal of Counseling & Development, 85,* 269–276.

Corey, G. (2008). *Theory and practice of counseling and psychotherapy* (8th ed.). Pacific Grove, CA: Thompson.

Drucker, J. (2008, July 23). Richest Americans see their income share grow. *The Wall Street Journal,* p. A3.

Duncan, G. T., & Smeeding, T. M. (1992). The incredible shrinking middle class. *American Demographics, 14*(5), 34–39.

Epel, E. S., Lin, J., Wilhelm, F. H., Wolkowitz, O. M., Cawthon, R., Adler, N. E., et al. (2006). Cell aging in relation to stress arousal and cardiovascular disease risk factors. *Psychoneuroendocrinology, 31,* 277–287.

Hopps, J. A., & Liu, W. M. (2006). Working for social justice from within the health care system. In R. L. Toporek, L. H. Gerstein, N. A. Fouad, G. Roysricar, & T. Israel (Eds.), *Handbook for social justice in counseling psychology: Leadership, vision, and action* (pp. 318–337). Thousand Oaks, CA: Sage.

Kumari, M., Head, J., & Marmot, M. (2004). Prospective study of social and other risk factors for incidence of Type 2 diabetes in the Whitehall II Study. *Archives of Internal Medicine, 164,* 1873–1880.

Kuo, L. E., Kitlinksa, J. B., Tilan, J. U., Li, L., Baker, S. B., Johnson, M. D., et al. (2007). Neuropeptide Y acts directly in the periphery on fat tissue and mediates stress-induced obesity and metabolic syndrome. *Nature Medicine, 13,* 803–811.

Lewis, J. A., Arnold, M. S., House, R., & Toporek, R. L. (2002). *ACA Advocacy Competencies.* Retrieved August 12, 2008, from http://www.counseling.org/Publications/

Liu, W. M. (2001). Expanding our understanding of multiculturalism: Developing a social class worldview model. In D. B. Pope-Davis & H. L. K. Coleman (Eds.), *The intersection of race, class, and gender in counseling psychology* (pp. 127–170). Thousand Oaks, CA: Sage.

Liu, W. M. (2002). The social class-related experiences of men: Integrating theory and practice. *Professional Psychology: Research and Practice, 33,* 355–360.

Liu, W. M. (2006). Classism is much more complex. *American Psychologist, 61,* 337–338.

Liu, W. M. (in press). Developing and social class and classism consciousness. In E. Altmaier & J. I. Hansen (Eds.), *Handbook of counseling psychology.* New York: Oxford University Press.

Liu, W. M., & Ali, S. R. (2005). Addressing social class and classism in vocational theory and practice: Extending the emancipatory communitarian approach. *The Counseling Psychologist, 33,* 189–196.

Liu, W. M., & Ali, S. R. (2008). Social class and classism: Understanding the impact of poverty and inequality. In S. D. Brown & R. W. Lent (Eds.), *Handbook of counseling psychology* (4th ed., pp. 159–175). New York: Wiley.

Liu, W. M., Ali, S. R., Soleck, G., Hopps, J., Dunston, K., & Pickett, T., Jr. (2004). Using social class in counseling psychology research. *Journal of Counseling Psychology, 51,* 3–18.

Liu, W. M., & Arguello, J. (2006). Social class and classism in counseling. *Counseling and Human Development, 39*(3), 1–12.

Liu, W. M., Fridman, A., & Hall, T. (2008). Social class and school counseling. In H. L. K. Coleman & C. Yeh (Eds.), *Handbook of school counseling* (pp. 145–156). Mahwah, NJ: Erlbaum.

Liu, W. M., & Hernandez, J. (2008). Social class and educational psychology. In N. J. Salkind (Ed.), *Encyclopedia of educational psychology.* Thousand Oaks: Sage.

Liu, W. M., Hernandez, J., Mahmood, A., & Stinson, R. (2006). The link between poverty, classism, and racism in mental health. In D. W. Sue & M. G. Constantine (Eds.), *Racism as a barrier to cultural competence in mental health and educational settings* (pp. 65–86). Hoboken, NJ: Wiley.

Liu, W. M., Pickett, T., Jr., & Ivey, A. E. (2007). White middle-class privilege: Social class bias and implications for training and practice. *Journal of Multicultural Counseling and Development, 35,* 194–207.

Liu, W. M., & Pope-Davis, D. B. (2003). Understanding classism to effect personal change. In T. B. Smith (Ed.), *Practicing multiculturalism: Internalizing and affirming diversity in counseling and psychology* (pp. 294–310). New York: Allyn & Bacon.

Liu, W. M., Soleck, G., Hopps, J., Dunston, K., & Pickett, T. (2004). A new framework to understand social class in counseling: The social class worldview and modern classism theory. *Journal of Multicultural Counseling and Development, 32,* 95–122.

Liu, W. M., & Toporek, R. L. (2004). Advocacy in rehabilitation counseling. In D. R. Maki & T. F. Rigger (Eds.), *Rehabilitation counseling: Profession and practice* (3rd ed., pp. 188–198). New York: Springer.

Lott, B. (2002). Cognitive and behavioral distancing from the poor. *American Psychologist, 57,* 100–110.

Lustig, D. C., & Strauser, D. R. (2007). Casual relationship between poverty and disability. *Rehabilitation Counseling Bulletin, 50,* 194–202.

Meyers, J. E., & Sweeney, T. J. (2004). Advocacy for the counseling profession: Results of a national survey. *Journal of Counseling & Development, 82,* 466–471.

O'Connell, W., & Shupe, M. (2007). A method to teaching counselors to be social advocates in the age of modern behavioral health care. *Counseling and Values, 51,* 82–92.

Robinson, T. L. (2009). *The convergence of race, ethnicity, and gender: Multiple identities in counseling* (3rd ed.). Columbus, OH: Merrill Prentice Hall.

Rosenthal, D. A., & Kosciulek, J. F. (1996). Clinical judgment bias due to client race or ethnicity: An overview with implications for rehabilitation counselors. *Journal of Applied Rehabilitation Counseling, 27*(3), 30–37.

Sapolsky, R. (2005, December). Sick of poverty. *Scientific American, 293*(6), 92–99.

Smith, L. (2005). Psychotherapy, classism, and the poor: Conspicuous by their absence. *American Psychologist, 60,* 687–696.

Smith, L. (2006). Addressing classism, extending multicultural competence, and serving the poor. *American Psychologist, 61,* 338–339.

Smith, L., Foley, P. F., & Chaney, M. P. (2008). Addressing classism, ableism, and heterosexism in counselor education. *Journal of Counseling & Development, 86,* 303–309.

Stern, S. M. (2008, May 15). *Poverty dynamics: 2001–2003.* Retrieved July 24, 2008, from www.census.gov/hhes/www/poverty/publications.html.

Sue, D. W., Arredondo, P., & McDavis, R. J. (1992). Multicultural counseling competencies and standards: A call to the profession. *Journal of Counseling & Development, 70,* 477–486.

Toporek, R. L., Lewis, J. A., & Crethar, H. C. (2009). Promoting systemic change through the Advocacy Competencies. *Journal of Counseling & Development, 87,* 260–268.

U.S. Census Bureau. (2000). *Disability and American families 2000.* Retrieved July 10, 2007, from http://www.census.gov/prod/2005pubs/censr-23.pdf

U.S. Census Bureau. (2003). Poverty in the United States: 2002. In *Current Population Reports, P60-222.* Washington, DC: U.S. Department of Commerce.

U.S. Census Bureau. (2007). *Household incomes rises, poverty rate declines, number of uninsured up.* Retrieved July 10, 2007, from http://www.census.gov/Press-Release/www/releases/archives/income_wealth/010583.html

Chapter

6

ACA Advocacy Competencies With Culturally Diverse Clients

Cirecie A. West-Olatunji

This chapter examines the role of counselor advocacy in ameliorating the psychological effects of systemic oppression for culturally diverse individuals. Beginning with a presentation of inequities in education, I discuss systemic oppression within the context of traumatic stress and its resultant health disparities and psychological outcomes. Transgenerational trauma is presented as a lens through which clinical conceptualization, intervention, and assessment can be conducted with culturally diverse clients. I integrate clinical competence that incorporates advocacy and social justice into the discussion to place emphasis on client and community empowerment, sociopolitical context, and the co-construction of presenting client issues as well as resolution of those issues.

Introduction

Despite major civil rights efforts, members of culturally diverse groups continue to be socially marginalized, resulting in qualitatively different life experiences in educational, vocational, and health areas, among others (Sue & Sue, 2008). It has been stated that much of the macrosystemic problems experienced by many African Americans, Latino Americans, Native Americans, and Asian Americans stem from long-term and pervasive oppression-related historical trauma (Bryant-Davis & Ocampo, 2005). Moreover, particularly within low-income communities, associations have also been made between discrimination and poorer health-related behaviors (J. P. Harrell, Hall, & Taliaferro, 2003).

Traditional responses from counselors and other mental health service providers have been to conceptualize these clients from a Eurocentric perspective that focuses on an individual's intrapsychic processes and minimizes the systemic forces that influence clients' available choices and sense of empowerment (Lewis, Lewis, Daniels, & D'Andrea, 2003; Sue & Sue, 2008). In contrast, the American Counseling Association (ACA) Advocacy Competencies emphasize clients' strengths, environmental context, community support, and ecosystemic interventions (Lewis, Arnold, House, & Toporek, 2002). Hence, counselors who integrate advocacy into their professional identity are apt to enhance their clinical efficacy by reducing the associated stress experienced by many socially marginalized individuals. Advocacy-competent counselors can also expect increased expediency when attempting to resolve clients' presenting concerns.

A Historiography of Miseducation, Systemic Oppression, and Transgenerational Trauma

Educational Hegemony

Nowhere is systemic oppression more evident, pervasive, or influential in shaping the quality of life for culturally diverse individuals than in the area of education. The National Center for Education Statistics (NCES, 2003) reports that wide gaps in achievement exist among cultural and ethnic groups. Those students most affected by the achievement gap are Native Americans, specific Asian American subgroups (in particular, Vietnamese and Pacific Islanders), Latino Americans, and African Americans.

The historiography of Native Americans includes placement in government-run boarding schools that has resulted in widespread suspicion of school-based programs designed for native people, specifically those run by outsiders (Lomawaima, 1995). Although these types of boarding schools are not as prevalent today, current schools continue to be unresponsive to the cultural needs of Native American students (Ward, 2005). Many schools serving these students have curricula that (a) focus on vocational training, (b) do not reflect this population's values and beliefs, and (c) serve as tools to assimilate Native Americans into the lower strata of U.S. culture (Deyhle, 1995; Ward, 2005). These culturally insensitive practices contribute to the low achievement of Native American students and other underinvestigated ethnocultural groups, such as Asian Pacific Americans.

Researchers often ignore or minimize within-group differentiation when investigating Asian Americans. Viewed monolithically as a model minority, Asian American students receive less-than-adequate attention in educational research literature (W. Kim, 2003). Their academic performance has been described as bimodal because, although a large part of this population is represented in high-achieving groups, a substantive number of Asian Pacific students are also represented in the low academic achievement groups (Delucchi & Do, 1996). For example, in some school districts this population has both the highest school dropout rates and the highest grade point averages (H. Kim, Rendon, & Valadez, 1998). In particular, Pacific Islanders and children from Indochina (Vietnam, Cambodia, and Laos) face many problems in schools because of acculturation and language barriers (Marshall, 2002). While little has been written about Native American and Asian American students' underperformance, literature abounds in the area of African American and Latino American student achievement.

Latino American students face a number of obstacles, both in and out of schools. One such problem is poverty; Latino American students are more likely than their White counterparts to live in poor areas (NCES, 2003). When comparing academic achievement levels, Latino American students score considerable lower than their White counterparts (Keith, 1999). Even more alarming are the high dropout rates for Latino American students. For the past three decades, Latino American students have had the highest school dropout rates of all the cultural groups (Kaufman, Alt, & Chapman, 2004; NCES, 2003).

Such disparities are also evident among African American students. In addition to chronic underachievement on standardized tests, African American students are overrepresented in mentally retarded, learning disabled, and emotionally disturbed categories and underrepresented in gifted programs (Civil Rights Project, 2002; U.S. Department of Education, 2002). These students also experience high rates of school suspension, corporal punishment, and other behavioral referrals. Such disciplinary actions undermine African American students' self-esteem and can lead to underachievement and even dropping out altogether (Steele & Aronson, 1995; Townsend, 2000).

Systemic Oppression and Psychological Hegemony

Understanding systemic oppression is an important step toward reconceptualizing mental health and overall functioning for culturally diverse people as well as other socially marginalized groups. Inherent in the definition of systemic oppression is an awareness of the overt and covert ways in which members of culturally diverse groups are violated (Burstow, 2003). Lack of access to institutional resources and lack of power to control those institutions create a cycle of sociocultural abuse that threatens the psyche of culturally diverse individuals (Sue & Sue, 2008). Yet, mental health professionals have been slow in defining issues within the context of normality outside of a Eurocentric framework (Holdstock, 2000; Ibrahim, Roysircar-Sodowsky, & Ohimshi, 2001; Kambon, 1996; Whitbeck, 2006). For culturally diverse clients, this has meant diagnoses based on models of normalcy for middle-class Whites.

One example of psychological hegemony that typifies the profession's confluence with sociocultural oppression is illustrated in the historiography of African Americans, beginning with diagnoses during enslavement. Diagnoses such as *drapetomania* and *dysaesthesia aethiopica* formed the scientific rationale for the antebellum South. *Drapetomania* was a term used to explain the "flight from home madness" of runaway Africans enslaved on plantations. *Dysaesthesia aethiopica,* also known as "rascality," refers to the mental affliction of enslaved Africans who exhibited behaviors in which they disrespected the rights of the slave master's property and resisted the forcible labor imposed on them (Thomas & Sillen, 1971). These foundling diagnoses were intended to support and reproduce cultural dominance by labeling acts and thoughts of self-preservation as dysfunctional. Moreover, the psychological effects of this abuse are frequently passed on from generation to generation.

Transgenerational Trauma

The notion of transgenerational trauma was initially developed from the investigation of the ways in which Jewish Holocaust survivors' children were affected by their parents' traumatic experiences (Danieli, 1998). The predominance of mental health interventions for these children in the late 1960s ignited impact research in Canada, the United States, and Israel. Explorations of transgenerational trauma have included families of veterans from World War II and the Vietnam War (Aarts, 1998; Bernstein, 1998; Rosenheck & Fontana, 1998), indigenous peoples (Duran, Duran, Yellow Horse Brave Heart, & Yellow Horse-Davis, 1998; Raphael, Swan, & Martinek, 1998), survivors of child abuse and domestic violence (Frazier, West-Olatunji, St. Juste, & Goodman, 2008; Schechter, Brunelli, Cunningham, Brown, & Baca, 2002; Simons & Johnson, 1998; Walker, 1999), and disaster survivors (Goodman & West-Olatunji, 2008).

The internment of Japanese Americans during World War II, the enslavement of people of African descent, and genocidal acts against indigenous peoples are three poignant illustrations of transgenerational trauma in the United States (Dass-Brailsford, 2007). Of note, these historical experiences continue to affect the mental health of those descendants. In a contemporary context, significant mental health effects, such as depression, anxiety, hypervigilance, low self-esteem, suicidal ideation and behavior, substance abuse, violence, and loss of cultural identity, have been cited (Dass-Brailsford, 2007; Duran et al., 1998; Felsen, 1998; Raphael et al., 1998; Simons & Johnson, 1998). Within this context, scholars have advocated for culturally sensitive conceptualization (West-Olatunji, 2008), interventions (Pedersen, 1991), and assessment (Dana, 1993; Ibrahim et al., 2001; Suzuki, Meller, & Ponterotto, 1996).

Current models of counseling and psychotherapy now shy away from ethnocentric monoculturalism and emphasize culture-centeredness as a focus for research, assessment, and treatment of culturally diverse clients (Comstock et al., 2008; Garcia, Cartwright, Winston, & Borzuchowska, 2003; Pedersen, 1991). For culturally diverse clients, this suggests a culture-centered framework for counseling theory and practice that reflects a cultural worldview rooted in clients' own historical experiences. Emphasizing collaboration between the counselor and client, practitioners and theorists seek to empower culturally diverse individuals and communities (Utsey, Bolden, & Brown, 2001).

Culture-centered theories and interventions move beyond adapting conventional, Eurocentric counseling theories of personality to developing therapeutic frameworks that centralize cultural values and worldviews as the basis for normalcy. Use of culturally informed interventions, from Native American (Garrett, Brubaker, Torres-Rivera, West-Olatunji, & Conwill, 2008; Whitbeck, 2006), Latino American (Constantino, Malgady, & Rogler, 1986; Yeh, Hunter, Madan-Bahel, Chiang,

& Arora, 2004), Asian American (Reynolds, 2001; Yoshikawa et al., 2003), and African American frameworks (West-Olatunji, Shure, Garrett, Conwill, & Torres, 2008; Williams-Clay, West-Olatunji, & Cooley, 2001), have been presented. Common themes in these culture-centered counseling models are reciprocity of healing between the counselor and the client, use of support networks, and advocacy for one's self and one's group. The Advocacy Competencies also emphasize the development of self-advocacy skills as an important component in the counseling process.

Social Justice and Advocacy in Counseling

An emerging emphasis on conceptualizing clients within the context of their sociopolitical realities was borne out of discourse in multicultural counseling (Bemak & Chung, 2005; Vera & Speight, 2003). Understanding sociopolitical context is especially important when working with socially marginalized individuals and communities (Constantine, Hage, Kindaichi, & Bryant, 2007; Hage, 2003; Sue & Sue, 2008). In 1999, ACA created a new division, Counselors for Social Justice, that further highlighted the importance of social justice in counselor identity. Advocacy and social justice in counseling underlines three critical actions: (a) empowering clients, (b) raising public awareness of systemic issues affecting clients' lives, and (c) fostering sociopolitical change that will improve the lives of marginalized persons (Bemak & Chung, 2005; Kiselica & Robinson, 2001; Lewis et al., 2002).

Recommendations

For the most part, traditional perspectives in the behavioral sciences have focused on the client as a poorly functioning individual. An ecological approach considers the possibility of a malfunctioning system and its impact on the client (Pardeck & Chung, 1997). In analyzing some hypotheses to explain why clinicians have been slow to incorporate systemic interventions into their roles and responsibilities, one study suggested that clinicians may "underestimate the power of resources other than their values, skills, and personalities" (Eriksen, 1999, p. 33).

An ecosystemic perspective in examining trauma aids in understanding and conceptualizing the needs of culturally diverse communities. Concentrating on the African American experience, researchers have begun investigating the correlates between historical trauma and oppression (Danoff-Burg, Prelow, & Swenson, 2004; S. P. Harrell, 2000; Rich & Grey, 2005; Scott, 2003). Additional work in this area by Seaton (2003) revealed that, because of racism in particular, African Americans experience more stressful events than European Americans. In summarizing the differential exposure hypothesis, Seaton suggested that racism, bias, and discrimination are detrimental to African Americans because they are disproportionately placed at higher risk for psychological disorders. Ecosystemic interventions incorporate an understanding of those external influences that have an impact on individuals' functioning (Pardeck & Chung, 1997).

Over the past decade, mental health practitioners across all disciplines have become increasingly aware of the need for clinicians to involve themselves in the role of advocate for their clients (Bryant-Davis & Ocampo, 2005; Constantine & Sue, 2006; Griffen, 1993). Clinicians need to consider their clients within the context of their families and communities as well as their social, cultural, and religious systems (Boydell & Volpe, 2004; Sklarew, Twemlow, & Wilkinson, 2004). Additionally, assessment and treatment models are needed to intervene with clients who have been affected by systemic oppression. Clinicians can explore relevant themes to address the context of systemic oppression and the related traumatic experiences. Intervening for trauma due to systemic oppression is necessary for recovery. Through their expanded awareness of sociocultural oppression, clinicians can become healers as well as advocates for their clients (Griffin, 1993).

Next Steps

Prior lack of emphasis on the relationship between individuals and their ecosystems may be, in part, attributed to clinicians' inadequate training in the area of client advocacy (Eriksen, 1999; Kiselica

& Robinson, 2001). Current discussions in the fields of counseling and psychology suggest that individuals and communities are better served when social advocacy is used (American Association for Marriage and Family Therapy, 2004; American Counseling Association, 2005; American Psychological Association, 2002; Council for Accreditation of Counseling and Related Educational Programs, 2001; Osborne et al., 1998; Savage, Harley, & Nowak, 2005).

With the establishment of ACA's Counselors for Social Justice division, more counselor educators have begun to integrate social justice into their counselor identity. The approval of the Advocacy Competencies in 2003 also served to broaden counselors' emphases by offering guidelines for competent practice in social justice advocacy. As an outcome, increased scholarship in the areas of social action and advocacy have emerged within counseling literature (Kiselica & Robinson, 2001; Lee, 1998; Watson, Collins, & Correia, 2004). To date, the majority of these publications rely on anecdotal experiences and conceptual papers offering novel approaches. More scholarship is warranted that provides empirical investigation of the impact of advocacy competence on client presenting problems. The imperative for academicians is to actively engage in collaborative research in communities and use their involvement as a form of engaged scholarship (Emihovich, 2005). Such a reciprocal relationship with clients has the capacity to transform communities, augment counselor trainees' development, and advance counseling scholarship.

In Whitbeck's (2006) work with Native Americans to devise guidelines for culturally specific research, he cautioned researchers not to replace culturally specific values and ways of being with those imposed by the majority culture when planning interventions: "Cultural ways and knowledge must be viewed as equal to social science prevention knowledge" (p. 185). This emphasizes the importance of community ownership and collaboration in defining problems and creating and implementing interventions. Collaboration with the community is important because it enables accurate information, as the community is the best source of information about itself. Furthermore, "community members are the ideal agents for solving the critical psychological, social, and economic problems occurring in their neighborhoods" (Lewis et al., 2003, p. 111). Involving community members in solution development empowers the community instead of relegating them to the role of passive recipient of assistance (Freire, 2000; Goodman & West-Olatunji, 2009; Utsey et al., 2001).

An example of such scholarship is the outreach work jointly sponsored by the Association for Multicultural Counseling and Development and the Association for Counselor Education and Supervision. These ACA divisions have partnered to develop immersion experiences for counselor educators, practitioners, and students to collaborate with individuals in disaster-affected communities in South Africa and Botswana. Other social-justice-oriented initiatives led by individual researchers have focused on regional disasters, such as post-Katrina disaster response work in New Orleans (Goodman & West-Olatunji, 2008, 2009). Outcomes of these outreach experiences for participants include increased awareness of sociopolitical context, enhanced cultural competence, and a deeper understanding of the role of advocacy when intervening with clients and communities. What characterizes these clinical outreach projects is an acute emphasis on problem identification and resolution in partnership with clients. This results in a more client-centered, client-empowered, transformative experience for both the client and the counselor. Given this reciprocity in outcomes, counselor training would do well to include more practitioner-oriented collaborative research. As the Advocacy Competencies gain a central role in the counseling profession, it is likely that new strategies will permeate actual practice across settings and specialties.

Conclusion

This chapter presented systemic oppression and transgenerational trauma as focal points for discussing the role of advocacy and social justice when working with culturally diverse clients. In my view, more engaged scholarship is needed in which counselors collaborate with clients to foster empowerment and change within an ecosystemic framework. Recommendations were provided for counselor educators to expose counselor trainees to multidisciplinary experiences to create solutions that are informed by an understanding of sociocultural oppression. Suggestions for future research center on engaged scholarship that allows clinical researchers to step out of the ivory tower to investigate real problems in real communities with real people.

References

Aarts, P. G. H. (1998). Intergenerational effects in families of World War II survivors from the Dutch East Indies: Aftermath of another Dutch War. In Y. Danieli (Ed.), *International handbook of multigenerational legacies of trauma* (pp. 175–187). New York: Plenum.

American Association for Marriage and Family Therapy. (2004). *AAMFT core competencies.* Alexandria, VA: Author.

American Counseling Association. (2005). *ACA code of ethics.* Alexandria, VA: Author.

American Psychological Association. (2002). *Ethical principles of psychologists and code of conduct.* Washington, DC: Author.

Bemak, F., & Chung, R. C. (2005). Advocacy as a critical role for urban school counselors: Working toward equity and social justice. *Professional School Counseling, 8,* 196–202.

Bernstein, M. M. (1998). Conflicts in adjustment: World War II prisoners of war and their families. In Y. Danieli (Ed.), *International handbook of multigenerational legacies of trauma* (pp. 119–124). New York: Plenum.

Boydell, K., & Volpe, T. (2004). A qualitative examination of the implementation of a community–academic coalition. *Journal of Community Psychology, 32,* 357–375.

Bryant-Davis, T., & Ocampo, C. (2005). The trauma of racism: Implications for counseling, research, and education. *The Counseling Psychologist, 33,* 574–578.

Burstow, B. (2003). Toward a radical understanding of trauma and trauma work. *Violence Against Women, 9,* 1293–1317.

Civil Rights Project. (2002, June). *Racial inequity in special education: Executive summary for federal policy makers.* Los Angeles: University of California, Los Angeles, The Civil Rights Project. Retrieved May 1, 2008, from http://www.civilrightsproject.ucla.edu/research/specialed/IDEA_paper02.php

Comstock, D. L., Hammer, T. R., Strentzsch, J., Cannon, K., Parsons, J., & Salazar, G., II. (2008). Relational-cultural theory: A framework for bridging relational, multicultural, and social justice competencies. *Journal of Counseling & Development, 86,* 279–287.

Constantine, M. G., Hage, S. M., Kindaichi, M. M., & Bryant, S. M. (2007). Social justice and multicultural issues: Implications for the practice and training of counselors and counseling psychologists. *Journal of Counseling & Development, 85,* 24–29.

Constantine, M. G., & Sue, D. W. (2006). Factors contributing to optimal human functioning in people of color in the United States. *The Counseling Psychologist, 34,* 228–244.

Constantino, G., Malgady, R. G., & Rogler, L. H. (1986). Cuento therapy: A culturally sensitive modality for Puerto Rican children. *Journal of Consulting and Clinical Psychology, 54,* 639–645.

Council for Accreditation of Counseling and Related Educational Programs. (2001). *CACREP accreditation standards and procedures manual.* Alexandria, VA: Author.

Dana, R. H. (1993). *Multicultural assessment perspectives for professional psychology.* Boston: Allyn & Bacon.

Danieli, Y. (1998). Introduction: History and conceptual foundations. In Y. Danieli (Ed.), *International handbook of multigenerational legacies of trauma* (pp. 1–20). New York: Plenum.

Danoff-Burg, S., Prelow, H. M., & Swenson R. R. (2004). Hope and life satisfaction in Black college students coping with race-related stress. *Journal of Black Psychology, 30,* 208–228.

Dass-Brailsford, P. (2007). *A practical approach to trauma: Empowering interventions.* Thousand Oaks, CA: Sage.

Delucchi, M., & Do, H. D. (1996). The model minority myth and perceptions of Asian Americans as victims of racial harassment. *College Student Journal, 30,* 173–196.

Deyhle, D. (1995). Navajo youth and Anglo racism: Cultural integrity and resistance. *Harvard Educational Review, 65,* 402–444.

Duran, E., Duran, B., Yellow Horse Brave Heart, M., & Yellow Horse-Davis, S. (1998). Healing the American Indian soul wound. In Y. Danieli (Ed.), *International handbook of multigenerational legacies of trauma* (pp. 341–354). New York: Plenum.

Emihovich, C. (2005). Fire and ice: Activist ethnography in the culture of power. *Anthropology and Education Quarterly, 36,* 305–314.

Eriksen, K. (1999). Counselor advocacy: A qualitative analysis of leaders' perceptions, organizational activities, and advocacy documents. *Journal of Mental Health Counseling, 21,* 33–49.

Felsen, I. (1998). Transgenerational transmission of effects of the Holocaust. In Y. Danieli (Ed.), *International handbook of multigenerational legacies of trauma* (pp. 43–68). New York: Plenum.

Frazier, K. N., West-Olatunji, C., St. Juste, S., & Goodman, R. (2008). Transgenerational trauma and CSA: Reconceptualizing cases involving young survivors of child sexual abuse. *Journal of Mental Health Counseling, 31,* 22–33.

Freire, P. (2000). *Pedagogy of the oppressed.* New York: Continuum.

Garcia, J. G., Cartwright, B., Winston, S. M., & Borzuchowska, B. (2003). A transcultural integrative model for ethical decision making in counseling. *Journal of Counseling & Development, 81,* 268–277.

Garrett, M. T., Brubaker, M., Torres-Rivera, E., West-Olatunji, C., & Conwill, W. (2008). Ayeli centering technique for group work. *Journal of Specialists in Group Work, 33,* 179–198.

Goodman, R. D., & West-Olatunji, C. (2008). Transgenerational trauma and resilience. *Journal of Mental Health Counseling, 30,* 121–136.

Goodman, R. D., & West-Olatunji, C. (2009). Cultural competency and disaster response. *Journal of Counseling & Development, 87,* 458–465.

Griffin, B. (1993). Promoting professionalism, collaboration, and advocacy. *Counselor Education and Supervision, 33,* 2–9.

Hage, S. M. (2003). Reaffirming the unique identity of counseling psychology: Opting for the "road less traveled by." *The Counseling Psychologist, 31,* 555–563.

Harrell, J. P., Hall, S., & Taliaferro, J. (2003). Physiological responses to racism and discrimination: An assessment of the evidence. *American Journal of Public Health, 93,* 243–248.

Harrell, S. P. (2000). A multidimensional conceptualization of racism-related stress: Implications for the well-being of people of color. *American Journal of Orthopsychiatry, 70,* 42–57.

Holdstock, T. L. (2000). *Re-examining psychology: Critical perspectives and African insights.* Philadelphia: Routledge.

Ibrahim, F. A., Roysircar-Sodowsky, G., & Ohimshi, H. (2001). Worldview: Recent developments and needed directions. In J. G. Ponterotto, J. M. Casas, L. A. Suzuki, & C. M. Alexander (Eds.), *Handbook of multicultural counseling* (2nd ed., pp. 425–456). Thousand Oaks, CA: Sage.

Kambon, K. K. K. (1996). The Africentric paradigm and African American psychological liberation. In D. A. ya Azibo (Ed.), *African psychology in historical perspective and related commentary* (pp. 57–69). Trenton, NJ: Africa World Press.

Kaufman, P., Alt, M. N., & Chapman, C. (2004). *Dropout rates in the United States: 2001* (NCES 2005-046). Washington, DC: U.S. Department of Education, National Center for Education Statistics.

Keith, T. (1999). Effects of general and specific abilities on student achievement: Similarities and differences across ethnic groups. *School Psychology Quarterly, 14,* 239–262.

Kim, H., Rendon, L., & Valadez, J. (1998). Student characteristics, school characteristics, and educational aspiration of six Asian American ethnic groups. *Journal of Multicultural Counseling and Development, 26,* 166–176.

Kim, W. (2003). Ethnic variations in mental health symptoms and functioning among Asian Americans (Doctoral dissertation, University of Washington, 2003). *Dissertation Abstracts International Section A: Humanities and Social Sciences, 63*(8-A), 3004.

Kiselica, M. S., & Robinson, M. (2001). Bringing advocacy counseling to life: The history, issues, and human dramas of social justice work in counseling. *Journal of Counseling & Development, 79,* 387–398.

Lee, C. C. (1998). Counselors as agents of social change. In C. C. Lee & G. R. Walz (Eds.), *Social action: A mandate for counselors* (pp. 3–14). Alexandria, VA: American Counseling Association.

Lewis, J. A., Arnold, M. S., House, R., & Toporek, R. L. (2002). *ACA Advocacy Competencies.* Retrieved August 1, 2008, from http://www.counseling.org/Publications/

Lewis, J. A., Lewis, M. D., Daniels, J. A., & D'Andrea, M. J. (2003). *Community counseling: Empowerment strategies for a diverse society* (3rd ed.). Pacific Grove, CA: Brooks/Cole-Thomson.

Lomawaima, K. T. (1995). Educating Native Americans. In J. A. Banks & C. A. McGee-Banks (Eds.), *Handbook of research on multicultural education* (pp. 331–347). New York: Macmillan.

Marshall, P. L. (2002). *Cultural diversity in our schools.* Belmont, CA: Wadsworth/Thomson Learning.

National Center for Educational Statistics. (2003). *The condition of education 2003* (NCES 2003-067). Washington, DC: Author.

Osborne, J. L., Collison, B. B., House, R. M., Gray, L. A., Firth, J., & Lou, M. (1998). Developing a social advocacy model for counselor education. *Counselor Education and Supervision, 37,* 190–202.

Pardeck, J. T., & Chung, W. S. (1997). Treating powerless minorities through an ecosystem approach. *Adolescence, 32,* 625–634.

Pedersen, P. B. (1991). Multiculturalism as a generic approach to counseling. *Journal of Counseling & Development, 70,* 6–12.

Raphael, B., Swan, P., & Martinek, N. (1998). Intergenerational aspects of trauma for Australian Aboriginal people. In Y. Danieli (Ed.), *International handbook of multigenerational legacies of trauma* (pp. 327–339). New York: Plenum.

Reynolds, D. K. (2001). Morita psychotherapy. In R. J. Corsini (Ed.), *Handbook of innovative therapy* (2nd ed., pp. 392–400). New York: Wiley.

Rich, J. A., & Grey, C. M. (2005). Pathways to recurrent trauma among young Black men: Traumatic stress, substance abuse, and the "code of the street." *American Journal of Public Health, 95,* 816–824.

Rosenheck, R., & Fontana, A. (1998). Warrior fathers and warrior sons: Intergenerational aspects of trauma. In Y. Danieli (Ed.), *International handbook of multigenerational legacies of trauma* (pp. 225–242). New York: Plenum.

Savage, T. A., Harley, D. A., & Nowak, T. M. (2005). Applying social empowerment strategies as tools for self-advocacy in counseling lesbian and gay male clients. *Journal of Counseling & Development, 83,* 131–137.

Schechter, D. S., Brunelli, S. A., Cunningham, N., Brown, J., & Baca, P. (2002). Mother–daughter relationships and sexual abuse: A pilot study of 35 days. *Bulletin of the Menninger Clinic, 66,* 39–60.

Scott, L. D., Jr. (2003). Cultural orientation and coping with perceived discrimination among African American youth. *Journal of Black Psychology, 29,* 235–256.

Seaton, E. K. (2003). An examination of the factor structure of the index of race-related stress among a sample of African American adolescents. *Journal of Black Psychology, 29,* 292–307.

Simons, R. L., & Johnson, C. (1998). An examination of competing explanations for the intergenerational transmission of domestic violence. In Y. Danieli (Ed.), *International handbook of multigenerational legacies of trauma* (pp. 553–570). New York: Plenum.

Sklarew, B., Twemlow, S., & Wilkinson, S. (2004). *Analysts in the trenches: Streets, schools, and war zones.* Hillside, NJ: Analytic Press.

Steele, C. M., & Aronson, J. A. (1995). Stereotype threat and the intellectual test performance of African Americans. *Journal of Personality and Social Psychology, 69,* 797–811.

Sue, D. W., & Sue, D. (2008). *Counseling the culturally diverse: Theory and practice* (5th ed.). New York: Wiley.

Suzuki, L. A., Meller, D. J., & Ponterotto, J. G. (1996). Multicultural assessment: Present trends and future directions. In L. A. Suzuki, D. J. Meller, & J. G. Ponterotto (Eds.), *Handbook of multicultural assessment: Clinical, psychological, and educational applications* (pp. 673–684). San Francisco: Jossey Bass.

Thomas, A., & Sillen, S. (1971). *Racism and psychiatry.* New York: Citadel Press.

Townsend, B. L. (2000). The disproportionate discipline of African American learners: Reducing school suspensions and expulsions. *Exceptional Children, 66,* 381–391.

U.S. Department of Education, Office of Special Education Programs. (2002). *Twenty-fourth annual report to Congress on the implementation of the Individuals With Disabilities Education Act.* Retrieved October 23, 2006, from http://www.ed.gov/about/reports/annual/osep/2002/index.html

Utsey, S. O., Bolden, M. A., & Brown, A. L. (2001). Visions of revolution from the spirit of Frantz Fanon: A psychology of liberation for counseling African Americans confronting societal racism and oppression. In J. G. Ponterotto, J. M. Casas, L. A. Suzuki, & C. M. Alexander (Eds.), *Handbook of multicultural counseling* (2nd ed., pp. 311–336). Thousand Oaks, CA: Sage.

Vera, E. M., & Speight, S. L. (2003). Multicultural competence, social justice, and counseling psychology: Expanding our roles. *The Counseling Psychologist, 31,* 253–272.

Walker, M. (1999). The inter-generational transmission of trauma: The effects of abuse on the survivor's relationship with their children and on the children themselves. *European Journal of Psychotherapy, Counseling and Health, 2,* 281–296.

Ward, C. J. (2005). *Native Americans in the school system: Family, community, and academic achievement.* Lanham, MD: AltaMira Press.

Watson, A. L., Collins, R. L., & Correia, F. C. (2004). Advocacy and social action in the context of ecological counseling. In R. K. Conyne & E. P. Cook (Eds.), *Ecological counseling: An innovative approach to conceptualizing person–environment interaction* (pp. 289–313). Alexandria, VA: American Counseling Association.

West-Olatunji, C. (2008). Multicultural case conceptualization. In C. Lee, D. Burnhill, A. Butler, C. P. Hipolito-Delgado, M. Humphrey, O. Munoz, & H. J. Shin (Eds.), *Elements of culture in counseling: Theory and practice* (pp. 163–176). Boston: Allyn & Bacon.

West-Olatunji, C., Shure, L., Garrett, M., Conwill, W., & Torres, E. (2008). Rite of passage programs as effective tools for fostering resilience among low-income African American male adolescents. *Journal of Humanistic Counseling, Education and Development, 47,* 131–143.

Whitbeck, L. B. (2006). Some guiding assumptions and a theoretical model for developing culturally specific preventions with Native American people. *Journal of Community Psychology, 34,* 183–192.

Williams-Clay, L., West-Olatunji, C., & Cooley, C. (2001). *Keeping the story alive: Narrative in the African-American church and community.* (ERIC Document Reproduction Service No. ED462666)

Yeh, C. J., Hunter, C. D., Madan-Bahel, A., Chiang, L., & Arora, A. K. (2004). Indigenous and interdependent perspectives of healing: Implications for counseling and research. *Journal of Counseling & Development, 82,* 210–219.

Yoshikawa, H., Wilson, P. A., Hsueh, J., Rosman, E. A., Chin, J., & Kim, J. H. (2003). What front-line CBO staff can tell us about culturally anchored theories of behavior change in HIV prevention for Asian/Pacific Islanders. *American Journal of Community Psychology, 32,* 143–158.

Chapter 7

Advocacy Counseling With the Multiracial Population

Kelley R. Kenney and Mark E. Kenney

This chapter addresses the American Counseling Association (ACA) Advocacy Competencies (Lewis, Arnold, House, & Toporek, 2002) for the multiracial population, a population that includes interracial couples, multiracial individuals, and multiracial families including transracial adoptive families. We include a brief discussion of the demographic trends within the multiracial population and the history of the multiracial movement in the United States. We also include information on the national grassroots advocacy efforts that have been conducted within and by members of the multiracial population. We discuss the application of the Advocacy Competencies to the multiracial population and incorporate ways that counselors can join in these efforts and work collaboratively with the population.

The multiracial population is one of the fastest growing segments in the United States today. Census data reveal that 7.4% or 4 million U.S. married couple households have spouses of different racial backgrounds and heritages. The 2000 Census marked the first time that people in the United States could identify themselves as being of more than one racial category. The census data revealed that 7 million people or 2.4% of the U.S. population were identified as being of two or more racial heritages. Statistics on transracial adoption indicate that 8% of all adoptions include parents and children of different racial backgrounds. Approximately a third of the children adopted through the foster care system are adopted by parents or families of different racial backgrounds (Steinberg & Hall, 2000).

Support for the notion and role of advocacy in the context of counseling grew out of the professional literature and work of the community, multicultural, and feminist counseling fields (Toporek, 2000). The topic and discussion of advocacy for the multiracial population in the context of counseling, the counseling profession, and other human services professions are extremely limited. In fact, much of the advocacy work that has been provided to and for the multiracial population has come out of grassroots advocacy organizations created by members of the multiracial population for the multiracial population (DaCosta, 2007). These organizations include the Association of Multiethnic Americans (AMEA) and their affiliate organizations across the country; Project RACE (Reclassifying All Children Equally); and MAVIN Foundation, *Mavin* being a word that has its roots in the Yiddish language and means "one who understands." There are other grassroots advocacy organizations in communities across the United States as well as a host of web and Internet-based organizations (DaCosta, 2007; Kenney, 2000; Kenney & Kenney, 2009; Root & Kelley, 2003).

In discussing the application of the Advocacy Competencies to the multiracial population, we need to first examine the counseling profession's interaction with and response to the growing multiracial population. Lewis, Lewis, Daniels, and D'Andrea (1998) suggested that advocacy "serves two purposes: (1) increasing clients' sense of personal power and (2) fostering environmental changes that reflect greater responsiveness to their personal needs" (p. 172). Before the last century, the counseling profession's involvement with and focus on the multiracial population were quite limited, and although by definition and composition the multiracial population is a multicultural population, the professional counseling literature on multiculturalism and diversity failed to include this diverse population. Much of the research and professional literature on counseling the multiracial population, and the counseling profession's overall focus on the multiracial population, are a result of the insistence and persistence of members of the multiracial population who are also members of the counseling profession. The efforts of these members are evidence of advocacy in that they have increased the counseling profession's overall focus on the issues, needs, and concerns of the multiracial population, provided guidance on how to competently and effectively address the needs of the multiracial population, and improved the image of the profession within the multiracial population.

Along with the dramatic increases in the number of interracial marriages and multiracial individuals since the U.S. Supreme Court's landmark *Loving et ux. v. Virginia* (1967) decision that struck down laws against interracial unions has come a societal shift of greater tolerance for these unions and their offspring (DaCosta, 2007; Kennedy, 2003; Taylor, Funk, & Craighill, 2006). However, interracial couples and mixed-race individuals—depending on socioeconomic status, educational background, and the communities in which they live—continue to encounter challenges and difficulties (DaCosta, 2007; Kennedy, 2003; Kenney & Kenney, 2009; Root, 2001; Wehrly, Kenney, & Kenney, 1999). Similarly, the topic of transracial adoption, despite the increasing numbers, meets with controversy and scrutiny (Bradley & Hawkins-Leon, 2002; Kennedy, 2003; Steinberg & Hall, 2000). The challenges and difficulties, and the continued opposition to interracial unions and transracial adoption reported by some members of the population, stem from the myths and stereotypes and other forms of misinformation that prevail in society and unresolved issues around race in the United States (Kennedy, 2003; Root, 2001; Wardle, 1999).

Empowerment and Advocacy for Clients From the Multiracial Population

Microlevel advocacy counseling requires that counselors empower as well as support and take action on behalf of their clients (Lewis et al., 2002). Wehrly et al. (1999) indicated that as members of the general society, counselors do not live in a vacuum and have therefore been subjected to the myths, stereotypes, and other forms of misinformation that have consumed society regarding the multiracial population. Hence, Kenney (2002, 2006, 2007), Kenney and Kenney (2009), Wehrly (1996), and Wehrly et al. (1999) have provided guidelines for applying the Multicultural Counseling Competencies espoused by Sue, Arredondo, and McDavis (1992) to the multiracial population. These guidelines stress the importance of counselors examining their own beliefs and attitudes about interracial unions and transracial adoptions and having awareness of the harmful impact that prevailing myths and stereotypes about interracial unions and transracial adoption have on the healthy functioning and well-being of members of the multiracial population. They also emphasized the need for counselors to acquire knowledge of the historical and sociopolitical contexts surrounding interracial unions and transracial adoption; the varied identity models useful for understanding the development of interracial couples, multiracial individuals, and multiracial families, including transracial adoptive families; and the varied worldview experiences of members of the multiracial population. A valuable resource for such knowledge is the Mixed Heritage Center (http://www.mixedheritagecenter.org), which was developed via the joint efforts of AMEA and MAVIN Foundation. The center is an Internet-based resource providing information available on the multiracial population through an array of media.

Both awareness and knowledge are essential for the delivery of effective and appropriate services that empower the multiracial population (Kenney, 2000, 2002, 2006, 2007; Kenney & Kenney, 2009; Wehrly, 1996; Wehrly et al., 1999).

Dinkmeyer (1991) discussed the positive role of psychoeducation in counseling and suggested that such an approach can be useful for counselors in their attempts to help clients understand and navigate the complexities of their environments. Psychoeducation involves the dissemination of information that promotes insight and stimulates new ideas and ways of thinking that ultimately results in growth and change (Dinkmeyer & Dinkmeyer, 1993). The popular press is replete with books and magazines involving the personal stories of multiracial couples, individuals, and families. In addition, numerous websites have been established to provide opportunities for personal sharing on the part of members of the multiracial population (Kenney & Kenney, 2009). Counselors need to familiarize themselves and their clients with these resources, which can be used to facilitate dialogue and discussion that produce new insights, learning, and empowerment. Information in and of itself is empowering.

A psychoeducational approach with the multiracial population is one in which the counselor demonstrates awareness and knowledge of the issues, concerns, challenges, and strengths of the multiracial population; is familiar with resources available to assist, support, and affirm the experiences of this population; and can provide this information in the context of counseling (Ibrahim, 1998). Another psychoeducational approach that leads to empowerment entails teaching and equipping members of the multiracial population with specific skills and strategies for dealing with and confronting the harsh realities of racism head on (Rockquemore & Laszloffy, 2003; Steinberg & Hall, 2000). Personal narrative approaches where couples, individuals, and families are given opportunities to share their stories may also provide empowering benefits (McDowell et al., 2005; Milan & Kelley, 2000).

Finally, Root (1996) espoused a Multiracial Bill of Rights meant to promote the rights and freedom of choice that multiracial individuals and families have to exist in the world, identify as they wish, and build connections across boundaries. Similarly, Triggs (1996) espoused a Transracially Adopted Child's Bill of Rights that speaks to the fundamental rights to which transracially adopted children are entitled. Both of these documents when presented to and used with members of the multiracial population can be powerful sources of empowerment. Other tangible measures that contribute to the empowerment of the multiracial population include empathizing with and validating the experiences of multiracial couples, individuals, and families (Tubbs & Rosenblatt, 2003; Wardle & Cruz-Janzen, 2004) as well as assisting them in assessing and acknowledging their strengths and skills and the sources of support available to them for addressing and responding to issues and concerns (Kenney & Kenney, 2009; Laszloffy, 2005).

Advocating on behalf of members of the multiracial population entails assessing the extent to which systems of primary intervention, including schools, community agencies, and so on, are available, understand, and are equipped to address the needs and concerns of the multiracial population. As the issues and concerns of the multiracial population have only recently been brought to the forefront, schools, community agencies, and other institutions are just beginning to understand this population and to grasp their complex issues and concerns. Hence, the likelihood of services and resources being limited or nonexistent is great in many areas of the country. In these instances, counselors need to take steps to educate, create, and aid in the establishment of these services and resources (Ibrahim, 1998; Kenney, 2000; Kenney & Kenney, 2009; Wardle & Cruz-Janzen, 2004). This requires counselors to be knowledgeable about their communities and the services or opportunities that exist in their communities and nationally to serve the needs of members of the multiracial population.

Community Collaboration and Systems Advocacy for the Multiracial Population

Advocacy counseling involves moving across a continuum from work that involves empowering and advocating on behalf of our individual clients or groups of clients to collaborating within our communities and working to bring about change to the often oppressive structures of the systems and institutions with which our clients interact (Lewis et al., 2002). Counselors have had little knowledge of and contact with the various national and community resources that have historically been available to provide support for the multiracial population. As we begin this discussion of how counselors can advocate for the multiracial population at the community level and collaborate with other organizations, it is important to provide knowledge and background information about these organizations and resources. Hence what follows is the history and current status of the various grassroots national and community advocacy efforts for the multiracial population.

The development of multiracial community organizations seen in many parts of the United States began in 1978 with an organization that still exists today, called Interracial/Intercultural Pride or I-Pride, located in San Francisco, California. This and other notable organizations—including Biracial Family Network of Chicago; Interracial Family Circle of Washington, DC; Multiracial Americans of Southern California; Project RACE; Hapa Issues Forum (*hapa* in the Hawaiian language means a portion or part of, and it also means a person of mixed descent; the organization, which no longer exists, had focused on concerns of multiracial Asians and Pacific Islanders); and the array of smaller organizations that sprang up across the country through the 1980s and early 1990s—were developed for purposes of social interaction, political activism, and networking around issues related to the multiracial worldview experience (Douglass, 2003). In the late 1980s, as the issues of interracial couples and families were becoming more prominent, members of these groups became more vocal and mobilized around issues of multiracial civil rights, and the idea for the formation of a national grassroots advocacy organization to raise public awareness and consciousness around multiracial issues emerged. According to Douglass (2003), the AMEA was formed in 1988 as an umbrella association for 14 member multiracial organizations across the United States, with its purpose being that of an education organization "promoting positive awareness of interracial and multiethnic people and families" (AMEA mission statement 1988–1999). From 1988 to 1995, AMEA focused primarily on

a) incorporating and obtaining 501c 3 nonprofit status; b) testifying before Congress through its Political Action Committee (PAC) on the necessity for creating a multiracial/multiethnic category on all federal forms that requested racial data; c) creating an educational/legal advisory board with connections to prestigious institutes of learning; and d) forming strategic alliances with other national advocacy groups to monitor local, state, and federal activities affecting interracial communities. (Douglass, 2003, p. 14)

During the mid-1990s through the year 2000, the primary focus of the aforementioned organizations and leaders of the multiracial community was that of advocacy for the interests and civil rights of multiracial families and multiracial individuals, specifically related to a multiracial category. Although it was considered a compromise by some factions of the multiracial community, it was the census lobbying efforts of the AMEA, under the presidency of Ramona Douglass, that resulted in the decision by the Office of Management and Budget to allow for a "check one or more" policy for the 2000 Census and on all government agency forms (Douglass, 2003).

Also in the mid-1990s, college campuses in many parts of the United States were beginning to see an increased number of multiracial college students. Many of these students, having observed the networking, activism, and/or challenges faced by their parents and families, were moved to organize and provide support on behalf of their mixed-race and transracially adopted peers. For example, *MAVIN* magazine was created in 1998 by Matt Kelley during his freshman year at Wesleyan University. The magazine was established both as a resource and an opportunity for multiracial college students to share their stories. In addition, beginning in 1996, Hapa Issues Forum and the Pan Collegiate Conference began to hold annual conferences for multiracial and transracial adoptive college students. By 2000, Wesleyan graduate Jen Chau had established Swirl Incorporated, with several chapters across the country, and Matt Kelley had incorporated and founded MAVIN Foundation. Both organizations and their affiliate organizations on college campuses were established as social networks celebrating and supporting the experiences of multiracial college students. In 2003 these organizations working together created a national coalition of multiracial college student organizations. More recently, both organizations have expanded their work and mission to include the broader multiracial community, focusing not only on social networking but also on health and political action (Douglass, 2003). For example, in addition to MAVIN Foundation's Campus Awareness and Compliance Project, a project whereby the organization both monitors and assists colleges and universities in their efforts to allow students to check more than one racial category on admissions applications and other relevant forms, the organization has also launched two community projects. MAVIN Foundation's Community Mixed-race Action Plan (MAP) is geared to assisting communities in conjunction with schools and agencies in assessing their multiracial population and developing a plan of action based on the population's needs. MAVIN has also taken the lead with the Matchmaker Bone Marrow Project, a national program geared toward the recruitment of mixed-race bone marrow donors (Evans, 2005).

Evans (2005) estimated that over 50 college and community organizations exist across the United States to provide a sense of community and conversation around mixed-race issues and concerns. While most of the aforementioned organizations have incorporated the issues, concerns, and experiences of transracial adoptees and their families, an array of national and community organizations have been developed specifically to address this segment of the multiracial population (Steinberg & Hall, 2000). Again, a host of websites have been developed with regulated and facilitated chat-rooms that serve as opportunities for networking and support as well (Kenney, Kenney, & Wehrly, 2000).

The national, community, and web-based organizations formed for the multiracial population have the expressed purpose of collaborating and dialoguing with other communities to educate, support, and advocate for the multiracial population (Douglass, 2003). Members of the multiracial population continue to be ostracized and misunderstood as well as subjected to both overt and covert forms of racism and discrimination. This is evidenced by the experiences that members of the population report encountering as they attempt to navigate their local communities, schools, social agencies, and services (DaCosta, 2007; Root, 2001; Steinberg & Hall, 2000; Wardle & Cruz-Janzen, 2004).

Advocacy counseling for members of the multiracial population at the community and systems level requires counselors first to familiarize themselves with the existence, work, and resources of the aforementioned national, campus, community, and web-based organizations that have been established for members of the multiracial population and then to form linkages and allegiances with those organizations that may be appropriate for the needs of the multiracial populations in their locales. As a purpose and benefit of these organizations is education related to issues and concerns of the multiracial population, linkages and allegiances can aid counselors as they attempt to both educate their clients and intervene for their clients by educating and informing the systems with which their clients interact (Kenney, 2000; Wardle & Cruz-Janzen, 2004). While the number of college campus and community-based multiracial organizations and multiracial Internet websites has grown, these resources and their value are still too few and recent to be of benefit to the entire population and the communities in which they live across the United States. The larger national advocacy organizations have resources and templates for establishing campus and community-based groups and organizations (DaCosta, 2007). Counselors can both collaborate with the multiracial population of their campuses and communities and intervene for them by assessing the need for such groups and organizations and, in instances where it is determined that the need exists, promote and assist in their development (Kenney, 2000, 2007; Nishimura, 1998; Root & Kelley, 2003).

Another form of systems advocacy requires that counselors involved in collaborative and other work with the multiracial population assess the need for specific services for the multiracial population within their communities and assess the quality of services that may already exist. Related to the availability and quality of services are the topics of how schools, colleges and universities, and social and service agencies collect demographic data; how multiracial individuals and families are identified and categorized; and how the data collected are interpreted and used in planning for and delivering programs and services (Douglass, 2003; Wardle & Cruz-Janzen, 2004). Despite the legislation mandating that organizations that receive federal aid and collect racial data provide options for the selection of more than one racial category on their forms and applications (Douglass, 2003), individuals and families continue to report examples where this option has not been provided or where how the individual or family chooses to identify has not been accepted or respected (Wardle & Cruz-Janzen, 2004). A systems advocacy approach requires that counselors be knowledgeable of this legislation, assure that multiracial individuals and families with whom they are involved are knowledgeable, and assess the extent to which the schools, colleges and universities, and social and service agencies with which the multiracial individuals and families of their communities interact have knowledge of this legislation, are abiding by it, and are using the information appropriately. In instances in which knowledge and application of this legislation do not exist, counselors need to educate and offer assistance with the implementation of a plan of action for assuring compliance. Both the AMEA and MAVIN Foundation can be consulted for assistance with these processes. Similarly, counselors need to have knowledge of federal and state legislation related to adoption, specifically transracial and international adoption, and be prepared to intervene in circumstances where it is clear that knowledge of the legislation does not exist or is being ignored. Counselors working in school and college and university settings may also need to assess the extent to which course curricula address multiracial issues and to serve as a resource and provide resources that can be added to the curriculum of current courses and/or aid in the development of separate courses. In summary, counselors who are culturally aware and knowledgeable of the issues, concerns, challenges, strengths, and worldview experiences of the multiracial population need to assert themselves to provide consultation related to the needs of the population and to the delivery of culturally competent and effective education and services for the population (Kenney, 2000; Kenney & Kenney, 2009; Wallace, 2003; Wardle & Cruz-Janzen, 2004; Wehrly et al., 1999).

Public Information and Social/Political Advocacy for the Multiracial Population

Discussion of advocacy for the multiracial population involving public information entails revisiting what has occurred within the counseling and other human services professions relative to these professions' focus on and work with the multiracial population. The counseling and other human services professions have only in the last 15 to 20 years begun to acknowledge the growing prevalence of the multiracial population (Wehrly, 1996, 2003; Wehrly et al., 1999). Despite the efforts aimed at increasing their members' awareness and understanding of the multiracial population evidenced through the conference programs and workshops, professional literature, interest networks, mission statements, and professional collaborations of the ACA, the American Psychological Association, the American College Personnel Association, and the National Association of Social Workers, more work needs to be done (Kenney, 2000; Renn, 1998; Renn & Shang, 2008; Wardle, 1999; Wardle & Cruz-Janzen, 2004; Wehrly, 1996, 2003; Wehrly et al., 1999). Although all of these organizations have made admirable strides, the impact of these efforts has been somewhat limited and has failed to permeate all entities of these professions. Hence, securing services from professionals in these groups who are culturally competent to work with multiracial couples, individuals, and families, including transracial adoptive families, remains an issue (Wardle, 1999; Wardle & Cruz-Janzen, 2004; Wehrly, 2003; Wehrly et al., 1999).

Edwards and Pedrotti (2008) conducted a study and review of articles from six major professional journals that included counseling and multicultural topic areas. Their review of articles from the *Journal of Counseling Psychology, Journal of Counseling & Development, The Counseling Psychologist, Professional Psychology: Research and Practice, Cultural Diversity and Ethnic Minority Psychology,* and *Journal of Multicultural Counseling and Development* spanning volumes as far back as 1806 up to 2006 yielded only 18 articles directly pertaining to multiracial issues. The authors acknowledged the following limitations of their research: the possibility of overlooked citations, the purposeful inclusion of the only two journals from the ACA with broad readership and likely to have articles about these topics, and the purposeful exclusion of books and book chapters (Edwards & Pedrotti, 2008). As the multiracial population continues to grow, there is a greater likelihood that counselors will find themselves working with members of this population (Kenney, 2000; Wehrly, 2003; Wehrly et al., 1999). Hence, counselors with knowledge and expertise must advocate for the multiracial population by lobbying their profession to increase efforts in the areas of new theory development and research leading to increased professional literature, conference presentations, and workshops geared toward the enhancement and improvement of professional practice with this population (Edwards & Pedrotti, 2008; Kenney, 2000; Wardle & Cruz-Janzen, 2004). These efforts would also enhance and improve the public information competencies of counselors by providing them with the knowledge and expertise necessary to hold educational and informational forums and conduct workshops for the multiracial population in their communities as well as for personnel working with the population in schools, colleges and universities, and social agencies (Wallace, 2003; Wardle & Cruz-Janzen, 2004; Steinberg & Hall, 2000). Another area that would be influenced by these efforts is the course curricula of the graduate training programs.

The public information domain of the Advocacy Competencies also requires counselors and other human services professionals to collaborate with the stakeholders and community (Lewis et al., 2002). Counselors and counseling organizations have collaborated with AMEA, MAVIN Foundation, and other grassroots multiracial advocacy organizations and have thus modeled for their members the benefits of doing so for the professions, for the professions' image, and ultimately for the services that members of these professions provide to the multiracial population. Examples of these collaborative efforts include the ACA's financial contribution to MAVIN Foundation's 2005 Generation Mix Tour. The donation added to funds that enabled MAVIN Foundation to train and send five mixed-race young adults across 15 U.S. cities engaging college campuses and communities in a dialogue about race. The AMEA Loving Conference, held in June 2007, celebrating the 40th anniversary of the Supreme Court's *Loving* decision received financial and other sponsorship from the ACA. In addition, leaders and members of ACA, the American College Personnel Association (ACPA), the American Psychological Association, and the National Association of Social Workers were involved in the program planning and presentations given during this historic conference. The ACPA multiracial and multiple identities conference also involved collaboration with and support from MAVIN Foundation and AMEA. And the 2008 ACA conference, held in Honolulu, Hawaii, the state with the largest multiracial population, marked the first time that the conference's exhibit area offered an exhibit and information from both AMEA and MAVIN Foundation. Finally, the multiracial interest networks of the ACA and ACPA have established liaison relationships with AMEA, MAVIN Foundation, and other grassroots multiracial advocacy organizations to allow for continued dialogues, information and resource sharing, and collaborative efforts geared toward improving members' public information sharing at all levels.

The steps taken by the ACA through its multiracial interest network to collaborate and partner with national grassroots advocacy organizations like AMEA and MAVIN Foundation on efforts they are taking to affect social and public policies are examples of social/political advocacy. For example, ACA's collaborative work with the AMEA resulted in ACA sending a letter to the California state legislature supporting AMEA's lobbying for a multiracial category for the state. As mentioned in previous paragraphs, the work of the AMEA, MAVIN Foundation, and their affiliate organizations include efforts of social/political lobbying and other forms of political action, many of these activities specifically related to how multiracial people are allowed to identify and to transracial adoption legislation (Douglass, 2003, Evans, 2005). Counselors should become aware of opportunities to become involved in these efforts at the national as well as at the state and local levels. They must also be willing to initiate steps toward policy change in instances where it is determined that such changes are necessary and appropriate. Again, both AMEA and MAVIN Foundation are available for consultation and support on these matters.

There are also examples of collaboration across counseling organizations sharing with each other in the dissemination of information and other work that they do with the multiracial population. The following are examples of some of these collaborations as well as suggestions for how they need to be continued and increased. In February 2008, ACPA, a professional organization of college student affairs practitioners and counselors, once a division of the ACA, held a conference on multiracial and multiple identities. The success of this conference lies in the dialogue and resource sharing that took place between the leadership of ACPA and ACA on behalf of members of both groups. This has opened up opportunities for dialogue, sharing, and collaboration on the part of members of the multiracial interests networks that both associations have established. Similarly, during the February 2008 Multicultural Winter Roundtable at Columbia University's Teacher's College, a 3-hour panel session was held that addressed research, theory, and practice with the multiracial population. This session was successful in bringing together practitioners from the fields of counseling, psychology, and social work that have decided to organize and are continuing to dialogue, share information, and collaborate.

There have been strides in our society's acknowledgment and recognition of the multiracial population, including AMEA's voice and presence on the U.S. Census Advisory Board that brought about the historic "check one or more" option on the 2000 census and resulted in 6.8 million Americans self-identifying with more than one race. Yet, according to current AMEA president, Jungmiwha Bullock (personal communication, August 7, 2008), the preparation period for the 2010 census provides another important opportunity to provide enlightenment and education about the increasing numbers of multiracial individuals and families. Cultural competency training around multiracial issues has been suggested for census advisory board members and nationwide census takers. Cultural competence is a value of the counseling profession as observed through the endorsement of the Multicultural Counseling Competencies by the ACA and its divisions and regions (Lewis, 2003). The profession's value of cultural competence is further observed through the recently released standards of the Council for Accreditation of Counseling and Related Educational Program (2009) that require all accredited programs to infuse cultural competency throughout the curriculum of graduate counseling programs. The commitment to cultural competence by the profession, as well as the increased inclusion of information about the multiracial population in multicultural counseling texts and other professional counseling literature and resources, may promote and enhance the cultural competence of a growing number of professional counselors and counseling trainees. Hence professional counselors and counseling trainees may be in a unique position to provide the cultural competency training needed for the census and to become involved in the census-gathering efforts that will be taking place across the country.

Conclusion

This chapter discussed the Advocacy Competencies at the client, community, and public arena levels and how they can be applied to advocacy counseling addressing the issues and concerns faced by interracial couples, multiracial individuals and families, and transracial adoptees and families. The chapter offers guidelines and strategies that individual counselors, members of the national and branch counseling associations, and the counseling profession can use in providing advocacy counseling for the multiracial population.

References

Bradley, C., & Hawkins-Leon, C. G. (2002). The transracial adoption debate: Counseling and legal implications. *Journal of Counseling & Development, 80*, 433–440.

Council for Accreditation of Counseling and Related Educational Programs. (2009). *2009 standards*. Retrieved February 26, 2009, from http://www.cacrep.org/2009standards.html

DaCosta, K. M. (2007). *Making multiracials: State, family, and market in the redrawing of the color line.* Stanford, CA: Stanford University Press.

Dinkmeyer, D. (1991). Mental health counseling: A psychoeducational approach. *Journal of Mental Health Counseling, 13*, 37–42.

Dinkmeyer, D., & Dinkmeyer, D. (1993). Family therapy and psychoeducation. In T. S. Nelson & T. S. Trepper (Eds.), *101 interventions in family therapy* (pp. 188–192). New York: Haworth Press.

Douglass, R. E. (2003). The evolution of the multiracial movement. In M. P. P. Root & M. Kelley (Eds.), *Multiracial child resource book: Living complex identities* (pp. 13–17). Seattle, WA: MAVIN Foundation.

Edwards, L. M., & Pedrotti, J. T. (2008). A content and methodological review of articles concerning multiracial issues in six major counseling journals. *Journal of Counseling Psychology, 55,* 411–418.

Evans, M. (2005). Mixed race history 101. *MAVIN, 8,* 21–23.

Ibrahim, F. A. (1998, March). *Counseling multiracial adolescents.* Paper presented at the annual conference of the American Counseling Association, Indianapolis, IN.

Kennedy, R. (2003). *Interracial intimacies: Sex, marriage, identity, and adoption.* New York: Pantheon.

Kenney, K. R. (2000). Multiracial families. In J. Lewis & L. Bradley (Eds.), *Advocacy in counseling: Counselors, clients, community* (pp. 55–70). Greensboro, NC: ERIC/CASS.

Kenney, K. R. (2002). Counseling interracial couples and multiracial individuals: Applying a multicultural counseling competency framework. *Counseling and Human Development, 35*(4), 1–12.

Kenney, K. R. (2006). Counseling multiracial individuals and families. In C. C. Lee (Ed.), *Multicultural issues in counseling* (3rd ed., pp. 251–266). Alexandria, VA: American Counseling Association.

Kenney, K. R. (2007). Strategies and counselor competencies in counseling multiracial students. In J. A. Lippincott & R. B. Lippincott (Eds.), *Special populations in college counseling: A handbook for mental health professionals* (pp. 77–88). Alexandria, VA: American Counseling Association.

Kenney, K. R., & Kenney, M. E. (2009). Counseling multiple heritage couples and families. In R. C. Henriksen, Jr., & D. A. Paladino (Eds.), *Counseling multiple heritage individuals, couples, and families* (pp. 111–124). Alexandria, VA: American Counseling Association.

Kenney, K. R., Kenney, M. E., & Wehrly, B. (2000, March). *Examining website support resources for the multiracial population and their efficacy.* Paper presented at the annual conference of the American Counseling Association, Washington, DC.

Laszloffy, T. A. (2005, March–April). Multiracial families. *Family Therapy Magazine,* 38–43.

Lewis, J. A. (2003). The competent practice of multicultural counseling: Making it happen. In G. Roysircar, D. S. Sandhu, & V. E. Bibbins, Sr. (Eds.), *Multicultural competencies: A guidebook of practices* (pp. 261–267). Alexandria, VA: American Counseling Association.

Lewis, J. A., Arnold, M. S., House, R., & Toporek, R. L. (2002). *ACA Advocacy Competencies.* Retrieved May 16, 2009, from http://www.counseling.org/Publications/

Lewis, J. A., Lewis, M. D., Daniels, J. A., & D'Andrea, M. J. (1998). *Community counseling: Empowerment strategies for a diverse society.* Pacific Grove, CA: Brooks/Cole.

Loving et ux. v. Virginia, 18 U.S.S.C. R. Ann. 1010 (1967).

McDowell, T., Ingoglia, L, Serizawa, T., Holland, C., Dashiell, J. W., & Stevens, C. (2005). Raising multiracial awareness in family therapy through critical conversations. *Journal of Marital and Family Therapy, 31,* 399–411.

Milan, S., & Kelley, M. K. (2000). Biracial youth and families in therapy: Issues and interventions. *Journal of Marital and Family Therapy, 26,* 305–315.

Nishimura, N. J. (1998). Assessing the issues of multiracial college students on college campuses. *Journal of College Counseling, 1,* 45–53.

Renn, K. (1998, November). *Check all that apply: The experience of biracial and multiracial college students.* Paper presented at the annual meeting of the Association for the Study of Higher Education, Miami, FL.

Renn, K. A., & Shang, P. (2008). *Biracial and multiracial students: New directions for student services.* San Francisco: Jossey-Bass.

Rockquemore, K. A., & Laszloffy, T. L. (2003). Multiple realities: A relational narrative approach to therapy with Black-White mixed-race clients. *Family Relations, 52,* 119–128.

Root, M. P. P. (Ed.). (1996). *The multiracial experience.* Thousand Oaks, CA: Sage.

Root, M. P. P. (2001). *Love's revolution: Interracial marriage.* Philadelphia: Temple University Press.

Root, M. P. P., & Kelley, M. (2003). *Multiracial child resource book: Living complex identities.* Seattle, WA: MAVIN Foundation.

Steinberg, G., & Hall, B. (2000). *Inside trans-racial adoption.* Indianapolis, IN: Perspectives Press.

Sue, D. W., Arredondo, P., & McDavis, R. J. (1992). Multicultural counseling competencies and standards: A call to the profession. *Journal of Counseling & Development, 70,* 477–486.

Taylor, P., Funk, C., & Craighill, P. (2006, March 14). *Guess who's coming to dinner: 22% of Americans have a relative in a mixed-race marriage* (Social Trends Report). Washington, DC: Pew Research Center.

Toporek, R. L. (2000). Developing a common language and framework for understanding advocacy in counseling. In J. Lewis & L. Bradley (Eds.), *Advocacy in counseling: Counselors, clients, and community* (pp. 5–14). Greensboro, NC: ERIC/CAPS.

Triggs, L. S. (1996, Fall). *A transracially-adopted child's bill of rights.* Oakland, CA: Pact, An Adoption Alliance Press. Retrieved from http://www.pactadopt.org/press/articles/rights.html

Tubbs, C. Y., & Rosenblatt, P. C. (2003). Assessment and intervention with Black-White multiracial couples. In V. Thomas, T. A. Karis, & J. L. Wetchler (Eds.), *Clinical issues with interracial couples: Theories and research* (pp. 115–129). New York: Haworth.

Wallace, K. (2003). Contextual factors affecting identity among mixed race heritage college students. In M. P. P. Root & M. Kelley (Eds.), *Multiracial child resource book: Living complex identities* (pp. 86–93). Seattle, WA: MAVIN Foundation.

Wardle, F. (1999). *Tomorrow's children.* Denver, CO: Center for the Study of Biracial Children.

Wardle, F., & Cruz-Janzen, M. I. (2004). *Meeting the needs of multiethnic and multiracial children in schools.* Boston: Pearson/Allyn & Bacon.

Wehrly, B. (1996). *Counseling interracial individuals and families.* Alexandria, VA: American Counseling Association.

Wehrly, B. (2003). Breaking barriers for multiracial individuals and families. In F. D. Harper & J. McFadden (Eds.), *Culture and counseling: New approaches* (pp. 313–323). Boston: Pearson/Allyn & Bacon.

Wehrly, B., Kenney, K. R., & Kenney, M. E. (1999). *Counseling multiracial families.* Thousand Oaks, CA: Sage.

Chapter 8

Religion and Spirituality and the ACA Advocacy Competencies

Marsha I. Wiggins

In the United States, freedom of religion is one of the rights guaranteed by the First Amendment of the Constitution. This amendment reads, "Congress shall make no law respecting an establishment of religion or prohibiting the free exercise thereof." While volumes have been written about the interpretation of these 16 words, one of the main purposes of the clause was to keep the government from establishing a national religion that would then limit the "free exercise" of those who did not belong to it (Neuhaus, 2008). When one considers the centrality of the freedom of religion principle in the United States and its concomitant ramifications, it becomes obvious that counselors may have both the opportunity and the obligation to advocate for clients regarding issues of religion and spirituality or the absence of it.

Religion and Spirituality in Counseling: An Overview

The very terms *spirituality* and *religion* create myriad images and meanings in the minds of the beholders. Indeed, any attempt to define spirituality seems antithetical to it. However, clarifying terms at the beginning of this chapter will assist readers in understanding the significance of the advocacy competencies in relation to spirituality and religion in counseling. *Spirituality* is a word grounded in the Greek term *pneuma* and the Hebrew word *ruach*, both meaning wind, breath, life, spirit (Delbane & Montgomery, 1981; Roth, 1990). While these connotations suggest physical animation, they also imply a transcendence of mere physical, organic existence to include awe, wonder, "the other," or "the holy" (Otto, 1958). Spirituality, then, encompasses the search for meaning, purpose, and value in life, and it may or may not include a deity or higher power (Frame, 2003). Challenged by the limiting aspects of definitions, in 1995, the Summit on Spirituality provided a description of spirituality rather than a definition:

> The animating force in life, represented by such images as breath, wind, vigor, and courage. Spirituality is the infusion and drawing out of spirit in one's life. It is experienced as an active and passive process. Spirituality also is described as a capacity and tendency that is innate and unique to all persons. This spiritual tendency moves the individual towards knowledge, love, meaning, hope,

transcendence, connectedness, and compassion. Spirituality includes one's capacity for creativity, growth, and the development of a values system. Spirituality encompasses the religious, spiritual, and transpersonal. ("Summit Results," 1995, p. 30)

Religion, on the other hand, is more easily defined. A *religion* refers to the beliefs and practices of an organized religious institution (Shafranske & Maloney, 1990). Religion is corporate, cognitive, behavioral, public, ritualistic, external, and institutional (Richards & Bergin, 1997). Although *spirituality* often includes *religion*, the two terms are not identical. In fact, religion may be only one way in which some people express their spirituality. Others may find their spirituality to be more private, individualistic, internal, and emotional. Thus, one may be spiritual without being religious or vice versa (Frame, 2003). Further, one may claim to eschew both religion and spirituality.

Rationale for the Advocacy Competencies

The American Counseling Association (ACA) Advocacy Competencies (Lewis, Arnold, House, & Toporek, 2002) involve counselors in both individual empowerment and systemic change on behalf of clients/students through both direct service and activities as advocates and allies. Counselors may be called upon to act as advocates for clients/students for whom spirituality and religion are core values and for those for whom they are not. In the individual domain of direct service, counselors need advocacy skills so they may help clients/students affirm and make use of the known positive benefits of spirituality and religion in physical and mental health (Benson & Stark, 1996; Koenig, 2004; Torosian & Biddle, 2005) and as coping resources (Somlai et al., 1996; Wiggins, Uphold, Shehan, & Reid, 2008). In addition, counselors may need to provide support for clients and students who maintain a secular worldview and wish to be free from others' imposition of religious and spiritual values in their lives. In the environmental domain, when clients/students for whom spirituality and/or religion is significant come up against barriers to receiving services, counselors may need to advocate on their behalf. Counselors may also need to negotiate for services for those who do not ascribe to a particular religious or spiritual belief or value set to assist them in protecting their rights not to self-identify as religious or spiritual persons.

Counselors may work with community organizations as allies for clients'/students' spiritual and religious concerns to increase awareness of current issues facing their clients and to collaborate with community partners in addressing these concerns. For example, sports organizations regularly schedule games on Saturdays and Sundays that conflict with various religious worship services. Counselors who want to support their clients' involvement in community sports as well as in their religious activities may wish to advocate with these organizations regarding ways to honor their clients' religious practices while not excluding them from participating in sports competitions. Similarly, some nonreligious and nonspiritually oriented clients may need advocacy as they confront the decidedly religious perspectives in organizations to which they belong.

In addition, counselors may find themselves in a position to advocate for clients/students in the public arena by providing information through the media and by engaging in social and/or political activities that aim at systems change. Sharing research results regarding the positive effects religion and spirituality have on physical and mental health is one area in which counselors can have an impact on the public domain. Although freedom of religion is protected by the U.S. Constitution, freedom *from* religion is often minimized in the public milieu. Counselors may choose to be advocates for their clients and students who do not embrace religion and/or spirituality to affect policy that may marginalize them as a result of their secular perspectives.

Counselors have the opportunity and the obligation to become informed about their clients'/students' religious and spiritual worldviews, and the lack thereof, and how these orientations affect their clients'/students' physical, mental, and emotional health, and how to empower individuals in self-advocacy. Moreover, counselors may act as allies and give voice to those whose voices are not heard in the public discourse, whether in community organizations or the larger sociopolitical context in which they find themselves. These examples form the rationale for applying the Advocacy Competencies when working with clients'/students' religious and spiritual concerns.

Operationalizing the Advocacy Competencies Regarding Religion and Spirituality

The Advocacy Competencies are applied at several levels of intervention: the client/student, school/community, and public arena. When considering clients/students for whom religion and spirituality are especially significant (or not significant), counselors have many opportunities to assume advocacy roles.

Client/Student Level

At the client/student level, there are many opportunities to implement the Advocacy Competencies in terms of both empowerment (acting with) and advocacy (acting on behalf) of one's clientele regarding religion and spirituality or the absence of these constructs.

Empowerment

Counselors can identify client strengths and resources found in their religious or spiritual perspectives. Counselors can encourage clients to make use of their religious or spiritual practices to manage stress, address depression, and increase their overall well-being. The following questions, adapted from Walsh (1999), may help counselors work with clients' religious or spiritual concerns:

- How important are spiritual beliefs in clients' lives?
- To what extent do the clients identify with a spiritual orientation?
- How do past or present spiritual beliefs and practices contribute to presenting problems or block healing and growth?
- How has adversity or trauma wounded the spirit?
- How might a spiritual void or disconnectedness from religious roots exacerbate suffering or alienation?
- How can past, current, or potential spiritual resources be identified or drawn upon to ease distress, provide support, aid in problem-solving, help clients to accept what cannot be changed, and foster healing? (pp. 35–36)

In addition, counselors can learn about various models of faith development, including those of Fowler (1981), Oser (1991), Genia (1995), and others, that may help clients understand how religious and spiritual worldviews develop and change as one matures. Knowledge of these developmental models may assist clients as they make transitions in their understanding and integration of religion and spirituality in their lives. For example, counselors working with adolescents or adults who are exploring and possibly questioning their religious or spiritual beliefs could share Fowler's (1981) model that includes the *individuative-reflective stage* related to critically examining belief systems, values, and commitments. In this stage, people claim their own personal stance with regard to their religious or spiritual heritage. By sharing these models, counselors can empower clients/students to understand the normative process of growing in one's faith.

Further, helping clients learn the characteristics of religion and spirituality that impair health and well-being (Clinebell, 1984) could also be useful. For example, Clinebell suggested counselors ask some of the following questions regarding clients' religion or spirituality:

Do the religious [spiritual] beliefs, attitudes, and practices of persons…

- give people meaning, hope, and trust in the face of life's tragedies?
- provide creative values and ethical sensitivities for personally and socially responsible living?

- nurture the transcendent aspects of people's lives?
- inspire reverence and love of life and nature?
- provide for renewal of a sense of trust and belonging in the universe?
- bring inner growth and enrichment from peak experiences?
- offer growth-enabling community of caring?
- build bridges with people of different values and faith systems?
- improve love and self-acceptance rather than fear and guilt? (pp. 118–119)

In this way, clients can evaluate the degree to which their personal religious or spiritual beliefs and practices contribute to or assuage their distress.

Counselors could also engage in empowerment by having clients complete a spiritual genogram (Frame, 2000). This tool enables clients to review three generations of family history for patterns that reveal ways that religion and spirituality have been sources of strength and resilience as well as barriers to interfamilial relationships and personal growth.

Advocacy

Counselors have the opportunity to practice advocacy for religious/spiritual clients and students in systems in which they find themselves. For example, counselors may need to be advocates with their colleagues regarding integrating religion and spirituality into their work because some counselors may be tempted to dismiss religion and/or spirituality as inappropriate for the psychological arena and better dealt with by clergy and other spiritual leaders. Counselors who take seriously the importance of addressing clients'/students' religious and spiritual worldviews can help their colleagues understand the importance of this aspect of human experience and thus pave the way for clients and students to receive comprehensive services.

In addition, counselors may need to advocate on behalf of those who either have no religion or who practice religions other than Christianity. In the United States, Christianity is the dominant religion and is so interwoven with cultural values and patriotism that it is often difficult to recognize Christian privilege (Blumenfeld, 2006; Schlosser, 2003). Indeed, counselors have the opportunity to advocate on behalf of non-Christian clients who may have internalized oppression by not being part of the dominant religion. They may experience guilt, shame, and exclusion in communities where religion, especially Christianity, is the norm. For example, counselors may need to advocate for students who prefer not to recite the pledge of allegiance because of the reference to God or for students to be excused from classes and examinations on religious (non-Christian) holidays, such as Yom Kippur. On the other hand, school counselors may be called to advocate on behalf of religious students in schools who wish to organize prayer groups or Bible studies.

School and Community Level

Community Collaboration

At the school and community level, counselors may wish to use their knowledge, skills, and experience to advocate on behalf of religious and nonreligious clients through community collaboration. One of the best opportunities counselors have in schools is to serve as consultants to teachers, administrators, and staff regarding child development, family dynamics, child abuse, and other mental health issues that affect students. For example, counselors may assist teachers in identifying characteristics of physical abuse in children so that they may intervene on behalf of children's safety. Also, counselors may function as consultants to clergy and other religious/spiritual leaders regarding similar issues. For example, many clergy may not know the characteristics of the cycle of intimate partner violence and the statistics regarding its prevalence. In fact, some clergy may run the risk of putting their parishioners in harm's way by suggesting they stay with abusive partners. Counselors may assist clergy and other religious/spiritual leaders in learning about issues that affect families and community resources available for assistance.

Similarly, school counselors may collaborate with school administrators, teachers, and staff when religious issues arise in the school setting. For example, they may help school personnel become aware of the various religious and spiritual holidays and their associated rituals and practices. Moreover, school counselors may provide both education and support for increasing sensitivity to these religious and spiritual observances and help school personnel plan for and integrate them into the life and calendar of the school.

Systems Advocacy

Counselors may also work with systems to ensure that clients for whom religion and spirituality are significant forces receive attention in this important dimension of their lives. Fortunately, the Association for Spiritual, Ethical, and Religious Values in Counseling has developed a set of competencies (Miller, 1999) for counselors who wish to address religious and spiritual issues with their clients. Counselors may need to advocate in university systems so that courses are offered that help preservice counselors gain knowledge and skills to work with clients and students regarding these concerns. Further, they may wish to advocate with the Council for Accreditation of Counseling and Related Educational Programs to have these competencies taken seriously and integrated significantly into program standards.

In the community mental health system, counselors may need to advocate for inservice training for program directors and administrators of mental health centers to learn the importance of addressing religious and spiritual issues in counseling and to learn the skills necessary to provide competent services. In turn, counselors may work with accrediting bodies of community mental health centers, the Joint Commission on Accreditation of Healthcare Organizations, for example, to move them toward including the religious and spiritual dimension in their accreditation of hospitals and mental health clinics. Counselors may also have input into client rights documents and policies that would increase clients' awareness of their right to have all of their concerns addressed, even religious and spiritual ones. In this way, serving religious and spiritual clients would cease to be considered an "alternative treatment," a "fad," or an approach on the fringe of mental health services. Instead, it would be considered central and standard. Thus, religious and spiritual clients would be more likely to be served if the current systems were both challenged and supported as they make changes that would increase the acceptance and quality of treatment of this population.

Public Arena

Public Information

Counselors have the opportunity to use the media to inform consumers about the availability of mental health services that integrate religion and spirituality and that are provided to clients by trained and competent professionals, not solely by religious or spiritual leaders. For example, counselors could write opinion articles for the editorial section of their local newspapers informing readers that many secular counselors do have training to work with clients' religious and spiritual concerns, and that such training is not intended to criticize clients' beliefs or to convert them to other religions. Such use of public media could aid in reducing the stigma for religious clients seeking mental health services. Further, the use of the media could also inform nonreligious clients that their concerns about life's purpose and meaning are an appropriate reason for seeking counselors' services.

In addition, counselors may work with national mental health organizations such as the National Association for the Mentally Ill and state mental health associations to publicize mental health services that address the religious or spiritual dimension of clients' lives. Counselors may also develop multimedia resources for public use that inform consumers of mental health services of the spiritual and religious counseling competencies and how to find a competent provider.

Social/Political Advocacy

Counselors may find themselves in the position to act as political allies with others who share a common commitment to social justice. For example, counselors may seek political support for faith-based organizations that provide counseling and other services to underserved populations when they seek public funding for their endeavors. Assuming these organizations meet the same standards as secular organizations seeking state and federal monies for their projects, counselors may work with funders to support grassroots organizations' missions that would provide community mental health services to clients with religious/spiritual concerns.

Another area for social or political advocacy involves school counselors who may wish to work with their local school boards regarding policies that affect religious and nonreligious students. For example, school counselors may advocate on behalf of religious or nonreligious students who are harassed by peers because of their participation (or nonparticipation) in religious groups, clubs, or activities.

In addition, school counselors may also work with school boards on policies regarding youths who attempt to recruit their peers into street gangs. Because gangs provide a sense of purpose and belonging, in many ways they provide a social structure and function somewhat like religions for their adherents. Indeed, according to Venkatesh (1997), "[the] gang can be a substitute for poorly functioning familial structures; its value orientation offers a moral chart for those youth excluded from cultural systems" (p. 89). Counselors may become allies with state social service departments, juvenile justice systems, law enforcement, municipalities, and courts to address this particular population and its activity in school settings.

Multicultural and Diversity Issues

In contemplating and implementing advocacy interventions with religious (and nonreligious) clients, counselors must also consider the entire sociopolitical context in which they and their clients find themselves. Issues of race, sexual orientation, and ability often intersect with issues of religion and spirituality, such that counselor advocates may find themselves facing a multitude of concerns when taking on such roles.

The relationship between religion/spirituality and race is rich and multifaceted. For example, the Black church has played an enormous role in advocating for social justice for African Americans, and many of these clients are deeply religious (Burke, Chauvin, & Miranti, 2005). In fact, spirituality is considered the whole of life for many African Americans (Frame & Williams, 1996). Counselors working with African Americans may find allies among pastors of Black churches because personal and social transformations are two of the major aspects of African American Christianity (Frame & Williams, 1996).

Another aspect of the intersection of multicultural concerns and religion/spirituality is related to indigenous healers. Many cultures have persons within their communities who wear the mantle of spiritual healer for their people. Counselors can advocate in the established mental health system on behalf of *curanderas*, medicine men, shamans, and practitioners of Santeria and voodoo to help legitimate these ancient cultural approaches to healing. Moreover, counselors may advocate for their clients of color by consulting and partnering with indigenous healers on behalf of their clients' well-being (Lee & Armstrong, 1995).

Lesbian, gay, bisexual, and transgender (LGBT) persons have experienced significant oppression by religious institutions that believe that homosexuality is a "sin" or an "abomination" and do not welcome them in worship or other areas of religious life. Moreover, some religious leaders espouse reparative therapies that purport to change one's sexual orientation from gay to heterosexual (Barret & Logan, 2002). Despite this discrimination, many LGBT individuals hold deep religious and spiritual beliefs and long for an integration of their sexual and spiritual identities (Heermann, Wiggins, & Rutter, 2007). Counselors can become knowledgeable about the barriers for individuals who identify as LGBT to full participation in their religious communities and may choose to advocate for their acceptance into the life and leadership of their particular religious or spiritual groups.

Persons with disabilities (mental, physical, psychological) also have experienced exclusion from their religious and spiritual organizations. Some of this discrimination is the result of a lack of awareness about the barriers persons with disabilities face. However, there is a long tradition in Jewish and Christian religious communities that equate disabilities with sin or punishment (Fitzgerald, 1997), and in Eastern religions, disabilities were considered the result of fate, karma, or misfortunes sent by deities (Miles, 1995). Counselors may become allies with others in their communities to advocate with religious organizations on behalf of persons with disabilities so that appropriate accommodations may be made for them.

In addition to taking on advocacy roles on behalf of others, counselors who are members of target groups themselves (e.g., people of color, women, LBGT, disabled, elderly) will be aware of the tendency of the dominant culture to attempt to squelch their voices as they advocate for others in marginalized positions vis-à-vis the political or religious establishment. Finding support and seeking allies is a necessary step in self-care for counselors whose own sociopolitical position is at the margins.

Challenges

One of the major challenges for anyone in an advocate role is that of speaking truth to power. Counselors often feel more comfortable in their therapeutic roles with individual clients and students than they do in their roles as advocates in larger systems. Most counselors need more training to prepare them for advocacy roles (Toporek, Lewis, & Crethar, 2009), and many are insecure in taking on the tasks of advocacy. Learning to find one's voice and being able to harness one's expertise and passion for social justice are significant challenges for counselors in all settings.

In becoming an advocate for clients for whom religion and spirituality are central concerns, counselors face a particular challenge of gaining knowledge and skills to work with this particular population. If counselors did not receive such training in their preservice educational experiences, then it is incumbent on them to participate in continuing education seminars and conferences to gain the competence they need for all aspects of client/student advocacy.

A major challenge for those working in advocacy roles regarding religion and spirituality concerns is the issue of the separation of church and state. Whenever the topic of religion or spirituality arises in a public arena in the United States, there are those who are quick to cite the separation of church and state as a reason for dismissing these issues. Moreover, some within the mental health professions may view advocacy for this population as inappropriate. Therefore, counselors must be prepared to address these issues and develop a strong rationale for providing services, public information, and policy changes on behalf of these clients.

Since the first amendment to the U.S. Constitution guarantees both freedom of religion and freedom from the imposition of religion, it is important for counselors to advocate for clients on both sides of the religion and spirituality fence. It may be a difficult challenge for some counselors to advocate for both religious and nonreligious clients simultaneously. Being able to adopt multiple perspectives on issues that affect different types of clients is critical in being an effective advocate for this population.

Finally, avoiding burnout is a considerable challenge to counselors who adopt advocacy roles around religion and spirituality. Learning to work in systems is time consuming and exhausting. Finding allies and supportive colleagues is paramount to both effectiveness and survival in this area. Practicing self-care, setting appropriate boundaries, and celebrating victories, however small, are extremely important aspects of avoiding burnout.

Benefits

One of the important benefits of counselors acting in advocacy roles is that clients for whom religion and spirituality are central dimensions will get more attention from mental health agency administrators and providers. Thus, they should receive more services and increased quality in those services.

In addition, another noteworthy benefit of advocacy is that the sociopolitical dimensions and ramifications of religion and spirituality in counseling will be made known in the public arena. As a result, these issues may enter public discourse in new and refreshing ways. Furthermore, the public and the profession will become more aware of the intersection of religion and spirituality with issues of multiculturalism and diversity. Counselor advocacy can be a means for addressing the compartmentalization that often occurs between special interest groups. It can also be a bridge for understanding the interrelationships in these issues and for generating person power and momentum for addressing the panoply of social justice concerns.

Ultimately, as a result of advocacy efforts in the area of religion and spirituality, counselors' influence and impact will increase beyond the 50-minute session and the counseling office into the wider community. Therefore, more people will be served through these efforts than could be served in individual counseling. Being visible as counselor advocates in the community may serve both to demystify and to expand the role of counselors in the public domain. As a by-product of advocacy initiatives, counselors will feel less isolated as they garner support for individual and systemic change.

Conclusion

Religion and spirituality are central to a majority of citizens in the United States. In fact, more than half of Americans reported religion is important to them, attend religious services regularly, and pray daily (Pew Forum, 2008). It is not surprising, then, that issues of religion and spirituality are significant for a considerable number of counseling clients and students. Counselors who assume the role as advocates for these clients (and for those for whom religion and spirituality are not significant) have an opportunity to address these issues in individual counseling, thus treating the whole person and integrating religious and spiritual concerns into the psychotherapeutic process. Moreover, when counselors advocate for their clients in this area, they increase the likelihood that these clients will receive services not previously provided. When counselors take on the role as advocates in the school or community, they are able to collaborate with community organizations and act as allies in working for organizational change. Similarly, counselors functioning as systems advocates can affect mental health systems and school systems in ways that take seriously the concerns held by clients for whom religion and spirituality are important. Finally, counselors who venture into the public arena may increase public awareness of the interface of religion and spirituality and psychotherapy and of the mental health services that are available that address these concerns. These counselors may also take on sociopolitical challenges and advocate for clients' needs in a way that brings down systemic barriers and opens the doors for increased opportunities for widespread social change.

References

Barret, B., & Logan, C. (2002). *Counseling gay men and lesbians: A practice primer.* Belmont, CA: Brooks/Cole.

Benson, H., & Stark, M. (1996). *Timeless healing: The power and biology of belief.* New York: Fireside.

Blumenfeld, W. J. (2006). Christian privilege and the promotion of "secular" and not-so "secular" mainline Christianity in public schooling and the larger society. *Equity and Excellence in Education, 39,* 195–210.

Burke, M. T., Chauvin, J. C., & Miranti, J. G. (2005). *Religious and spiritual issues in counseling: Applications across diverse populations.* New York: Bruner/Routledge.

Clinebell, H. (1984). *Basic types of pastoral care and counseling.* Nashville, TN: Parthenon Press.

Delbane, R., & Montgomery, H. (1981). *The breath of life: Discovering your breath prayer.* San Francisco: Harper & Row.

Fitzgerald, J. (1997). Reclaiming the whole: Spirit, self, and society. *Disability and Rehabilitation: An International Multidisciplinary Journal, 19,* 407–413.

Fowler, J. W. (1981). *Stages of faith.* New York: Harper & Row.

Frame, M. W. (2000). The spiritual genogram family therapy. *Journal of Marital and Family Therapy, 26,* 211–216.

Frame, M. W. (2003). *Integrating religion and spirituality into counseling: A comprehensive approach.* Pacific Grove, CA: Brooks/Cole.

Frame, M. W., & Williams, C. B. (1996). Counseling African Americans: Integrating spirituality into therapy. *Counseling and Values, 41,* 16–28.

Genia, V. (1995). *Counseling and psychotherapy of religious clients: A developmental approach.* Westport, CT: Praeger.

Heermann, M., Wiggins, M. I., & Rutter, P. A. (2007). Creating a space for spiritual practice: Pastoral possibilities with sexual minorities. *Pastoral Psychology, 55,* 711–721.

Koenig, H. G. (2004). Religion, spirituality, and medicine: Research findings and implications for clinical practice. *Southern Medical Journal, 97,* 1194–1200.

Lee, C. C., & Armstrong, K. L. (1995). Indigenous models of mental health intervention: Lessons from traditional healers. In J. G. Ponterotto, J. M. Casa, L. A. Suzuki, & C. M. Anderson (Eds.), *Handbook of multicultural counseling* (pp. 441–456). Thousand Oaks, CA: Sage.

Lewis, J. A., Arnold, M. S., House, R., & Toporek, R. L. (2002). *ACA Advocacy Competencies.* Retrieved August 15, 2008, from http://www.counseling.org/Publications/

Miles, M. (1995). Disability in an Eastern religious context: Historical perspectives. *Disability and Society, 10,* 52.

Miller, G. (1999). The development of the spiritual focus in counseling and counselor education. *Journal of Counseling & Development, 77,* 498–501.

Neuhaus, R. J. (2008, February 27). Freedom for religion. *New York Sun.* Retrieved September 7, 2008, from http://www.nysun.com/arts/freedom-for-religion/71945

Oser, F. K. (1991). The development of religious judgment. In F. K. Oser & W. G. Scarlett (Eds.), *Religious development in childhood and adolescence* (pp. 5–25). San Francisco: Jossey-Bass.

Otto, R. (1958). *The idea of the holy.* New York: Oxford University Press.

Pew Forum on Religion and Public Life. (2008). *U.S. religious landscape survey.* Washington, DC: Author.

Richards, P. S., & Bergin, A. E. (1997). *A spiritual strategy for counseling and psychotherapy.* Washington, DC: American Psychological Association.

Roth, N. (1990). *The breath of God: An approach to prayer.* Cambridge, MA: Cowley.

Schlosser, L. Z. (2003). Christian privilege: Breaking a sacred taboo. *Journal of Multicultural Counseling and Development, 31,* 44–51.

Shafranske, E. P., & Maloney, H. N. (1990). Clinical psychologists' religious and spiritual orientations and their practice of psychotherapy. *Psychotherapy, 27,* 72–78.

Somlai, A. M., Kelly, J. A., Kalichman, S. C., Mulry, G., Sikkema, K. J., McAuliffe, T., et al. (1996). An empirical investigation of the relationships between spirituality, coping and emotional distress in people living with HIV/AIDS. *Journal of Pastoral Care, 50,* 181–191.

Summit results in formation of spirituality competencies. (1995, December). *Counseling Today,* p. 30.

Toporek, R. L., Lewis, J. A., & Crethar, H. A. (2009). Promoting systemic change through the ACA Advocacy Competencies. *Journal of Counseling & Development, 87,* 260–268.

Torosian, M. H., & Biddle, V.R. (2005). Spirituality and healing. *Seminars in Oncology, 32,* 232–236.

Venkatesh, S. A. (1997). The social organization of street gang activity in an urban ghetto. *American Journal of Sociology, 103,* 82–111.

Walsh, F. (1999). Opening family therapy to spirituality. In F. Walsh (Ed.), *Spiritual resources in family therapy* (pp. 28–58). New York: Guilford Press.

Wiggins, M. I., Uphold, C. , Shehan, C. L., & Reid, K. (2008). The longitudinal effects of spirituality on stress, depression, and risk behaviors among men with HIV infection attending three clinics in the southeastern United States. *Journal of Spirituality and Mental Health, 10,* 1–24.

Chapter 9

ACA Advocacy Competencies and Women

Kathy M. Evans

The U.S. Census Bureau (2008) reported that women outnumbered men by 4.2 million in 2007. Today, women own 28% of nonfarm businesses and employ more than 7.1 million people. According to the Census Bureau report, more women graduate from high school and college than men; more women hold positions in managerial, professional, and related occupations than men; 15% of the armed forces are women; the participation of girls in sports has doubled in the past 30 years to approximately 3 million; and more women voted in the 2008 presidential election than men (Lopez & Taylor, 2009). As the slogan says, "We've come a long way, baby."

Title VII of the Civil Rights Act of 1964 prohibits employers from discriminating against women in decisions on hiring, promotion, training, and discipline and also prohibits paying women lower salaries than men (U.S. Equal Employment Opportunity Commission, n.d.). With the passage of Title IX of the Education Amendments in 1972, educational institutions that received federal funding were required to offer equal educational opportunities for boys and girls (U.S. Department of Justice, n.d.). Therefore, programs offerings that were denied to girls prior to that time were required to be opened to them and an equal amount of money had to be spent on extracurricular activities for girls and boys. With these kinds of laws on the books, so many opportunities opened for women that most people do not believe discrimination against women still exists. In fact, it is not uncommon to hear women themselves make statements like Sally's:

> I don't know why women are considered a minority group, I don't feel like I've been oppressed. I have never been discriminated against because of my sex and I have never been sexually harassed, either. I think some women are just too sensitive about things that just don't matter. They should just get over themselves.

The awful truth is that the advocacy issues for women today do not differ much from those faced 40 years ago during the second wave of the feminist movement. This is not to say that there have not been significant advances made that have lessened the intensity of oppression. The face of oppression has changed but it exists, and the need for advocacy still remains.

Today's Advocacy Issues for Women

Today's women face discrimination at all levels in hiring in the United States, although it is less likely than 40 years ago that it will occur at the entry level or even at the mid-management level. Discrimination is more likely to occur at the highest levels of management and administration (Herlihy & Watson, 2006). This phenomenon is also known as the glass ceiling. According to Alksnis, Desmarais, and Curtis (2008), there is a lingering belief that women are not capable of handling high-level management positions because of physical limitations (menstruation), personality (too emotional), or cognition (not logical). In 2007, U.S. women earned 77.8 cents for every dollar a White man made (National Committee on Pay Equity, 2008). The wage gap has been even greater for African American women and for Latinas, with Latinas in 2004 earning just 58.8 cents as compared with all men (AFL-CIO, 2006, p. 2). It is understandable that half of the families living in poverty are headed by single women.

Although women have increased their numbers in male-dominated professions, they remain in the minority, and in those professions that have moved from male dominated to 30% female, salary levels and status of those professions have dropped (Reskin & Roos, 1990). Fewer men enter the lower paying, traditionally female-dominated fields, but men who do earn more than women (Atkinson & Hackett, 1998). Even so, more women are segregated in the lower paying fields of education and social assistance than any other occupation (U.S. Census Bureau, 2008). The bottom line is that women are paid significantly less than men at every level of employment in every field. This lower pay is a manifestation of a gender socialization in a society that devalues women's work. The results of a study by Alksnis et al. (2008) support this notion: College students assigned lower salaries to jobs they perceived to be performed in a feminine domain even though the job titles and job duties were exactly the same as the jobs they perceived to be in a masculine domain.

If employment and wage discrimination are against the law, how is it that there is a wage gap and job segregation? One explanation could be that many women may not choose to risk alienating their employers or losing a potential job by seeking equitable pay. Instead women are likely to believe that they can get the job and subsequently prove themselves worthy of a substantial raise (Herlihy & Watson, 2006). Another reason could be that women fail to negotiate salaries commensurate with those negotiated by men, or if they do negotiate, they are less likely to get a job offer. As it stands, the equal-pay dilemma is still being fought by women and its nuances are being addressed in Congress at this writing.

According to Herlihy and Watson (2006), "sexual harassment has been called the single most widespread occupational hazard for women . . . 35–70 percent of women have experienced sexual harassment on the job" (p. 370). However, as compared with 40 years ago, women are more likely to report sexual harassment and more likely to get support, and there are more consequences for the behavior. The insidious issue with sexual harassment is that many people believe that the only definition of sexual harassment is quid quo pro: The person in power asks for sexual favors in exchange for employment, promotion, or privileges. However, Title VII of the Civil Rights Act of 1964 states that it includes verbal comments made when "such conduct has the purpose or effect of unreasonably interfering with an individual's work performance or creating an intimidating, hostile, or offensive working environment." The more subtle forms of sexual harassment (e.g., comments, images, and jokes that make for an uncomfortable work environment) do not meet the definition of harassment in most people's eyes. Uninformed women make statements like Sally's regarding sexual harassment and are less likely to submit a grievance for behavior they do not recognize as harassment. It does not help matters that the more subtle forms of harassment are more difficult to prove because they must be proven to unreasonably interfere with work. This means the harassment needs to happen often enough and be severe enough that the individual's work is impaired. Incidences that occur once a week, for example, probably would not be considered sexual harassment. It is the responsibility of the employer to set criteria that will protect women from such intermittent harassment; if not addressed early on, it is likely to escalate.

On the home front, over 70 million women (59%) were employed outside the home in 2006. The reasons women work have evolved over the years. Today's woman is more likely to work outside the home because she may be a single parent or her income is needed for family survival or to maintain the lifestyle her family desires (Evans, 2006). In fact, one of the reasons the wage gap has diminished over the years is not just because women's wages have increased but also because men's wages have declined (Costello & Stone, 2001).

More men are taking on home responsibilities of child care and home maintenance; however, women spend more hours on household tasks. Women are still more likely than men to be stay-at-home spouses (Evans, 2006; Gilbert, 1985; U.S. Census Bureau, 2008).

Educators have contributed to differential treatment of girls and young women to reinforce appropriate gender role stereotypes. Research reveals that teachers provide boys with more feedback and attention than they do girls, and they allow boys to talk more and answer higher level questions than they do girls (Maher & Ward, 2002). Educators in general see girls, but not boys, as quiet, neat, and emotional.

Unfortunately, the mental health field has not been exempt from bias against or oppression of women. To begin with, the theories used on women have traditionally been created by men and have devalued women's experiences in favor of male norms (Worell & Remer, 2003). Counselors and psychotherapists are not immune to socialization and the sex role orientation that all children receive. As a result, they have been found to believe in the stereotypes for men and women. In a landmark study, Broverman, Broverman, Clarkson, Rosenkranz, and Vogel (1970) found that men who fit the stereotype of independent, aggressive, and strong and women who fit the stereotype of submissive and dependent were considered psychologically healthy. The aggressive, independent woman and the submissive, dependent man were not considered healthy because they possessed characteristics desirable only for the opposite gender. Although this study was completed almost 40 years ago, more recent studies indicate that not much has changed in the gender role stereotypes held by counselors and psychotherapists (Eriksen & Kress, 2008). What this means for women is if they try to develop masculine, socially desirable characteristics, they will be considered unhealthy, and if they remain with the socially acceptable feminine characteristics, they will remain powerless and dependent. When counselors help to perpetuate these stereotypes, they inflict more harm than good on their clients.

Advocacy Issues for Culturally Diverse Women

Women of Color

The oppression of women of color is more severe than it is for White women. The well-used term of *double jeopardy* comes to mind—meaning that women of color are twice as likely to be discriminated against, once for gender and once for race. In general, women of color earn less than White women, are less educated, occupy lower level positions, and are more likely to be single parents and poor (American Association of University Women, 2008; U.S. Census Bureau, 2007a, 2007b, 2007c, 2007d, 2007e). In addition, they are as likely as White women to be sexually harassed and experience domestic violence and more likely to be diagnosed with severe mental illness than White women (Sue & Sue, 2008).

Women of color were ignored by the feminist movement and subsequently by feminist theorists until their voices were heard in the latter part of the 1980s and early 1990s (Brown, 1995; Brown & Root, 1990). Diversity issues became a major focus of the counseling field in general at that time and of feminist therapy specifically. Women of color had little use for the feminist movement because it was seen as a middle-class White woman's movement (Evans, Kincade, Marbley, & Seem, 2005). African American women, especially, were more invested in the oppression of their racial group than they were of their gender. Because their husbands, brothers, fathers, and sons were as oppressed as they were, African American women saw no reason to join with what they thought were privileged White women who oppressed Blacks as much as the White women's husbands, brothers, fathers, and sons did.

Historically, women of color have been treated as if they were invisible in the United States, and it seems evident that not much has changed in the first years of the 21st century. To most people, the term *women* means White women. This assumption is illustrated whenever an employer advertises a job vacancy with wording such as "women and minorities are encouraged to apply." If women of color were assumed to be included in the term *women*, the advertisements would read: "women and minority men are encouraged to apply." It is interesting to note that the more accurate statement, "minorities are encouraged to apply" is not accepted because many White women, like Sally, do not consider themselves part of a minority group.

The connection that minority women have to the men of their culture is personally relevant and reflects their collective oppression. They empathize more with the men in their lives, who suffer from that oppression, than they do with White women. For example, it is a well-known fact that White women earn only 77% of what White men earn. However, a much less publicized fact is that African American men and Latinos earn even less, at 75% and 66% of White men's earnings, respectively (American Association of University Women, 2008). The gender socialization of women of color is not isolated from their racial socialization. They learn to be African American women, Latinas, Asian American women, or Native American women. They learn to live as a female member of a minority group surrounded by the dominant group that holds privileges and power. Women of color learn that only cultural solidarity has helped their people survive that dominance.

Lesbians

Although lesbians are protected against sexual discrimination by Titles VII and IX, there is no federal protection for lesbian, gay, bisexual, and transgendered (LGBT) individuals. However, several states, local governments, and industries have instituted nondiscriminatory legislation and practices (Whitcomb, Wettersten, & Stolz, 2006). Because of the severe homophobia in U.S. society, there seems to be a two-steps-forward, one-step-back approach to LGBT rights. Lesbians are discriminated against in hiring, housing, health, and legal unions (marriage). In addition, they are liable to be physically attacked for their sexual orientation. Lesbians are multiply oppressed in that they suffer all the oppressions of other women with the added homophobic oppressions. With no federal protection, many lesbians are careful about disclosing their sexuality to others (especially those at work) because it is not unreasonable for them to assume that they will be "outed" and fired for their sexual orientation. Lesbians involved in committed relationships without the benefit of marriage are unlikely to get consideration for the partner's career when taking on a new job, nor will they have spousal privileges from that employment (such as insurance). Finally, lesbians are prohibited from adopting children in many states because of the misguided belief that their same-sex relationships will be detrimental to children. It does not seem to matter that research has proved that children who grow up with same-sex parents are as well adjusted as those who have heterosexual parents (Patterson, 1996).

Counselors contribute to the oppression of lesbians when they have homophobic reactions to their clients. Some behaviors counselors need to monitor are focusing on sexuality as the source for any problem that the client may bring up, failing to understand the coming-out process, and assuming the client is heterosexual and apply heterosexual relationship norms to their lesbian clients.

Advocacy and Internalized Oppression

Ethnic and cultural minority groups teach more than values to their members. Through cultural socialization, individuals learn how to function in U.S. society where it is generally assumed that being different is not acceptable. In fact, being different is often equated to being inferior to the dominant White middle-class culture (Sue & Sue, 2008). Successful cultural socialization results in individuals learning to live with society's views of their culture but to reject those attitudes about themselves.

Societal expectations regard a person who is African American, Latino, American Indian, gay or lesbian, or disabled as incapable of performing up to "normal" standards. It has been found that culturally diverse individuals "are more likely to be evaluated more negatively in our schools and workplaces. Culturally diverse groups may be seen as less intelligent, less qualified, and more un-popular, and as possessing more undesirable traits" (Sue & Sue, 2008, p. 86). While these beliefs are also true of White women, race/ethnicity, sexual orientation, and ability status are all further evidence of this so-called inferiority in the eyes of our society. Minority individuals with limited cultural socialization may internalize these negative beliefs, resulting in lowered self-efficacy and self-deprecating behaviors.

Recent literature addresses multiple identities—especially those women who identify with multiple oppressed groups, for example, a Latina who is poor, disabled, and lesbian. Multiple identities go beyond double jeopardy and require the counselor's awareness and understanding of the complexity of these women's daily existence. With multiple identities may come multiple beliefs of internalized oppression. Vasquez and Magraw (2005) stated,

> Self-abuse, eating disorders, depression, unhealthy relationship choices, domestic violence, drug and alcohol abuse, academic failure, gang involvement, hopelessness and despair, and so on can all be manifestations of the internalization or mistreatment experienced in the larger society. Internalized oppression may contribute to clients' beliefs that they are not smart enough, not beautiful enough, not deserving enough, that they are, in fact, less human than people in the dominant culture. (pp. 75–76)

Feminist Therapy and Advocacy for Women

In my view, advocating on behalf of the client should be a part of every treatment plan. However, most of the traditional approaches to counseling and psychotherapy focus only on changing the individual while maintaining the oppressive environmental status quo (Goodman et al., 2004). The counselor or therapist would need to go beyond the dictates of those theories if he or she wishes to advocate on behalf of female clients. According to Goodman et al. (2004), the feelings of alienation, disempowerment, or despair experienced by so many oppressed people "cannot truly be resolved without changing the systems and structures from which they arise" (p. 798). Several of the more recently developed theories are responsive to environmental influences (e.g., narrative therapy; constructivists theories such as multicultural counseling theory and feminist therapy). Feminist therapy is the obvious choice for a chapter on advocacy for women not only because of its focus on women's issues but also because its primary treatment strategy is advocacy.

Feminist therapists have always had a commitment to and involvement with advocating for women. In fact, the development of feminist therapy itself is considered an act of advocacy. In response to the oppressive treatment of women from practitioners who devalued women and their experiences in a way that mirrored that of the larger society, feminist therapy was created to give women a mechanism to be validated and empowered in counseling (Worell & Remer, 2003). A basic assumption of feminist therapy is that the personal is political. In other words, the personal problems that women face are due to gender socialization, oppressive societal expectations, and sexist institutional policies. The only way to completely remedy these problems is to empower clients to become involved in social action and the political process. Feminist therapists assist their clients in planning and implementing social justice activities to empower them and to make a difference.

This is not a chapter on feminist therapy, but a brief review of its basic tenets is helpful in understanding how the American Counseling Association (ACA) Advocacy Competencies (Lewis, Arnold, House, & Toporek, 2002) fit in with feminist philosophy. According to Worrell and Remer (2003), there are a number of basic principles of feminist therapy. To begin with, feminists therapists believe that they should disclose their values as feminists. They have a commitment to keep the client informed and to engage the client as a partner in her therapy. As part of that informed consent, feminist therapists will inform clients of alternatives available to them in terms of treatment, and a contract is always a part of the process. Feminist therapists try to make the relationship between their clients and themselves as equal as possible with the knowledge that the client–counselor relationship is inherently unequal. They also promote equality in other parts of clients' lives. In terms of treatment, feminist therapists use empowerment with clients while encouraging self-nurturance. They view clients as competent experts on their own lives and individuals who have strengths to draw upon. The focus of therapy is not for personal adjustment but for change, especially social change. Feminist therapists value diversity among women and include men in their practice as well.

Feminist therapists have been using the empowerment competencies long before the Advocacy Competencies were published. In the client's first visit, the goal is to empower the client who comes to counseling in a vulnerable state. Feminist therapists successfully use a number of techniques that are helpful in achieving this goal. Aware that knowledge is power, feminist therapists treat informed consent as part of the therapy process. Therapy is demystified by the information therapists give clients. The therapist gives information not only about how counseling will proceed but also about his or her beliefs and values. Clients are given credit for being adults, and they are informed of their choices, one of which is deciding whether to continue seeing the feminist therapist. Feminist therapists educate the potential client about counseling approaches and provide other information to help her to become an informed consumer. Feminist therapists will help the client to understand what to look for in a counseling relationship, the questions that should be asked, and situations she might wish to avoid. This approach empowers the client because she is the one who makes the choices about her own life. In addition, because knowledge is power, the client's increased understanding of the counseling process not only takes away the mystique but also reduces the power differential between client and therapist.

To promote an egalitarian relationship and thus empower the client, the feminist counselor is authentic and may use self-disclosure and immediacy while demonstrating to the client that the counselor values the client's knowledge of herself. For some clients, an egalitarian relationship is culturally inappropriate and uncomfortable. In those instances, the counselor can maintain the professional distance the client needs and still empower the client by promoting the client's knowledge and experience and letting her know she is trusted to make informed decisions on her life.

The strength of the feminist therapy models is that they are designed to specifically address the empowerment competencies regarding social, political, and cultural influences on behavior. During the first session with a client, a feminist therapist will listen to the client's presenting problem and then explore with the client information that will lead to an understanding of the social, environmental, and cultural factors that influence her behavior. In hearing the client's story, a feminist therapist will look for systemic and internalized oppression to understand how the personal-is-political assumption applies to that particular client. Once the counselor has an understanding of the cultural and environmental influences on the client, the counselor can help the client identify her external barriers and develop advocacy skills. The techniques involved in this strategy are gender role, power, and cultural analyses.

Gender Role Analysis

Gender role analysis is a technique that is unique to feminist therapy. According to Enns (2004), it "involves exploring the impact of gender and other identity statuses (e.g., age, sexual orientation, race) on the psychological well-being. It also involves exploring the costs and benefits of role-related behaviors and engaging in decision making about future behaviors that the client hopes to enact" (p. 43). To conduct a gender role analysis, the counselor needs to be knowledgeable about gender role socialization. Regardless of culture, from the time one is born, one is given information about the appropriate behavior and values one should have related to one's gender. In the United States, males are socialized to be independent, logical, emotionally restrained, achievement oriented, and competitive. Females are socialized to be caring, selfless, nurturing, supportive, communicative, helpful, and physically attractive to men. Deviating from these prescribed roles causes problems for the individual in terms of his or her development, career, position in society, self-esteem, and relationships. The feminist therapist helps the client to take a look at how she has internalized gender roles and how she has used her depression, anxiety, eating, and so on to cope with expectations. The counselor will help the client to decide whether her perceived gender roles are helpful or harmful; for the roles the client determines are harmful, she will decide if something needs to change. At this point, the client probably may be ready to start the process of "resocialization." In resocialization, the client learns to reject the beliefs and values that have been problematic and to adopt new beliefs and values whether or not they are sanctioned by the larger society.

Power Analysis

Both men and women exercise power; however, they typically do so within the confines of their gender socialization. Men are most likely to use power directly, women are most likely to use it indirectly. In our society, power is believed to be finite, and everyone must compete for a piece of that fixed entity. The more power one has, the higher his or her status. Because the United States is a patriarchal society, masculine forms of power are highly valued, and because power is believed to be finite, it is hoarded and protected rather than shared. This hoarding results in denying power to those in subordinate positions, like women. Because subordinate groups use their power in a way that does not overtly undermine the power of others, it can often seem manipulative.

In power analysis, counselors assist the client in defining power and identifying inequities in power among subordinate groups (e.g., women, ethnic minority men, people living in poverty, senior citizens). They also discuss how men and women exert power differently and how the client uses her power. Part of the discussion is how gender role socialization implants internal messages and affects use of power. Ultimately, the client will have a better understanding of power and will be able to decide which power strategies she will develop, keep, or put aside. A client who is able to exert her power in a way that is congruent with her image of herself and contributes to her belief in her self-worth is more likely to become involved in social justice beyond simple self-change.

Cultural Analysis

Earlier in the chapter the terms *multiple identities* and *multiple oppressions* were used. It is important to determine these identities and oppressions with a client to do an effective cultural analysis. In keeping with the gender and power analyses, the counselor will assist the client in identifying the values, beliefs, and behaviors she was socialized to adopt as a child. Then the counselor and client will examine the values the client has internalized, paying special attention to the ones that present the greatest amount of concern for the client.

Hays (2008) presented a strategy for identifying and organizing these identities in counseling through her ADDRESSING model, which include the following factors: *a*ge, developmental *d*isabilities or acquired *d*isabilities, *r*eligion and spirituality, *e*thnicity, *s*ocioeconomic status, *s*exual orientation, *i*ndigenous heritage, *n*ational origin, and *g*ender. In each identity a client can be part of a privileged group or an oppressed group. According to Hays, counselors should assess every client for these identities because of the powerful impact any type of oppression can have on an individual. When clients can see oppression from the viewpoint of both the oppressor and the oppressed, they have a better understanding of themselves and the role of oppression in their lives. Hays suggests that exploring clients' "salient identities" (those they hold most dear and have the most effect on their life) helps lead to discovering the clients' worldview and values. The cultural genogram (Hardy & Laszloffy, 1995) is also an excellent tool to assist in this process because it allows clients to learn how cultural socialization is related to their oppression.

Counselors can use cultural analysis to assist the client in understanding where her feelings originated. It can also be used to understand Whites in that the client and counselor can explore the concepts of privilege and White identity. Such discussion could take the sting out of oppression for some clients. Cultural analysis helps the client to become an advocate on her own behalf and change her behavior to cope with the problem in a healthier way than she has chosen in the past.

Implementing the ACA Advocacy Competencies

Client/Student Advocacy

When a client is in a crisis situation, it is often necessary to advocate on the client's behalf. In such a case, the counselor may believe it is important to negotiate with the client's contacts with police, social services, school administration, and other institutions because the client is in immediate need and unable to represent herself. If a client is not in crisis, it is important to connect the client with the information and the people she needs. Sometimes that means simply giving a telephone number of a direct contact when a client is getting the "run around." Sometimes it means a face-to-face introduction, and sometimes it means that the counselor will go with the client to make certain that the client's issues are heard. The situations that warrant each approach depend on the client and her problem. When a bureaucracy is intimidating enough to immobilize a client or the client is unable to communicate because of linguistic barriers, the counselor will need to be more proactive and present (Vera & Speight, 2007). Some counselors believe that acting on behalf of the client takes away that client's power, but there are situations when the opposite is true. Vera and Speight (2007) pointed out that "advocacy can be an important additional tool that can help in minimizing external stressors that affect marginalized clients. In fact, the goal of advocacy is ultimately self-empowerment of the client" (p. 377).

Counselors can make the largest impact by becoming involved in advocacy training in their roles as supervisors. They can help fill the needed knowledge gap on the oppression of women, assess students' biases toward women, and work toward a nonsexist if not feminist approach to counseling. In addition, counselors may want to organize or challenge an existing student organization to devote time and energy toward advocating for girls and women. Finally, counselors serving as supervisors can arrange the practicum and/or internship experience so that they can model Advocacy Competencies for their supervisees.

Community Collaboration

When counselors help clients connect with others in the community who can lend support, oftentimes that very act results in the clients' involvement in advocacy. Community organizations are typically proactive in providing needed services that help enhance the lives of members. For a counselor to be involved as an advocate, she or he would need to be proactive. This would involve identifying a need not being met and working to see that something is done to change that fact. For example, if a large employer in the community has an unequal pay scale for men and women, the counselor may want to connect with a union if there is one or other organization within the company to discuss this injustice and encourage some kind of action toward change. The counselor could offer the organization her or his expertise in communicating with management, data collection, or organization of the effort.

To address the lack of women entering more high-paying careers, counselors may want to work with schools to design programs to encourage girls to consider careers in math and science. Such programs can promote efficacy in these subjects. School counselors would be ideally placed for such an advocacy approach. They could work with teachers on their attitudes toward girls and women and enlighten the teachers about any discouraging messages they may be inadvertently sending to students. Counselors can run sensitivity training for teachers and other counselors and perhaps can apply for grants to secure funds for their efforts.

For sexual harassment concerns, an ideal approach is for counselors to educate adolescent males and females about what constitutes harassment through youth organizations, men's organizations, and women's organizations, among others. Teachers and parents could also be targeted to ensure that they recognize and can stop this kind of behavior before it takes hold. Such contacts would be helpful in educating men and women about the necessity of equally dividing work at home among the partners.

Counselors can promote responsible parenting and partnering by running educational and practical workshops on child care and other household responsibilities.

Advocacy in the Public Arena

At the societal level, counselors can get involved in advocating for women in many different ways. Perhaps the most effective is to become active in one or more of the already effective national women's advocacy groups. An individual may become involved locally or regionally in most national organizations. One of the organizations that has been particularly active in women's rights is the National Organization for Women (www.now.org), whose goal is to advocate on behalf of women for abortion and reproductive rights, economic justice, an end to sex discrimination, and lesbian rights, as well as promoting diversity and working against violence against women. The American Association of University Women (www.aauw.org) has as its mission to fight for equity for girls and women through education, research, and advocacy. This organization has been involved in fighting for ending wage discrimination against women for over 50 years.

Challenges

The counselor's attitude about advocacy may be the biggest challenge to implementation. Gainor (2005) suggested that for individuals to become advocates, they first have to have a strong sense of moral outrage. Stimulating moral outrage about women's issues these days is definitely a challenge when women's oppression is not seen by many as critical (after all, what is so bad about not being promoted to high-level management when one earns $250,000 per year?). Instead, counselors need to develop outrage because "women's" work educating children who will be the future of the country and caring for those who cannot care for themselves is not seen as important enough to pay on par with a plumber or electrician. If all of these jobs are important, why shouldn't "women's" careers be worth more than they are? Why should women have to endure sexual harassment to get jobs or promotions? As advocates, we need to do a better job of training future counselors so that they understand better the injustices in our society and develop that moral outrage.

Other reasons why counselors are not involved in social advocacy have been outlined by Fox (2003). These factors include (a) fear of reprisals from employers who are not as dedicated to social justice, (b) risk of being ridiculed and harassed by colleagues as a bleeding heart, (c) alienating potential resources instead of gaining support from them, and (d) fear of losing one's job. In addition, Vera and Speight (2007) suggested that many people believe that they should keep their politics to themselves or that advocacy is not their job but the job of social workers. These authors also mentioned that counselors may have learned to work within the system so well that they cannot see its flaws.

Perhaps the most depressing challenge is Gainor's (2005) suggestion that counselors may not get involved in advocacy because, as privileged individuals, they are unwilling to change a system and lose those privileges. It would be a sad state for professionals in a helping field to be so protective of their privilege. An argument against Gainor's suggestion is Blustein, McWhirter, and Perry's (2005) charge that because counselors are so privileged in our society, they have the moral obligation to promote social justice.

Finally, the challenge is that the Advocacy Competencies themselves have not been taught to most counselors. It is difficult to embark on a journey without a map, and counseling programs have not provided their students with that map. Vera and Speight (2007) proposed using service learning components in courses and/or community immersion plans. However, Evans (2008) pointed out that service brings awareness to the issue but is not proactive. Advocacy involves taking action to promote change. Therefore, students also need instruction and experience in advancing the notion of change.

Other challenges for implementing the Advocacy Competencies for women clients and students include (a) inability getting support from the women themselves, (b) difficulty getting access to community organizations that distrust counselors and their institutions, and (c) denial of oppression by those in power or having the more critical problems with women far down the list of priorities.

Conclusion

Although the past 40 years have been phenomenal for women in terms of their advances in society, the work is far from over. Counselors see clients every day with depression, anxiety, insomnia, fatigue, posttraumatic stress, and other problems that are directly or indirectly attributed to the injustices women experience today. The more counselors and their clients can contribute to bringing about the social change needed to correct those injustices, the more they contribute to the mental health of the female population.

References

AFL-CIO. (2006). *Fact sheet: Professional women: Vital statistics*. Retrieved March 15, 2009, from http://www.pay-equity.org/PDFs/ProfWomen.pdf

Alksnis, C., Desmarais, S., & Curtis, J. (2008). Workforce segregation and the gender wage gap: Is "women's" work valued as highly as "men's." *Journal of Applied Social Psychology, 38,* 1416–1441.

American Association of University Women. (2008). *Paycheck Fairness Act.* Retrieved July 31, 2008, from http://www.aauw.org/advocacy/issue_advocacy/upload/LC-PaycheckFairnessAct072408.pdf

Atkinson, D. R., & Hackett, G. (1998). *Counseling diverse populations* (2nd ed.). Boston: McGraw-Hill.

Blustein, D. L., McWhirter, E. H., & Perry J. C. (2005) An emancipatory communitarian approach to vocational development theory, research and practice. *The Counseling Psychologist, 33,* 141–179.

Broverman, I. K., Broverman, D. M., Clarkson, F. E., Rosenkranz, P. S., & Vogel, S. R. (1970). Sex-role stereotypes and clinical judgments of mental health. *Journal of Consulting and Clinical Psychology, 34,* 1–7.

Brown, L. S. (1995). Cultural diversity in feminist therapy: Theory and practice. In H. Landrine (Ed.), *Bringing cultural diversity to feminist psychology: Theory, research, and practice* (pp. 143–161). Washington, DC: American Psychological Association.

Brown, L. S., & Root, M. P. (1990). *Diversity and complexity in feminist therapy.* New York: Harrington Park Press.

Costello, C. B., & Stone, A. (Eds.). (2001). *The American woman, 2001–2002: Getting to the top.* New York: Norton.

Enns, C. Z. (2004). *Feminist theories and feminist psychotherapies: Origins, themes, and diversity* (2nd ed.). New York: Haworth Press.

Eriksen, K., & Kress, V. E. (2008). Gender and diagnosis: Struggles and suggestions for counselors. *Journal of Counseling & Development, 86,* 152–162.

Evans, K. M. (2006). Career counseling with couples and families. In D. Capuzzi & M. D. Stauffer (Eds.), *Career counseling: Foundations, perspectives and applications* (pp. 336–359). Boston: Pearson Education.

Evans, K. M. (2008). *Gaining cultural competence in career counseling.* Boston: Lahaska Press.

Evans, K. M., Kincade, E. A., Marbley, A. F., & Seem, S. R. (2005). Feminism and feminist therapy: Lessons from the past and hopes for the future. *Journal of Counseling & Development, 83,* 269–277.

Fox, D. (2003). Awareness is good but action is better. *The Counseling Psychologist, 31,* 299–304.

Gainor, K. A. (2005) Social justice: The moral imperative of vocational psychology. *The Counseling Psychologist, 33,* 180–188.

Gilbert, L. A. (1985). *Men in dual-career families: Current realities and future prospects*. Hillsdale, NJ: Erlbaum.

Goodman, L. A., Liang, B., Helms, J. E., Latta, R. E., Sparks, E., & Weintrab, S. R. (2004). Training counseling psychologists as social justice agents: Feminist and multicultural principles in action. *The Counseling Psychologist, 32*, 793–837.

Hardy, K. V., & Laszloffy, T. A. (1995). The cultural genogram: Key to training culturally competent family therapists. *Journal of Marital and Family Therapy, 21,* 227–237.

Hays, P. A. (2008). *Addressing cultural complexities in practice: Assessment, diagnosis, and therapy* (2nd ed.). Washington, DC: American Psychological Association.

Herlihy, B. R., & Watson, Z. P., (2006). Gender issues in career counseling. In D. Capuzzi & M. D. Stauffer (Eds.), *Career counseling: Foundations, perspectives and applications* (pp. 363–385). Boston: Pearson Education.

Lewis, J. A., Arnold, M. S., House, R., & Toporek, R. L. (2002). *ACA Advocacy Competencies*. Retrieved May 16, 2009, http://www.counseling.org/Publications/

Lopez, M. H., & Taylor, P. (2009). *Dissecting the 2008 electorate: Most diverse in U.S. history.* Washington, DC: Pew Research Center. Retrieved June 11, 2009, from http://pewresearch.org/assets/pdf/dissecting-2008-electorate.pdf

Maher, F. A., & Ward, J. V. (2002). *Gender and teaching*. Mahwah, NJ: Erlbaum.

National Committee on Pay Equity. (2008). *The wage gap over time: In real dollars women see a continuing gap*. Retrieved March 15, 2009, from http://www.pay-equity.org/info-time.html

Patterson, C. (1996). Lesbian mothers and their children. In J. Laird & R. Greed (Eds.), *Lesbians and gays in couples and families: A handbook for therapists* (pp. 420–437). San Francisco: Jossey-Bass.

Reskin, B. F., & Roos, P. A. (1990). *Job queues, gender queues: Explaining women's inroads into male occupation.* Philadelphia: Temple University Press.

Sue, D. W., & Sue, D. (2008). *Counseling the culturally diverse: Theory and practice* (4th ed.). Hoboken, NJ: Wiley.

U.S. Census Bureau (2007a). *The American community: American Indian and Alaska Natives: 2004.* Retrieved from http://www.census.gove.prod/2007pubs/acs-07.pdf

U.S. Census Bureau (2007b). *The American community: Asians: 2004.* Retrieved from http://www.census.gov/prod/2007pubs/acs-05.pdf

U.S. Census Bureau (2007c). *The American community: Blacks: 2004.* Retrieved from http://www.census.gov/prod/2007pubs/acs-04.pdf

U.S. Census Bureau (2007d). *The American community: Hispanics: 2004.* Retrieved from http://www.census.gov/prod/2007pubs/acs-03.pdf

U.S. Census Bureau (2007e). *The American community: Pacific Islanders: 2004.* Retrieved from http://www.census.gov/prod/2007pubs/acs-06.pdf

U.S. Census Bureau. (2008). *Fact for features: Women's history month.* Retrieved July 15, 2008, from http://www.census.gov/Press-Release/www/releases/archives/cb08ff-03.pdf

U.S. Department of Justice. (n.d.). *Title IX of the Education Amendments of 1972.* Retrieved July 27, 2008, from http://www.usdoj.gov/crt/cor/coord/titleixstat.htm#(a)

U.S. Equal Employment Opportunity Commission. (n.d.). *Title VII of the Civil Rights Act of 1964.* Retrieved July 27, 2008, from http://www.eeoc.gov/policy/vii.html

Vasquez, H., & Magraw, S. (2005). Building relationships across privilege: Becoming an ally in the therapeutic relationship. In M. P. Mirkin, K. L. Suyemoto, & B. F. Okun (Eds.), *Psychotherapy with women: Exploring diverse contexts and identities* (pp. 64–83). New York: Guilford Press.

Vera, E. M., & Speight, S. L. (2007). Advocacy, outreach, and prevention: Integrating social action roles in professional training. In E. Aldarondo (Ed.), *Advancing social justice through clinical practice* (pp. 373–388). Mahwah, NJ: Erlbaum.

Whitcomb, D. H., Wettersten, K. B., & Stolz, C. L. (2006). Career counseling with gay, lesbian, bisexual, and transgender clients. In D. Capuzzi & M. D. Stauffer (Eds.), *Career counseling: Foundations, perspectives and applications* (pp. 386–420). Boston: Pearson Education.

Worell, J., & Remer, P. (2003). *Feminist perspectives in therapy* (2nd ed.). Hoboken, NJ: Wiley.

Chapter 10

Advocacy for Older Clients

Jane Goodman

As counselors, if we work with older adults, we know that advocacy must play a central role in our work. Our clients are sometimes discounted, often marginalized, and always subject to the possibility of discrimination. In this chapter, I examine some key demographic trends regarding aging, make the case for advocacy, review a number of practical strategies, and provide a list of valuable advocacy-focused resources. I begin by first asking, who are our clients, and how do we perceive them?

Who Are Our Clients?

How old are you? Your answer to that question will provide a lens for how you read this chapter. Is it about *them?* Or is it about *us?* All of us are in some way connected to older adults. If we are not yet "old," we certainly hope to acquire that status! Ageism may be the one form of discrimination that all of us who live long enough may encounter. Being old is the one marginalized group that we wish to join. For the purposes of this chapter, I use the age of 65 and over to be "old" while recognizing that other definitions may apply. The United States protects workers over age 40 from age discrimination. AARP (www.aarp.org), known until 1998 as the American Association of Retired Persons, invites people over age 50 to join. Movie theaters and other public places, such as museums or hotels, often give discounts to people over 55, 60, 62, as well as 65. The reality is that our aging population necessitates some new ways of thinking about what it means to be old and even what "old" is.

Let us look at some demographics. Even though the United States is aging at a slower rate than some other countries (Haas, 2008), a major demographic trend is clearly the aging of the population.

- According to U.S. Census Bureau projections, the elderly population will more than double between 2000 and 2030, growing from 35 million to over 70 million.
- Much of this growth is attributed to the baby boom generation, which will enter their elderly years between 2010 and 2030 (University of North Carolina, 2006).
- The national median age rose to 37.9 in 2007, up 1.4 years since 2000 (Jones & Overberg, 2008).

- The "oldest old"—those age 85 and over—are the most rapidly growing elderly age group.[1]
- The oldest old represented 12.1% of the elderly population in 2000 and 1.5% of the total population. In 2050, they are projected to be 24% of elderly Americans and 5% of all Americans.
- Centenarians—those 100 years old or more—represent a small but growing number of elderly Americans. The 1990 census reported 37,000 centenarians, while the 2000 census reported 50,000 centenarians in the United States (University of North Carolina, 2006).

It is not just increasing numbers that make it important for us to serve as advocates for older adults. Close your eyes for a moment and think about the images that come to your mind when you think about old people. I am guessing that many more are negative—slow, frail, sick, weak, confused, boring, stuck in their ways, out of touch—than positive—wise, mature, understanding. What is known in actuality is that older adults are *more* diverse than younger adults as they have had more years to develop their differences. They run the gamut from athletic to frail, from wealthy to poor, and from socially active to socially isolated.

People of color are disparately affected by aging and poverty and therefore are even more in need of advocacy efforts. For example, in looking at data about who is at risk for poverty at age 65, one finds that 25% of Black females, 22% of Hispanic females, 20% of Black men, and 17% of Hispanic men fall into that category, compared with 11% of White women and 6% of White men. Similarly, although life expectancy for all has increased dramatically since 1900, the disparities have also increased. In 1900 the two most disparate life expectancies at age 65 were Black men (10½ years) and White women (12½ years), a 2-year difference. In 2003 the two most disparate were still Black men and White women, but there was a 5-year difference: life expectancies at age 65 were 15 and 20 years, respectively (University of North Carolina, 2006). The University of North Carolina described the following implications of these data: First, the effects of aging are compounded by the additional effects of race, class, and gender and result in higher risks for health and social problems; and, second, major implications include increased demand for support services, greater need for long-term care solutions, and higher expenditures for health care and services.

Why Advocacy?

Older adults, particularly women and people of color, are often marginalized by society, sometimes patronized, other times ignored. Many older women can attest to feeling invisible as younger people are served first at shops, listened to differently at meetings, or otherwise treated as if they are not there. (Younger women and men of color describe this experience also, but the invisibility seems to be exaggerated for older women.) Elderly women outnumber elderly men. By age 85, 72% of the population is female, compared with 59% at age 65 and 51% of all ages (University of North Carolina, 2006).

Many older adults are vulnerable because they are less experienced with technological ways of dealing with bureaucracies or are more intimidated by authority compared with younger people. These differences will probably diminish, however, as the cohort of baby boomers becomes old. Other vulnerabilities may increase as more people live to be old-old. Vision, hearing, and dexterity do diminish with age for most people. Elder abuse is also a growing problem, often triggered when families are stressed beyond their coping capacities by partners, parents, or other relatives who require extensive care.

On the positive side, there is evidence that advocacy works. Mandatory retirement has been eliminated, giving those who wish to work after 65 that opportunity. Whether it is this opportunity or the lack of finances, growing numbers of U.S. workers are delaying retirement.

---

[1]I thank Elinor Waters for her help with this chapter. She was my coauthor on an earlier book chapter from which much of this chapter was drawn: "Advocating on Behalf of Older Adults," by J. Goodman & E. B. Waters (2000). In J. Lewis and L. Bradley (Eds.), *Advocacy in Counseling: Counselors, Clients, and Community* (pp. 79–87). Greensboro, NC: CAPS Publications.

According to the U.S. Census Bureau, there were 5.5 million workers 65 and older in the labor force in 2006, or about 23% of people ages 65 to 74. That figure is up 20% from 8 years ago. The number of people 65 and older in the workforce is expected to reach 10.1 million by 2014 (American Counseling Association, 2008). Social Security now pays benefits not only to wives and widows but also to divorced women who were married for 10 or more years.

Advocacy efforts can run the gamut from simple to extensive. For example, a simple act of advocacy is to make sure that there are white lines on the front of each stair in an office building or apartment complex. This can make the difference between ease and difficulty of accessibility for older adults. On a more complex level, arranging for "call a ride" services can allow a modicum of independence for older adults who can no longer drive and who live in areas without mass transit.

There are some other demographic data that are important to know as one examines advocacy for older adults. For example, (a) the elderly are becoming more racially and ethnically diverse, just as U.S. society as a whole is becoming more diverse; (b) poverty rates rise with advancing age; and (c) older women are more likely to live alone (University of North Carolina, 2006).

Many older adults have serious mental health problems, with depression being the most common. Estimates are that nearly 15% of community-living older adults and at least 25% of nursing home residents suffer from depression. Other problems include anxiety disorders, substance abuse, and cognitive impairment. Older adults commit suicide at a rate higher than any other age group in the United States. People age 85 and older have the highest rates, the next highest rates are among people age 75 to 84. Unfortunately, many of these mental health needs are unmet. According to the National Institute of Mental Health, 20% of older Americans have a diagnosable mental illness, but fewer than a quarter get any mental health attention or appropriate care (National Association of Social Workers, 2004). This stems, in part, from the reluctance of many in this age cohort to seek mental health assistance. Counselors may need to encourage service providers to provide more informal "consultation" or "by-the-way counseling" to people who may be reluctant to seek formal mental health services. One counselor I know changed the name of her services to consultation and greatly increased the number of older adults who sought her out. An advocacy program run by the Continuum Center at Oakland University some years ago trained staff members at senior residences in basic listening skills. These newly trained staff members, with their new listening skills, found that people who stopped by the office at their senior residence, ostensibly to ask for logistical help, began to talk about their more serious problems.

There is a corollary problem of service providers' reluctance to provide help to older adults. I recently heard a story of a woman seeking assistance for increasing memory loss. The psychiatrist she consulted told her and her husband there was no way to determine the cause and nothing to do and, much to their distress, gave the impression of a lack of interest. Although there may not be "cures" for this condition, there are ameliorative activities and coping mechanisms that could have been useful to both the woman and her spouse. There should also have been a medical work-up to rule out physical problems that can be addressed, such as overmedication for other conditions or, as alluded to above, depression.

Other factors include the scarcity of both community-based preventive programs and institutionally based treatment programs, the fact that health insurance plans typically give short shrift to mental health benefits, and the lack of coordination between the aging network, the mental health network, and the primary care delivery system. While all these factors point to the need for counselors to advocate for the needs of older adults and their families, I want to caution against treating older adults merely as people to be served. Advocacy may mean helping older adults to advocate for themselves as well as intervening for them. By definition, older adults are survivors, and one of the jobs of counselors and advocates is to help them identify and utilize the repertoire of coping skills they have developed over a lifetime. The American Counseling Association (ACA) Advocacy Competencies (Lewis, Arnold, House, & Toporek, 2002), discussed next, begin with acting *with* the client in an empowering mode.

Advocacy Strategies

The Advocacy Competencies provide a conceptualization for advocacy strategies. To advocate for older adults, counselors need first of all to be knowledgeable about the needs and concerns of this population and familiar with the aging network that encompasses the array of services for older adults. For example, counselors should know how to contact the Eldercare Locator (http://www. eldercare.gov), a national organization that "can help older persons and their families access home and community-based services like transportation, meals, home care, and caregiver support services" (Eldercare locator, para. 1). It is also important to have contacts with the Area Agency on Aging or local service providers who can effectively direct older adults or family members through the maze of services.

Help Older Adults to Advocate for Themselves

A look at the three levels of advocacy suggested by the Advocacy Competencies confirms that the empowerment level is particularly important for older adults. It is imperative that counselors not belittle older adults by assuming that they must be "taken care of." Although people often face the prospect or the reality of having to be taken care of as they age, as long as an individual is capable of advocating for him- or herself, one needs to foster that independence. To do so, counselors may need to teach clients advocacy skills and attitudes. That is, counselors need to empower older adults. As the Advocacy Competencies suggest, counselors may need to help older adults develop a contextual awareness and an understanding of both external and internalized oppression. Group self-hatred is endemic in this population. Few people greet the statement "You are looking old today" as a compliment! Counselors may help older clients develop awareness by teaching them skills such as assertiveness, by helping them believe that they have the *right* to receive assistance, and by helping them understand the political process. Counselors may also help their older clients understand the differences between being passive, aggressive, and assertive and teach them specific communication techniques for asserting their rights.

Age cohort issues may arise here as many of today's older adults are part of a tradition of independence. Often this includes a "don't make waves" approach. These generations of older adults often saw needing assistance beyond the family as a sign of weakness or vulnerability. Different cultures have different terms for this idea of protecting privacy. "Don't air your dirty linen in public" is a common one. Among Jewish families the statement, "It's a shonda for the goyim," expressed the idea that it would bring shame if a Jew ever let "outsiders" know about their unmet needs. Other families express their pride in independence with such statements as "I kept food on the table during the Depression; my family was never hungry."

Helping older adults with these kinds of traditions understand their entitlements can be an important role for counselor advocates. As today's younger people age, these kinds of issues may disappear. But I suspect that the strong independence value fostered in American culture will continue to influence many people and make it harder for them when some sort of dependence becomes necessary. The cultural differences among older adults with different ethnic traditions need to be mentioned here. Those older adults from traditions where interdependence and connectedness are higher values than independence may not fit this Western mold. This may be an asset as they face having more needs, but counselors who themselves are from independent Western traditions will have to be extremely careful not to impose their values. Similarly, counselors from more relationship-oriented traditions will need to be extra cautious when working with clients for whom independence is a prime value.

Assisting older adults to advocate for themselves can take many forms. Coaching or role-playing may help individuals (caregivers as well as older adults themselves) ask for what they need from health care providers, public and private bureaucracies, or other organizations. Groups of older adults can also be taught, or reminded to use, political advocacy and community organizing skills. Remember that many trade unions and important advocacy groups were started by people who are today "older adults." A sparkling example of an "older"-run advocacy group is the Gray Panthers (www.graypanthers.org). They describe themselves as "an intergenerational, multi-issue organization working to create a society that puts the needs of people over profit, responsibility over power and democracy over institutions" (Gray Panthers, n.d.). The Gray Panthers was founded in 1970 by Maggie Kuhn, who is well known for stating, "Old age is not a disease—it is strength and survivorship, triumph over all kinds of vicissitudes and disappointments, trials and illnesses." The Gray Panthers annual conference includes such empowering topics as publicity and influencing elected officials.

Abused elders may need special assistance as they may not be aware of their rights or may be afraid to ask for help because they perceive themselves as dependent on their abusers. Abuse hotlines, more accustomed to serving women and children, may need education and training in handling this special group. This kind of outreach is an example of community collaboration, which I discuss next.

Community Collaboration

The second area in the Advocacy Competencies is that of community collaboration. Lewis et al. (2002) wrote,

> Their ongoing work with people gives counselors a unique awareness of recurring themes. Counselors are often among the first to become aware of specific difficulties in the environment. Advocacy-oriented counselors often choose to respond to such challenges by alerting existing organizations that are already working for change and that might have an interest in the issue at hand. In these situations, the counselor's primary role is as an ally.

Knowing about others' efforts is a necessary adjunct to an advocacy-oriented counselor's efforts, but it is not sufficient. Counselors need to lend their expertise and knowledge to these efforts. The special training counselors receive and the skills counselors develop in the profession make them particularly qualified to hear the needs of diverse groups, manage inevitable conflict about priorities, and present clear and convincing statements of needs, based on real information from clients. Counselors need, obviously, to protect clients' privacy, but nonetheless the specific case examples may be the most persuasive information available.

Some examples of counselors enhancing their effectiveness by working with existing organizations follow:

1. Counselor advocates can contact the aging network in their community or state for information on available services. Federal funding for services for older adults is funneled through state offices of aging and regional Area Agencies on Aging, known as AAAs or triple As. In planning distribution of these funds, AAAs hold annual hearings that represent an excellent opportunity to advocate for those services older clients most need. Such contacts also represent an opportunity to advocate for licensing for facilities that serve older adults and for standards of staff training and performance.
2. Counselor advocates can locate coalitions of mental health and aging organizations at the national, state, and local level. The National Coalition on Mental Health and Aging includes representatives of:

- professional associations, such as ACA, the National Association of Social Workers, the American Psychiatric Association, the American Psychological Association, the American Society on Aging, and the National Council on Aging;
- government organizations, such as the Administration on Aging, the National Association of State Units on Aging, the National Association of Area Agencies on Aging, and the National Institute of Mental Health; and

- aging organizations, such as AARP, the National Council of Senior Citizens, the National Caucus and Center on Black Aged, and the aforementioned Gray Panthers.

Many states have similar coalitions that can be contacted through the state department of aging and/or mental health department. At the local level, it may be easiest to contact the area agency on aging.

3. Counselor advocates can locate, recommend, and publicize innovative services. Two examples follow:

- In some communities the Eden Alternative represents an approach to long-term care designed to make facilities more like homes and less like institutions. Nursing homes that adapt this approach bring pets and plants into the facility and give residents responsibility for their care. Young children are typically brought in to engage in joint activities with residents.
- Other communities are experimenting with providing mental health services in physical health care settings. Such an approach is designed to address the reluctance of many older adults to seek traditional mental health services. To evaluate this approach, the U.S. Substance Abuse and Mental Health Services has provided a number of grants to assess the effectiveness of this kind of integrated model of treatment in the primary care setting itself.

4. Counselor advocates can work with organizations that represent older adults. For example:

- AARP is one of the largest membership organizations in the United States, with an active corps of volunteers, newsletters and magazines that reflect the interests of members, and a staff who lobbies on behalf of those members. Both the Washington office and regional offices will supply information and contacts.
- Founded in 2001, the Alliance for Retired Americans (www.retiredamericans.org/) is intended to be a more progressive representative of older adults than the mainstream AARP. The mission of the alliance is to "ensure social and economic justice and full civil rights for all citizens so that they may enjoy lives of dignity, personal and family fulfillment and security. With the help of our members, the Alliance aims to influence government through action on retiree legislative and political issues at the federal, state and local levels" (Alliance for Retired Americans, n.d.). They state that they are not in competition with AARP but are "an organization of retirees who are committed to activism and want to influence the policies of government that affect all older Americans."
- A much smaller organization, the Older Women's League (OWL; www.owl-national.org/) is "The only national grassroots organization to focus solely on issues unique to women as they age" (OWL, n.d.-b). It has a platform that calls for a national universal health care system, economic security including Social Security and pensions, full access to appropriate housing and housing alternatives, ending violence against women and the elderly, staying in control through all of life, and combating discrimination in the workplace. OWL has a Washington office and local chapters throughout the United States. OWL has instigated an Older Americans' Mental Health Week that promotes 10 facts about mental health and aging. These facts are as follows:

  - Mental health problems are not a normal part of aging.
  - Mental health is as important as physical health.
  - Healthy older adults can continue to thrive, grow, and enjoy life.
  - Mental health problems are a risk for older adults regardless of history.
  - Suicide is a risk among older adults.
  - These symptoms call for consultation with a health care professional.

- Older adults can be helped with the same success as younger people.
- Our health care system is not adequately helping older adults with mental disorders.
- Misdiagnosis and avoidance are common.
- Older adults have specific mental health needs. (OWL, n.d.-a)

Advocate at the Public Arena Level

The third leg of the Advocacy Competencies tripod is public information and social political advocacy within the public arena. Political advocacy takes many forms. As counselors, we can monitor proposed legislation at the national and state level that would affect benefits and services for older adults and let our views be known. For example, the news media is currently full of ideas for revamping Social Security programs, often with a view toward privatization. Counselors need to be aware that such proposals may negate the safety net provided by Social Security, particularly for women. Many older women rely on Social Security, and women of color are even more likely to live in poverty and depend on Social Security than are White women.

Another much discussed issue of extreme importance to older adults concerns financing of health care. When HMOs decide they cannot afford to serve older adults, a crisis is at hand which necessitates broad-based advocacy. Medicare and Medicaid only partially fill this gap. The looming shortage of family doctors and doctors who specialize in internal medicine will probably aggravate this problem, as these are the practitioners who typically provide coordination of an individual's care, even when specialists become involved. An all-too-frequent problem for older adults is taking medicine that conflicts with or counteracts other medicines or having several prescription drugs prescribed for the same complaint. Having one doctor or other health professional monitoring all care becomes imperative in these circumstances.

In an article in the AARP newsletter, Kirchheimer (2008) described a growing practice of asking people to pay a percentage of their health care costs up front, before they receive the service. These costs, which can run into the tens of thousands, or occasionally more, are often prohibitive for older people, who may then choose to forgo the health care. This is an example of where advocating at the public arena level intersects with advocating for an individual. Kirchheimer suggested that patients (and/or their advocates) contact the hospital's social worker or patient navigator as well as ask for at least some of the price break that insurance companies receive on the costs. He stated that companies typically get a 60% price break and that individual patients may be able to negotiate a 30% discount. It is my opinion that charging individuals more than double what large companies pay is unconscionable and ought to be the focus of someone's advocacy efforts.

To maximize the impact we have as counselors, it is important to work with some of the groups that already do political advocacy. I have already mentioned one very large group, the AARP; one medium-sized group, the Alliance for Retired Americans; and one small group, OWL. All three have lobbyists in Washington and chapters in local areas. ACA, and in particular one of its divisions, the Association for Adult Development and Aging, addresses issues of older adults when they intersect with the needs of counselors or the services counselors can provide. Working with such organizations is crucial to successful political advocacy. It is one way to work to include age in all nondiscriminatory statements.

I have not addressed advocacy at the international level at all in the foregoing, but it is important to at least recognize that efforts by the U.S. government in international policy have an impact on other countries and domestically. In a provocative article, Haas (2008) pointed to a potential "Pax Americana Geriatrica" as a result of different rates of aging and immigration. He stated that, for example, policies that encourage reduced fertility in developing nations would diminish violence in their countries and in the United States. He stated that young people, "especially in the context of economic deprivation and political oppression, frequently feel that they have little to lose by engaging in violent acts designed to change the status quo" (p. 38). The kinds of policies mentioned include women's rights, education and employment opportunities, and increased access to birth control, all areas that could by fostered by U.S. foreign policies.

Further Client Advocacy

As counselors consider how life can be improved for many older adults, it is important to think broadly about the many entities with which they interact. Service locations from grocery stores to department stores, libraries to senior centers, and Social Security offices to doctor's offices all need to be aware of, and responsive to, normal age-related sensory losses. Such responsiveness should involve making sure that printed material is easy to read, that auditory distractions are minimized, and that chairs are firm and easy to get in and out of it. Several websites dedicated to the needs of older adults have a button on their home page to allow the reader to increase the font size. If all public sites did this, it would be helpful not only to older adults but also to others with vision problems.

An important role for counselor advocates might be to encourage managers at all kinds of facilities to ask their older consumers what would make their services more hospitable. One might hear about needs for better lighting, wider aisles to accommodate wheelchairs, or programs held during daylight hours and accessible by good public transportation. Many older adults enjoy attending classes and artistic performances. Some may need reduced tuition or admission fees.

Conclusion

As counselors, we can be better advocates for older adult clients if we picture ourselves as older adults and consider what would make our lives less complicated and more fulfilling. What could we do for ourselves with the assistance of groups of various kinds? What do we experience as a member of a minority group or as women that will be or is exacerbated by aging? The challenge for us then is to determine how we can improve the quality of life for the older adults whom we serve. It is my hope that the information in this chapter will make it easier for counselors to enter into advocacy roles.

Counselors do not have to carry out the advocacy role alone, without assistance. There is often help from community resources and advocacy organizations. The following list of suggested resources will provide a start.

Suggested Resources

Professional Associations

American Counseling Association
    5999 Stevenson Avenue
    Alexandria, VA 22304
    Phone: (800) 347-6647
    www.counseling.org

American Society on Aging
    833 Market Street, Suite 511
    San Francisco, CA 94103
    Phone: (415) 974-9600
    www.asaging.org
        This organization includes a Mental Health and Aging Network (http://www.asaging.org/networks/index.cfm?cg=MHAN), "the largest organization of multidisciplinary professionals in the field of aging. Our resources, publications, and educational opportunities are geared to enhance the knowledge and skills of people working with older adults and their families."

National Council on Aging
    409 Third Street, SW
    Washington, DC 20024
    Phone: (202) 479-1200
    www.ncoa.org

Membership and Advocacy Organizations

AARP (formerly known as the American Association of Retired Persons)
  601 E Street, NW
  Washington, DC 20049
  Phone: (202) 434-2277
  www.aarp.org

Alliance for Retired Americans
  815 16th Street, NW, Fourth Floor
  Washington, DC 20006
  (202) 637-5399
  www.retiredamericans.org

Bazelon Center for Mental Health Law
  1101 15th Street, NW, Suite 1212
  Washington, DC 20005
  (202) 467-5730
  www.bazelon.org
    "The mission of the Judge David L. Bazelon Center for Mental Health Law is to protect and advance
    the rights of adults and children who have mental disabilities. The Center envisions an America
    where people who have mental illnesses or developmental disabilities exercise their own life choices
    and have access to the resources that enable them to participate fully in their communities."

Gray Panthers
  3635 Chestnut Street
  Philadelphia, PA 19104
  Graypanthers.org
    The mission of the Gray Panthers is to "Work for social and economic justice and peace for all
    people."

National Caucus and Center on Black Aged
  1220 L Street, NW, Suite 800
  Washington, DC 20005
  (202) 637-8400
  www.ncba-aged.org

Older Women's League (OWL)
  666 11th Street, NW, Suite 700
  Washington, DC 20001
  (202) 783-6686 or 1-800-0825-3695
  www.owl-national.org/

Recommended Readings

The AARP Guide to Internet Resources Related to Aging
    Available from AARP (mailing address above) or through www.aarp.org/cyber/
    guide1.htm
    A comprehensive listing of websites divided into such categories as World Wide Web, government
    and government related, health related, housing and living arrangements, income related, law re-
    lated, leisure activities, and social services. Also includes listings for listservs, Usenet newgroups,
    newsletters, and electronic magazines related to aging.

Wacker, R. R., Roberto, K. A., & Piper, L. E. (1998). *Community Resources for Older Adults: Programs and Services in an Era of Change.* Thousand Oaks, CA: Pine Forge Press.

> A useful overview of the legislative basis for programs, services, and benefits for older adults. Chapters on various services (e.g., information and referral, senior centers and recreation, respite services, and nursing homes) contain descriptions of services, examples of best practices, case studies, national organizations, and Internet resources for each topic area.

References

Alliance for Retired Americans (n.d.). *Frequently asked questions.* Retrieved August 12, 2008, from http://www.retiredamericans.org/ht/display/ShowPage/id/333/pid/333

American Counseling Association. (2008, August 12). Fast fact: Retirement delayed for growing numbers of U.S. workers. *ACAeNews, X,* Issue No. 16. Retrieved August 13, 2008, from http://www.counseling.org/PressRoom/PressReleases.aspx?AGuid=6d669ed0-3a49-4e49-8f2d-df88295424b7

Gray Panthers. (n.d.) *Gray Panthers are.* Retrieved August 7, 2008, from http://graypanthers.org/index.php?option=com_content&task=blogcategory&id=27&Itemid=17

Haas, M. L. (2008, August). Pax Americana geriatrica. *Miller-McCune Center for Research and Public Policy,* 31–39.

Jones, C., & Overberg, P. (2008, August 7). Demographic landscape shifts across United States. *USA Today,* p. 7A.

Kirchheimer, S. (2008, July–August). Cash before care. *AARP Bulletin*, pp. 20–23.

Lewis, J. A., Arnold, M. S., House, R., & Toporek, R. L. (2002). *ACA Advocacy Competencies.* Retrieved May 16, 2009, from http://www.counseling.org/Publications/

National Association of Social Workers. (2004). *NASW promotes older Americans Mental Health Week.* Retrieved August 3, 2008, from www.socialworkers.org/pressroom/2004/051104.asp

Older Women's League. (n.d.-a). *Ten facts about mental health and aging.* Retrieved August 3, 2008, from http://www.mentalhealthweek.org/Ten_Facts_about_Mental_Health.html

Older Women's League. (n.d.-b). *The OWL agenda.* Retrieved August 3, 2008, from http://www.owl-national.org/Agenda.html

University of North Carolina. (2006). *United States aging demographics.* Chapel Hill: University of North Carolina, Institute on Aging. Retrieved July 29, 2008, from http://www.aging.unc.edu/infocenter/slides/usaging.ppt

Chapter 11

ACA Advocacy Competencies in School Counseling

Hugh C. Crethar

This chapter provides an overview of the role of student advocacy within school counseling as approached historically and through use of the American Counseling Association (ACA) Advocacy Competencies (Lewis, Arnold, House, & Toporek, 2002). I begin with an overview of the history of student advocacy in the field of school counseling, focusing on its historical centrality. This is followed with an overview of current perspectives on student advocacy among school counseling leaders as reflected in the literature and the American School Counselor Association (ASCA) National Model (ASCA, 2005). I then operationalize the use of the Advocacy Competencies through the use of a detailed vignette from a school counseling setting. Finally, I discuss challenges of implementing the Advocacy Competencies in the school setting.

Introduction

Student advocacy has long played a central role in the field of school counseling. From the onset of the development of the field, Frank Parsons's work served as part of the progressive movement in education within the United States (Zytowski, 2001). Parsons and his followers focused their work on providing both vocational guidance intended to prepare students to be effective in the workplace and vocational assistance for those who had dropped out of school. Early school counselors offered developmental services to youths that provided vocational guidance and enhanced self-understanding and growth. An underlying focus of this work was to provide vocational services to many students who otherwise would not likely receive any help, thus closing gaps in services.

Owing to the popularity of the nondirective or person-centered approach of Carl Rogers throughout the middle of the 20th century, the majority of school counselors came to view their role as increasingly clinical in nature (Baker & Gerler, 2008). During this era, school counselors focused much more of their energy on one-to-one, individualized counseling interventions rather than broader developmental guidance. In the 1980s and 1990s, student advocacy moved to the forefront of counseling through the work of advocates for multicultural competency in counseling. This work resulted in ASCA publishing a position statement in 1998 calling for school counselors to strengthen their abilities to facilitate student development by developing multicultural competence (ASCA, 1998). This statement is paired with calls for counselors to broaden their focus from the primarily intrapsychic focus of Carl Rogers to a more extrapsychic focus on forces that deter and hinder student development and success (House & Hayes, 2002; Kiselica & Robinson, 2001; Lee, 1998). This call was due to counselors falling into the habit of focusing too narrowly on the wellness of individuals while ignoring the barriers to growth, encountered by students, that were both systemic and systematic in nature. A focus that is overly intrapsychic can lead to a phenomenon not much unlike that of "blaming the victim," wherein students are held responsible to overcome obstacles that are ultimately out of their control. The ACA Advocacy Competencies (Lewis et al., 2002) respond to this call, ultimately helping school counselors focus their energies on pertinent systemic change.

Although the work of school counselors eventually broadened to include personal/social and educational concerns, it has never really lost its focus on advocating for the welfare of all students. The ASCA National Model incorporates into its framework four themes that reflect this enduring focus: leadership, advocacy, collaboration and teaming, and systemic change (ASCA, 2005). These themes emphasize the importance of school counselors working within each area as student advocates and systems advocates to ensure access and equity to rigorous education for all students (Martin, 2002).

Key assumptions within the ASCA National Model include the belief that effective school counseling programs reach every student and are comprehensive in scope, developmental in nature, and preventative in design (ASCA, 2005). School counseling services within the ASCA National Model are to be rendered across the three domains of academic, career, and personal/social development as clarified through standards, competencies, and indicators that student competencies have been met. Comprehensive, outcome-based service to every student that takes into account varying needs and abilities based on development is perfectly aligned with use of the Advocacy Competencies. The Advocacy Competencies provide a structure of domains of service that school counselors should consider to assure that students are educated and empowered to live successful and fulfilling lives. The structure of the Advocacy Competencies focuses school counselors' energy into six domains, helping them visualize their students within the reality of their broader systemic context. Conceptualizing student challenges within the Advocacy Competencies allows school counselors to target collaborative systemic change efforts in a manner most responsive to student needs in the present as well as to prevent problems in the future. The Advocacy Competencies align well with the ASCA National Model as they provide tools for school counselors to use to assure that students have every opportunity to meet the competencies clarified in the model.

Numerous scholars and leaders in school counseling have argued that school counselors should adopt an approach that makes social advocacy central to their work (Bailey, Getch, & Chen-Hayes, 2007; Bemak & Chung, 2005; Brown, 2005; Eriksen, 1997; House & Martin, 1999; Ratts, DeKruyf, & Chen-Hayes, 2007). Lee (2007) argued that school counselors have both a moral and an ethical responsibility to advocate for students and serve as agents for social and political change. Stone and Dahir (2007) posited that school counselors need to actively promote equitable access to quality education for all students and identify and ameliorate patterns and behaviors that impede the success of all students.

Operationalizing the ACA Advocacy Competencies

When applied in the school counseling setting, the Advocacy Competencies readily come to life. One of the reasons this is true is because competent school counselors focus on all students within their schools and not only those who are perceived to need remediation. School counselors oriented toward social justice are able to see the connections between individual challenges and systemic issues. Such insight and focus align well with the framework of the Advocacy Competencies. The following vignette is based on an actual situation faced by a practicing school counselor. The vignette is accompanied by a set of responses that are based on applications of the six domains of the Advocacy Competencies. The vignette provides an example of the manner in which a school counselor might implement the Advocacy Competencies at a number of levels.

Vignette of Paulo

At a school in a suburb of Chicago, one of the administrators has referred Paulo, a fifth-grade student, to the school counselor for "behavior problems." Paulo transferred to the school at the beginning of the school year when he and his family moved from Chicago to a suburb that does not have very many Latino residents. Paulo's primary language is Spanish. He speaks enough English to get by but not enough to allow him to excel in his classes. His parents speak even less English and thus have not been able to help him sufficiently with his classes. They have also not been able to intervene successfully on his behalf, in part because the school staff has not done a good job of explaining Paulo's struggles to them. They appear to have assumed that the problems lay with Paulo even though he did well academically when he was a fourth-grade student in the Chicago Public Schools. The transition to the new school has affected Paulo's grades, which continue to decline as the second half of the school year begins. This semester, he has been reported for "ignoring the teacher," "doing whatever he wants," and "not following the class rules" on three separate occasions. Paulo comes across as both frustrated and despondent when the school counselor speaks with him. At present, Paulo's school does not offer bilingual services because it has not been perceived to be a need by the school administration. This appears to be largely due to the assumption that Spanish-speaking students attend schools in a neighboring district, where a much larger percentage of the Latino population lives. Although the school counselor is able to speak beginning Spanish from having taken a few classes in undergraduate studies, it is not enough to communicate at a higher level with Paulo and his family regarding the teachers with whom he is having trouble.

Response to Vignette of Paulo

School counselors who are versed in the Advocacy Competencies as well as the ASCA National Model are likely to conceptualize their responses to situations that arise from a systemic viewpoint while taking into account students' individual needs. Such school counselors realize that their students' functioning responds to situational contexts within which they are placed. In the case of Paulo, it is likely that a competent school counselor will focus on most, if not all, of the domains within the Advocacy Competencies if the counselor functions within the themes of the ASCA National Model. Effective counselor response in such situations requires action in all four thematic areas of leadership, advocacy, collaboration and teaming, and systemic change.

Client/Student Domain: Empowerment and Advocacy

As student advocates, a school counselor's primary responsibility is to help students reach their academic, career, and personal/social potential. In the case of Paulo, the school counselor would do well by initially focusing on his immediate needs. Paulo was referred to the counselor because he was having trouble achieving academically since his transfer to a suburban school. His successful academic history prior to transfer suggests that the transition is deterring him from remaining successful in school. Social justice–oriented counselors would note that Paulo has strengths as a student, despite the reputation that has developed among his teachers since his arrival at his new school.

The client/student advocacy domain calls for counselors to work with students, empowering them in their environments and helping them develop skills so they may advocate for themselves. It is evident that Paulo has had a difficult time finding effective responses to the changes in his scholastic environment. Time spent with Paulo will likely uncover frustration that he is experiencing due to the language gap that has emerged as a result of his move to a school that does not currently offer effective English Language Learner (ELL) services. Time should be spent with Paulo assessing the strengths that he brings as a student as well as any deficits or challenges he also encounters.

To empower Paulo and equip him with the skills needed to be successful, school counselors may want to consider following five basic steps of empowerment (adapted from Crethar, Bellamy, Bicknell-Hentges, & Giorgis, 2002; McWhirter, 1994). This entails first focusing on increasing Paulo's and his family's awareness of the power dynamics at work in their life context, including any institutional and social barriers that exist as well as assets they already bring into the situation or have at their access. This step has often been referred to as raising the critical consciousness of the clientele (Freire, 1970). Simply put, critical consciousness entails a state of in-depth understanding about the world and the way things work that results in an experience of freedom from oppression (Friere, 2005). A key issue within this process is making sure that Paulo and his family come to understand how things systemically affect them without internalizing the inequities that exist within the system.

The second step involves helping Paulo and his family develop skills to gain control over Paulo's life and life context within the constraints of his new environment. Third, a related part of the empowerment process would include helping Paulo and his family recognize areas where they could begin to exercise individual control as well as areas where they might need to begin building allied support to confront institutional barriers, such as the lack of bilingual services in their public school. Fourth, this all needs to be done without infringing on the rights or freedoms of others in the community, as empowerment does not mean the disempowerment of others. Finally, effective counselors will help Paulo and his family develop supportive connections to others around them in a manner that helps develop the empowerment of others in the community. The entire client/student empowerment process is most effectively carried out over the length of the counseling relationship and integrated with other components of the Advocacy Competencies.

Effective advocacy requires counselors to develop and maintain collaborative relationships with the people for whom they advocate. This is particularly true in K–12 settings where the power differential between the school counselor and student is more distinct than it is between a community counselor and her or his adult client. School counselors are generally in ideal positions to advocate for students they serve because they have access to relevant data, contact with key personnel, access to the entire student body, and relative flexibility in how they can approach their work. The most effective advocacy efforts are built from the understanding that develops out of a good counseling relationship. Also, the underlying goal of counseling is to help clients develop their strengths toward increasingly effective independence from the need for counseling. Collaborative work helps clients develop perspective, understanding, skills, and confidence necessary for such independent success.

School counselors working with Paulo to empower him within his environment take care to assure that Paulo and his family are actively involved in selecting any advocacy efforts. A key reason for this has to do with the notion that advocacy efforts can readily become misguided when not done in harmony with those for whom one advocates. This requires that the school counselor maintain an egalitarian relationship with Paulo and his family. A counselor applying the Advocacy Competencies in the case of Paulo would find a way to care for his immediate needs up front. With this in mind, it is important that school counselors explore with Paulo the source of his difficulties at school; this includes his trouble understanding everything that happens in the classroom as well as difficulty communicating his needs with his teachers. Both of these areas can be remedied largely through working directly with Paulo. How, when, and why the difficulties that are translated into "misbehavior" occur should be explored with Paulo. From these conversations, the school counselor and Paulo can come to collaborative decisions on how to improve his relationships with his teachers and develop an appropriate course of action. Any actions that the counselor takes on behalf of the Paulo should emerge from the collaborative process in the client/student domain of the Advocacy Competencies. It is preferable to do as much advocacy as possible with the student rather than on behalf of the student. This approach can be empowering because it allows Paulo to become an active part of the change process, thereby helping him develop self-confidence and problem-solving skills that he can use in the future.

Of course, not all client advocacy efforts can be done with the client. This is particularly true in the school counseling setting. In the case of Paulo, the school counselor will likely need to work on behalf of Paulo with his teachers, the school psychologist, administration, and his parents. All significant players appear to need help seeing how the difficulties Paulo is having may result from a current language barrier. Paulo may need help from anyone bilingual in Spanish within the school system or from a resource in the community until appropriate ELL services are offered. This effort leads to the community/school domain of the Advocacy Competencies.

Community/School Domain: Community Collaboration and Systems Advocacy

The dilemma Paulo presents suggests systemic deficits within the school environment. When working with, and on behalf, of Paulo, it is critical that school counselors investigate whether systemic barriers exist for children whose primary language is not English. Using schoolwide data to determine how many ELL students are struggling academically can aid in this effort. Examining for potential systemic barriers aligns with the ASCA National Model and the philosophy of the Education Trust (Martin, 2002) in that the school counselor addresses issues of equity and access for all students.

Upon determining the need for systemic change within the school, the counselor's next step is to look into working in a collaborative fashion with faculty, administration, and staff of the school to bring about such change. In this case, for some reason the school has apparently not yet budgeted nor prepared to equitably serve students who are native Spanish speakers. This calls for investigation as to why the system has not responded to this need to date, including whatever forces might exist to maintain things as they currently are. The school counselor may need to work with a number of key players in the school and possibly the school district to help those key players understand how and why the provision of services to language learners is an issue of equitable education for all students. Despite the fact that there are legal requirements in place for equitable treatment for language learners, "reasonable accommodations" are interpreted differently throughout the United States. These discussions are particularly important, as Paulo is likely not the only student within the school and district who has need for services due to language differences. It is also quite possible that more children will move into the school and district with similar needs, possibly who speak different languages than Spanish. Using schoolwide data to determine this and sharing the data with key personnel is an important advocacy intervention at the school/community level. The work done with the school and district to develop systemic change responsive to the needs of language learners is invaluable and ultimately serves as a form of preventive work by the counselor.

The process of developing new paradigms with school leaders regarding equitable services for ELL students may lead school counselors to work on behalf of the school system in the community. Experts in school counseling commonly recommend the collaborative-interdependent model wherein school counselors develop an interdependent problem-solving process, with family members, students, and members of the broader community contributing equivalently (Erford, 2007). This approach requires the development of a relationship grounded on trust and understanding across all parties involved in the collaborative process. This is particularly important in the enactment of the systems advocacy domain of the Advocacy Competencies in a school setting, as long-term, effective systemic change requires the "buy-in" of all stakeholders on a given issue. This approach to systems advocacy is where all four themes of the ASCA National Model come into play at once. The school counselor provides *leadership* through working to pull stakeholders together toward a shared vision, and response and generation of this response require effective *collaboration and teaming.* Furthermore, any effective *advocacy* for *systemic change* will only occur when all stakeholders feel that they have sufficient input into the vision and solution that they feel a sense of ownership in it (Brigman, Mullis, Webb, & White, 2005; Kampwirth, 2006). One of the most important issues for school counselors to consider is that efforts toward teaming and collaboration outside the school context are most successful when done with the support of administration. Thus, for school counselors, it is generally recommended that efforts in the systems advocacy domain of the Advocacy Competencies occur after work has been done in the community collaboration domain.

In the case of Paulo, it is important that any reaching out to the community be done with the administration's support, as action taken otherwise might create unnecessary barriers and thus not produce the desired results. Systems advocacy in this case may include reaching out to community members who are bilingual for tutoring and in-school help, working with neighboring districts that might have more significant ELL programs in place, and seeking external funding to bring in more ELL services. A key issue to consider in systems advocacy and community collaboration efforts relevant to the case of Paulo is to work toward systemic change that serves not only Paulo but also all other students in the present as well as the future of Paulo's school.

Public Domain: Public Information/Social/Political Advocacy

Although not every dilemma that requires systemic change also requires advocacy at levels beyond the school and immediate community, many do call for such broader efforts. Resistance at the school and community levels is often based on misunderstandings or problematic interpretations of public policy and legislation. In the case of Paulo, it appears that the administration at his school has been interpreting the law and associated policy in a way that does not serve students whose primary language is Spanish. Instead of taking an approach that blames the school administration for malice in the way it has interpreted the law, school counselors would do well by working with school personnel to clarify how others have interpreted the law and how it has been implemented in various districts. In such a situation, school counselors should focus their energy on sharing relevant information regarding ELL students and their academic development. For example, school counselors should highlight research findings that provide evidence that ELL students thrive when they are provided education that allows them to transition from their language of origin to English. Students with English learning needs tend to not do as well when not provided education in a language transitional situation.

School counselors seeking systemic change need to remain current on research relevant to the area or areas in which they seek change. Furthermore, they need to be prepared and willing to seek out situations wherein they inform the public about factors that are conducive of healthy development as well as those that serve as deterrents. Well-prepared presentations that provide clear explanations of the roles of specific environmental factors in children's development can serve to change perspectives about these issues and ultimately diminish opposition. It is critical that school counselors also reach out to others through written materials and other public forums, adjusting their language and approach to best fit the needs of a given target population. In the case of Paulo, this information would be centered on the benefits of appropriate language learner services to students such as Paulo as well as to all students within the system. The best approach to take in such instances is that of information sharing, wherein the conclusions made from the information are garnered from the audience to maximize buy-in.

The final domain of the Advocacy Competencies, social/political advocacy, will vary in pertinence and necessity depending on the issue at hand. In the issue emanating from the dilemma that Paulo faces, school counselors might consider the federal and state laws and associated policies relevant to serving all students enrolled in public, federally funded schools. As states throughout the United States vary in their legislation and policy on serving those who speak English as a second language, the amount of social and political advocacy that a counselor should consider will vary as well. For example, in the state of Arizona, recent legislation (Arizona Department of Education, 2003) has been enacted and subsequently included in educational policy that has left ELL students increasingly underserved and behind native English speakers (Wright, 2005). Because of the passage of such legislation, school counselors working in Arizona should recognize a need to advocate at the state level for the needs of ELL students. This may likely be best carried out through the state school counseling associations, as school counselors have much better impact on legislative issues when their voices are unified and heard together. If school counselors in Arizona find it difficult to get their state association to take a lobbying stand on this issue, they may need to step back into the public information domain and work specifically on helping other school counselors in their state understand how effective and research-based ELL services are in sync with the mission of school counselors in the ASCA National Model.

Once effectively unified, school counselors can and should act as a lobbying body to work to change policies and legislation that may not be in the best interest of the academic, career, and personal/social development of all students. On issues revolving around Paulo's struggles, there are many states that require implementation of an effective public information and political advocacy campaign, as counselors hands are tied from doing much work in the community/school domain when working against current legislation and policy.

Multicultural and Diversity Issues

School counselors will find the Advocacy Competencies particularly useful in conceptualizing student and systemic needs across cultural and other forms of diversity. This is particularly important given Sue and Sue's (2008) assertion that students from marginalized populations require both microlevel and macrolevel interventions. This is an important point to note given that school counselors are responsible for the academic, career, and personal/social development of all students (ASCA, 2005). For these reasons it is critical that school counselors pay particular attention to all populations of students who might be currently underserved (Ratts et al., 2007). For example, in recent years, school violence has increasingly caught the nation's attention, with highly publicized accounts of violence in Colorado, Arkansas, Virginia, and Oregon. As professionals with comprehensive service in mind, school counselors have a duty to address issues of school violence in all of its forms ranging through-out physical, media, cultural, racial, sexual, and gender violence (Daniels, Arredondo, & D'Andrea, 1999). Similarly, a significant issue in U.S. schools has long been violence and harassment against lesbian, gay, bisexual, transgender, and questioning (LGBTQ) students (Kosciw, Diaz, & Greytak, 2007; O'Conor, 1994). It has been estimated that at least 1 in 20 adolescents attending U.S. public schools is lesbian or gay (Ginsberg, 1998; Kosciw et al., 2007). These students are at high risk due to a number of variables within and without the school, and they have significantly less social support available from peers, school personnel, and family than straight students (Mufioz-Plaza, Crouse Quinn, & Rounds, 2002). An estimated 26% of these students are forced to leave home because of conflicts with the families regarding their sexual orientation (Remafedi, 1987). In school, these students are the most frequent victims of hate crimes (O'Conor, 1994), experiencing a much higher incidence of fights that require medical attention than heterosexual students (23% vs. 3%; Massachusetts Department of Education, 1995), and generally are quite underprotected by teachers. For example, in a survey in Iowa, despite the fact that students reported hearing antihomosexual epithets 25 times a day, teachers failed to respond all but 3% of the time (Carter, 1997). For some reason, these issues were left out of the federally funded 2005 update of the Youth Risk Behavior study (Eaton et al., 2006).

It is difficult for students to reach their academic, career, and/or personal potential when they are concerned for their welfare. Researchers have consistently concluded that victimization is associated with various issues, including diminished self-esteem, rejection, loneliness, and depression (Boulton & Smith, 1994; Graham & Juvonen, 2002; Nansel et al., 2001; van der Wal, de Wit, & Hirasing, 2003). It is the duty of all those who work in schools, particularly school counselors, to be proactive change agents who work to create a safe and inclusive learning environment for all students. The U.S. Supreme Court ruled this to be the case in 1999 with a decision that federally aided schools can be held liable when they demonstrate indifference to harassment that is "so severe, pervasive and objectively offensive that it denies its victims the equal access to education" (*Davis v. Monroe County Board of Education,* 1999, p. 650). School counselors must become attuned to both the prevalence and incidence of harassment based on sexual/affectional orientation in their schools. This can be accomplished by using the Advocacy Competencies as a template to guide their systemic response to this issue. Examples of effective applications of the Advocacy Competencies at different levels with regard to sexual/affectional orientation include the LGBTQ affirmative training for school counselors (Whitman, Horn, & Boyd, 2007) and LGBTQ affirmative training of school professionals by school counselors (Bauman & Sachs-Kapp, 1998).

There are many other diversity-related issues that school counselors should consider. For example, the needs of students with different physical needs are not necessarily being addressed nationwide. Many schools' and districts' accommodations for different physical needs are not appropriately attended to because of perceptions that retrofitting of old school buildings are not "readily achievable" given district funding. Federal law does not require schools to make unreasonable accommodations if it can be demonstrated that they are not "readily achievable" (American With Disabilities Act of 1990).

Related to the issue of how readily an appropriate educational environment can be offered is the issue of inequities in school funding around the United States. For example, funding varies dramatically between states as well as within states (U.S. General Accounting Office, 2002). Despite the arguments of some that school funding does not matter when looking at student outcomes, research has provided evidence that both poor school funding and student poverty negatively affect student achievement (Payne & Biddle, 1999). In states with higher per capita of people who speak English as a second language, some have argued that the children from these families are holding down the achievement outcomes of schools they attend. This is an overly simplistic perspective; students designated as ELL commonly attend public schools that have relatively low standardized test scores; these scores are not solely attributable to poor achievement by ELL students. The same schools tend to report poor achievement by many of their other students as well. These schools commonly have a set of characteristics associated generally with poor standardized test performance, including high levels of students living in or near poverty and high student–teacher ratios (Fry, 2008).

Thus, an issue for school counselors to consider is the ongoing inequity perpetuated by school funding based on the wealth of a given school district or area. This issue is reflective of the values within the ASCA National Model as well as those of the Advocacy Competencies. The ASCA National Model calls for school counselors to work for systemic change that creates accountable service for all students. Education that limits resources to children based on the income of their parents is ultimately not in the best interest of all students but instead treats students with differential bias, affording separate and unequal educational opportunities and ultimately separate and unequal career prospects. School counselors can utilize the Advocacy Competencies by considering educational opportunity for all students to focus energy on the public domain. Thus, school counselors can work together to educate at the meso- and macrolevels of the advocacy, offering accurate public information regarding the effects of policies that are not in the best interests of all students. They can also work together to advocate for public policy and legislative action that remedy such inequities.

Nowhere does this become more apparent than in the design of the No Child Left Behind Act of 2001, wherein students are guaranteed an opportunity to change from their failing schools to other schools that are not failing *within* a given school district. Such legislation does not take into account the fact that numerous school districts nationwide only have one school for students to attend. This law effectively reinforces interdistrict funding inequities by design in the way it overlooks these inequities perpetuated by the general funding of schools through property taxes. Many challenges that students face could be partially ameliorated through more equitable access to quality education for *all* students, regardless of the wealth of their caregivers.

Challenges in Implementing the Advocacy Competencies in Schools

There are a few key challenges that school counselors might face when implementing the Advocacy Competencies in the school counseling setting. A likely challenge school counselors might encounter is resistance from within the ranks of school counselors undereducated on the data regarding the needs of underserved and diverse populations. This particular challenge is key when school counselors are faced with issues that require intervention in the public information and social/political advocacy domains, as the most effective approach at this level requires a unified and well-informed approach.

School counselors are also likely to face pressure from their administration to not "rock the boat" by highlighting needs for systemic change. Such pressure might come in the form of stifling the voice of school counselors by burying them in administrative tasks and other duties that are not counseling related or even through direct pressure to leave things as they have always been. Some administrators do not understand that the mission of school counselors is to serve all students and not some preordained subset, such as those who are presumed to be college-bound or those with behavior problems.

Related to the above challenge is the reality that advocacy at all levels requires working to change something that is generally attached to the status quo. With advocacy work, it is very likely that school counselors will come up against individuals or groups who are invested in the status quo for varying reasons and thus are likely to become activated in opposition to the school counselors' work.

Conclusion

The greatest benefit of the Advocacy Competencies in school counseling is how well they align within the themes, standards, and delivery system of the ASCA National Model (ASCA, 2005). The Advocacy Competencies provide a template for school counselors to develop a balanced approach between more individualized services (Individual Student Planning and Responsive Services) and more global work and concerns (School Guidance Curriculum and System Support). The Advocacy Competencies encourage a focus on student empowerment and individual student advocacy while reminding school counselors that leadership must be provided for systems change that will prevent needless repetition of problems.

Experienced counselors will often find that many student problems have a tendency to both repeat and reemerge. The Advocacy Competencies fit well within the role of the transformed school counselor as they provide a mechanism for conceptualizing both student and systemic needs, particularly as they intersect. Such conceptualization enables counselors to develop intentional responses to problems that are tied to systemic issues, encouraging cooperative work that will ultimately be comprehensive in scope, preventative in design, and developmental in nature.

References

American School Counselor Association. (1998). *Position statement: Cultural diversity.* Retrieved November 13, 2008, from http://www.schoolcounselor.org/content.asp?contentid=249

American School Counselor Association. (2005). *The ASCA national model: A framework for school counseling programs* (2nd ed.). Alexandria, VA: Author.

Americans With Disabilities Act of 1990, 42 U.S.C. 12101–213.

Arizona Department of Education. (2003). *Arizona LEARNS: A step by step guide to calculating an achievement profile.* Phoenix: Arizona Department of Education Research & Policy.

Bailey, D. F., Getch, Y. Q., & Chen-Hayes, S. F. (2007). Achievement advocacy for all students through transformative school counseling programs. In B. T. Erford (Ed.), *Transforming the school counseling profession* (2nd ed., pp. 98–120). Upper Saddle River, NJ: Pearson Education.

Baker, S. B., & Gerler, E. R., Jr. (2008). *School counseling for the twenty-first century* (5th ed.). Upper Saddle River, NJ: Pearson/Merrill Prentice Hall.

Bauman, S., & Sachs-Kapp, P. (1998). A school takes a stand: Promotion of sexual orientation workshops by counselors. *Professional School Counseling, 1*(3), 42–45.

Bemak, F., & Chung, R. C. Y. (2005). Advocacy as a critical role for urban school counselors: Working toward equity and social justice. *Professional School Counseling, 8,* 196–203.

Boulton, M. J., & Smith, P. K. (1994). Bully/victim problems in middle-school children: Stability, self-perceived competence, peer perceptions and peer acceptance. *British Journal of Developmental Psychology, 12,* 315–329.

Brigman, G., Mullis, F., Webb, L., & White, J. (2005). *School counselor consultation: Skills for working effectively with parents, teachers, and other school personnel.* Hoboken, NJ: Wiley.

Brown, J. T. (2005). Advocacy competencies for professional school counselors. *Professional School Counseling, 8,* 259–265.

Carter, K. (1997, March 7). Gay slurs abound. *Des Moines Register*, p. 3.

Crethar, H. C., Bellamy, F., Bicknell-Hentges, L., & Giorgis, T. (2002, March). *Issues and strategies in counseling urban populations.* Paper presented at the annual meeting of the American Counseling Association, New Orleans, LA.

Daniels, J., Arredondo, P., & D'Andrea, M. (1999, June). Expanding counselors' thinking about the problem of violence. *Counseling Today, 41,* 12, 17.

Davis v. Monroe County Board of Education, 526 U.S. 629 (1999).

Eaton, D. K., Kann, L., Kinchen, S., Ross, J., Hawkins, J., Harris, W. A., et al. (2006). Youth Risk Behavior Surveillance—United States, 2005. *Journal of School Health, 76,* 353–372.

Erford, B. T. (2007). Consultation, collaboration, and parent involvement. In B. T. Erford (Ed.), *Transforming the school counseling profession* (2nd ed., pp. 211–235). Upper Saddle River, NJ: Pearson/Merrill Prentice Hall.

Eriksen, K. (1997). *Making an impact: A handbook on counselor advocacy.* Philadelphia: Taylor & Francis.

Freire, P. (1970). *Pedagogy of the oppressed.* New York: Continuum.

Freire, P. (2005). *Education for critical consciousness.* New York: Continuum.

Fry, R. (2008, June). The role of schools in the English Language Learner achievement gap. *Pew Hispanic Center Report,* 1–27.

Ginsberg, R. W. (1998). Silenced voices inside our schools. *Initiatives, 58,* 1–15.

Graham, S., & Juvonen, J. (2002). Ethnicity, peer harassment, and adjustment in middle school: An exploratory study. *Journal of Early Adolescence, 22,* 173–199.

House, R. M., & Hayes, R. L. (2002). School counselors becoming key players in school reform. *Professional School Counseling, 5,* 249–256.

House, R. M., & Martin, P. J. (1999). Advocating for better futures for all students: A new vision for school counselors. *Education, 119,* 284–291.

Kampwirth, T. J. (2006). *Collaborative consultation in the schools: Effective practices for students with learning and behavior problems* (3rd ed.). Upper Saddle River, NJ: Pearson/Merrill Prentice Hall.

Kiselica, M. S., & Robinson, M. (2001). Bringing advocacy counseling to life: The history, issues, and human dramas of social justice work in counseling. *Journal of Counseling & Development, 79,* 387–398.

Kosciw, J. G., Diaz, E. M., & Greytak, E. A. (2007). *The 2007 National School Climate Survey: The experiences of lesbian, gay, bisexual and transgender youth in our nation's schools.* Washington, DC: Gay, Lesbian and Straight Education Network.

Lee, C. C. (1998). Counselors as agents for social change. In C. C. Lee & G. R. Walz (Eds.), *Social action: A mandate for counselors* (pp. 3–16). Alexandria, VA: American Counseling Association.

Lee, C. C. (Ed.). (2007). *Counseling for social justice* (2nd ed.). Alexandria, VA: American Counseling Association.

Lewis, J. A., Arnold, M. S., House, R., & Toporek, R. L. (2002). *ACA Advocacy Competencies.* Retrieved May 16, 2009, from http://www.counseling.org/Publications/

Martin, P. J. (2002). Transforming school counseling: A national perspective. *Theory Into Practice, 41,* 148–153.

Massachusetts Department of Education. (1995). *Youth risk behavior study.* Boston: Author.

McWhirter, E. H. (1994). *Counseling for empowerment.* Alexandria, VA: American Counseling Association.

Mufioz-Plaza, C., Crouse Quinn, S., & Rounds, K. A. (2002). Lesbian, gay, bisexual and transgender students: Perceived social support in the high school environment. *The High School Journal, 85,* 52–63.

Nansel, T. R., Overpeck, M., Pilla, R. S., Ruan, W. J., Simons-Morton, B., & Scheidt, P. (2001). Bullying behaviors among U.S. youth: Prevalence and association with psychosocial adjustment. *Journal of the American Medical Association, 285,* 2094–2100.

No Child Left Behind Act of 2001, Pub. L. No. 107-110.

O'Conor, A. (1994). Who gets called queer in school? Lesbian, gay and bisexual teenagers, homophobia, and high school. *The High School Journal, 77,* 7–12.

Payne, K. J., & Biddle, B. J. (1999). Poor school funding, child poverty, and mathematics achievement. *Educational Researcher, 28*(6), 4–13.

Ratts, M. J., DeKruyf, L., & Chen-Hayes, S. F. (2007). The ACA Advocacy Competencies: A social justice advocacy framework for professional school counselors. *Professional School Counseling, 11,* 90–97.

Remafedi, G. (1987). Male homosexuality: The adolescent's perspective. *Pediatrics, 79,* 326–330.

Stone, C. B., & Dahir, C. A. (2007). *School counselor accountability: A MEASURE of student success* (2nd ed.). Upper Saddle River, NJ: Pearson/Merrill Prentice Hall.

Sue, D. W., & Sue, D. (2008). *Counseling the culturally diverse: Theory and practice* (4th ed.). Hoboken, NJ: Wiley.

U.S. General Accounting Office. (2002). *School finance: Per pupil spending differences between selected inner city and suburban schools varied by metropolitan area.* Washington, DC: Author.

van der Wal, M. F., de Wit, A. M., & Hirasing, R. A. (2003). Psychosocial health among young victims and offenders of direct and indirect bullying. *Pediatrics, 111,* 1312–1317.

Whitman, J. S., Horn, S. S., & Boyd, C. J. (2007). Activism in the schools: Providing LGBTQ affirmative training to school counselors. *Journal of Gay and Lesbian Psychotherapy, 11,* 143–154.

Wright, W. E. (2005). English language learners left behind in Arizona: The nullification of accommodations in the intersection of federal and state policies. *Bilingual Research Journal, 29,* 1–30.

Zytowski, D. G. (2001). Frank Parsons and the progressive movement. *The Career Development Quarterly, 50,* 57–65.

Chapter 12

Advocacy in College and University Settings

Matthew A. Diemer and Ryan D. Duffy

Advocacy in college and university settings aligns with, yet is also distinct from, counseling centers' traditional emphases on campus outreach and psychoeducational programming. Outreach and psychoeducation have increasingly become a part of counseling center practice since approximately the mid-1980s (Stone & Archer, 1990) until today. Outreach and psychoeducation may include activities such as consulting to campus fraternity and sorority organizations regarding healthy relationships or conducting campus depression screenings. These psychoeducational approaches are worthy endeavors that attend to students' well-being more broadly and may prevent the onset of mental health concerns. Indeed, one assumption embedded in outreach and psychoeducation is that by remediating barriers to well-being and facilitating positive development, college and university counseling centers might prevent the onset of some mental health concerns and therefore reduce the need for traditional face-to-face counseling services. In a context of increasing complexity and severity of presenting problems on college campuses (Diemer, Wang, & Dunkle, 2009) and tightening counseling center budgets, the application of outreach as a prevention mechanism has gained increasing popularity. Campus outreach and psychoeducation practices that aim to foster systems change or advocate for marginalized groups may align with aspects of the American Counseling Association (ACA) Advocacy Competencies (Lewis, Arnold, House, & Toporek, 2002; Toporek, Lewis, & Crethar, 2009).

Advocacy differs from campus outreach and psychoeducation in its clear recognition of and more explicit orientation toward social, political, economic, and cultural inequality and contextual barriers. For example, the most recent iteration of the *ACA Ethics Code* (American Counseling Association, 2005) details advocacy as a domain of ethical counselor practice, noting that "counselors advocate at individual, group, institutional, and societal levels to examine potential barriers and obstacles that inhibit access and/or the growth and development of clients" (p. 5). Stone and Archer (1990) argued that outreach and psychoeducation should include systematic efforts to change aspects of the campus environment that constrain development and well-being. However, outreach and psychoeducation generally pay little attention to inequitable social structures, discriminatory practices, and environmental barriers. Outreach and prevention focus instead on helping people adapt to their environment rather than helping them become more conscious of their environment or fostering their skills to alter their environment. This more "value-neutral" practice does little to help students negotiate social, political, cultural, and economic inequality and social structures (E. H. McWhirter, 1994).

Advocacy is a social justice–oriented practice wherein counselors work (with or on behalf of clients) to change social structures that constrain well-being and help clients develop a consciousness of and skills to negotiate contextual barriers (Lee & Walz, 1998; Lewis et al., 2002; Toporek et al., 2009). In college and university settings, advocacy represents a social justice–oriented approach with the potential to alter campus structures and practices that constrain well-being and help students be conscious of, negotiate, and change contextual barriers. This attention to context complements and extends the attention to internal factors that has historically been the focus of campus outreach and prevention efforts (Stone & Archer, 1990). The Advocacy Competencies emphasize macrolevel inequality, cultural factors, and local structures that constrain well-being, which provides counselors with a conceptual framework to promote social justice in their respective campus communities.

Below we describe the unique developmental needs of students, outline how advocacy may be conceptualized in college and university settings, and conclude this chapter by using a case study to illustrate the application of the Advocacy Competencies in college settings.

Developmental Needs of College and University Students

Students enrolled in college and university settings face a similar set of developmental challenges. These include establishing social networks, solidifying a personal and educational identity, transitioning from high school or the working world into higher education, and deciding on one's major and career path. However, the salience and form of these concerns for students likely differ based on a number of factors. First, the college setting itself (4-year college and university vs. community college) likely attracts different types of student populations. For example, students at 4-year institutions may be more likely to enter college right out of high school, whereas those in community college may already have experience in the workforce and enroll as part-time students. Second, individual student characteristics are important to consider; these include, but are not limited to, a student's cultural background, economic stability, age, and family circumstances. It is therefore critical that discussions of college student development, and in particular advocacy, are inclusive of all student populations.

Scholars within the college student development literature have recently begun to pay more attention to the varying needs and concerns for students at 4-year institutions versus those attending community colleges (Cohen & Brawer, 2008). Research has shown that of the approximately 17 million students enrolled in college, 60% currently attend 4-year institutions and 40% attend community college (U.S. Census Bureau, 2006). Along with a host of differences within the institutions themselves, students at community colleges tend to be older, are more likely to go to school part time, are more diverse in terms of race and ethnicity, are more likely to be working full time, are more likely to be married and have children, are more likely to be living with family members, and tend to have less economic resources than students at 4-year institutions (Cohen & Brawer, 2008; Simon & Tovar, 2004). While these findings suggest that the typical profile of a 4-year and community college student differs, it is important not to assume that all 4-year students will be young and live way from home or that all community college students will be parents and be working full time.

Generally speaking, each student population's demographic differences entail varying developmental needs and, in turn, differential applications of the Advocacy Competencies. The developmental challenges facing traditional-age college and university students (ranging from ages 17–23 years) surround the struggle to reconcile and develop a coherent sense of identity in their transition from adolescence to adulthood (Arnett, 2000). These include learning to be autonomous from one's parents or family, establishing more serious romantic relationships, deciding if and when to engage in risky behaviors, and attempting to figure out the best major or career path. For some of these students, challenges often occur in what has been stereotyped as a "bubble," whereby students are surrounded by a college or university community that partially shields them from the strain and pressures of the outside world. However, this stereotype is likely heavily influenced by the location of a student's institution (e.g., urban vs. rural) as well as by whether the student lives on campus or commutes to school from home.

For students attending community colleges, more often than not they are living outside of the college or university bubble. As very few community colleges even have on-campus residencies, community college students are more likely to live at home with friends, parents, siblings, spouses, and children. This likely results in an increase of multiple roles and responsibilities that students need to fulfill on a daily basis and, in turn, heightened role-related stress (Cohen & Brawer, 2008; Hagedorn, Maxwell, & Hampton, 2001). Given that community college students often work full time, these students may be more likely to struggle fitting in time to complete school-related work. Additionally, as students may be coming to college with more work experience, they may have a firmer idea of their vocational plans and be more focused on achieving a particular career goal.

Finally, given that community college students are often older than 4-year students, their general sense of social or personal identity may be more established (Cohen & Brawer, 2008; Simon & Tovar, 2004). These students may be much more likely to have progressed to taking on traditionally labeled adult roles. However, it is important to note that despite their (comparably) more advanced age, community college students still contend with sweeping demographic changes in the United States. Young people as a whole are more likely to delay the onset of initiating long-term and committed relationships and/or establishing their financial independence more than previous generations; that may lead many adult-age community college students to not subjectively *feel* like adults (Arnett, 2000). We note these demographic changes to highlight that identity struggles may be less salient for community college students than 4-year students, but this population may also struggle with managing multiple demands and establishing a firm identity as adults.

These general differences in 4-year and community college students underscore the need for advocacy interventions to be uniquely tailored to students at particular college or university settings. Students at traditional 4-year institutions may be best described as transitioning from adolescence to adulthood, and college may be a time to solidify their social, ethnic, personal, and vocational identities. Advocacy efforts for this population should be geared toward providing opportunities for and addressing systemic barriers that constrain development in these domains. Community college students may more often be concerned with balancing their school, work, and family roles. Advocacy efforts for this population may focus on giving voice to these common struggles among community college students as well as helping to change institutional barriers that exacerbate these struggles. As the community college student population is generally more diverse in terms of age, racial/ethnic background, life experience, and work experience, it is critical that these differences be understood and integrated into advocacy efforts.

For example, advocacy in a community college setting might entail advocating for affordable day care on campus for students with children. While students at community colleges may be older developmentally, their academic development likely parallels those from 4-year universities. For students with children, their ability to progress academically will likely hinge, in part, on how well they are able to fit their courses and class assignments into their family responsibilities. By advocating for affordable, on-site day care, a counselor would be secondarily promoting the academic development of students trying to balance school and family demands.

In sum, these two unique college settings serve to highlight potentially different needs that students have in college. We recommend that, regardless of the setting, advocates understand the developmental concerns of the populations they serve.

Applying the ACA Advocacy Competencies: Changing the Campus Racial Climate

The expanse of advocacy opportunities available to professionals in 4-year and community colleges is vast. Within this expanse, the contextual and social justice emphases of the Advocacy Competencies open up new vistas for practice. Advocating for changes in campus structures and practices does diverge from the historical focus on helping students adapt to their environment in campus outreach and psychoeducation (Stone & Archer, 1990), but some problems are so systemic in nature that counselors must go beyond business as usual.

Outreach and psychoeducation do little to address entrenched and longstanding injustices such as racism. Therefore, we have chosen the issue of campus racial climate to illustrate social justice advocacy in action. The campus racial climate is a key feature of the college and university environment that affects students' well-being and development, particularly for students of color (Gurin, 1999; Worthington, Navarro, Loewy, & Hart, 2008). Research with high school students of color suggests that school racial climate also affects their well-being (Diemer, Hsieh, & Pan, 2009). Racial and ethnic discrepancies in postsecondary academic performance and attainment (National Center for Education Statistics, 2005) may also be explained by an inhospitable racial climate for students of color. Rather than focusing on helping students of color adapt to a hostile campus racial climate, we focus here on altering the campus racial climate itself.

We have elected to target White students to change the campus racial climate because we believe Whites contribute more to an inhospitable campus racial climate than students of color do. We recognize other contributors to campus racial climate—including faculty and staff, admissions policies, and support for ethnic minority student organizations—but we focus here on peers, given the salience of peers at this stage of the life course and in students' social relationships (Arnett, 2000). White students obviously have more power to negatively affect the campus racial climate, but a strong advocacy effort can incorporate their capacity to take responsibility for the racial environment and to act as allies for change. White students are the racial and ethnic majorities at many colleges and universities (National Center for Education Statistics, 2005) and are in the dominant position in the racial/ethnic hierarchy of the United States (Fine, Weis, Powell, & Wong, 1997). Their numerical majority and social status afford Whites a greater capacity to affect campus racial climate than students of color (Spanierman, Poteat, Beer, & Armstrong, 2006). Given a history of racial oppression and discrimination against persons of color, White expressions of racism also have more noxious effects on students of color than "reverse racism" directed at Whites (Fine et al., 1997). Finally, devoting attention to those granted socially valued power and privilege provides an important complement to emphases on fostering self-determination and liberation among marginalized groups in the pursuit of social justice (E. H. McWhirter, 1994; Prilleltensky, 1994). Despite this focus on targeting White students, our ultimate "clients" in this case example are students of color, who are more overtly affected by the campus racial climate than White students.

To understand how campus racial climates may be changed, one needs to first examine how Whites contribute to the development of campus racial climates. The college setting, with its new challenges, social roles, and opportunities for autonomy and decision making, challenges and reshapes the identity and worldview of many students in the "emerging adulthood" phase of development (Arnett, 2000). Many students' cultural identity and worldview are also challenged in the campus environment. Students from homogeneous cultural backgrounds (particularly White students from predominantly White communities) are challenged by a move into a more ethnically and racially diverse and (often, but not always) more politically progressive campus environments (Worthington et al., 2008). These same issues of cross-cultural contact remain salient in nonresidential community colleges. Although students in these colleges might have a more concrete sense of their ethnicity or culture because of their chronological age, the racial/ethnic diversity present on community college campuses may serve as a greater challenge to ingrained worldviews. Social psychology research suggests that in group interactions, the more diverse individuals are demographically, the greater the likelihood is of interpersonal conflict (Dixon, Durrheim, & Tredoux, 2005). Given that individuals' worldviews may become more solidified as they age (Kruglanski, 2004), it may be especially important to attend to racial climate on community college campuses.

With this understanding of how Whites contribute to campus racial climate, and the potential differences in these processes among 4-year and community colleges, we illustrate below how counselors' advocacy at the client/student, school/community, and public arena levels may alter the campus racial climate (Lewis et al., 2002). More specifically, we detail below a multipronged antiracist intervention designed to improve White students' contributions to a positive campus racial climate. Given our focus on campus racial climate, the focus of the advocacy program detailed below will be the school/community level of the advocacy model. We define White racial consciousness by the development of White antiracist attitudes (e.g., empathy for and understanding of the experiences of persons of color, coupled with low levels of irrational fear of persons of color), as conceptualized by Helms (1992) and Spanierman et al. (2006). The Advocacy Competencies are applied to illustrate how focusing on White students may create a more hospitable campus climate for our ultimate clients—students of color on campus. Given the multifaceted nature of the campus racial climate and benefits of campus diversity for all students, the effort detailed below should be complemented by admissions policies considerate of racial/ethnic and socioeconomic disparities in educational resources and opportunities; collaboration with student organizations such as Black Student Unions, Latino/Latina Student Associations, Native American student groups, Asian Student Associations, or ethnic studies departments; campuswide efforts to recruit, retain, and graduate students of color (e.g., mentoring and/or supportive services); and culturally competent counseling center staff (Gurin, 1999; Worthington et al., 2008).

Case Example: Applying the ACA Advocacy Competencies

The following case example is provided to illustrate the application of the Advocacy Competencies in the pursuit of social justice in college and university settings. Dr. McNulty is a counseling center staff member at a public, 4-year university with a predominantly White student population. Recent years have brought a rising tide of covert and overt acts of racism against students of color at this university; in some instances the perpetrator(s) have been identified and appropriately sanctioned and/or dismissed by the university. Increasing numbers of students of color have presented at the counseling center secondary to these incidents (either directly affected or indirectly affected and becoming increasingly uncomfortable with the campus racial climate). Given limited time and energy, Dr. McNulty struggles with whether to situate his advocacy efforts directly with the students of color affected by these acts of racism or to target the broader community of White students on campus.

After much deliberation, Dr. McNulty decides to situate his advocacy efforts by mainly targeting White students on campus while also directly addressing the needs of students of color. Viewed from the lens of prevention, the campus racial climate is viewed as pathological, and an appropriate primary prevention response is to alter the milieu where the disorder of White racism is manifesting (J. J. McWhirter, McWhirter, McWhirter, & McWhirter, 2007). From this perspective, changing the context in which these actions occur may prevent or reduce the onset of further expressions of the disorder of White racism. Recognizing that a broader campuswide advocacy effort will not greatly affect students with deeply entrenched racist attitudes, the advocacy campaign is designed to alter the broader campus milieu that indirectly supports these expressions of White supremacy. That is, advocacy here is designed to alter the global campus climate that supports (or at the least does not repudiate) expressions of White supremacy; this analysis is most reflective of the systems advocacy component of the Advocacy Competencies.

The assumption guiding this advocacy effort is that these acts of racism are being conducted by White students in a campus climate that indirectly supports these overtly racist actions. White students generally do not problematize these actions, and White students' campus social norms do not exclude the students who perpetrate these actions. By conducting advocacy efforts explicitly designed to attend to both the conscious and subconscious racist tendencies of White college students, these efforts may affect the campus racial climate.

Further, students of color on this campus report a more general feeling of being "unwelcomed" or unsupported by White students. Given that school racial climate appears to affect the well-being of students of color (Diemer, Hsieh, & Pan, 2009; Gurin, 1999), the advocacy effort is intended to affect students of color by changing the campus racial climate and reducing the onset of further expressions of White supremacy. The advocacy effort will also encompass outreach efforts to minority student organizations on campus as well as ethnic studies departments, continued counseling services to students of color, and action in the public arena. Expanding this effort may include working collaboratively across campus to foster support for organizations through which students of color are able to take action on their own behalf. This multipronged effort aims to change the campus racial climate to facilitate the well-being, retention, achievement, and attainment of all students on campus (Gurin, 1999).

Application of the Advocacy Competencies

Here we illustrate the application of the Advocacy Competencies to this scenario, considering each domain (discussed below) of the 3 × 3 advocacy model conceptualized by Lewis et al. (2002) and further discussed by Toporek et al. (2009).

Public Information

This domain represents acting with clients in the public arena. In this case, Dr. McNulty would work with student organizations to design interventions to address White students. For example, Dr. McNulty could present to campus organizations and residence halls information regarding automatic processes of stereotyping that occur (Bargh & Ferguson, 2000) or the processes of White racial identity development (Helms, 1992). If this were a community college setting, it may be more appropriate for Dr. McNulty to present in classes to obtain a broad range of exposure. In advocating with the client or community, as reflected in this domain of the Advocacy Competencies, Dr. McNulty may engage students of color and White students in the planning process to identify issues that could be the focus of this type of presentation. It is a powerful and affirming message to convey to students that stereotyping may be a somewhat automatic cognitive process but that human beings have agency and control in how they relate to others despite the activation of culturally based stereotypes. This may help White students (a) overcome their fear of "saying something offensive" in cross-racial interactions, (b) affirm their capacity to reflect on and move beyond cultural messages they have internalized, and (c) understand their own sense of agency—to move beyond the reliance on stereotypes to understand and relate to those who are culturally different from themselves—despite the presence of automatic cognitive stereotypes. The first and third of these three potential outcomes correspond respectively to the theorized behavioral and cognitive components of the perceived cost of racism to Whites model (Spanierman & Heppner, 2004).

Sociopolitical Advocacy

This domain refers to using counselors' skills and knowledge to act as change agents in the broader policy arena, drawing upon data and counselors' communication expertise, on behalf of clients. In this case, Dr. McNulty could draw upon scholarship suggesting that racially diverse and harmonious campus environments are associated with academic motivation, advances in higher level critical thinking, and postbaccalaureate educational aspirations of White students (Gurin, 1999) and that positive school racial climates are associated with the well-being of students of color (Diemer, Hsieh, & Pan, 2009), among other outcomes. This scholarship could be used to lobby the campus administration for resources and energy devoted toward the improvement of the campus racial climate at this university. Similarly, advocacy could be directed toward the campus newspaper and/or local community newspaper. Sociopolitical advocacy plays a particularly important portion of advocacy here in that White racism is generally unquestioned and unchallenged (Fine et al., 1997; Helms, 1992).

Community Collaboration

This domain represents working with students at the community level to develop alliances and effect change at the campus level (Smith, Baluch, Bernabei, Robohm, & Sheehy, 2003). For example, Dr. McNulty could develop collaborative relationships with campus groups that share similar antiracist agendas, such as the women's resource center, racial and ethnic minority student organizations, and social justice–oriented campus groups. These alliances could build on the programming and advocacy these groups already conduct to avoid duplicative efforts and to tap into mutual strengths to affect the campus community. Further, this linkage could augment or initiate campus-based "difficult dialogues" groups that seek to foster intergroup contact, cross-cultural understanding, and racial identity development among participants. Dr. McNulty could draw upon working relationships with campus groups to involve students of color affected by, or invested in, changing the campus racial climate. It is important to note that these types of collaborations may be more difficult to build in a community college setting, because the general community college population may be less linked in with campus organizations. In this case, it would be advised that Dr. McNulty seek to form alliances with student leaders on campus and use their expertise to touch as many other students as possible.

Systems Advocacy

This domain refers to working to alter microlevel systems that constrain healthy development and well-being. As this advocacy project is primarily focused on systems advocacy (changing the overall campus racial climate), we focus here on the potential sources of resistance and emphasize the need for persistence and vision in initiating systems-level change, particularly when addressing White racism. Advocacy that addresses and challenges White racism is likely to elicit resistance in the campus community. For example, White students would likely resent the implication that they are racist and that their cultural worldview is in need of attention (Helms, 1992). Further, White students tend to have more positive views of campus racial climate than students of color do (Worthington et al., 2008). Anticipating this resistance, and effectively and constructively addressing White students' affect associated with White guilt and fears of being branded a racist, would be essential in the implementation of this advocacy campaign.

It is also important to consider sources of power and influence in counselors' advocacy work. Although campus administrators would likely repudiate expressions of overt White racism, the notion that the campus racial climate needs to be altered may inspire resistance from multiple sources. For example, it is likely that expressions of White supremacy may be regarded as "isolated incidents" rather than a shared campus problem in need of attention. Further, the notion of campus racial climate is not in a metric that many campus administrators would generally be concerned with (as opposed to finances and achievement data). One way to address this potential resistance from university or college power brokers is to use extant scholarship to suggest the ways diverse and harmonious campus climates facilitate academic achievement for all and the well-being of students of color. Additionally, given the likelihood of resistance to this initiative, we believe it will be important for Dr. McNulty to seek out and create sources of support for this advocacy initiative. The opportunity to safely express frustrations related to the advocacy work may help to sustain this advocacy initiative in the face of multipronged resistance.

Client/Student Advocacy

This domain is concerned with helping individual clients negotiate contextual barriers that constrain their development and well-being by the identification of allies and the securing of necessary resources. This advocacy approach may be especially useful if this occurred in a community college setting, where students are likely to have much more interaction with diverse students. Dr. McNulty would advocate on behalf of individual students of color to alter the campus racial climate but target students of color and White students to do so.

Students could be provided access to allies in antiracist campus or community organizations, to campus speakers who address White racism, or to educational experiences that help them acknowledge and work through racism (internalized or overt) learned in an inherently racist society (Helms, 1992). White racism also constrains individual White student's well-being and development, such as producing anxiety in cross-racial interactions and limiting social networks (Spanierman et al., 2006). We recognize that students with entrenched racist attitudes would likely not access these resources and services, but individual White students and students of color may benefit from this form of advocacy. Advocating on behalf of individual students in this manner is another mechanism to alter the broader campus racial climate and address the needs of students of color. Students engaging in Dr. McNulty's intervention efforts may carry these messages to other students in less formal settings (i.e., dormitory, cafeteria), which may be a safer place for some students to process these issues.

Client/Student Empowerment

This domain represents working with individual students in counseling to help them understand the social, political, economic, and cultural factors that affect them. This may involve helping students of color develop the "psychological armor" (Perry, 2008) to negotiate racism in interactions with White peers. Many students of color have likely learned from their parents how to negotiate relationships with predominantly White authority figures, such as teachers and law enforcement officers (Helms, 1992). However, some students of color may be less prepared to address and effectively negotiate "microaggressions" from White students in everyday social interaction (Sue et al., 2007). This may be particularly true for students of color who grew up in neighborhoods and attended schools where most of their peers were not White. Dr. McNulty may process and address negotiating these micro-aggressions with students of color in counseling and encourage fellow counselors to also be cognizant of these issues. Further, he could create a process group where White students and students of color collaboratively discuss and process recognizing and overcoming (internalized or overt) racism in everyday social interaction and campus life.

Client/student empowerment would also encompass helping White clients understand whether their behaviors and presenting problems may reflect responses to structural or internalized oppression (Lewis et al., 2002). For White students, this would entail understanding White privilege and developing a consciousness of themselves as racial beings (Fine et al., 1997; Helms, 1992). This process is aimed both at increasing White students' understanding of how White privilege operates and at developing their cultural empathy (E. H. McWhirter, 1994). It also entails helping White clients to understand the psychological costs—for example, more limited friendship groups, creation of more chilly campus climates—associated with White racism (Spanierman et al., 2006).

An important caveat is that counseling for empowerment is not the imposition of the counselor's worldview but a collaborative process of dialogue and reflection regarding the client's micro- and macrolevel context and the manner in which it affects him or her (E. H. McWhirter, 1994). Further, fostering White students' racial consciousness and fostering students' of color capacity to address microaggressions would not supersede clients' presenting problems or treatment plan in face-to-face counseling but serve as adjunctive treatment goal. From a counseling perspective, both can be viewed as "developmental nutrients" or aspects of positive youth development that inform the counseling process. Empowering individual clients is intended to alter the broader campus milieu by empowering White students to question or challenge the racism they see in other White students on campus and empowering students of color to effectively negotiate White racism.

Conclusion

The potential advocacy interventions for students at colleges and universities are diverse and likely need to be tailored according to the specific student population. A great deal of research has been completed on the developmental needs of students at 4-year institutions and community colleges. While counselors recognize the heterogeneity in each population, students at 4-year institutions may generally be best served by advocacy interventions that foster a student's personal, social, ethnic, and vocational identities, whereas students at community colleges may generally be best served by advocacy interventions that foster the balance of a student's work, family, and school roles as well as solidify their emerging identity as adults (Arnett, 2000; Simon & Tovar, 2004). It is critical the professionals working in either 4-year institutions or community colleges recognize the unique concerns of populations within their institutions (Cohen & Brawer, 2008).

One area in which advocacy interventions can have meaningful effects is in the racial climate of colleges and universities. For professionals working in these settings, it is likely that advocacy efforts to promote a safer racial climate could have positive effects on White students, students of color, and the campus in general. Coupled with supportive services (e.g., mentoring programs and/

or culturally competent counseling services), a positive racial climate may help address racial/ethnic disparities in postsecondary retention, performance, and attainment (Worthington et al., 2008). The example presented in this chapter served to highlight how professionals working in college or university settings may implement advocacy efforts around one particular topic. We feel that this type of intervention may be appropriate for students at 4-year institutions, who are developing their sense of racial/ethnic identity, and community college students, who are likely attending school in a more diverse atmosphere. Regardless of the exact type of intervention, we encourage college professionals to develop advocacy efforts that attend to each domain of the ACA advocacy model.

References

American Counseling Association (2005). *ACA code of ethics*. Alexandria, VA: Author.

Arnett, J. J. (2000). Emerging adulthood: A theory of development from the late teens through the twenties. *American Psychologist, 55,* 469–480.

Bargh, J. A., & Ferguson, M. L. (2000). Beyond behaviorism: On the automaticity of higher mental processes. *Psychological Bulletin, 126,* 925–945.

Cohen, A. M., & Brawer, F. B. (2008). *The American community college*. San Francisco: Jossey-Bass.

Diemer, M. A., Hsieh, C., & Pan, T. (2009). School and parental influences upon sociopolitical development among poor adolescents of color. *The Counseling Psychologist, 37,* 317–344.

Diemer, M. A., Wang, Q., & Dunkle, J. H. (2009). Counseling center problem checklists at academically selective institutions: Practice and measurement implications. *Journal of College Student Psychotherapy, 23,* 1–16.

Dixon, J. A., Durrheim, K., & Tredoux, C. (2005). Beyond the optimal strategy: A "reality check" for the contact hypothesis. *American Psychologist, 60,* 697–711.

Fine, M., Weis, L., Powell, L. C., & Wong, L. M. (1997). *Off White: Readings on race, power and society*. New York: Routledge.

Gurin, P. (1999). *The compelling need for diversity in education*. Expert report prepared for the lawsuits *Gratz and Hamacher v. Bollinger, Duderstadt, the University of Michigan, and the University of Michigan College of LS&A,* U.S. District Court, Eastern District of Michigan, Civil Action No. 97-75231; and *Grutter v. Bollinger, Lehman, Shields, the University of Michigan and the University of Michigan Law School,* U.S. District Court, Eastern District of Michigan, Civil Action No. 97-75928. Retrieved August 7, 2008, from: http://www.umich.edu/urel/admissions/legal/expert/gurintoc.html

Hagedorn, L. S., Maxwell, W., & Hampton, P. (2001). Correlates of retention for African-Americans in community colleges. *Journal of College Student Retention, 3,* 243–263.

Helms, J. E. (1992). *A race is a nice thing to have: A guide to being a White person or understanding the White persons in your life*. Framingham, MA: Microtraining Associates.

Kruglanski, A. W. (2004). *The psychology of closed mindedness*. New York: Psychology Press.

Lee, C. C., & Walz, G. R. (Eds.). (1998). *Social action: A mandate for counselors*. Alexandria, VA: American Counseling Association.

Lewis, J. A., Arnold, M. S., House, R., & Toporek, R. L. (2002). *ACA Advocacy Competencies*. Retrieved July 21, 2008, from http://www.counseling.org/Publications/

McWhirter, E. H. (1994). *Counseling for empowerment*. Alexandria, VA: American Counseling Association.

McWhirter, J. J., McWhirter, B. T., McWhirter, E. H., & McWhirter, R. J. (2007). *At-risk youth: A comprehensive response* (4th ed.). Pacific Grove, CA: Brooks/Cole.

National Center for Education Statistics. (2005). *Condition of education 2005*. Washington, DC: U.S. Government Printing Office.

Perry, J. C. (2008). School engagement among urban youth of color: Criterion pattern effects of vocational exploration and racial identity. *Journal of Career Development, 34,* 397–422.

Prilleltensky, I. (1994). *The morals and politics of psychology.* Albany: State University of New York Press.

Simon, M. A., & Tovar, E. (2004). Confirmatory factor analysis for the Career Factors Inventory on a community college sample. *Journal of Career Assessment, 12,* 255–269.

Smith, L., Baluch, S., Bernabei, S., Robohm, J., & Sheehy, J. (2003). Applying a social justice framework to college counseling center practice. *Journal of College Counseling, 6,* 3–13.

Spanierman, L. B., & Heppner, M. J. (2004). Psychosocial Costs of Racism to Whites scale (PCRW): Construction and initial validation. *Journal of Counseling Psychology, 51,* 249–262.

Spanierman, L. B., Poteat, V. P., Beer, A. M., & Armstrong, P. I. (2006). Psychosocial costs of racism to Whites: Exploring patterns through cluster analysis. *Journal of Counseling Psychology, 53,* 434–441.

Stone, G. L., & Archer, J. (1990). College and university counseling centers in the 1990s: Challenges and limits. *The Counseling Psychologist, 18,* 539–607.

Sue, D. W., Capodilupo, C. M., Torino, G. C., Bucceri, J. M., Holder, A. M., Nadal, K. L., & Esquilin, M. (2007). Racial microaggressions in everyday life: Implications for clinical practice. *American Psychologist, 62,* 271–286.

Toporek, R. L., Lewis, J. A., & Crethar, H. C. (2009). Promoting systemic change through the Advocacy Competencies. *Journal of Counseling & Development, 87,* 260–268.

U.S. Census Bureau. (2006). *School enrollment.* Retrieved August 28, 2008, from http://www.census.gov/population/www/socdemo/school.html.

Worthington, R. L., Navarro, R. L., Loewy, M., & Hart, J. (2008). Color-blind racial attitudes, social dominance orientation, racial-ethnic group membership and college students' perceptions of campus climate. *Journal of Diversity in Higher Education, 1,* 8–19.

Chapter 13

Advocacy and the Private Practice Counselor

A. Michael Hutchins

People are living in difficult and complex times, and rapid change has become a common theme in society. The social changes that are emerging are reflected in the counseling profession as well. As counselors, particularly as private practice counselors, we are challenged to be on the cutting edge of change.

Counselors in private practice face unique dynamics as the provision of mental health services evolves. Throughout the history of the profession, social justice advocacy has been a part of a counselor's identity. The American Counseling Association's (ACA's) mission statement challenges counselors "to enhance the quality of life in society by . . . using the profession and practice of counseling to promote respect for human dignity and diversity" (ACA, 2005, p. 2). When the ACA Governing Council endorsed the ACA Advocacy Competencies developed by Lewis, Arnold, House, and Toporek (2002) in March 2003, the association acknowledged the importance of advocacy and social justice counseling in contemporary society. This acknowledgment has particular implication for counselors in private practice.

In an article in the June 2008 issue of *Counseling Today*, Crethar and Ratts (2008) wrote, "Issues of social justice are integral to counseling because our clients do not exist as individuals independent of society, culture, and context" (p. 24). They further pointed out that the 2005 *ACA Code of Ethics* clarifies the need for social justice advocacy and that ethical practice includes such advocacy. The Advocacy Competencies provide a framework within which such counseling can emerge. In the cover story of the July 2008 issue of *Counseling Today*, Jonathan Rollins (2008) explored the emerging issues in counseling with counselors and counselor educators from a variety of settings and sites. The themes that emerged in this article include the dynamics of technology and cyber issues; changing racial and ethnic demographics; war and violence and the traumatic impact on individuals, families, and the community at large; individual and group trauma; stress related to marginalization, discrimination, and oppression; addiction in its varied forms; the changing world of work and responses to such change; changing family dynamics; and the role of aging in the majority culture. Beneath clients' presenting issues, private practice counselors are experiencing the effects of fear, anger, shame, loneliness, and emotional pain. Additionally, counselors encounter individuals and groups whose cognitive processes either enhance or inhibit healthy growth and development. Individuals and communities have learned ways of internalizing core feelings and beliefs, sometimes effectively, at other times in damaging ways. These cognitive and affective processes are then translated into helpful or damaging behavioral patterns. The Advocacy Competencies provide a framework for exploring how to integrate behavior, affect, and cognitions in ways that can create a sense of empowerment and change for individuals, families, and communities.

Counselors in private practice face unique challenges as advocates and in applying the Advocacy Competencies. In many cases, counselors work with clients who depend on health insurance to pay for services. These companies primarily reimburse for services based on the diagnosis of pathology rather than on growth, development, and advocacy. Even when a counselor in private practice works with self-paying clients, advocacy work may be outside of the most common scope of practice. In many ways, counselors in private practice work with a more privileged client population than do counselors in school and community settings, and this difference makes the practice of the advocacy even more complicated. Where schools and community agencies may have contacts to larger systems and structures, private practitioners who want to enhance their effectiveness as advocates must develop their own networks of resources within the community. The challenges and the benefits of advocacy in the private-practice milieu show themselves clearly in the case study that forms the heart of this chapter.

Operationalizing the Advocacy Competencies

Counselors who want to put the Advocacy Competencies into action have to begin by understanding the depth and difficulty of the stressors faced by their clients. When clients are affected by multiple oppressions, their life situations can make effective counseling challenging. The case of Carlos, which follows, illustrates the complexity of the helping process but also highlights the importance of multilevel advocacy.

Case Study

Carlos is a 34-year-old Mexican American male who presents for counseling in Tucson, Arizona, after having recently moved from Phoenix, where he worked in community theatre. He is living with his mother and two brothers. Carlos moved "home" after being fired for "insubordination" at his job with a Phoenix theatre company. His 50-year-old Anglo lover, Todd, did not move to Tucson with Carlos, and there are some questions about whether or not that relationship will continue. Carlos's family does not know about his relationship with Todd, although they have been partners for several years. Carlos reports that he has been very depressed since his move. He says that he has difficulty coming out of his room and that he spends several hours on the Internet daily. He reports that he has created an online "character" and is beginning to develop several "cyberfriends" with whom he is in daily contact. He reports that the character he has created is outgoing, fit, and creative. Carlos says that he has entered counseling at the request of his mother, who is very concerned about him. He reports that he moves back and forth from anxiety to depression. He reports that the director for whom he worked in Phoenix discriminated against him because his English was sometimes confused and because he is male. He is considering filing a lawsuit against her and the theatre company.

Carlos was born in Mexico and lived in California during much of his early life. His father was a migrant farmer, and his mother worked in the fields while raising Carlos and his brothers and sisters. He reports that his parents do not speak English, and the family crossed the California–Mexico border seasonally when he was very young. He reports that, at times, he went to elementary school in the worker camps, and when he was old enough, he attended high school and worked in the fields. By that time, his father was drinking heavily and frequently was abusive to Carlos's mother and the children. During this time, his mother moved in with her sister's family in Tucson. Carlos quit high school but did obtain his GED and would like to go to college to learn skills so that he can help other Latinos, but he is afraid to apply to the University of Arizona for fear of being deported. Carlos began being sexually active with men as an adolescent and was "very popular" in the gay community in Tucson before moving to Phoenix. Additionally, he reports that he has been sexually active with men he has met through the Internet and is afraid to be tested for sexually transmitted diseases because he read that if he showed up at a local health clinic, he could be sent back to Mexico. He reports that he has not "come out" to his family but he believes that they suspect that he is gay. He also reports that he knows that he drinks "too much" and may become "as angry" as his father was. He says that he has always been afraid of anger and conflict and will do anything to avoid getting angry. Carlos has connected with some of his "theatre friends" from Tucson and has been offered the opportunity to work on a community theatre production as an assistant stage manager. He is afraid that if he takes advantage of the opportunity, he will get "too anxious or depressed" to be able to follow through with the responsibilities.

The case above indicates some of the complexities for a gay-identified Mexican American male in the United States. In particular, it demonstrates how forces such as poverty, racism, classism, heterosexism, sexism, immigration policies, and the insidious dynamics of terrorism affect personal, social, career, and educational development and integration. Additionally, the case addresses the need to focus on advocacy and empowerment for the individual client and on addressing issues in the larger community. What follows is a possible path a counselor might take to empower and advocate for Carlos and his family.

Client/Student Level

Client/Student Empowerment

In keeping with the Advocacy Competencies, the counselor works intensively with Carlos to enhance his sense of empowerment and to build his self-advocacy skills. The counselor begins working with Carlos by focusing on the daily management of his life and then exploring the strengths that it has taken for him to have accomplished all that he has already achieved. Carlos is encouraged to explore the resilience and courage it has taken for him to move forward with life goals and plans to the extent that he has. He explores the underlying dynamics of his depression and anxiety and examines ways of refocusing his strengths to redirect his life. Carlos appears to have some connections with a gay community and, depending on where he is in his identity development, is supported in building on the healthy connections within that community. He is also encouraged to examine the role that the Internet plays in his development. The counselor encourages Carlos to make use of resources in the lesbian, gay, bisexual, and transgender (LGBT) community center, Latino/Latina community organizations, his extended family, the church, and community leaders.

Carlos explores those concerns that are unique to him and those that reflect dissonance in the larger community. The counselor helps him to examine the impact of discrimination on the basis of immigration status, race, language, and sexual orientation. In response to terrorism, some of the recent legislation in the United States affecting undocumented workers is appropriately anxiety producing and is not necessarily an indication of individual pathology. It is also important to demonstrate how discriminatory laws reinforce bias against non-English-speaking individuals and families in employment, housing, education, and health care services and how local laws may be in conflict with state and federal laws. Helping Carlos to distinguish between his own personal responses and those of a culture over which he has no control can create a path to developing a plan of action.

Carlos believes that he was terminated from his employment as a result of poor English skills. The family also reflects problems related to discrimination on the basis of language and social class. These may manifest themselves in the anxiety and depression Carlos reports. They may also be reflected in the family pattern of alcoholism and abuse. Additionally, relationship problems between Carlos and Todd may reflect internalized homophobia and complications in sexual identity development, in the men and in the community at large. Employment concerns may also reflect the dynamics of discrimination. All of these dynamics reflect internalized and systemic oppression. Several approaches may be helpful in addressing these dynamics. Carlos can explore his history through narrative therapy, expressive therapy, or cognitive–behavioral approaches examining the boundaries of responsibility.

It is important for Carlos to be able to see his situation in context. He may pathologize and internalize dynamics that are external and, while they affect him, are not dynamics that are endemic to his personality. It is important that Carlos recognize that his responses may be healthy responses to an unhealthy system, and that the problems begin in the system and not with his personal sense of self. The counselor helps Carlos to cognitively restructure his world experiences and to come to a fuller understanding of how discriminatory practices and policies affect him. He is then introduced to practices that can assist him from internalizing oppression. He learns to appropriately integrate healthy thoughts, feelings, and behaviors wherein he becomes accountable for himself and articulates healthy boundaries.

The counselor collaborates with Carlos in developing personal tools that are informed by the Multicultural Counseling Competencies developed by Sue, Arredondo, and McDavis (1992). He learns appropriate problem-solving and conflict-resolution skills and is encouraged to participate in activities through the LGBT community center. He is also encouraged to enroll in programs through the community college with the intent to follow through with the University of Arizona. The community theatre system has many opportunities for bilingual individuals. Carlos has the intellectual skills to explore possibilities through the Immigration Law Center at the University of Arizona. Through these programs, he obtains a clearer understanding of the possibilities of resolving his concern about his job discrimination experience. Carlos is also encouraged to explore online support groups for men in situations similar to his own.

Together Carlos and his counselor develop a clear plan of action based on developing resources within the community. Carlos begins by collaboratively developing a diet and exercise plan with his counselor. Such a plan focuses on addressing the physical dynamics of depression and anxiety. He develops a realistic education and career plan. With the assistance of the Immigration Law Center, he explores issues related to employment discrimination, health services, and educational opportunities. The LGBT community center has a series of groups and other activities to address the concerns Carlos has expressed about finding a "healthy gay community." Carlos can practice interview and problem-solving skills in a group counseling setting, receiving feedback from his peers about his presentation of self and his impact on others.

At this point, the counselor's role is to encourage, guide, and support the individual in creating and carrying out a realistic, attainable, and measurable path toward a clear and concise vision. It is important to consistently review goals and strategies and explore ways of altering those in nonjudgmental ways to encourage the growth of the client's self-esteem and connectedness to a community.

Although the client/student level of direct services would appear on the surface to fit easily into the private-practice environment, the counselor faces challenges that may be unique to this work setting. To develop the plan of action and to guide and support the client, the counselor must be aware of community resources. In the case of Carlos, many of the services that the counselor provides may not fall into the services reimbursed by insurance companies. To ensure quality services, counselors in private practice may work with sliding-fee scales that are consistent with the *ACA Code of Ethics*.

Client Advocacy

As Carlos articulates his plan, the counselor collaborates with him in clarifying his visions and pathways. Where resources do not exist, the counselor works with Carlos and appropriate community resources to develop such resources. This may include assisting Carlos identify appropriate resources and may also include having the counselor work within the community to integrate services and arrange opportunities for discussion and development. An example of such an intervention may be to work with the LGBT community center to develop bilingual groups for men who have had the experience of early childhood abuse. Another opportunity is to work with the Immigration Law Center to help legal volunteers develop intervention skills.

When appropriate resources have been identified, the counselor uses his or her resources to create culturally appropriate opportunities for Carlos. For counselors, it is essential to have a network of resource professionals and volunteers to assist in creating realistic action plans. In this case, these include, but are not limited to, career specialists, English as a Second Language programs, immigration and discrimination law specialists, employment law resources, health care professionals, social service resources in the LGBT community, community college and university resources, group work opportunities, and resources throughout the Spanish-speaking community.

It is important to recognize that Carlos is likely to run into resistance from his family and from the community. Helping him to understand his situation in context is part of the counseling relationship as well. He can run into resistance because of the family's history of being undocumented workers. The fear that exists in the community at large since 9/11 concerning undocumented workers has magnified. Current state and federal legislation reflects this fear and affects the decision-making process of legislators as well as citizens. Some of these barriers may be easily overcome; others may be addressed and resolved with greater difficulty; others may not be overcome at this time. Helping Carlos to get a realistic picture of prospects can be critical to his mental health and that of his family.

By working together, Carlos and his counselor can develop a specific action plan for addressing barriers. Again, the counselor needs to be familiar with, and connected to, resources within the community. It is extremely difficult to anticipate roadblocks and solutions if the community resources are not in place. The counselor encourages Carlos to use the Internet to identify community resources in addition to making the contacts face to face in the community. They then identify a path with specific contacts and strategies, anticipating difficulties and developing problem-solving plans.

On his own, Carlos risks being tossed back into isolation, fear, anxiety, and depression. With assistance, he becomes empowered. The community center has a core of bilingual volunteer physicians, counselors, attorneys, social service professionals and paraprofessionals, health care workers, and others who encourage participation from members of the community and who can provide information. The Spanish-speaking community and the community college also provide realistic parameters. The City of Tucson has an advisory commission to the mayor and city council that advises these city officials on issues related to the citizens of the community. Collaboratively, Carlos and his counselor create a plan of action.

Carlos and his counselor work through the action plan, knowing that, at times, the plan will be revised and edited. The process of working through the plan assists Carlos in learning to integrate thoughts, feelings, and behaviors; helps him to learn to establish culturally appropriate boundaries; and facilitates a clearer understanding of who he is in the world and how the world functions. Perhaps most important, Carlos gains a clarity regarding who he is and how he can make a significant contribution to the community in which he lives.

Community Level

In addition to using the Advocacy Competencies on the micro level, the *ACA Code of Ethics* requires that counselors address the community dynamics that affect clients and their world. In the case of Carlos, the counselor participates in the community at large, becoming a resource and networking with other resources to be part of a fabric for healthy change. As a private practitioner, it is incumbent on the counselor to go beyond the counseling office and be an active part of the community. Where a school or community agency counselor may have access to systemic information, the counselor in private practice will need to have a personal network in all parts of the community. In this case, the counselor will need to have connections in the Spanish-speaking, the LGBT, the employment, the immigration law, the religious, the medical, and the legal communities. Some of these resources are available through different community agencies with which the counselor may be familiar. Additionally, the counselor is well advised to know who in the community can serve as advocates with and for the client.

Community Collaboration

In exploring Carlos's case, one needs to recognize the environmental factors affecting Carlos and his family. These include the reported discrimination on the basis of language and gender in his job loss; the impact of fear concerning undocumented workers and other diverse communities in contemporary society, and the history of such fear; the lack of understanding and acceptance of sexual diversity in the majority culture and in dynamics of sexual diversity in the Spanish-speaking community; the dynamics of sexual identity development in individuals and communities; the dynamics of immigration and racial discrimination; the health care dynamics of sexually diverse individuals and communities; the political and social climate affecting diverse communities; the impact of socioeconomic decisions and actions taken on the local, state, and federal levels; the relationships in Mexican American families; the state of educational and training opportunities; the availability of mental health facilities; and legal/legislative issues in the community. To be an effective counselor, one has to develop a network within the community wherein calls can be made and contacts arranged that, when needed, can be called into play when the occasion arises. In this case, the counselor needs to explore possible resources throughout the community as Carlos develops his action plan with the counselor. When appropriate, and with appropriate regard for confidentiality, the counselor contacts the community to alert colleagues that a case may be developing. In this case, it can include inquiring into the availability of support groups in the community center and/or contacting resources in the Immigration Law Center.

It is critical to develop alliances with other professionals who are active in all aspects of the community. Counselors have skills to bring to community groups and can facilitate change on the community level. In Carlos's situation, the counselor is active in one or more community groups that allow access to other community support systems. The counselor is in regular contact with the colleagues at Immigration Law Center and the LGBT community center, community college and university, and members of the religious and social structures in the Latino community. Additionally, it is important to use Internet resources to keep abreast of changes and additions to programs and other resources in the community.

Counselors bring their skills to the community by serving on boards and commissions or performing volunteer activities in different capacities. Counselors acknowledge community colleagues in many ways. They work with counseling associations to recognize and acknowledge the work of colleagues on local, state, and national levels. This recognition may be something as simple as letters of acknowledgment to individual colleagues or their superiors for "work well done" or recommending them for local recognition. Counselor advocates take the opportunity to provide training within the community and serve on community boards and associations that explore ways to address the impact of marginalization and oppression. It can mean being willing to expose one's own vulnerabilities and lack of understanding of problems and having a willingness to learn from colleagues, consistently seeking feedback and shared observations from peers and supervisors in the community. As practitioners, counselors continue developing ongoing collaborative referral bases and continue to be in clinical supervisory relationships to address their own vulnerabilities. Providing community services may be seen as additional services for the counselor in private practice. However, participation in such activities creates a larger resource and referral base for counselors.

Systems Advocacy

Working in the community implies that the counselor tries to develop systemic change when the current systems perpetuate paradigms and procedures that contribute to marginalization, discrimination, and oppression. In this case, the counselor works with professional colleagues to explore community conditions that either enhance or inhibit growth and development for gay, Spanish-speaking, undocumented working individuals and their families and the community. By collaborating with agencies and other groups, the counselor can articulate community dynamics. The counselor presents anecdotal and other research evidence indicating work that has been done and needs to be done when meeting with colleagues and other leaders in the community. The City of Tucson passed an antidiscrimination ordinance in 1977, and this ordinance has been revised and updated. Through city commissions, the atmosphere is continually monitored, with data needing continual revision and updating. Counselors and others on these commissions work within the city to coordinate campaigns and programs to address underlying problems of discrimination and oppression within the community. Drawing on the expertise of career, educational, and legal professionals, the counselor in this case explores the dynamics of workplace discrimination and encourages educational opportunities for citizens who believe they have been the targets of discrimination in the workplace. Community action groups create a community vision and plan of action.

The counselor can effect community change by working with the sexual minority, educational, and legal communities to assess the most effective ways to address the underlying dynamics of Carlos's case. The Latino/a community has strong resources and can provide critical support. Limited resources are available in the mental health community, and greater long-range action needs to be taken. By using group work skills, the counselor participates in planning sessions to create communitywide education and training sessions, supported by elected city officials and community service organizations to improve the life climate for diverse populations within the city.

Not all parts of the community will initially be supportive of programs to include sexually diverse individuals. It is important to build alliances from the religious, Spanish-speaking, mental health, and education communities to support creating a safe place for all people to live. When appropriate, the counselor invites Carlos to be involved in a "Safe Schools" program for GLBT students.

Nor will all parts of the community agree on the integration of undocumented workers into the community. The counselor collaborates with the Immigration Law Center to develop educational programs for undocumented workers and their families. Additional work involves being active in supporting legislation to address inequity; integrating group decision-making/problem-solving skills as a contribution to community building; inviting those who will be in opposition to join in the discussion and planning to create long-term change; and participating in assessing the progress of community action plans.

The Broader Public Arena

Public Information

Addressing the impact of oppression, the counselor in this case collaborates with others in the community to develop health, mental health, educational, and legal services that can become part of community education. The City of Tucson has historically provided educational opportunities for all city employees to address discrimination, diversity, and oppression. The Gay, Lesbian, Bisexual and Transgender Commission in collaboration with the Human Relations and Women's Commissions have developed educational media to share with organizations throughout the community. Counselors in private practice have been active members in each of these commissions. School districts, the community college, and the University of Arizona all work with community groups to conduct research and to educate the community. A coalition of religious congregations is involved in providing support for diverse populations. Counselors in private practice are involved in all of these endeavors. Strong connections have been made through the University of Arizona, and research continues to evolve. Counselors can provide research results and other material to community groups and can collaborate in community education and publication. Developing relationships with media personnel is an important resource. By getting to know members of the media, the counselor may be the "go to" person when incidents arise in the community. The counselor can also publish material in community publications to address issues. Counselors and colleagues are developing blogs and other Internet material that can easily be accessed by community leaders and others in the community. Regularly, collaborators meet to assess changes in strategies, determine whether action plans are coming to fruition, explore needed changes, and determine what steps need to be taken. While participation as described above is not always easy, counselors in private practice enhance their personal reputations and those of their practice and profession by engaging in such activities.

Social/Political Advocacy

Counselors need to be in regular communication with legislators on the local, state, and federal levels to influence legislation. An example related to this case includes the counselor contacting a state legislator from his district concerning a bill in the state legislature addressing bullying in schools. The bill did not include reference to sexual and gender identity, and the counselor was able to provide research information that affected the way the bill was drafted. Mental health services continue to be inadequate, and legislation to improve services continues to be needed. As the nation explores the possibility for universal health care, we as counselors, and our allies in other helping professions, need to be vigilant on the local, state, and federal levels. As counselors, we continue to see the impact of fear-based legislation and must be active participants in addressing the more universal problems as we ask our allies to help us with specific concerns. We have greater impact by serving on community boards and being elected to community positions. We can bring emerging research results to the attention of decision makers across the entire spectrum of the community. We can further enlist corporate colleagues in addressing specific and more universal issues. There will be those in our society who wish to perpetuate fear-based systems. It is our charge to engage in the difficult discussion of advocacy. In times of crisis, more counselors in private practice will be called upon as resources when we allow our voices to be heard.

Multicultural and Diversity Issues

The issues identified in Carlos's case address concerns that many counselors are facing. A growing number of people in the community come from cultures that are not primarily English speaking. Many have migrated, legally and illegally, to the United States in search of a more harmonious lifestyle. Immigration is a hot topic in contemporary society, and Carlos's family and community reflect some of the dynamics of that struggle. Carlos and his family have encountered the dynamics of fear and anger in a population that already lives here. In this case, Carlos and his family have been in Arizona and California for much of their lives, and Carlos has attempted to integrate into the community and become a productive member of the community. He experiences some of the stress of discrimination based on language and ethnicity. Members of the larger community have a reality-based fear that must also be addressed through education and advocacy. His family began in poverty, and family members have made efforts to become productive members of the community. They continue to confront the limited resources available on the basis of socioeconomic class. Carlos begins to describe abuse and trauma in his family. It is critical to explore the cultural trauma that provides the background for the familial and personal trauma and abuse. Carlos also identifies the dynamics of substance abuse that he saw in his father and that he suspects could be part of his personal development. He identifies that he is afraid to receive appropriate health care. This can complicate his integration personally and into the larger community. Carlos has attempted to become a citizen but reports being afraid to pursue citizenship because he believes he may be deported even though he has lived most of his life in the United States and he and his family have always attempted to be productive members of the community. Carlos has attended school in California and Arizona, but resources have become more restricted and he is afraid to pursue higher education. The issue of public education for undocumented immigrants continues to be a critical problem for individuals and communities in the United States.

Sexual orientation is a significant dynamic in this case. Carlos has grown up in a traditional Spanish-speaking migrant family that has close connections to the Catholic church. He has "come out" in the community but has not disclosed his sexual orientation to his family. He describes a fear of losing familial support and also reports that he avoids conflict and anticipates dissonance, which will "tear the family more apart than it already is" if he comes out. Although Tucson as a community is relatively accepting of sexual and gender diversity, individuals, families, and subgroups within the community are not. Additionally, Carlos has been in a cross-cultural relationship with an Anglo man who is significantly older than he is. It is possible that the couple has experienced additional stress as a result of racism within the gay community. It would be helpful to explore the dynamics of age-different relationships as well.

Carlos is developing a life on the Internet. He reports that he is meeting other people and has developed a group of cyberfriends with whom he feels close connections, although he has never met any of them. He identifies that he does this from loneliness and sees the amount of time he spends on the Internet as problematic. The Internet community introduces a new set of cultural dynamics with which counselors must become familiar.

Challenges

Significant challenges face the counselor in private practice when exploring this case. Some of the challenges are addressed below.

Many of the concerns presented by Carlos have historically been identified as intrapsychic issues. Carlos identifies "anxiety and depression" and has learned to pathologize his responses to environmental dynamics. He can begin to explore how his responses may be appropriate responses to external dysfunction. The counselor may receive limited support for challenging systems that are in place. Counselors have been taught to view the world in a framework of growth and development. Counselors are often expected to interpret the world using a medical model that frames the world in terms of individual pathology. In many cases, only counselors who use this model of pathology to determine "progress toward a treatment goal" will be financially reimbursed by health insurance companies. The counselor's challenge may be to integrate these divergent approaches to enhance client growth while being reimbursed for services. Additionally, a challenge can be to work with provider panels to open the discussion of alternative worldviews and to work with state licensing boards to broaden the view of encouraged practices that are culturally appropriate and effective. It may also mean working with those organizations that provide counselor liability insurance to broaden insurance coverage for counselors providing a wider scope of practice.

Counselors in private practice may also be challenged to broaden their view of who their client is. An individual may present for services and expect to be seen in the counselor's office. Operating within the framework of the *ACA Code of Ethics* (American Counseling Association, 2005), the counselor may need to see the family and community as "clients" as well. This implies becoming involved in community and professional activity to change the climate within which individuals live. This work will bring the counselor into contact with a wider network of community decision makers and provide the opportunity to engage in meaningful dialogue with those who see and experience the world in more diverse ways. Creating hope in a culture of fear can be a significant challenge.

Counselors in private practice encounter different views of the role of counselors in the community from within the counseling profession itself. Many within the profession challenge the appropriateness of social justice advocacy. It becomes critical to tie the community advocacy work into the commitment, from the ACA mission statement, "to enhance the quality of life in society by… using the profession and practice of counseling to promote respect for human dignity and diversity," and the revised *Code of Ethics*.

A significant challenge is to become an active voice for change by being in regular contact with community decision makers and elected officials to encourage legislation that supports the inclusion of all people in combating fear-based actions and replacing those with decisions based on respect and dignity. It may mean having counselors seeking political office to create community change.

Counselors often work with clients and others to assist them in balancing their lives. A challenge for counselors is to maintain balance in their own lives. If counselors support clients in living healthy lives on many levels, they must remember to do the same.

Benefits

As counseling practitioners, when we create an advocacy-based practice, we build on the profession's roots in human growth and development. As a result of operating from a growth and advocacy model, we distinguish ourselves from other helping professions and clarify the role of counselors within the community. We become collaborators in shifting individuals, families, and the community from fear-based styles of being-in-the-world to worldviews based on respect, dignity, and hope.

In the short term, we begin to affect the way the counseling profession is seen in the community and become resources for individual and community change. As private practitioners, we are instrumental in operationalizing concepts that we have learned in more theoretical settings and putting the concepts to the test. In collaboration with colleagues, we provide the research data to support systemic change. Counselors in private practice have sometimes reported that the work can be lonely. With an advocacy model, we become more increasingly part of a community of change.

Many of us in private practice counseling are highly skilled, and the benefits to our community are great. We bring a perspective of health and hope to community decision making and challenge fear-based approaches. If we live "advocacy," we are challenged to create balance in our lives, becoming mentors for others.

Conclusion

As we step into the future, we are challenged as counselors to build a culture of hope. Counselors have identified fear-based concerns and have developed strategies for working with clients to integrate thoughts, feelings, and behaviors and to create hope. As counselors in private practice, we are actively engaged in advocacy on the client level. It is critical for us to expand our worldview and see the community as our client as well. Our challenge is to be active collaborators in changing the world in which we and our clients live, becoming advocates in the larger community. This means broadening our definition as private practitioners. The Advocacy Competencies provide a paradigm for expanding that view. The demographics of our client population are changing, and we must creatively change in culturally appropriate manners. The path of creative change is not an easy one, but it is an exciting one. When we clearly articulate an approach based on dignity, respect, and hope, we are collaborators in creating social change, making our world more inclusive and hopeful.

References

American Counseling Association. (2005). *ACA code of ethics*. Alexandria, VA: Author.

Crethar, H. C., & Ratts, M. J. (2008, June). Why social justice is a counseling concern. *Counseling Today*, 24–25.

Lewis, J. A., Arnold, M. S., House, R., & Toporek, R. L. (2002). *ACA Advocacy Competencies*. Retrieved January 29, 2009, from http://www.counseling.org/Publications/

Rollins, J. (2008, July). Emerging client issues. *Counseling Today*, 30–41.

Sue, D. W., Arredondo, P., & McDavis, R. J. (1992). Multicultural counseling competencies and standards: A call to the profession. *Journal of Counseling & Development, 70*, 477–486.

Chapter

14

From Passion to Action: Integrating the ACA Advocacy Competencies and Social Justice Into Counselor Education and Supervision

Judith C. Durham and Harriet L. Glosoff

There has been an increased focus in the past several years on integrating not only multiculturalism in the counseling profession but also advocacy and social justice. Although the focus on social justice advocacy in relation to counselor education and supervision is fairly recent, the theme of advocacy and social justice has been an integral part of the history of the counseling profession.

This chapter begins with a rationale for integrating a social justice advocacy orientation in counselor education and supervision, followed by a discussion of the American Counseling Association (ACA) Advocacy Competencies (Lewis, Arnold, House, & Toporek, 2002) as being the optimal construction for the integration of an advocacy focus across the counselor education curriculum. Information is included on strategies for infusion believed to be important for students and supervisees as they develop and implement advocacy interventions. The chapter concludes with challenges to implementing Advocacy Competencies in counselor education and supervision. We include a focus on strategies for developing a culture of advocacy in counselor education programs, administrative and pedagogical considerations, and the general challenges of operationalizing the Advocacy Competencies and adopting a social justice advocacy orientation.

Rationale for Infusing the Advocacy Competencies Into Counselor Education and Supervision

The increased emphasis by counselors on multiculturalism over the past several years has naturally led to a focus on social justice and advocacy. According to Vera and Speight (2003), it is through expanding the definition of multiculturalism that one easily comes to an understanding of social justice. As one becomes aware of cultural and contextual differences or social locations in people's lives, one cannot help but see oppression, inequities, and injustices. Sue et al. (1998) stated that "multiculturalism is about social justice, cultural democracy, and equity" (p. 5). Arredondo (1999) articulated how specific Multicultural Counseling Competencies (Sue, Arredondo, & McDavis, 1992) might be used as tools to address oppression and racism. She detailed how specific Multicultural Counseling Competencies necessitate that counselors become aware of issues of power, privilege, oppression, and bias in their own and clients' lives. Although the Multicultural Counseling Competencies do speak to issues of oppression, they say little specifically about how one is to become a counselor advocate.

This concern can be more appropriately addressed through the Advocacy Competencies developed by Lewis et al. (2002).

The advocacy competence model consists of six different domains: empowerment, client advocacy, community collaboration, systems advocacy, public information, and social and political advocacy (Lewis et al., 2002), each of which may have an affinity for integration into specific courses as well as cross courses. However, training students to be social justice advocates is not as simple as integrating new course content or creating assignments designed around social advocacy interventions, although these are fine strategies. Education to develop advocates for social change requires attention to issues of curricular process as well as content. Thus, the primary focus of this chapter is on strategies for establishing a foundational culture of advocacy within counselor education programs while using the Advocacy Competencies as a framework.

A critical first step in developing an advocacy orientation is for counselor educators and supervisors to recognize the negative consequences of oppression in the lives of targeted populations and to assist developing counselors in acquiring the necessary skills to effect social change (Constantine, Hage, Kindaichi, & Bryant, 2007; Vera & Speight, 2003). Counselors are then challenged to address issues of social injustice within all areas of counseling practice and must have the expertise to respond in creative, innovative, and intentional ways, often within new roles. These roles are defined within the Advocacy Competencies and described from both a micro and a macro orientation. Students need to be challenged to think about the inequities and power structures within society as well as the issues of marginalization, disenfranchisement, subjugation, and systemic barriers that are too often part of everyday experience. As advocates, counselors are mandated to go beyond their roles of direct service providers attending not only to those who express need (microlevel) but also to the larger social and contextual forces that create and continue to oppress, victimize, and give rise to mental health issues (macrolevel). We now shift attention to the various ways in which counselor educators and supervisors can apply the Advocacy Competencies in the training and supervision of future counselors, including a focus on administrative and pedagogical considerations, the integration of an advocacy social justice focus in supervision, and the challenges of a social justice advocacy orientation.

Administrative Considerations of a Social Justice Advocacy Orientation

Integrating the Advocacy Competencies into counselor training is one critical step in the development of a culture of advocacy within counseling programs. For an increasing number of counselor education programs, issues of advocacy and social justice are not only content areas to be included in curricula but also ideals around which programs are making all decisions, including administrative policy (Bemak & Chung, 2007; Goodman et al., 2004; Osborne et al., 1998; Rogers & Molina, 2006; Shin, 2008; Talleyrand, Chung, & Bemak, 2006). Faculty in counselor education programs have a responsibility to be aware of their own positions of power within their institutions and to advocate for socially just policies with regard to recruitment, admissions, retention, and personal survival (Shin, 2008). The issue of retention of a diverse student body highlights the need for faculty to use and model systemically focused advocacy skills. As Shin (2008) questioned, "How many students of color have been dismissed from programs because it was determined that they had some psychological, emotional, or intellectual deficiency when a more significant problem was the failure of the White faculty to adjust their approaches in a way that would create a welcoming environment?" (p. 185). Understanding the educational and other inequities that students of color may bring with them requires being open to hearing about their struggles without being defensive. In addition, it involves changing departmental pedagogical structures in new and unique ways that make the educational environment inclusive of these students. These are examples of social justice advocacy interventions that can empower and liberate students of color at the client/student level of the Advocacy Competencies.

Numerous institutions, including Boston College, Penn State University, Ball State University, Loyola University Chicago, Oregon State University, and Marquette University, have adopted mission statements and made programmatic and curricular changes to address issues of diversity and social justice in their programs (Osborne et al., 1998; Talleyrand et al., 2006). Boston College and George

Mason University (GMU) have addressed issues of advocacy and social justice in recruitment and retention of students and faculty as well as in all aspects of their curriculum. GMU provides fieldwork and internship placements designed to assist students in developing a systems advocacy and public information perspective. Students in this program work in various governmental organizations, the U.S. Office for Refugee Resettlement, and the Peace Corps and gain practical advocacy experiences in the school/community and public arena advocacy levels. In addition, an interdisciplinary collaboration includes an emphasis on public policy, public health, political science, and anthropology as critical components in integrating the theoretical aspects of an advocacy orientation (Bemak & Chung, 2007; Talleyrand et al., 2006). These experiences provide students with numerous opportunities to learn about and experience advocacy at the school/community and public arena levels.

Pedagogical Considerations of a Social Justice Advocacy Orientation

Curricular Process

In academia, attention needs to be given to curricular content and the process of learning. Educators should model the tenets of social justice through their classroom delivery (Kiselica, 2004). Classrooms designed to promote principles of social justice are structured in an egalitarian manner in which faculty do not set themselves up as the experts possessing all the knowledge and power. In the tradition of Freire (1993), a socially just pedagogy does not seek to indoctrinate but rather shares the process of learning with students. Just as students must be empowered to embrace both traditional and nontraditional approaches to helping, faculty members need to design learning strategies that embrace a constructivist orientation while integrating the Advocacy Competencies into the curriculum. One of the most essential elements in creating a climate focusing on advocacy is for students to develop critical thinking skills, critical consciousness, or cognitive complexity (Vera & Speight, 2003). Without these skills, one cannot develop a reflective attitude toward the injustices in the lives of those who are oppressed and marginalized and enact the Advocacy Competencies.

McDowell and Shelton (2002) contended that classes should be structured to assist students in developing the critical thinking skills necessary to engage in "dialogues of difference" (p. 313). They noted that such skills are essential for examining how the dominant paradigm shapes experiences for all—faculty, students, and clients. For example, the use of clinical cases of individuals and families from marginalized groups is one way to shape classroom discussion for critical examination of issues of power, privilege, and oppression. Faculty can direct discussion to how existing social structures perpetuate and maintain unjust systems, power and privilege, and the associated intersection with oppression (McDowell & Shelton, 2002). It is only through critical analysis that students can "recognize the impact of social, political, economic, and cultural factors on human development" (Toporek, Lewis, & Crethar, 2009, p. 262), a necessary step in being able to provide direct and indirect individual advocacy interventions as articulated in the Advocacy Competencies.

Fostering Critical Consciousness and Reflective Thinking

Vera and Speight (2003) stated that the development and application of critical thinking skills (cognitive complexity) are essential in analyzing social conditions and policies that maintain the injustices in the lives of those who are marginalized or oppressed. In addition, the literature indicates that reflective practice and critical thinking skills are essential for the competence of any counselor (Connor-Greene, 2000). Reflective practice includes processing, debriefing, providing feedback, and journal writing, and it assists students in the development of cognitive complexity or the movement from dichotomous to contextual thinking. Such reflection not only enhances critical thinking but also promotes overall professional growth (Adams, Bell, & Griffin, 1997).

Equally essential to the development of cognitive complexity is that counselor educators and supervisors model this critical consciousness, not only in exploring the lives of others, but also in self-examination relating to issues of power and privilege in their own lives (Kiselica, 2004). McDowell and Shelton (2002) pointed out that students and faculty must be respectful of different cultural values, social locations, and experiences of privilege and oppression that they bring with them into the classroom. Faculty, as well as students, must be open and vulnerable to exploring their own biases, values, and assumptions. Just as the process of challenging and changing bias, oppression, and ethnocentrism can be complicated in the community, so can it also be with students. However, when faculty model openness and vulnerability to such exploration, students will develop the aptitude for critical reflection more quickly (Kiselica, 2004) and be able to transfer these skills to advocating for clients.

Drawing from literature on teaching for multicultural competence, counseling courses that are instructive of an advocacy orientation should contain affective and reflective components that go beyond the typical knowledge acquisition seen in many training programs (Sue & Sue, 1990) or that embrace a balance of emotional and cognitive components of learning (Adams et al., 1997). Courses should include experiential activities that give rise to affective learning that challenges ethnocentrism; helps students bring feelings, attitudes, and values to the surface (Arthur & Achenbach, 2002); and assists students in the development of cultural empathy (Pope-Davis, Breaux, & Liu, 1997; Ridley & Lingle, 1996) and an understanding of the need to adopt an advocacy stance as articulated in the Advocacy Competencies. As previously noted, using clinical cases of people from marginalized groups is one way to shape classroom discussion for critical examination of advocacy-related issues and ways to intervene at the client/student, school/community, and public arena levels. All of these aforementioned suggestions allow students to better understand how to integrate the Advocacy Competencies in their work with clients.

Curricular Content

In designing courses that infuse an advocacy or social justice orientation, educators must be mindful that "teaching and learning about social justice are not destinations that once achieved are to be checked off as accomplishments; rather they are processes of continuous growth and understanding" (Harley, Alston, & Middleton, 2007, p. 44). Kiselica and Robinson (2001) asserted that counselors need to possess skills in consultation, group dynamics, coalition building, and organizational change as well as specific skills such as outreach, prevention, mediation, lobbying, and marketing. Training programs, therefore, must provide students with opportunities to develop these skills while integrating roles beyond the traditional service provider for individual and client groups. Client empowerment and advocacy—the role of adviser, consultant, or social justice change agent—require skills that students must also develop throughout their programs of study (Constantine et al., 2007). Courses also need to include mechanisms for involvement in advocacy projects, community outreach, and public policy-making activities for marginalized and disenfranchised groups in order for developing counselors to broaden their repertoire of roles for professional behavior (Vera & Speight, 2003). In addition, counseling faculty should consider including educational, legal, and public policy institutions as experiential or in vivo learning sites during practicum or internship while encouraging students to take elective courses in those areas. All of these suggested strategies are examples of how the client/student, school/community, and public arena levels of the Advocacy Competencies are operationalized.

Similar to the Multicultural Counseling Competencies, the Advocacy Competencies should not just be introduced or taught in a single unit in a social or cultural counseling course. Rather, the Advocacy Competencies need to be infused across the counseling curriculum. Kiselica (2004) recommended that a balance of preventive and empowering strategies be taught, just as faculty should use a balance of support with empathic confrontation. Romano and Hage (2000) suggested several training domains relevant to prevention that could be infused into course content. These include community collaborations, social and political history, protective factors and risk reduction strategies, systemic interventions, psychoeducational groups, and prevention research and evaluation. For instance, assessment classes might include exercises that investigate prevention research with an eye toward critically examining the extent to which the prevention programs successfully address systemic barriers experienced by client groups (Romano & Hage, 2000). This is an example of the public arena level of the Advocacy Competencies. Similarly, school counseling students can be required to not just develop individual and group activities and/or guidance lessons aimed at prevention in foundational courses but also implement and assess the effectiveness of such prevention activities in practicum and/or internship.

Courses that instruct students regarding the practice of consultation, whether mental health, school, or industrial/organizational consultation, need to be concerned with how race, culture, ethnicity, gender, and sexual orientation, along with associated issues of power and inequities, affect individuals and organizations within society. Such a focus assists students in developing the critical consciousness that is necessary for becoming a counseling advocate as well as knowing how to respond to such challenges through their consultant role. Sue (2008) presented a model of consultation from a social justice advocacy perspective that should be an integral part of any course in consultation and leadership. The model begins with acknowledging that as the demographics of the society change, so too does the composition of organizations within the society. Thus, consultants must be prepared to provide consultative services to enhance the organization's ability to adapt to and use diversity to maintain or improve effectiveness in a manner that provides equal access and opportunity for all (Sue, 2008).

Service Learning as Advocacy Curricular Content

Service learning experiences are one example of the type of curricular activity that can help students actualize the Advocacy Competencies. Moreover, service learning might be used to provide students with opportunities to critically analyze power structures and oppressive practices both perpetuated and challenged within the organizations (Harley et al., 2007). Service learning experiences could also begin to provide students with the knowledge and skills necessary to effectively engage in the practice of advocacy and prevention and could easily be incorporated early in a student's program, for example, in a foundations or introduction to the profession class, and then be continued throughout the curriculum. Such experiences can provide students with a practical and real-world understanding of how to enact the Advocacy Competencies. Students are able to identify societal inequities, a necessary precursor to becoming an advocate, as well as develop an understanding of intervening on a systemic level (Vera & Speight, 2003).

Lee (1997) asserted that mental health professionals should become better trained to understand social justice issues from a global perspective. This broadens the advocacy role from what is traditionally envisioned to one that embraces global connections and the need to understand these connections in developing a broader sociopolitical advocacy orientation. As global interconnectedness is becoming increasingly apparent, training programs should focus on worldwide social transformation and the need for mental health or counseling interventions not only at the individual, group, or societal level but also at international levels. This might be explored in classes in consultation and leadership or multicultural counseling, and advocacy skills could be developed through service learning, practicum, and internship opportunities outside the borders of the United States.

Summary and Examples

In summary, preparing students to be counselor advocates is not as simple as integrating new course content or creating assignments designed specifically around the Advocacy Competencies but, rather, includes developing a culture of advocacy throughout the counseling program. Education to develop counseling advocates or advocates for social change requires attention to issues of pedagogy and curricular process as well as the continual infusion of content that adopts the philosophy of an advocacy orientation. Faculty are encouraged to be creative in their integration of curricular content focusing on issues of advocacy. It is our hope that the following examples will be used as jumping-off points for the creation of a culture of advocacy rather than ends in themselves:

- Introduce students to the Advocacy Competencies as early in their programs as possible, preferably during orientation (preclasses) and in a foundations or introductory class.
- Include specific reading assignments on systems advocacy, sociopolitical advocacy, community collaboration, and evidence-based advocacy throughout the curriculum, related to course-specific topics.
- In an introductory course, have students review the history of the counseling profession from a social advocacy perspective, including an analysis of the positive and negative influence of laws and regulations on the delivery of counseling services. Encourage students to continue to explore such issues in all of their other courses.
- Have students plan and implement an advocacy poster project. Working in teams, they develop posters presenting a course-relevant issue, a summary of related literature, and a description of proposed advocacy roles in addressing the issues and challenges associated with advocating for a specific population across the six Advocacy Competency domains. This can be integrated in a number of classes, such as introduction to the profession, counseling children, career counseling, and so on.
- In an assessment and diagnosis class, have students review a diagnostic category from a socio-political historical perspective, noting trends regarding tendencies for any particular classifications of individuals to be under- or overrepresented with that diagnosis. Include a project in which students research and describe a proposed advocacy strategy that addresses the needs of clients with a specific diagnosis, the associated issues and challenges, and/or the delivery of services.
- Have students participate in legislative training and "legislative days" offered by state counseling professional associations and submit a paper on their experience, including how the training may influence their work with clients and their work setting.
- Across courses, use case studies that include individuals from disenfranchised or marginalized populations, including individuals with disabilities, as a way to help students begin to think about their roles as social advocacy counselors.

Doctoral Preparation for Future Counselor Educators, Researchers, and Supervisors

It cannot be assumed that students who enter doctoral programs have had adequate exposure to concepts of advocacy and social justice during their master's programs. For this reason, we would like to note two important points with regard to recruitment and admissions processes: (a) not relying solely on traditional admissions requirements (Shin, 2008) and (b) including specific questions that help faculty assess the goodness of fit between candidates and the program's goals related to social justice (Osborne et al., 1998). Counselor educators teaching in doctoral programs are in the position to prepare future faculty and supervisors with the advanced knowledge and skills necessary so they may, in turn, prepare master's-level counselors to become competent social justice advocates. To meet this challenge, faculty members need to assess the cultural and advocacy competence of doctoral students once they are admitted and provide opportunities for them to gain advanced knowledge and skills in cultural issues, social change theory, and advocacy action planning. In the following section, we discuss possible strategies to accomplish this end.

Requiring advanced-level courses specific to diversity, advocacy, and leadership provides one venue for both assessing and advancing knowledge and skills of doctoral students pertinent to their own competencies as social advocate counselors. Also important, however, is helping doctoral students develop a strong orientation of conceptualizing their own counseling from a social advocacy perspective. For example, during advanced counseling practicums, it is helpful for students to be required to address how they are using the Advocacy Competencies (from the microlevel to the macrolevel) to guide their case conceptualizations and treatment plans during case presentations and in their case notes. Having students analyze and discuss problems they have experienced with regard to conflicts between organizational or insurance policies and what may be considered "best counseling practices" can also help develop their ability to discern the influence of cultural factors, oppression, and privilege on counseling services. For each example students provide, we suggest they be required to (a) examine when they have acted with clients in the role of "supporter/encourager"; (b) identify when it was or might have been more effective to collaborate with or on behalf of clients in working with school, agency, or community leaders to address issues; and (c) explore the identified issue or problem from a historic and systemic perspective, including delineating laws and written or unwritten policies that may influence the lives of clients. Finally, to prepare doctoral students for their future roles, it is important to facilitate discussions about how they can apply these same types of exercises in their work with master's students both in classes and during supervision.

Doctoral teaching internships are another way for future counselor educators to develop and demonstrate their ability to assess the needs of counselors in training and develop strategies to help students become culturally competent social justice advocates. At the University of Virginia, as is true in many other programs, teaching interns colead master's-level courses with faculty members. This offers an excellent vehicle for students to learn how to address both the Multicultural Counseling Competencies and Advocacy Competencies by coconstructing with their faculty supervisors learning objectives, activities, and assignments that can increase master's-level students' development of advocacy skills and increase their understanding of social justice issues related to specific course topics. Having doctoral students coteach a variety of master's-level courses that infuse a social justice perspective is an excellent way to help doctoral students see how to integrate the Advocacy Competencies across the master's curriculum and in their supervision of counselors-in-training.

With regard to research, Sedlacek (2007) contended that although research alone cannot create social change, it can make a critical difference in advocacy efforts. Counselor educators can foster doctoral students' scholarship related to social justice issues. This can include a wide variety of research topics, focusing on the microadvocacy level (e.g., case studies on welfare recipients who followed certain paths) to the macroadvocacy level (e.g., research on how early detection of HIV/AIDS can be cost-effective for governments and insurance companies). In addition to taking required research classes, students ought to have opportunities to work with faculty members who themselves model a commitment to social justice by the types of research projects they undertake. This provides students an opportunity to learn effective protocols that they can later apply to their own research.

Finally, counselor educators must pay attention to the process of training future supervisors. It is our belief that supervision is equally important to what takes place in the classroom in the development of a social justice advocacy orientation in counselors and that the Advocacy Competencies offer guidance for counseling supervisors as well as for counselors. Because of space limitations, however, our discussion of how supervisors can effectively integrate the Advocacy Competencies into their practice will be brief. We believe that everything previously mentioned with regard to preparing social justice counselors holds true for supervisors and supervision practice. It is also our hope that previous discussions in this chapter provide a foundation from which to envision ways to use the supervisory process to create a culture of advocacy. Following are just a few examples of ways in which faculty and site supervisors can focus their supervision to prepare counselor advocates:

- Intentionally facilitate discussions that foster supervisees' development of critical consciousness. It is easy to get caught up in reviewing cases, logistical matters, discussing what may be happening at practicum or internship sites, and addressing specific questions posed by supervisees. It is important for supervisors to ensure that there is time in supervision to also reflect on issues of oppression and privilege throughout the supervisory relationship (Garcia, Kosutic, McDowell, & Anderson, 2007).
- Use issues of power inherent in most supervisory relationships to help supervisees explore their own issues of power, oppression, and privilege. Empowering supervisees to voice their opinions and understand their own knowledge and expertise and building on their strengths are critical factors to modeling what we hope they do with clients.

- Asking questions that cause supervisees to examine issues of culture and privilege can facilitate the ability of supervisees to recognize power dynamics that may be at play in the lives of their clients (Garcia et al., 2007) as well as in the counseling and supervisory relationships (Borders & Brown, 2005). An example of a reflective question that can be used in supervision is, "How might your personal understanding of growing up in an economically disadvantaged home influence your proposed treatment plan and actions in empowering (or advocating for) this client?"
- Have supervisees analyze the intake or request for services form used in their training clinic or practicum/internship site for indications of assumptions of heterosexism and classism.

Challenges to Implementing the Advocacy Competencies in Counselor Education and Supervision

Taking on the mantle of a culturally competent social justice advocate, counselor, or supervisor is often fraught with multiple emotions as well as role confusion. Even those faculty and supervisors who consider advocacy and topics of power, privilege, and oppression to be important may be reluctant to initiate or engage in such discussions. A variety of reasons for such reluctance have been posited. For example, multicultural counseling and advocacy are relatively recent emphases in training, and supervisees may feel better prepared to engage in dialogue related to diversity and advocacy than their supervisors (Durham, 2002; Garcia et al., 2007; Gatmon et al., 2001). Gatmon et al. noted that some supervisors may deny the relevance of such dialogues to the supervisory process, whereas some may be concerned with being seen as overly concerned about diversity and advocacy, and others may be uncertain of their abilities to effectively manage such dialogues.

Whether one is a student, a faculty member, or a counseling supervisor, the process of becoming aware of one's privileged social location in terms of race, gender, ethnicity, class, sexual orientation, religion, and ability is not always easy or comfortable (Roysicar, Gard, Hubbell, & Ortega, 2005). For a faculty member or supervisor, the process of educating students regarding the issues of privilege, oppression, and inequities may mean opening oneself up to possible scrutiny. As students learn to perceive inequities in the world and the larger community, they may question faculty and challenge injustices they perceive in their program (Osborne et al., 1998). Faculty members and supervisors need to be able to model comfort with examination and scrutiny, both individual and programmatic.

As students become aware of the complexity of the racial/cultural inequities and injustices, their first emotional response may be one of anger. Too often this may lead to immobilization as the students experience the enormity of the task if they were to truly take on the mantle of being a multicultural or social justice advocate. Similarly, students may decide that their singular efforts will have no impact on such a momentous task, so they give up before beginning or find it easier to remain in their predisposed state of apathy (Bemak & Chung, 2008).

The emotional discomfort experienced by students who are examining issues of social injustice may also cause them to close off and thus impede the learning process from moving forward (Harley et al., 2007). Fear, personal apathy, guilt, being labeled as a troublemaker, anger, and powerlessness may all lead to ineffective or inappropriate responses to social injustices (Bemak & Chung, 2008). Fear may come from a number of sources, may interfere with the development of appropriate advocacy role skills, and may ultimately immobilize the developing counselor. There is also the fear of being stigmatized as troublemakers when actively engaged in promoting social justice advocacy and organizational change initiatives (Bemak & Chung, 2008). Other associated fears include the fear of being disliked, of being subjected to negative peer pressure, and of receiving poor performance evaluations or even losing one's job. As Bemak and Chung stated, counselors must be willing to move beyond the "nice counselor syndrome." Bemak and Chung further noted that challenges to the status quo by social justice advocates can lead those in power and even other counselors to raise questions about the counselor's professional competence or personal character. Some researchers have reported professional and character assassination strategies that have been used by organizational leaders to discredit social justice advocates willing to challenge aspects of the status quo that perpetuate unfair policies and practices (Daniels, D'Andrea, & Comstock, 2007). Similarly, others have reported experiencing a backlash from colleagues or harassment from intolerant individuals when they become social justice advocates working to decrease oppressive practices for marginalized populations (Kilselica & Robinson, 2001). Students need to be guided through their fear and discomfort to a place of empathic understanding, as it is that empathy that will assist them in becoming change agents in working with and on behalf of others (Harley et al., 2007).

In addition to the issues already noted, in the process of training for social justice and advocacy work, individuals may experience discomfort with these more nontraditional helping roles (Constantine et al., 2007). Being an advocate or social justice counselor often means that one must move beyond the confines of the office or the role of a direct service provider (microlevel) and into the community or even into governmental administrations (macrolevel) to work with those who have the authority and resources to ultimately effect change in the lives of clients (Kiselica & Robinson, 2001). As students examine their own cultural biases, sociopolitical systems, privileges, and the types of oppression that their clients may be facing, it is not uncommon to feel overwhelmed or powerless to effect significant social change. This may be especially true when students and supervisees think about effecting change beyond the microlevel of advocacy. In addition, there may be counselor educators and supervisors who question whether intervening beyond the microlevel is the responsibility of counselors. This may be due in part to a deficiency in the social justice literature or the ways in which many counselors interpret advocacy work. Kiselica and Robinson (2001) spoke to this issue in an interview with Ward (2006) by stating the following:

> It is important for counselors to identify a style of social justice work that is right for them. One of the shortcomings of the social justice literature is that it tends to create the erroneous impression that you must be extremely vocal to be an effective advocacy counselor. But some counselors advocate in very quiet yet persistent ways to make a positive difference. We must respect these different approaches to advocacy work. (p. 17)

Kiselica and Robinson suggested thinking about a continuum of advocacy work and emphasized the importance of individual comfort and style. In their view, all counselors have a place on that continuum. At the same time, counselor educators and supervisors are in the position to help students and supervisees more critically examine how they may quietly go about the business of effecting change in systems. Regardless of where on the social justice advocacy continuum counselors in training may fall, faculty and supervisors can reinforce the courage that it takes to develop critical consciousness and to practice advocacy, in whatever form that may take. Further, providing numerous opportunities for reflection and processing will assist everyone in developing comfort with their broadened professional role definitions. As students develop comfort with their multiple social locations, they will likely be more willing to adopt a broader array of professional roles and skills (Constantine et al., 2007).

Conclusion

We began this chapter with a focus on the importance of creating a culture of advocacy within counselor education programs. Infusing an advocacy orientation goes beyond merely putting new exercises within existing courses. Curricular process and content issues are addressed as well as administrative considerations. We described strategies for the inclusion of an advocacy orientation as conceptualized in the Advocacy Competencies within master's- and doctoral-level programs and within counseling supervision. We also addressed challenges to implementing the Advocacy Competencies in counselor education programs. In our review of literature related to these issues, it is clear that there has been an increased focus in the past several years of the integration of multiculturalism, advocacy, and social justice in the counseling profession. This focus reflects the passion of many professionals to maximize the likelihood of providing effective counseling services to an increasingly more diverse clientele. It is only recently, however, that the literature reflects a shift from passionate discussions about the importance of preparing culturally competent counselors to the necessity of preparing counselors who can both discern the need to expand the traditional role of counselor to include that of advocate and then also know how to act from an advocacy perspective. What is necessary now is more research on how to most effectively infuse issues of diversity, social justice, and advocacy across the counselor education curriculum and in counseling supervision. Time has come to focus our attention and efforts on developing best practices for the preparation and supervision of social justice counseling advocates.

References

Adams, M., Bell, L. A., & Griffin, P. (1997). *Teaching for diversity and social justice: A source book.* New York: Routledge.

Arredondo, P. (1999). Multicultural counseling competencies as tools to address oppression and racism. *Journal of Counseling & Development, 77,* 102–108.

Arthur, N., & Achenbach, K. (2002). Counselor preparation: Developing multicultural counseling competencies through experiential learning. *Counselor Education and Supervision, 42,* 2–14.

Bemak, F., & Chung, R. C. Y. (2007). Training counselors in social justice. In C. C. Lee (Ed.), *Counseling for social justice* (2nd ed., pp. 239–257). Alexandria, VA: American Counseling Association.

Bemak, F., & Chung, R. C. Y. (2008). New professional roles and advocacy strategies for school counselors: A multicultural/social justice perspective to move beyond the nice counselor syndrome. *Journal of Counseling & Development, 86,* 372–382.

Borders, L. D., & Brown, L. L. (2005). *The new handbook of counseling supervision.* Mahwah, NJ: Lahaska Press.

Connor-Greene, P. A. (2000). Making connections: Evaluating the effectiveness of journal writing in enhancing student learning. *Teaching of Psychology, 27,* 44–46.

Constantine, M. G., Hage, S. M., Kindaichi, M. M., & Bryant, R. M. (2007). Social justice and multicultural issues: Implications for the practice and training of counselors and counseling psychologists. *Journal of Counseling & Development, 85,* 24–29.

Daniels, J., D'Andrea, M., & Comstock, D. (2007, October). *Implementing social justice advocacy and change strategies: Research and practice.* Paper presented at the annual meeting of the Association for Counselor Education and Supervision, Columbus, OH.

Durham, J. (2002). Inclusion of multicultural and diversity issues by field supervisors. *Kentucky Counseling Association Journal, 21,* 27–34.

Freire, P. (1993). *Pedagogy of the oppressed* (Rev. 20th anniversary ed.). New York: Continuum.

Garcia, M., Kosutic, I., McDowell, T., & Anderson, S. (2007). *Critical supervision.* Unpublished manuscript.

Gatmon, D., Jackson, D., Koshkariahn, L., Martos-Perry, N., Molina, A., Patel, N., et al. (2001). Exploring ethnic, gender, and sexual orientation variables in supervision: Do they really matter? *Journal of Multicultural Counseling and Development, 29,* 102–113.

Goodman, L. A., Liang, B., Helms, J. E., Latta, R. E., Sparks, E., & Weintraub, S. R. (2004). Training counseling psychologists as social justice agents: Feminist and multicultural principles in action. *The Counseling Psychologist, 32,* 793–837.

Harley, D. A., Alston, R. J., & Middleton, R. A. (2007). Infusing social justice into rehabilitation education: Making a case for curricula refinement. *Rehabilitation Education, 21,* 41–52.

Kiselica, M. (2004). When duty calls: The implications of social justice work for policy, education, and practice in the mental health professions. *The Counseling Psychologist, 32,* 838–854.

Kiselica, M., & Robinson, M. (2001). Bringing advocacy counseling to life: The history, issues, and human dramas of social justice work in counseling. *Journal of Counseling & Development, 79,* 387–397.

Lee, C. C. (1997). The global future of professional counseling: Collaboration for international social change. *International Journal of Intercultural Relations, 21,* 279–285.

Lewis, J. A., Arnold, M. S., House, R., & Toporek, R. L. (2002). *ACA Advocacy Competencies.* Retrieved August 4, 2008, from http://www.counseling.org/Publications/

McDowell, T., & Shelton, D. M. (2002). Valuing ideas of social justice in MFT curricula. *Contemporary Family Therapy, 24,* 313–331.

Osborne, J. L., Collison, B. B., House, R. M., Gray, L. A., Firth, J., & Lou, M. (1998). Developing a social advocacy model for counselor education. *Counselor Education and Supervision, 37,* 190–203.

Pope-Davis, D. B., Breaux, C., & Liu, W. M. (1997). A multicultural immersion experience: Filling a void in multicultural training. In D. B. Pope-Davis & H. L. K. Coleman (Eds.), *Multicultural counseling competencies: Assessment, education and training, and supervision* (pp. 227–241). Thousand Oaks, CA: Sage.

Ridley, C. R., & Lingle, D. W. (1996). Cultural empathy in multicultural counseling: A multidimensional process. In P. Pederson, W. Lonner, & J. Draguns (Eds.), *Counseling across cultures* (pp. 21–45). Thousand Oaks, CA: Sage.

Rogers, M. R., & Molina, L. (2006). Exemplary efforts in psychology to recruit and retain graduate students of color. *American Psychologist, 61,* 143–156.

Romano, J., & Hage, S. (2000). Prevention and counseling psychology: Revitalizing commitments for the 21st century. *The Counseling Psychologist, 28,* 733–763.

Roysicar, G., Gard, G., Hubbell, R., & Ortega, M. (2005). Development of multicultural counseling trainees' multicultural awareness through mentoring English as a second language students. *Journal of Multicultural Counseling and Development, 33,* 17–36.

Sedlacek, W. E. (2007). Conducting research that makes a difference. In L. C. Courtland (Ed.), *Counseling for social justice* (pp. 223–237). Alexandria, VA: American Counseling Association.

Shin, R. Q. (2008). Advocating for social justice in academia through recruitment, retention, admissions and professional survival. *Journal of Multicultural Counseling and Development, 36,* 180–191.

Sue, D. W. (2008). Multicultural organizational consultation: A social justice perspective. *Consulting Psychology Journal: Practice and Research, 60,* 157–169.

Sue, D. W., Arredondo, P., & McDavis, R. J. (1992). Multicultural counseling competencies and standards: A call to the profession. *Journal of Counseling & Development, 70,* 477–486.

Sue, D. W., Carter, R. T., Casas, J. M., Fouad, N. A., Ivey, A. E., Jensen, M., et al. (1998). *Multicultural counseling competencies: Individual and organizational development.* Thousand Oaks, CA: Sage.

Sue, D. W., & Sue, D. (1990). *Counseling the culturally different: Theory and practice.* New York: Wiley.

Talleyrand, R. M., Chung, R. C.-Y., & Bemak, F. (2006). Incorporating social justice in counselor education programs. In R. L. Toporek, L. H. Gerstein, N. A. Fouad, G. Roysicar, & T. Israel (Eds.), *The handbook for social justice counseling in counseling psychology: Leadership, vision and action* (pp. 44–58). Thousand Oaks, CA: Sage.

Toporek, R. L., Lewis, J. A., & Crethar, H. C. (2009). Promoting systemic change through the ACA Advocacy Competencies. *Journal of Counseling & Development, 87,* 260–268.

Vera, E. M., & Speight, S. L. (2003). Multicultural competence, social justice, and counseling psychology: Expanding our roles. *The Counseling Psychologist, 31,* 253–272.

Ward, C. C. (2006, February). Catalysts to becoming a 'change agent': An interview with Mark Kiselica. *Counseling Today, 48*(8), 16–17, 23.

Chapter 15

Assessment in Counseling: A Tool for Social Justice Work

Chris Wood and Jerome V. D'Agostino

For many counselors in training, course work in assessment, tests and measurements, and appraisal is something of a bitter pill. For counselors operating from a social justice perspective, the use of assessment may also raise concerns about the further victimization and marginalizing of vulnerable and underserved individuals and groups in U.S. society. There can be no doubt that assessment has been used in horrible ways to justify policies of social injustice (Gould, 1981). However, assessment has also contributed to eliminating horribly unjust policy, as in the 1954 case of *Brown v. Board of Education* (Jackson, 2001). Counselors who do not understand assessment may be ill equipped to protect against the misuse of assessment to victimize individuals/groups (and may even unwittingly participate in using assessment to further victimize), and they may be unable to optimize the use of assessment as a tool in actualizing the American Counseling Association (ACA) Advocacy Competencies (Lewis, Arnold, House, & Toporek, 2002; Ratts, DeKruyf, & Chen-Hayes, 2007) and counseling for social justice.

This chapter examines the use of assessment as a strategy for employing the Advocacy Competencies. First, we discuss the use of assessment within the context of social justice. Second, we outline up-to-date knowledge requisite for a counselor to be competent in the area of assessment. Finally, we describe the connection between the Advocacy Competencies and assessment, illustrating assessment at the client/student level, the community/school level, and the public arena level.

Assessment in the Context of Social Justice

In the counseling profession, using assessment from a social justice perspective means that counselors can work to ensure assessments are not used to further social injustices, whether on the microlevel with students/clients or the macrolevel as part of discriminatory policies. Moreover, assessments can be used as a means for furthering social justice, whether empowering individuals, identifying the need for advocacy with and on behalf of clients/students, or initiating change at the systems level.

There have been emerging efforts from the counseling profession to use assessment in a socially just fashion. Vacc (1998) called for counselors to take a more profound exploration of assessment practices in the context of social justice: "Counselors need to examine the quality and usefulness of assessment activities that are available relative to how such assessments may negatively affect clients"

(p. 180). Sedlacek (1994) similarly warned of prevalent concerns regarding the use of assessments with diverse populations (e.g., labeling, single measures, sampling bias, lack of knowledge about diversity issues by assessment users, and nondevelopmental research on multicultural groups). Prediger (1994) postulated that assessment can be beneficial to culturally diverse populations when counselors follow the appropriate professional standards and guidelines. The Joint Committee on Testing Practices updated the *Code of Fair Testing Practices in Education* in 2004. This committee includes representation from the ACA, the American Educational Research Association (AERA), the American Psychological Association (APA), the American Speech-Language-Hearing Association, the National Association of School Psychologists, the National Association of Test Directors, and the National Council on Measurement in Education (NCME). The Association for Assessment in Counseling (2003) updated the *Standards for Multicultural Assessment*, building on Prediger's earlier work.

So, it would seem that the profession of counseling recognizes the necessity of providing guidelines and standards for counselors regarding the use of assessment to protect vulnerable populations. The Advocacy Competencies also provide guidelines for counselors using assessment. When assessment is used within the framework of the Advocacy Competencies, counselors can move beyond ensuring assessments are not used to victimize to ensuring they are used as instruments for social justice.

Requisite Knowledge in Assessment

To appropriately use assessment at the micro- or macrolevels, counselors must first have an understanding of assessment principles, including current knowledge in the field of assessment. Without an up-to-date understanding of assessment principles and psychometric properties of instruments, counselors will not be able to use assessment to assist with empowerment and advocacy at the individual, community/school, and public arena levels.

There are several resources describing what counselors need to know about assessment. The American Counseling Association (2003) published a policy statement outlining seven areas of requisite competence with respect to using tests. Similarly, Moreland, Eyde, Roberston, Primoff, and Most (1995) described 12 essential competencies for counselors using tests. Moreover, the Association for Assessment in Counseling and Education (2009) published guidelines and competencies in the following areas available via their website:

- Code of Fair Testing Practices in Education
- Standards for Multicultural Assessment
- Preemployment Testing and the American With Disabilities Act of 1990
- Responsibilities of Users of Standardized Tests
- Competencies in Assessment and Evaluation for School Counselors
- Standards for Qualifications of Test Users
- Test Taker Rights and Responsibilities

Krieshok and Black (2009) provided a practical checklist that counselors can use to evaluate their testing competencies and practices. This checklist was developed based on many of the standards described above as well as resources such as Sandoval, Frisby, Geisinger, Scheuneman, and Grenier's (1998) text, *Test Interpretation and Diversity: Achieving Equity in Assessment*. The relevant ethics and competencies outlined by professional associations such as the ACA, AERA, APA, and joint commissions from these and other professional associations are as important as the key knowledge we outline below.

Counselors should have, at a minimum, a basic understanding of how to evaluate reliability and validity evidence provided by publishers of tests, and they should be well grounded in how to interpret accurately and cautiously the test results. Graduate programs for counselors commonly require at least one course in measurement and testing, and the AERA, APA, and NCME (1999) have released the *Standards for Educational and Psychological Testing* about every 10 years since the mid-1950s.

Providing a detailed explication of the reliability and validity issues pertinent for counselors is beyond the scope of this chapter, but certain key principles are critical for the proper use and interpretation of tests for counselors. Many myths and misconceptions about tests and test scores exist throughout the professions, and it is important for counselors to avoid these potential pitfalls.

Perhaps the most pronounced misconception in testing is the belief that a test possesses a certain degree of reliability and validity, which holds across a variety of testing purposes and context. This belief is incorrect for two primary reasons. First, it is not the test itself that possesses reliability and validity, rather it is the scores from examinees that are the focus of reliability and validity analyses. This difference might seem minor, but quite the contrary. Scores from first-grade examinees from underserved backgrounds and scores from third graders from a rural community on the same test might differ dramatically in reliability and validity. Second, even for the same examinees, test scores might not be reliable and valid for all possible purposes and interpretations. For example, a state's standards-based assessment scores might accurately reflect the degree to which students attained the state standards but might not properly indicate placement in special education or gifted programs or the quality of a school's curriculum and instruction. Counselors should carefully read the information provided by test publishers, typically found in the test's manual, to determine the specific inferences that can be safely drawn about the scores for specific examinee populations. Usually, test sponsors and publishers collect reliability and validity evidence to support the proper use of the test within rather narrow contexts.

Another common myth about testing is that reliability is a uniform concept and that various reliability analyses will yield similar results. Reliability can refer to the repeatability of test scores yielded across time and testing circumstances (test–retest reliability), but it can also mean the consistency of examinees' performance on items from the same test taken in one sitting (internal consistency) or the consistency or agreement of judges or scorers (rater reliability). Typically, test publishers collect and disseminate information on internal consistency reliability, mainly because it requires only one test administration and is quite efficient to compute. Yet knowing that test scores possess respectable internal consistency reliability indicates little about the repeatability of scores over time or settings for a group of examinees. Hypothetically, the examinees could take the test again 2 weeks later and produce discrepant scores, even if the internal consistency was good on the first administration. Thus, if repeatability is an important characteristic of scores for the counselor, expect the publisher to provide test–retest reliability coefficients.

Not only can test–retest and internal consistency reliability values differ, but the several methods available to compute internal consistency reliability often render a range of coefficients. Some methods, such as the Kuder–Richardson Formula 21 or KR-21, systematically produce lower reliability estimates than other methods, such as the alpha coefficient or split-half procedure. It is advisable to use the average or median of the available internal consistency estimates and to consider the range of values when evaluating a test for a given purposes. The counselor should be leery of the technical manual that provides just one estimate of reliability.

Another myth is that test scores should have a specific reliability value. There is no reliability value that is acceptable across the array of tests, examinees, and testing situations. Scores based on shorter tests typically yield lower reliability estimates, as do scores from younger examinees (e.g., primary grade students) and tests that attempt to cover a broader range of topics and skills. Because tests that need to be scored by judges include the additional error attributed to raters, scores based on such tests commonly are less reliable than so-called objective exams. Counselors also should consider the stakes or consequences that will result from interpreting and using the scores. Tests used to select or place students in educational programs, diagnose learning deficiencies, or help students discover their career interest have high stakes for students' lives, so those exams should yield very reliable scores, such as .80 or higher internal consistency and test–retest values. Acceptable reliability estimates for scores from less consequential tests, such as an attitudinal survey, might be less than .80. Again, a test is not a test; the counselor must consider the testing circumstances and ramifications for examinees.

Often test users believe that reliability and validity are interchangeable terms. The concepts are related but not synonymous. As stated, reliability refers to the consistency of scores across items, time, situations, or judges. But just because scores are repeatable does not mean the scores possess adequate validity. The latter concept refers to the degree to which the scores accurately reflect the attribute the scores are expected to measure. Thus, career inventory scores would have good validity if the scores truly indicate the vocational interests of the examinee. Because most attributes measured by counselors are relatively enduring attributes, one should expect the scores to have acceptable reliability estimates. Reliability, therefore, is the basis for validity, but it is not sufficient to make a claim that test scores are measuring what they are expected to measure.

In terms of validity, it is commonly misconstrued that validity is a single, unitary concept. There are several facets of validity that work in concert to evaluate the soundness of validity claims. Besides yielding consistent scores, a test should contain items that accurately represent the domain that defines the attribute to be measured. For example, a test purported to measure mathematical problem solving should contain an adequate representation of items that require examinees to solve mathematical problems, and it should not possess a disproportional number of items that merely require the student to compute numbers. Often content validation is established in the test construction process, so the test publisher should provide a complete description about how items were generated in the technical manual.

Not only should the test contain an adequate sample of items representing the domain, it should not possess too many items that require knowledge, skills, or dispositions that cloud the measurement of the target attributes. For example, a problem-solving exam should not contain verbose or linguistically complicated items that demand good language skills to simply understand the problem. If it did, the test then would be as much a measure of comprehension as an indicator of problem solving. Such construct-irrelevant information often is the cause of item bias, in which an examinee from a certain group might be at a disadvantage in accurately expressing his or her target attributes. For instance, an English Language Learner would be disadvantaged while taking the verbose problem-solving test. To support social justice in testing, the counselor should appraise a test to determine whether the items contain any construct-irrelevant information that lead to unfair testing. Counselors should also expect test publishers to conduct item and test bias analyses and report the findings in the technical report.

Test publishers also should report evidence pertaining to the degree to which test scores converge with scores from other assessments designed to measure the same attributes and diverge with measures of dissimilar attributes. If certain groups are known to differ on a given attribute, the test publisher could document test scores differences between the groups. There is not one particular set of validity analyses that is suitable for all tests and circumstances, but instead, an argument supported by empirical evidence should be made to support the inferences to be drawn from test scores.

It is the counselor's responsibility to weigh the strength of the existing evidence to determine the soundness of the argument in favor of a test's use. Having a fundamental knowledge of assessment and social justice relative to different human populations is vital if the counselor can accurately evaluate the quality of evidence. As Sedlacek (1994) stated,

> There are many graduate programs that turn out methodologists with good technical and quantitative skills, but few of these graduates have even a rudimentary appreciation of racial and cultural variables, let alone any sense of how to measure them. Conversely, those most interested in cultural and racial variables tend to have little training or interest in quantification or assessment. (pp. 551–552)

Assessment as Advocacy Competencies in Action

Client/Student Level

Few interventions may be as empowering on the individual level as the use of career assessments, when used properly by a trained counselor as a part of broadening career opportunities for individuals from marginalized groups. Gysbers and Lapan (2009) proposed career assessments as a potentially powerful means to assist people in becoming self-advocates.

With respect to empowerment, the Advocacy Competency calls for identifying strengths and resources of clients/students as well as identifying oppressive environmental and social factors that affect the client/student. Administering the Strong Interest Inventory (SII), Skills Confidence Inventory (SCI), and StrengthsFinder 2.0 can illustrate how the use of career assessments exemplifies the Advocacy Competencies at the client/student level. The SII, SCI, and StrengthsFinder 2.0 are used below to provide specific examples of assessments. Yet there is a wide range of career assessments that a counselor can use as a foundation for client empowerment and client/student advocacy (Whitfield, Feller, & Wood, 2009).

The SII measures a client/student's career interests in six occupational areas, and the SCI measures an individual's perceived level of confidence in performing skills related to those same six occupational areas. The StrengthsFinder 2.0 is an online measure that investigates an individual's talents from 34 themes. The SII and StrengthsFinder 2.0 can be used by counselors to help individuals identify their career interests and areas of strength, and they can be used as a foundation for developing action plans to achieve personal vocational potential. Such action plans can (and should) involve self-advocacy from the client/student and may require the counselor advocating on behalf of and/or with the client/student to overcome institutional and social barriers. Similarly, the SCI can help to identify career areas of high interest where an individual lacks confidence. Often this lack of confidence is in response to systemic or internalized oppression. A counselor can subsequently explore the social, political, economic, and cultural factors that are affecting this discrepancy between interest and confidence to facilitate client/student empowerment and identify specific areas in need of client/student advocacy. Subsequently, a counselor may take such action as to help the individual access financial assistance in pursuit of career goals or contact government agencies such as the Equal Employment Opportunities Commission to help an individual overcome discriminatory practices that are preventing career goal advancement.

Community/School Level

At the community/school level, counselors can identify organizational issues by administering social climate instruments. In addition, counselors can recognize vulnerable groups in need of specialized counseling interventions by disaggregating assessment data. Consider the following community and school examples.

Community

A counseling agency director gave the counselors she supervises the Fundamental Interpersonal Relations Orientation–Behavior, more commonly referred to as FIRO-B (Schutz, 1958), to measure their perceptions of inclusion, control, and affection with respect to being members of the agency. She discovered that many of the counselors of color perceived less control and felt less included in the agency. Moreover, exploring the policies and procedures for client intake revealed inequities in assigned counselor caseloads.

An Employee Assistance Program (EAP) community counselor consulting with the human resources department of a local organization administered the Workplace Prejudice/Discrimination Inventory (James, Lovato, & Cropanzano, 1994). The results revealed that prejudices and discrimination existed. In response to the data, the organization conducted workshops on valuing diversity. In addition, the counselor increased the available support groups for employees and worked with the organization to enact more explicit policies to protect the employee rights of populations vulnerable to discrimination.

School

A high school counselor conducted a needs assessment of the students and teachers at her school. As part of this needs assessment, she included the Situational Attitude Survey (Sedlacek & Brooks, 1972) to explore how prejudice exists and toward what specific racial/ethnic groups. The needs assessment also explored school climate and safety concerns, specifically in the area of sexual harassment based on gender and sexual orientation. This needs assessment identified several areas of concern regarding maltreatment of students of color; lesbian, gay, bisexual, transgender, and questioning (LGBTQ) students; and students perceived to be LGBTQ in the school. Equipped with this knowledge, the school counselor worked with building administrators to help arrange for a schoolwide Safe Space training for teachers. The school counselor also presented the data to the school leadership team, which subsequently collaborated to develop clearer student conduct policies around the use of oppressive language and other discriminative behavior.

Archival school data can also be a source for using assessment toward greater social justice at the school level. One middle school counselor was able to disaggregate her school's achievement data beyond the typical gender and racial/ethnic categories. Given the diversity of the Asian student body, her school was able to disaggregate the data for students of Asian ancestry into the subgroups of South Indian, Chinese, Korean, Vietnamese, Hmong, Lao, and Japanese ancestry. This level of disaggregation identified an educationally vulnerable Hmong student population in need of specialized counseling support and educational interventions. As an example of community collaboration, the school counselor and principal conducted focus groups with the local Hmong community. Together, they strategized culturally responsive educational supports, including a lunchtime mentoring program and afterschool tutoring done in coordination with the Hmong community.

Public Arena Level

Each of the examples of using assessment to enact the Advocacy Competencies described above can be extended to exemplify advocacy at the public arena level. The same assessment data used to guide school/community-level advocacy efforts can also contribute to macrolevel advocacy in the form of both public information and the social/political advocacy domains.

Community

The EAP counselor described above could easily develop policy briefs as a form of providing public information to local media and state legislatures. At present, 30 of 50 states in the United States do not have specific laws prohibiting discrimination in the workplace based on sexual orientation. As a mental health expert with supporting relevant assessment data, the counselor's policy brief could be an important advocacy tool. Gysbers and Lapan (2009) proposed a two-page format for developing policy briefs oriented toward public advocacy.

Moreover, the counselor might also develop alliances with local agencies and political groups in making allies and supporting concerted efforts toward greater political change. As a mental health expert able to articulate the human costs of such maltreatment, the counselor is in a unique position to assist in efforts toward lobbying legislatures to help provide stronger legal protections for vulnerable clients. Moreover, a competent counselor can use assessment data to support the prevalence of the discrimination concerns.

School

The school counselor can make similar efforts to operate at the public arena level. A school counselor can also provide a policy brief for teachers, parents, and community as a means of increasing awareness. The building-level efforts might easily be replicated districtwide as mandatory trainings for educators. The school counselor can present at a school board meeting and lobby the school board toward developing district goals (and subsequent districtwide policies) aimed at ameliorating issues of injustice/inequity and protecting educationally vulnerable populations.

Benefits and Challenges

Using assessment presents both potential benefits and subsequent challenges. In summarizing some of the points made above, we conceptualize the benefits to using assessment in the categories of access, equity, and measurable objective.

Access

Through assessment, counselors can ensure that individuals and groups are receiving equitable access to programs and services. Counselors can ensure that assessments themselves (and assessments used to qualify individuals for educational programs or placement) are available in a language and format most optimal for a person or group.

Some assessments help individuals qualify for services. Without such an assessment, the individual might not receive necessary financial assistance or mental health services. Using knowledge of reliability and standard error of measurement for a given instrument, counselors have been known to advocate for an individual's access to an educational institution, a training program, and even specific social services.

Equity

Some individuals and groups are in positions of disadvantage in comparison with the dominant group in society. Assessment can help counselors identify individuals and groups in need of equity with respect to the majority or dominant group in society. The counselor using assessment as a means of striving for greater equity benefits from the data that illustrate such inequities. Using the data, counselors can access grants and external funding to better serve individuals or groups as well as advocate on different levels for additional services/programming for the underserved.

Measurable Objective

Sometimes issues of social justice are dismissed by counselors or administrators as being "too political" or a "soap box" issue from an individual counselor. Assessment results that identify issues of access and equity, however, present the problem in a concrete material fashion that cannot be dismissed as any one individual's agenda. Moreover, as the assessment results identify a lack of access or equity, a goal of ameliorating the inequity is established. One benefit of assessment, then, is that it creates a measurable objective.

Challenges

The counselor using assessment from a social justice perspective can expect to encounter several challenges. The first challenge may be the counselor's own lack of knowledge or training in assessment. Similarly, the counselor may lack similar knowledge about cultural diversity and issues of socioeconomic status as they relate to people in society or the field of assessment. Counselors must rise to defeat this challenge through professional development in assessment and culturally responsive counseling.

Counselors using assessment toward access and equity may be identifying issues and concerns that are unpopular in organizations or society. Administrators, leaders, and even colleagues sometimes do not want to hear about how professional counselors, schools, or agencies are perpetuating inequity or a lack of access through the improper use of assessment (or may refuse to respond to the call toward equity as identified through assessment). Counselors must remain ever vigilant and use the benefit of assessments results as a concrete and observable measure of inequity for all of us to address social justice in counseling practice.

Conclusion

In this chapter, we outlined the use of assessment as a means of putting into action the ACA Advocacy Competencies. Using assessment at the client/student, community/school, and public arena levels can assist in counseling for social justice. Although we provided an overview of necessary knowledge in the field of assessment and some parsimonious examples of how a counselor might use assessment at the macro- and microlevels, social justice and assessment are much more complicated issues than presented here. Wrenn (1962) in his seminal text, *The Counselor in a Changing World,* pointed out the importance of a counselor being an expert in socioeconomic issues as well as counseling theory. Similarly, as mentioned previously, Sedlacek (1994) highlighted the importance of experts in measurement being knowledgeable experts on diverse human groups and not abdicating responsibility for being an expert on assessment. Holzer and Ludwig (2003) pointed out that assessment methodologies used to identify discriminative practices in social enterprises such as housing and labor markets can be used to identify discrimination in education and even—dare we say it—discriminative practices in how counseling services and interventions are administered and how theoretical counseling orientations serve marginalized populations. Assessment can help ensure social justice in counseling just as counselors can use assessment for social justice.

References

American Counseling Association. (2003). *Standards for qualifications for test users.* Alexandria, VA: Author. Retrieved February 10, 2009, from http://www.theaaceonline.com/standards.pdf

American Educational Research Association, American Psychological Association, & National Council on Measurement in Education. (1999). *Standards for educational and psychological testing.* Washington, DC: American Educational Research Association.

Association for Assessment in Counseling. (2003). *Standards for multicultural assessment.* Retrieved February 10, 2009, from http://www.theaaceonline.com/multicultural.pdf

Association for Assessment in Counseling and Education. (2009). *Resources.* Retrieved March 5, 2009, from http://www.theaaceonline.com/resources.htm

Gould, S. J. (1981). *The mismeasure of man.* New York: Norton.

Gysbers, N. C., & Lapan, R. T. (2009). Using assessment for personal, program, and policy advocacy. In E. A. Whitfield, R. W. Feller, & C. Wood (Eds.), *A counselor's guide to career assessment instruments* (5th ed., pp. 35–42). Broken Arrow, OK: National Career Development Association.

Holzer, H. J., & Ludwig, J. (2003). Measuring discrimination in education: Are methodologies from labor and markets useful? *Teachers College Record, 105,* 1147–1178.

Jackson, J. P. (2001). *Social scientists for social justice: Making the case against segregation.* New York: New York University Press.

James, K., Lovato, C., & Cropanzano, R. (1994). Correlational and known-group comparison validation of a workplace prejudice/discrimination inventory. *Journal of Applied Social Psychology, 24,* 1573–1592.

Joint Committee on Testing Practices. (2004). *Code of fair testing practices in education.* Washington, DC: Author. Retrieved February 10, 2009, from http://www.theaaceonline.com/codefair.pdf

Krieshok, T. S., & Black, M. D. (2009). Assessment and counseling competencies and responsibilities: A checklist for counselors. In E. A. Whitfield, R. W. Feller, & C. Wood (Eds.), *A counselor's guide to career assessment instruments* (5th ed., pp. 61–68). Broken Arrow, OK: National Career Development Association.

Lewis, J. A., Arnold, M. S., House, R., & Toporek, R. L. (2002). *ACA Advocacy Competencies.* Retrieved February 10, 2009, from http://www.counseling.org/Publications/

Moreland, K. L., Eyde, L. D., Robertson, G. J., Primoff, E. S., & Most, R. B. (1995). Assessment of test user qualifications: A research-based measurement procedure. *American Psychologist, 50,* 14–23.

Prediger, D. (1994). Multicultural assessment standards: A compilation for counselors. *Measurement and Evaluation in Counseling and Development, 27,* 68–74.

Ratts, M. J., DeKruyf, L., & Chen-Hayes, S. F. (2007). The ACA Advocacy Competencies: A social justice advocacy framework for professional school counselors. *Professional School Counseling, 11,* 90–97.

Sandoval, J., Frisby, C. L., Geisinger, K. F., Scheuneman, J. D., & Grenier, J. R. (Eds.). (1998). *Test interpretation and diversity: Achieving equity in assessment.* Washington, DC: American Psychological Association.

Schutz, W. (1958). *FIRO: A three-dimensional theory of interpersonal behavior.* New York: Holt, Rinehart & Winston.

Sedlacek, W. E. (1994). Issues in advancing diversity through assessment. *Journal of Counseling & Development, 72,* 549–553.

Sedlacek, W. E., & Brooks, G. C. (1972). *Situational Attitude Scale (SAS) manual.* Chicago: Natresources.

Vacc, N. A. (1998). Fair access to assessment instruments and the use of assessment in counseling. In C. C. Lee & G. R. Walz (Eds.), *Social action: A mandate for counselors* (pp. 179–198). Alexandria, VA: American Counseling Association.

Whitfield, E. A., Feller, R., & Wood, C. (Eds.). (2009). *A counselor's guide to career assessment instruments* (5th ed.). Broken Arrow, OK: National Career Development Association.

Wrenn, C. G. (1962). *The counselor in a changing world.* Washington, DC: American Personnel and Guidance Association.

Chapter

16

Substance Abuse Counseling and Social Justice Advocacy

Judith A. Lewis and Jacqueline Elder

On occasion, we hear a counselor say something like, "I see all kinds of clients in my practice but I always steer clear of working with substance abuse or addictions." Of course, given the ubiquitous nature of substance abuse, no counselor could possibly avoid all of the students or clients who are affected by it. What these counselors might really mean is that they could never feel comfortable relating to people in the way that they imagine addiction counselors are forced to deal with their clients. And who could blame them?

In the field of substance abuse, a set of myths has been disseminated throughout the United States. This mythology as a whole is built on the premise that people who are grappling with issues related to addictions or substance abuse somehow belong in a different category of species from other human beings. The implication of the myths is that the collaborative partnerships that counselors like to build with their students and clients must suddenly be put aside when alcohol or other drugs find their way into the conversation. The stereotype about how substance abuse counselors must operate has become a self-propelling "conventional wisdom" that inspires avid belief with no basis in fact.

> The treatment of addictive behaviors has sometimes been thought to require aggressive confrontation, a tearing down of defenses, coercion, and a wariness to avoid being deceived or conned…. Such an approach casts the therapist in the role of powerful expert, who must impart to a passive and resistant addict the necessary knowledge, wisdom, insight, and motivation for change. (Miller, 1996, p. 840)

If counselors actually had to abide by this kind of conventional wisdom when working with addiction-related issues, advocacy-oriented counselors would obviously have to say, "Thanks, but no thanks."

- The American Counseling Association (ACA) Advocacy Competencies (Lewis, Arnold, House, & Toporek, 2002) tell us to help our clients find their own power, while the conventional wisdom wants them to disown their power of personal choice—even over the question of whether they have a need to change.

- The Advocacy Competencies tell us to help our clients recognize the impact of oppression, while the conventional wisdom wants them to find the source of all their problems within themselves.
- The Advocacy Competencies tell us to break down barriers to our clients' development, while the conventional wisdom insists that the clients—not the environment—must change.

Fortunately, the conventional wisdom fails to appear on any list of evidence-based practices for treating addictions. It has been known for decades that some of the most promising approaches include methods such as social skills training, behavioral self-control training, behavioral couples counseling, community reinforcement, and motivational interviewing (Holder, Longabough, Miller, & Rubonis, 1991), all of which can comfortably coexist with social justice advocacy. Although the old myths hang on in the public consciousness, the field of addictions has begun to move on.

Motivational Interviewing

Motivational Interviewing provides an example of a style of interaction that fits well with the empowerment orientation that is implicit in advocacy. Motivational Interviewing was introduced to substance abuse professionals when Miller and Rollnick (1991) published *Motivational Interviewing: Preparing People to Change Addictive Behavior*. For some counselors, this alternative to harsh confrontation seemed even then to be a breath of fresh air. The Motivational Interviewing "MI Spirit" brings to many counselors a sense of coming home to a philosophy that matches their own values and their own senses of how the change process works. Counselors are obviously comfortable with the notion that the client's ideas about change should be elicited and accepted. Counselors generally approve of the concept that the client's autonomy is worthy of support. Implicit in these ideas, however, is the assumption that clients are responsible for their own decisions about whether to change, when to change, and how to change. For many people in the substance abuse field, the thought that clients should be "allowed" to continue behaviors that were obviously dangerous was hard to take. They would have to believe or, even worse, say to a client, "You are free to do what you choose, it is your right to decide, and you may or may not decide to change." Motivational Interviewing must have seemed to many helping professionals like a radical change from existing philosophies for dealing with substance use and abuse. In fact, they were right. Adopting Motivational Interviewing represents an alteration of core assumptions about people, about addictions, and about the change process. Further, it forces the helper to move from a focus on diagnosable problems to the unlikely state of what W. R. Miller (personal communication, February 18, 2009) suggested is "pathological optimism." Motivational Interviewing, like an advocacy orientation, represents not a methodology to be added to existing tools but rather a new style of interaction based on different assumptions.

Over time, Motivational Interviewing has gradually moved to the center of accepted practice in working with substance abuse and other health risk behaviors. One of the explanations for this attitudinal transformation lies in the fact that the research studies supporting its efficacy became too numerous for even the most vociferous skeptics to ignore (Hettema, Steele, & Miller, 2005; Rubak, Sandboek, Lauritzen, & Christensen, 2005). Another reason—less measurable but perhaps just as compelling—is the fact that the number of counselors who were attracted to the idea of actually using their listening skills and empathy reached a critical mass, allowing for training opportunities and for mutual support in the face of pressure to conform.

Harm Reduction

The concept of harm reduction is just as controversial as Motivational Interviewing and even more relevant to advocacy. Harm reduction outreach is "the philosophy and practice of respectfully collaborating with people to assist any positive change as a person defines it for him/herself and begins where the person is at with no biases or condemnation for the person's chosen lifestyle" (Chicago Recovery Alliance, 2009). The principles underlying harm reduction include the following (Marlatt, 1998):

1. Harm reduction is a public health alternative to the moral/criminal and disease models of drug use and addiction (p. 49).
2. Harm reduction recognizes abstinence as an ideal outcome but accepts alternatives that reduce harm (p. 50).
3. Harm reduction has emerged primarily as a "bottom-up" approach based on addict advocacy, rather than a "top-down" policy promoted by drug policymakers (p. 52).
4. Harm reduction promotes low-threshold access to services as an alternative to traditional, high-threshold approaches (p. 54).

Most people assume that the "moral/criminal" and "disease" models are opposites. Both share, however, an assumption that drug use is inherently bad (whether sinful or pathological) and should be eliminated. Neither model recognizes the possibility of a shorter term solution: reducing the harm caused by drug use even when the ultimate goal of abstinence has not yet been achieved. Marlatt's (1998) suggestion that harm reduction is a bottom-up approach recognizes the fact that many practical harm reduction methods have come into being in response to informal needs assessments carried out by drug users, supportive community members, and concerned health care workers. An important example of this process involves the grassroots advocacy movement for the provision of clean needles. As long as policymakers and treatment providers withhold help from people who are not ready to take the abstinence route, new cases of HIV infection that could have been prevented will be ignored. And *ignored* is not too strong a word. Treatment programs built on the old conventional wisdom routinely require that clients abstain from drug use, not as a treatment outcome but as a precondition for receiving services. Setting this high a threshold for entry into treatment reflects a judgmental stance that could endanger those who are not ready to adhere to externally placed objectives.

A harm reduction approach can be very beneficial to individual clients and students. Van Wormer (1999) suggested that, in contrast with formulations that focus on problems, labels, and powerlessness, the harm reduction model, with its positive acceptance of the client's potential for growth, is entirely congruent with a strengths-based counseling style. Moreover, harm reduction has a great deal to add to a social justice perspective at the societal level. Just as narrow and judgmental views tend to make it difficult to meet the needs of individuals, they also have impact on policy at the national level. Several years ago, Senator Dick Durbin of Illinois responded to a rash of drug overdoses in Chicago that were brought about by heroin laced with fentanyl. He made these comments on the floor of the United States Senate, supporting a bill that did not pass at that time.

> The time has come to put an end to these tragedies. I urge my colleagues to join me in supporting the Drug Overdose Reduction Act to bring resources to community-based efforts to prevent unnecessary deaths by providing information about the dangers of drug abuse, how to find help to break addictions, and how to stay alive in the interim. (Durbin, 2006)

A harm reduction model, like a social justice advocacy model, recognizes that the lives of people who are addicted to heroin are worth saving, even if those lives do not fit one's assumptions about what a good lifestyle should be.

Advocacy-oriented counselors can make a tremendous difference in the lives of people who are affected by substance abuse. Although counselors might not feel comfortable with the old conventional wisdom regarding substance abuse, they can find allies among helpers whose work with clients and students is based on motivational interviewing, harm reduction, and other evidence-based practices.

Operationalizing the Advocacy Competencies

Counselors address substance-abuse-related issues across every setting and specialty of the counseling profession. A counselor might be a substance abuse specialist whose work takes place in a treatment facility or a counselor who deals with substance abuse only in response to needs among his or her clients. In either of these situations, an advocacy orientation is sorely needed. Advocacy can mean the difference between a student or client whose life is enriched and one whose life is sullied or even cut short. In this chapter, competent advocacy is exemplified by two very different counselors. One is a professional school counselor, the other a substance abuse counselor. One works in a suburban high school, the other in a van. What they have in common, as advocate counselors, far surpasses their differences.

The Case of Jason

Jason is a 17-year-old, African American high school junior who attends a large, suburban high school that has an excellent academic reputation. In fact, one of the reasons his parents decided to move to the suburb from Chicago was so that Jason and his younger siblings would have every possible chance to do well academically. They had lived in Chicago until Jason was in the ninth grade. Jason's parents have felt that their decision to move was the right one. Their son is an excellent student, taking all of the honors and advanced placement courses he can so that his dream of a top Ivy League university can become a reality. He will be the first person in his family to go to college, and he knows that he will have to get scholarships.

Although Jason has done well academically, he has not always been completely comfortable in this high school. The majority of the students in the school are White. Although there are other African American students in the school, Jason is one of only a few who are in honors and advanced placement classes. In fact, his family had to go to the school and complain because he was having a hard time getting into these classes. Ms. Jackson, a school counselor, had advocated for the family at that time, which is one of the reasons that she feels she knows Jason well.

Recently, Jason went to a school prom with his girlfriend, Courtney, who comes from a more affluent Black family and who shares his aspirations. At one point, Courtney went into the restroom with her girlfriends. While Jason waited for her, he was approached by Rob, another junior who was in his calculus class. Rob was a school leader: popular and athletic as well as academically superior. He let Jason know that several of the guys were outside. They had found someone to get them some beer, and they were waiting for Rob to come back out. He invited Jason to come along with him. Jason said that he was waiting for Courtney, but Rob told him not to worry; the girls would be in there forever.

Jason went along even though he really didn't like beer at all. He did manage to gulp down one can and then part of a second one before going back inside to look for Courtney. As he looked around for her in the hallway, a teacher walked up to him. Almost immediately the teacher confronted Jason, saying that he seemed to have been drinking. The teacher took him to a small side room and summoned the school principal. Jason was told that he would have to call his parents to come and pick him up and that he would have to report to the principal's office immediately on Monday before going to any classes.

Jason was mortified about what had happened. Not only was he in trouble at school but he was also in trouble with his parents, with Courtney, and with Courtney's parents. He was worried that his whole future might be in jeopardy. If he got suspended—or worse, expelled—there went his college scholarships. In fact, there went his recommendations even to get into college.

On Monday morning, Jason met with the principal. The principal told him that, since it was his first offense, school policy offered him only one possible resolution, which he should appreciate. Recently, the school had changed the zero-tolerance policy so that now a first-time offender could see a counselor before being disciplined. Jason could see Ms. Jackson about his possible drinking problem and then they would see what had to be done.

Student and Counselor

Jason came into Ms. Jackson's office in an angry and defensive mood. Although he was embarrassed and concerned about his relationship with his parents and his girlfriend, these feelings were overshadowed by his anger over the racism of the teacher who spotted him.

The conventional wisdom about substance abuse and addiction would dictate that the counselor turn Jason's attention away from the racism he perceived to focus on his own behaviors or his own alcohol problem. This counselor knew, however, that burying the issue of race would not only disrespect Jason's reality but might also place an obstacle in the path toward the student's ability to solve the problem at hand. As Franklin (1993) stated, "If the impact of racism is ignored, it's unlikely that therapy will go anywhere" (p. 36).

Ms. Jackson accepted Jason's viewpoint on the issue of racism and showed a willingness to explore what had happened from that perspective.

Jason: I'm really feeling angry about this because it's just obvious that a lot of guys were drinking at the dance. The only difference between them and me is that I drank a lot less than they did and I'm the African American. It seems pretty fishy that I was the one that was singled out.

Counselor: You're thinking that it was race that prompted that teacher to notice you and question you.

Jason: Exactly! I don't know this teacher. I don't think he teaches in the college prep. I think he teaches basic math or something. So he sees me in the hallway and he only sees one thing. He assumes I've been up to no good.

Counselor: This is something that you've seen as part of what goes on for you in school? That people have different expectations for you and are looking for something to be wrong?

Jason: Yes, it happens all the time. It happens in the hallways, it happens in the lunchroom. If people haven't known me for a long time they see who they want to see. I'm used to it. It doesn't surprise me anymore.

Counselor: But this time the stakes are very high. It isn't just somebody's opinion. It's your future that you're thinking might be in jeopardy.

Jason: My future, my relationship with my girlfriend, my parents being disappointed, people in the school knowing about it—everything that's bad. My parents being disappointed might be the worst thing. I just can't look my mother in the eye.

Counselor: So as much as you know that there's racism involved in this and you're mad about that, you're also mad at yourself for being in a position that this teacher could get at you.

Jason: I should never have let myself be in that position. Never.

Counselor: I'm interested in something you just said—about the fact that you shouldn't have let yourself get in a position where you'd be so vulnerable to racism. You've spent your whole school career making sure that doesn't happen. That's been a lot of pressure for you to handle.

Jason: Yeah. But you're probably thinking I'm all stressed out and under pressure so I was drinking. No chance.

Counselor: You hadn't been feeling like you'd like a drink.

Jason: No. I'd been feeling like I'd like to hang out with these other guys. Like maybe I didn't have to be so super-careful any more. What a joke. I wasn't brought up to ever think that.

Counselor: You weren't craving a drink. You were craving a chance to relax with some other people that you wanted to feel more comfortable with.

Jason: Right. I really don't drink. Just having that beer made me dizzy but I didn't want them to know it so I tried to have another one. I don't know…I probably was walking like I was dizzy but I still think the teacher was looking at me hard because he's racist. But there probably was something for him to see once he started looking at me. Damn, that was dumb. I'll never get out of this. One minute, one little thing that everybody does and my life is down the drain.

Counselor: This might be a good chance for us to look whether your life has to be down the drain. What do you think has to happen for your life to be salvaged?

Jason: Go back to last week and don't go to the dance?

Counselor: That would be good. Any other thoughts?

Jason: I have to find a way that I don't get suspended and that this isn't in my school record. That's the only way I can see that my college plans don't get fucked up. Sorry!

Counselor: That's okay. So the big thing is your school record. You're not as worried about getting some kind of disciplinary action as long as it's not part of your permanent record.

Jason: Yes. They can do anything to me. I just don't want to get kicked out of school and I don't want this in my records to keep me out of college. That's it.

Counselor: What about the fact that the other guys aren't getting punished? That bother you?

Jason: I don't care. I did it. I want out of this quagmire.

Counselor: You're starting to be a little bit more hopeful about that and I think you're right. I do think it's possible—not easy, but possible.

After this interaction, Jason and his counselor were at a point of readiness to explore the next steps that would involve both Jason's self-advocacy and the work that his parents and Ms. Jackson could do on his behalf. Jason described his parents' attitudes this way: "They're very upset, very disappointed, and very mad. They want to lock me in my room and keep me grounded forever—but they still want me to get into a good college." The counselor suggested that she set up a meeting with the principal that would involve herself, Jason, and Jason's parents. As she put it, "Maybe together we could hash this out and come out with a better strategy than giving up your dreams."

The School

In this situation, it was in the student's best interest to move on from the issue of racism to the practical problem solving that was needed for the sake of his future success. That does not mean, however, that the counselor let herself forget about the impact of racism on the school environment. She had had some success in addressing this in the past when the issue of equal access to advanced placement courses arose. She knew it was necessary to raise this point again, first as a key point in her advocacy on behalf of this particular student, and then in urging the principal to lead an in-depth exploration of the impact of race.

It is important to recognize, too, that Ms. Jackson would not have had the chance to work with Jason if the school's previous zero-tolerance disciplinary policy had still been in effect. Her advocacy, in concert with a group of parents and concerned teachers, had helped to make possible a policy that now provided options to the kinds of automatic disciplinary procedures that had failed to take individual differences or environmental factors into account. The group had been successful in convincing the school board and administration that

> we need teachers, educators, parents, and school boards to reclaim schools as sites of learning and growth—places where incidents of misbehavior, poor choices, wrongdoing, and, yes, even crimes are generally handled within the school setting based on principles of repairing the harm, recognizing the consequences, and developing talents and assets. (Ayers, Ayers, & Dohrn, 2001, p. xiii)

As the high school moved away from a rigid zero-tolerance policy, Ms. Jackson moved toward implementing substance abuse prevention curricula in collaboration with some of the teachers. She felt that the most successful curricula were the ones that focused on building positive skills and promoting health rather than using scare tactics. "Life Skills Training" (Botvin, 2009), for example, was designed to strengthen students' self-management, social, and drug-resistance skills. "Class Action" (Perry et al., 2000) used social-influence strategies to explore the consequences of substance abuse. "Positive Action" (Flay & Allred, 2003) was designed to improve academic outcomes as well as problematic behaviors. Ms. Jackson found that the administrators, teachers, and students all responded well to the curricula. What she, herself, noticed as well was the good fit between positive, skill-based curricula and the empowerment strategies she used with individual students like Jason.

The Public Arena

Attitudes toward student discipline are not created anew in each school district, nor can they be changed one school at a time. Punitive and discriminatory approaches to discipline tend to follow broader trends that are apparent at state and national levels.

> Fear of our children is at the heart of zero tolerance policies in our schools. Guided largely by fear, the education system has sought to exert power and control over our children, and has abdicated its responsibility to guide, nurture, and protect. Our greatest challenge, then, is to transcend a preoccupation with "power over" and to refocus energies toward developing the "power to do." Exerting "power over" children fuels the jail industrial complex but does nothing to advance our collective aspirations. The "power to do" all that we can to ensure that all youth have the opportunity to become self-sufficient and productive adults fuels the education industrial complex and utilizes scarce resources toward the task of empowering rather than punishing. "Power over" focuses attention on personal, rather than societal, misdeeds. (Jackson, 2001, p. vii).

At the national level, alternatives to punitive power games in educational systems do exist and can be used to support positive efforts toward fairness. The U.S. Department of Education's (2000) guide to safe schools suggests that schools should take the following steps in developing schoolwide policies:

- Develop a school-wide disciplinary policy that includes a code of conduct, specific rules, and consequences that can accommodate student differences on a case-by-case basis when necessary. . . . Be sure to include a description of school anti-harassment and anti-violence policies and due process rights.
- Ensure that the cultural values and educational goals of the community are reflected in the rules. These values should be expressed in a statement that precedes the school-wide disciplinary policy.
- Include school staff, students, and families in the development, discussion, and implementation of fair rules. Provide school-wide and classroom support to implement these rules.
- Be sure consequences are commensurate with the offense, and that rules are written and applied in a nondiscriminatory manner and accommodate cultural diversity.
- Make sure that if a negative consequence…is used, it is combined with positive strategies for teaching socially appropriate behaviors and with strategies that address any factors that might have caused the behavior. (p. 11)

These commonsense guidelines are quite conservative in nature but still adhere to the idea of the "power-to-do" orientation. In fact, it is the "power-over" zero-tolerance policies that differ so radically from what one would normally expect in a school environment. Counselors see the effects of this kind of policy differentiation when they work with students like Jason. Counselors, therefore, are in an ideal situation to take action.

The Case of Lucy

Lucy is a 26-year-old White woman who began drinking alcohol and using drugs at the age of 13. Lucy grew up in a middle-class neighborhood and always describes her childhood as reasonably happy. In high school, however, she began what she calls "really having fun" and became so rebellious that her parents, at wits' end, tried to get her under control by grounding her. She tried to escape by running away, but she was brought back and hospitalized in a residential adolescent treatment facility for 60 days.

At the age of 19, Lucy began using heroin, shooting intravenously and becoming very involved with other heroin intravenous (IV) users. Although she never finished high school, Lucy was intelligent and very street-smart as well. Initially, she earned money by working at grocery stores, warehouses, and diners, but she always lost her jobs quickly either because of absenteeism or stealing. She drifted into becoming a street worker. Although she had been raped or mugged by her clients several times, she found prostitution to be the easiest way to earn a living. Because her independence was valuable to her, she did not use a pimp and managed her own money well enough to cover the cost of drugs.

Covering these costs became more difficult as Lucy's tolerance to heroin increased. She was forced to spend more money and work longer hours. She was arrested several times. She could "kick" and go "cold turkey" in jail but would always start using again as soon as she got out.

Occasionally, Lucy would get probation and be sent for substance abuse assessment and treatment. Although she was far from satisfied with her life, she never accepted treatment as a viable option. She did not like being told what to do; she remembered with too much horror the inpatient treatment she had endured as an adolescent; and most of all, she felt that the treatment providers looked down on her because of her lifestyle. She tried Narcotics Anonymous (NA) but felt that nonusers were boring and cheered herself up after meetings by using.

Although Lucy was not attracted to NA or to treatment, she had begun to feel that she needed some kind of change in her life. She was worried about her health and was interested when she heard about a mobile van that would pull up and park, offering clean syringes, cookers, saline, and cotton. She had heard that this needle exchange program also helped people who were overdosing. She began to bring in her dirty needles for exchange. On one visit, she met a professional counselor named Jodie.

Client and Counselor

Jodie was a licensed counselor who had obtained her master's degree in community counseling, never dreaming that she would end up working in a harm reduction outreach program. She had always thought she would work in a community mental health agency or maybe even have a private practice. In the last year of her master's program, however, her professor took the class for a field trip to the needle exchange and the students served hot food for the clients and for people in the neighborhood. Jodie was so drawn to this surprisingly convivial atmosphere that she began doing volunteer work at the van. When the outreach program offered her a job, she accepted it. She thought this was a place where she could make a difference.

The fit between Jodie and Lucy really worked. When Lucy went to the needle exchange van for the first time, she noticed that the atmosphere was that of a block party. She felt comfortable, and when a counselor named Jodie approached her to ask what she needed, she did not feel that old sense of dread that she had always felt when someone wanted to "help" her. She had come in her "working clothes," which normally made people look down on her, and she was struck by Jodie's friendliness. Jodie took Lucy into the van, introducing her to other staff and clients, and put together a bag of syringes, condoms, and HIV testing supplies. Lucy always took good care of herself with regard to HIV and other sexually transmitted diseases and thought how nice it was that she could come here rather than to a health office. Jodie got Lucy a plate of food and asked her if she was interested in a free hepatitis A and B vaccination. Although they spoke for 30 minutes that first time, Jodie never said anything to Lucy about her drug use. Instead, she used the time to respond to Lucy's questions and to make sure that Lucy had plans for her own safety in the streets.

Lucy did not change immediately. She continued to shoot heroin and work the streets. She visited the needle exchange regularly, however, and she even gave Jodie her telephone number. If Jodie didn't see Lucy for a while, she called to make sure she was all right and to let her know that everyone missed her at the van.

Lucy had thought about quitting and about getting off the streets. She wondered what it would be like to have a normal life. Jodie would talk with her about that desire to quit and what it would take for that to happen. She always ended up by saying, "You are a smart gal. You will quit when you decide to quit. It is up to you." Lucy found that statement both encouraging and empowering. When she did feel ready to make a change—maybe even to reconnect with her family—she went to Jodie, who understood how difficult a decision this was. "New territory for you," said Jodie.

Jodie helped Lucy make an action plan. Among all the detoxification options, Jodie believed that a center using a short methadone-weaning procedure to make patients more comfortable through their withdrawal would be a good fit for Lucy. When Lucy decided on that option, Jodie made a call on her behalf, knowing that she could get the bed faster than Lucy could. Lucy came through feeling better and more hopeful than she had felt in years. Jodie and Lucy continued to work together, first on finding a place to live and then on putting together Lucy's first resume. Jodie and the needle exchange staff had put together a listing of job settings where felons and long-time addicts could be hired. Lucy did get a job and, eventually, started giving back some of what had been given to her by volunteering at the needle exchange.

In the Community

People with addiction-related problems have always been a stigmatized population, and "drug users are often viewed as morally corrupt or weak-willed individuals who engage in not only voluntary self- and socially-destructive behavior but also criminal activity" (National Institute on Drug Abuse, 2004). Harm reduction programs like the one that employs Jodie have at their core a belief that their clients should not have to be subjected to social stigmatization. Ironically, however, the stigma often carries over to the programs themselves, with staff and supporters often finding the need to respond to strong criticism from uninformed and frightened community members.

During Jodie's tenure at the needle exchange, attacks on the program occurred on a regular basis. At one point, an individual complained to the city council that the van was parked in an inappropriate place. As a result of this one complaint, the program director was told that the van was not welcome in the neighborhood. What the individual complainer did not understand was that the program had strong support from many people in the community, some of whom had been fed or helped by Jodie and her colleagues. It was time consuming but not difficult to gather a formidable group of people, including staff, clients, allies, and neighbors, to advocate on behalf of what had become a valuable community resource. The van was, of course, allowed to stay.

Public Policy

Stigma carries over into public policy, often making it necessary for substance abuse counselors to take part in macrolevel efforts at education and sociopolitical advocacy. The moving of the van made Jodie realize how the needle exchange could be affected by the whim of public opinion toward IV drug users, street workers, and other marginalized people. It had recently become legal to buy syringes in drug stores, but now a new fight had to be waged. Narcan, which reverses opiate overdoses immediately, was kept in the van and had been used successfully many times for overdose reversal. Unfortunately, Narcan was not available where and when it was most often needed: at the time and place of an overdose actually occurring. A few states had passed bills to make access to Narcan more readily available, usually in response to well-publicized deaths, but Jodie's state was not one of them. When a legislator agreed to introduce a bill, Jodie became one of a group of allies who would fight for the bill until it passed.

The scourge of stigma is also visible at the national level, where a policy banning the use of federal funds for programs involved in needle exchange remains in effect. Fortunately, the possibilities for more responsive approaches to substance abuse have begun to improve. Such policies, which can save or enhance the lives of people dealing with substance issues, clearly belong on the to-do lists of counselors who are social justice advocates.

Multicultural and Diversity Issues

People dealing with substance abuse-related issues are often subject to multiple oppressions. For instance, the stigma of substance abuse is magnified for people of color. Racial/ethnic minority populations are perhaps most adversely affected by this stigma and its effects, leading to misperceptions about drug abuse and addiction in minority communities….For example, the common perception is that minority groups, particularly Blacks and Hispanics, use drugs more than Whites even though epidemiologic data show little difference in overall use by race/ethnicity. In fact, in some instances minority groups are less likely to use licit or illicit drugs. There are, however, great differences in the consequences of drug use for racial/ethnic minorities, creating a great need to better understand the unique prevention, treatment, and health services needs of these communities. (National Institute on Drug Abuse, 2004)

The impact of multiple oppressions shows up clearly even in the two examples that have been reviewed in this chapter. The case of Jason highlights the vulnerability of an African American student to precisely the kind of false assumption identified by the National Institute on Drug Abuse. The case of Lucy also sheds light on the impact of multiple oppressions, this time illustrating the multiplier effect when stigma and sexism are combined.

In the broad public arena, policies and practices are complicit in the unequal treatment offered by the criminal justice system in virtually every state. The Drug Policy Alliance (2002), in a review of research related to the "war on drugs," reported the following :

- While African Americans constitute 13% of the nation's monthly drug users, they represent 35% of those persons arrested for drug possession, 55% of drug possession convictions, and 74% of those sentenced to prison for drug possession.
- Under federal legislation enacted in 1986, it takes 1/100 as much crack cocaine as powder cocaine to trigger equal mandatory minimum sentences. In 1995, although American crack users were 52% White and 38% African American, Blacks accounted for 88% of those sentenced for crack offenses and Whites just 4.1%
- Almost 1.4 million African American males, or 14% of the adult Black male population, are currently disenfranchised as a result of felony convictions. Black men represent more than 36% of the total disenfranchised male population in the United States, although they make up less than 15% of American males.

It is clear that this level of inequality and oppression calls for the implementation of a strong advocacy effort. Such an endeavor would be timely at this point because a new window of opportunity for change is opening. According to the White House (2009), "President Obama and Vice-President Biden will give first-time, non-violent offenders a chance to serve their sentence, where appropriate, in the type of drug rehabilitation programs that have proven to work better than a prison term in changing bad behavior." Moreover, "President Obama and Vice-President Biden believe the disparity between sentencing crack and powder-based cocaine is wrong and should be completely eliminated" (White House, 2009). In this environment, advocates and antiracist activists might have an uncommon chance for success.

Challenges

An advocate who seeks justice for people affected by substance abuse must be strong-minded and resolute because the challenges are daunting. Although alternatives are gaining ground, the conventional wisdom that addicts are incapable of change without coercion remains deeply entrenched, affecting both treatment models and the attitudes of the general public.

The stereotypes that are attributed to people with addiction-related problems are grounded in stigma. A treatment plan initiative under the auspices of the Center for Substance Abuse Treatment (2000) found the following:

- The stigma of alcohol or other drug addiction is a powerful, shame-based mark of disgrace and reproach.

- Prejudicial attitudes and beliefs generate and perpetuate stigma.
- The result is discrimination directed at individuals at risk for, suffering from, or in recovery from addiction to alcohol or other drugs, and those associated with them.
- People suffering from alcohol or other drug addiction and those in recovery are ostracized, discriminated against, and deprived of basic human rights.
- Often, individuals who are stigmatized internalize such attitudes and practices, making them part of their identity. (p. 43)

Of course, these attitudes are devastating when they affect individuals directly. Perhaps even more damaging, however, is the impact that this mindset has on community environments and public policy. The notion that a group of people is deserving of ostracism and discrimination brings with it a hardened political stance that has helped to fill prisons, endanger lives, and short-circuit dreams. What is it like to come up against entrenched politics? It is, by any definition, challenging.

Benefits

The benefits of advocacy in the context of substance abuse counseling arise in response to the difficult challenges described above. If individual clients are disempowered by helpers who are caught up in the myth of the change-resistant client, then counselor advocates are obligated not just to use different strategies themselves but also to change the dominant paradigm. If biases against substance-abusing clients infect the community, then advocacy-oriented counselors are mandated to find allies and make systemic changes. If the conventional wisdom about addiction means that people who should be receiving medical care are instead dealt with in the criminal justice system, then it is time for counselors to put their Advocacy Competencies to work in changing public policy.

Conclusion

In the past, the conventional wisdom about substance abuse counseling depended on the assumption that people with problems related to drugs were incapable of making decisions about their own lives. This myth affected both clinical approaches and public policy. Fortunately, the advent of newer approaches such as motivational interviewing and harm reduction models has begun to move the substance abuse field toward empowerment strategies that are more compatible with an advocacy orientation.

This chapter reviewed two case studies that would appear on the surface to be highly divergent: one a case involving a suburban high school student hoping for entry into an Ivy League university, the other involving a long-time IV drug user whose life was led on the urban streets. Both of these personal stories have in common, however, the need for advocacy on behalf of an individual affected by stigma and oppression. In each situation the counselor used competent advocacy strategies both to empower the individual client and to stand up for essential changes in community practices and public policy.

References

Ayers, W., Ayers, R., & Dohrn, B. (2001). Introduction: Resisting zero tolerance. In W. Ayers, B. Dohrn, & R. Ayers (Eds.), *Zero tolerance: Resisting the drive for punishment in our schools* (pp. vi–xvi). New York: New Press.

Botvin, G. (2009). *Life skills training: High school program.* Retrieved June 1, 2009, from http://www.lifeskillstraining.com/evaluation.php

Center for Substance Abuse Treatment. (2000). *Changing the conversation. Substance abuse treatment: The national treatment plan initiative* (DHHS Publication No. SMA 00-3479). Washington, DC: U.S. Department of Health and Human Services.

Chicago Recovery Alliance. (2009). *Community outreach.* Retrieved February 24, 2009, from http://www.anypositivechange.org/hro.html

Drug Policy Alliance. (2002). *Effectiveness of the war on drugs.* Retrieved February 24, 2009, from http://www.drugpolicy.org/library/factsheets/effectivenes/

Durbin, D. (2006, June 22). Floor statement accompanying the Drug Overdose Reduction Act, United States Senate.

Flay, B. R., & Allred, C. G. (2003). Long-term effects of the Positive Action program. *American Journal of Health Behavior, 27*(Suppl. 1), 6–21.

Franklin, A. J. (1993, July/August). The invisibility syndrome. *Family Networker,* 33–39.

Hettema, J., Steele, J., & Miller, W. R. (2005, April). Motivational interviewing. *Annual Review of Clinical Psychology, 1,* 91–111.

Holder, H., Longabough, R., Miller, W. R., & Rubonis, A. V. (1991). The cost effectiveness of treatment for alcoholism: A first approximation. *Journal of Studies on Alcoholism, 52,* 517–540.

Jackson, J. L., Sr. (2001). Foreword. In W. Ayers, B. Dohrn, & R. Ayers (Eds.), *Zero tolerance: Resisting the drive for punishment in our schools* (pp. vii–ix). New York: New Press.

Lewis, J. A., Arnold, M. S., House, R., & Toporek, R. L. (2002). *ACA Advocacy Competencies.* Retrieved February 24, 2009, from http://www.counseling.org/Publications/

Marlatt, G. A. (1998). Basic principles and strategies of harm reduction. In G. A. Marlatt (Ed.), *Harm reduction: Strategies for managing high-risk behaviors* (pp. 49–66). New York: Guilford Press.

Miller, W. R. (1996). Motivational interviewing: Research, practice, and puzzles. *Addictive Behaviors, 21,* 835–842.

Miller, W. R., & Rollnick, S. (1991). *Motivational interviewing: Preparing people to change addictive behavior.* New York: Guilford Press.

National Institute on Drug Abuse. (2004). *National Institute on Drug Abuse strategic plan on reducing health disparities.* Retrieved February 25, 2009, from http://www.drugabuse.gov/StrategicPlan/HealthStratPlan.html

Perry, C. L., Williams, C. L., Komro, K. A., Veblen-Mortenson, S., Forster, J. L., Bernstein-Lachter, R., et al. (2000). Project Northland high school interventions: Community action to reduce adolescent alcohol use. *Health Education and Behavior, 27,* 29–49.

Rubak, S., Sandboek, A., Lauritzen, T., & Christensen, B. (2005). Motivational interviewing: A systematic review and meta-analysis. *British Journal of General Practice, 55,* 305–312.

U.S. Department of Education. (2000). *Early warning, timely response: A guide to safe schools.* Retrieved March 13, 2003, from http://www.ed.gov/offices/OSERS/OSEP/earlywrn.html

Van Wormer, K. (1999). Harm induction vs. harm reduction: Comparing American and British approaches to drug use. *Journal of Offender Rehabilitation, 29,* 35–48.

White House. (2009). *Civil rights.* Retrieved February 26, 2009, from http://www.whitehouse.gov/agenda/civil_rights/

Chapter 17

Rehabilitation Counseling: A Continuing Professional Imperative for Multiculturalism and Advocacy Competence

Renée A. Middleton, Mona C. Robinson, and Ameena S. Mu'min

This chapter positions advocacy or social action as a skill intrinsic to the Multicultural Counseling Competencies (Sue, Arredondo, & McDavis, 1992). As such, multicultural counseling competency is viewed as an indispensable and obligatory precursor to engaging in effective advocacy. In this chapter, we provide a framework for understanding how advocacy has historically been embedded in the field of rehabilitation counseling and describe the ongoing gaps in services to many under-represented groups and our commitment to effective service delivery. We conclude by providing an overview of the challenges and benefits to implementing the advocacy competencies within the rehabilitation counseling profession.

Rehabilitation counseling is a systematic process that assists people with physical, developmental, cognitive, and emotional disabilities to achieve their personal, career, and independent living goals in the most integrated setting possible through the application of the counseling process. The counseling process involves communication, goal setting, and beneficial growth or change through self-advocacy, psychological, vocational, social, and behavioral interventions (Parker, Szymanski, & Patterson, 2005). "Rehabilitation counseling is a profession that assists individuals with disabilities in adapting to the environment, assists environments in accommodating the needs of individuals, and works towards full participation of persons with disabilities in all aspects of society, especially work" (Szymanski, 1985, p. 3).

Rehabilitation counseling has several distinctive aspects in that equal attention is given to personal and environmental factors. Historically, the medical model has located the social problem of the disability within the person rather than the environment or attitude of the system. The person with a disability is viewed as dependent and passive, and the disability is viewed as something that needs to be prevented, cured, and eliminated. The medical model often tends to focus on the individual in an attempt to minimize pathology and treat symptoms as opposed to focusing on reducing environmental barriers (Parker et al., 2005). In other words, the medical model tends to define the disability in terms of characteristics of the individual and ignores the environment. Therefore, the medical model does not provide a sufficient explanation for an inability of persons with disabilities to participate fully in society and is not a preferred model in the rehabilitation community (Parker et al., 2005).

Self-advocacy in the rehabilitation profession is generally thought to be the use of skills to enhance one's self-determination. In general, the individual exercises a willingness to seek multiple resources in an effort to retain self-dignity and sustenance of personal and social adjustment, which may or may not lead to employment. Self-advocacy (i.e., client) has been a core value and essential service component of the rehabilitation counseling profession for over three decades (Rehabilitation Act of 1973). In order for state vocational rehabilitation (VR) services agencies to receive Rehabilitation Act funds, a Client Assistance Program (CAP) that provides legal and advocacy services must be available to applicants and consumers/clients of VR services. The scope of services section of the Rehabilitation Act provides a summary of training and service options available to meet the individualized needs of consumers/clients with disabilities. Indeed, rehabilitation counselors have been urged to consider advocacy as an ethical imperative (Vash, 1987). Common issues addressed by CAP include the following:

- Agreement on an employment objective: when the state VR agency personnel do not agree with the consumer/client that a particular objective is achievable
- Appropriateness of training: disagreements on where and what type of training should be pursued
- Evaluations: contested inaccurate or incomplete evaluations, or a consumer/client is seeking a customized assessment
- Denial of services: consumer/client is found not eligible for services, denied specific services, or offered less-than-adequate services to meet needs
- Employment/placement: consumer/client wants assistance in finding employment, an integrated placement as opposed to a sheltered workshop setting, or to be trained for a career rather than an entry-level position
- Technology issues: client needs adaptive equipment or services to be employed or to benefit from VR services

According to Parker et al. (2005), the specific techniques and modalities utilized within this rehabilitation counseling process may include, but are not be limited to the following:

- Assessment and appraisal
- Diagnosis and treatment planning
- Career and vocational counseling
- Individual and group counseling treatment interventions focused on facilitating adjustment to the medical and psychosocial impacts of disability
- Case management, referral, and service coordination
- Program evaluation and research
- Interventions to remove environmental, employment, and attitudinal barriers
- Consultation services among multiple parties and regulatory systems
- Job analysis, job development, and placement services, including assistance with employment and job accommodations
- Consultation and access to rehabilitation technology

Although the importance of self-advocacy cannot be underestimated, historically, oppression due to race, class, gender, sexual orientation, and disability status has determined the institutional power accessible to many consumer/client groups. To this end, professional advocacy with and on behalf of the consumer/client cannot be underestimated as well. Counselors are in positions of institutional power and privilege in relation to clients, holding access and influence over resources, information, policy, and practice at a level often unattainable by clients (Alston, Harley, & Middleton, 2006). Therefore, advocacy with and on behalf of the consumer/client is an essential role of the counselor. Inherent within the receipt of services should be a reasonable expectation that counselors possess a keen sense for recognizing systematic oppression. Once recognized, the counselor accepts responsibility to engage in social action or advocacy necessary to facilitate the removal of external and institutional barriers impeding the consumer's/client's well-being. Multiculturally competent counselors are able to recognize oppression in all of its forms (individual, systemic, institutional, etc.).

Advocacy or social action is a skill intrinsic to the Multicultural Counseling Competencies (Sue et al., 1992) and the yet-to-be formally adopted Multicultural Rehabilitation Counseling Competencies and Standards (Multicultural Rehabilitation Counseling Competencies for short; Middleton et al., 2000). Toporek, Lewis, and Crethar (2009) correctly pointed out that the Multicultural Counseling Competencies (Sue et al., 1992) have paved the way for the American Counseling Association (ACA) Advocacy Competencies (Lewis, Arnold, House, & Toporek, 2002). Consequently, while the rehabilitation profession has led the way in embracing the concept of self-advocacy, two things are lacking. First, there is a lingering lack of endorsement of the Multicultural Rehabilitation Counseling Competencies (Middleton et al., 2000) that signals the unreadiness of a profession committed to ensuring the sustained presence and professional development of a cadre of multiculturally competent rehabilitation counselors. Second, there is a continuing absence or lack of acknowledgment regarding a need for the application of a common language and comprehensive set of minimum advocacy competencies that can serve as a framework for the various credentialing groups in the counseling profession (Toporek & Liu, 2001). Within the larger profession of counseling in general, there has been a lack of training and coherent agreement about philosophy, definitions, and methods of advocacy. The Advocacy Competencies (Lewis et al., 2002) provide a common philosophy and definition of advocacy and can serve as a tool for identifying ways in which a counselor might provide advocacy or identify professional development needs at a number of levels (individual/consumer-client, systems/ community, public arena/institutional) depending on the circumstances, context, resources, cultural factors, and sociopolitical skills of the counselor and consumer/client (Toporek et al., 2009).

Advocacy and Basic Values of Multiculturally Competent Rehabilitation Counseling

Rehabilitation counselors possess a unique set of skills that assist them in working with persons with disabilities. By combining their specialized knowledge of disabilities and the interaction of environmental factors with their counseling skills, they are able to effectively advocate for consumers of their services. Thus, rehabilitation counseling is often viewed as a specialty within the rehabilitation profession with counseling at its core, and this is what typically differentiates it from other types of counseling (Parker et al., 2005). This counseling partnership, which relies heavily on consumer/ client involvement, consists of communication, goal setting, and beneficial growth or change through self-sufficiency, psychological, vocational, social, and behavioral interventions.

To advocate for their consumers/clients, rehabilitation counselors must adhere to several basic values. These values consist of the facilitation of independence, integration, and inclusion of persons with disabilities. Namely, credence must be given to a commitment to equal opportunity of people with disabilities based on a model of accommodation that looks not only at the individual but also at the environment with the realization that participation of the person with a disability may be increased or diminished by environmental factors. Emphasis must be placed on the assets and not just the limitations of the individual with a disability. There must also be an understanding that the rehabilitation process is interdisciplinary in nature, and individuals with a disability have the right to provide input during the goal-setting stage and thereafter. Other important aspects include giving the consumer/client the opportunity to make informed choices regarding their services, services providers, and so on. No one should be excluded from services, regardless of the severity of the disability (Parker et al., 2005).

Rehabilitation Advocacy: Individual and Community Level

Advocacy is embedded in the very nature of the rehabilitation counseling field. Advocacy insists on a commitment to sponsorship and encouragement for the lives of others and that some level of change is necessary in order that a cause or effort be established to improve the livelihood of a person and/ or community. Rehabilitation counselors must be trained in a manner that prepares them to assist individuals with disabilities in adapting to the environment, assist environments in accommodating the needs of the individual, and work toward full participation of individuals with disabilities in all aspects of society, especially in work (Szymanski, 1985). Within this established commitment is a central and recurrent theme in rehabilitation counseling, which is that the Multicultural Rehabilitation Competencies are necessary if persons with disabilities from diverse ethnic backgrounds are to be well served by rehabilitation counselors (Middleton et al., 2000).

Rehabilitation counselors need to be versed in facets of Title I of the Americans With Disabilities Act of 1990 and the Age Discrimination in Employment Act of 1967 to assist persons navigating the employment application and hiring process. Dobren (1994) suggested that rehabilitation counselors become ecologically oriented and function as advocates for client causes, going into the client's environment and helping effect change. This can mean a more active role for the counselor in the employment process, especially in assisting older persons who come from diverse ethnic backgrounds.

Rehabilitation counselors frequently work with older clients with late-onset disabilities who face significant challenges, such as workplace discrimination, issues related to health care coverage, and concerns regarding finances and retirement planning. Unfortunately, older workers with disabilities need to remain in the workforce but are unable to return to their former position or their former employer at predisability wages without advocacy efforts from rehabilitation counselors. These may include people who have not engaged in recent job searches and may be unfamiliar with the labor market and contemporary job-seeking skills, and who may also lack experience with current technology, which can present significant barriers. Subsequently, rehabilitation counselors are able to offer specialized services related to vocational assessment, job placement, and job accommodations to assist their clients with return-to-work activities. One effective tool is the use of tailored resumes. Using a functional resume will allow older job applicants to give employers information about their experiences without allowing the employer to focus solely on their age (Finch & Robinson, 2003).

Another essential component that requires rehabilitation advocacy at the individual level is related to rehabilitation counselors who work with children and adolescents in schools providing transition services. Transition planning for a student with a disability typically begins at age 14. Transition services are a coordinated set of activities that assists students in moving from school to postschool activities such as work or college. Under the Individual With Disabilities Education Act, all students with disabilities who are receiving regular, vocational/career-technical, or special education and related services are entitled to receive transition services via the Individualized Education Plan. Many students work with a rehabilitation counselor and receive services through their local VR agency such as career planning and job development/placement activities. Without advocacy by the rehabilitation counselor, many students would not be able to access and therefore benefit from transition services (Ohio Rehabilitation Services Commission, 2001).

The heightened awareness of multicultural issues has thus made it necessary for rehabilitation counselors to go beyond merely assisting minority persons with disabilities find employment or make personal adjustments (Harley, Feist-Price, & Alston, 1996) to addressing continuity in both training and practice by adhering to the Multicultural Rehabilitation Counseling Competencies. These multifaceted lenses of the Advocacy Competencies and Multicultural Rehabilitation Counseling Competencies are beneficial to the field for the reason that they cyclically connect the counselor educator, student, clinician, and client through a process of empowerment, by way of self-awareness, values, biases, beliefs, and worldview as a guide.

Multicultural Rehabilitation Counseling Competencies: Policy Level Advocacy

The Multicultural Counseling Competencies (Sue et al., 1982) take into the account the worldview of the practitioner and its influence or impact on the client and include factors such as attitudes/beliefs, knowledge, skills, and relationships. Researchers and social advocates in the field of rehabilitation counseling (Alston & Bell, 1996; Alston et al., 2006; Matrone & Leahy, 2005) have continuously promoted the awareness and necessity of this multicultural infusion in both practice and training of rehabilitation counselors. Areas of focus include social justice advocacy (Alston et al., 2006), race-related matters (Mpofu & Harley, 2006), a historical overview of rehabilitation counselor competencies (Leahy & Szymanski, 1995), and a call to action to endorse the Multicultural Rehabilitation Competencies (Middleton et al., 2000). Advocacy is the common thread for each of these themes that, with respect to the training of rehabilitation counselors, begins with counselor educators.

The Multicultural Rehabilitation Competencies operate under the premise that trainees would become aware of their own assumptions, values, and biases as they are all relevant to working for persons with disabilities. Middleton et al. (2000) endorsed these competencies but additionally asserted the position that they be operationalized. In essence, the competencies are acknowledged and supported; in addition, the practical means by which they are adhered to are provided. This signifies a move in the direction of true multiculturalism, not simply to provide a standard that must be upheld, but also to develop a compass that one can use as a guide for how the competencies can be demonstrated.

Counselor educators play one of the most essential roles in the development, training, and advocacy initiatives of rehabilitation counselors across all domains that rehabilitation counselors encounter (public and private sector, school, community). Helping counseling students become more aware of the social, political, economic, and cultural factors (Lewis et al., 2002) that have the potential to affect the lives of their clients is critical. Promoting advocacy initiatives among counseling students, even at the grassroots level, empowers them to later become advocates for their clients on multiple levels.

To meet the needs of culturally diverse racial/ethnic groups, counselors must continuously recognize the value of the individual. Culturally competent rehabilitation counselors are often called upon to serve as advocates, thus emphasizing the need for operationalization of the multicultural competencies and standards endorsed by the field (Sue et al., 1992). In order for rehabilitation counselors to address the needs of the consumers/clients, the role of advocacy on behalf of the counselor is fundamental; more specifically, the multiple roles of culture are intertwined.

Challenges in Implementing Advocacy Competencies

One of the challenges that counselors face when implementing the Advocacy Competencies is a lack of critical knowledge that is necessary to work with diverse populations. The Advocacy Competencies are also crucial if counselors are to assist consumers/clients in meeting their basic needs, including access to public accommodations, transportation, education, employment, and health care. Another challenge that rehabilitation counselors face is the lack of adequate funding to provide services to the growing number of consumers/clients with disabilities.

With growing acknowledgment of disparities among minority and nonminority clients, rehabilitation and mental health practitioners have begun to consider the integration of culture, race, and other aspects of human socialization into mental health assessment and delivery (Locke, 1993; T. L. Robinson, 1999; Sue & Sue, 2003; Vontress & Epp, 1997). The U.S. government began a campaign in the 1960s to remove barriers that prevented equal access and opportunities for women and historically underrepresented racial and ethnic groups. Efforts to provide culturally competent services have intensified since the 1970s. Additionally, in an effort to ensure diversity within the rehabilitation workforce, Section 21 was included in the 1992 Amendments to the 1973 Rehabilitation Act. The goal of Section 21 was to ensure that governmental polices represented Americans with disabilities (Middleton et al., 2000; Paugh, 2003). Part of the initiative included funds from Rehabilitation Services Administration (RSA, 1993) to build and support rehabilitation counseling programs at higher education institutions serving predominantly minority students. Today, as a result of Section 21, there are 30 new programs on 22 campuses (Dan Hopkins, personal communication, July 2006). Nevertheless, despite some progress by RSA, the work in this area is far from over as there continues to be a need for research in the area of multicultural competencies, specifically as they relate to minority and nonminority treatment outcomes (T. L. Robinson, 1999; Sue et al., 1992; Sue & Sue,

2003; Vontress & Epp, 1997; Wheaton, Wilson, & Brown, 1996). Additionally, individuals who are dually diagnosed and are of minority status face formidable challenges in rehabilitation (Dunston-McLee, 2001; Paugh, 2003).

Advocacy and the Vocational Rehabilitation of Underrepresented Groups

Lewis, Lewis, Daniels, and D'Andrea (1998) suggested that advocacy "serves two primary purposes: (1) increasing the consumers'/clients' sense of personal power and (2) fostering environmental changes that reflect greater responsiveness to their personal needs" (p. 172). Vulnerable populations who are consumers/clients of VR services are often composed of individuals who have a primary diagnosis of a mental health disorder, reside in urban and rural areas, are dually diagnosed, and are persons of African American or Latino/Hispanic descent (Strohl, Robinson, & Wilson, 2008). These populations make up the greatest need for multicultural counseling competency, advocacy, and social justice. Frequently, VR services provided to underrepresented groups present a picture of disparity in existing services in terms of outcomes for these vulnerable populations. VR is the model with the longest history and serves the largest number of persons with a physical or mental illness. VR services can be traced back to the early 1900s. Recently, the federal and state VR system has come under scrutiny for its failure as a viable source of VR for persons with a severe mental illness. The National Alliance for Mental Illness published a report regarding the failure of the federal–state vocational system in meeting the VR needs of persons with a severe mental illness (Noble, Honberg, Hall, & Flynn, 1999). The report challenges us to rethink where we are heading regarding policy formulation and service delivery with persons with severe mental illness (Noble et al., 1999).

There is no doubt that issues of public accountability are crucial in the efficacy of the federal–state VR system. However, there needs to be more reliable information gathered. We need to know which VR services received by people with a primary diagnosis of a mental health disorder predict who will close successfully in Status 26 (employed 90 days or longer; Cook, 1999). Status 26 is a VR classification designation for case management, identifying the status of the case. In addition, there are many differences between urban and rural areas, yet the same standards of service delivery are used for differing populations. A thorough understanding of what is working with what population will help facilitate the allocation of scarce resources now and in the future (Bond, Drake, Becker, & Mueser, 1999; Conley, 1999; Cook, 1999).

Evidence suggests that access to VR is more difficult for racial minorities than for nonminorities/ White Americans in the United States (Strohl et al., 2008; Wilson, 2002; Wilson, Jackson, & Doughty, 1999). The lack of cultural competence has been suggested as one of the main reasons that historically underrepresented racially and ethnically diverse persons have experienced less-than-desirable outcomes as compared with their White counterparts within mental health and rehabilitation systems (Capuzzi & Gross, 2003; Granello, & Wheaton, 1998; M. Robinson, 2007; T. L. Robinson, 1999; Sue & Sue, 2003; Vontress & Epp, 1997; Watson & Collins, 1993; Wheaton et al., 1996). While the lack of cultural competency was considered as one of the main reasons why minorities experienced poorer outcomes, lack of an effective and competent advocate is also linked with affecting VR outcomes. Additionally, M. Robinson (2007) pointed to factors such as workplace discrimination and lack of access to appropriate vocational and academic experiences.

H. Robinson (2005) examined VR outcomes of people who were dually diagnosed with substance abuse and mental health disorders and noted that minority consumers/clients received less college services than nonminority consumers/clients. The findings suggested that a lack of multicultural competence on the part of rehabilitation counselors may have been a contributing factor. Rehabilitation counselors can demonstrate Advocacy Competencies by identifying strengths and weaknesses of the individual they are working with instead of making decisions on the basis of race. One way to accomplish this is by jointly formulating a rehabilitation plan with the consumer/client that allows the person the opportunity to try a college program for a specified period of time instead of denying it based on past unacceptable aptitude test scores or grades. If the individual is successful in college during the trial period, the plan can be amended to include the length of time necessary for degree attainment. The cultural diversity in the United States is continually increasing; it is estimated that by the year 2050, no more than 50% of the population will be of European American ancestry (D'Angelo & Dixey, 2001). In addition, advances in technologies have increased each person's ability and likelihood of interacting with people of cultural backgrounds quite different from his or her own (Bellini, 2002; D'Angelo & Dixey, 2001; Granello & Wheaton, 1998; T. L. Robinson, 1999; Sue et al., 1992). The implications for VR are magnified when one considers that racial minorities tend to have higher rates of disability than individuals from the majority group (Smart & Smart, 1997). H. Robinson (2005) conducted a study that sought to contribute to the understanding of the impact of multicultural issues on VR program outcomes for consumers/clients with a dual diagnosis (mental illness and substance abuse). The results of the study showed that there are differences in program outcomes for minority consumers/clients with a dual diagnosis as compared with their nonminority counterparts. Specifically, minorities continued to fare worse than their nonminority counterparts. Atkins and Wright (1980) were one of the first research teams to analyze VR acceptance by race (African Americans vs. White Americans). They found that African Americans with disabilities were accepted proportionately less for VR services than their White American counterparts (Strohl et al., 2008). The second research team to examine VR acceptance was Herbert and Martinez (1992), who were the first researchers to include the Hispanic ethnic group in VR eligibility studies. The purpose of Herbert and Martinez's study was to determine whether race/ethnicity (e.g., Native American, Alaskan Native, Asian/Pacific Islander, African American, or White) was correlated with case service statuses utilized by VR counselors, specifically, whether race played a role in consumers/clients not being accepted for VR services, being rehabilitated and closed successfully, being closed unsuccessfully after the Individual Plan for Employment (IPE) was written, and being closed for other reasons before the IPE was written. It is evident that a consensus began to emerge as Herbert and Martinez provided findings similar to those of Atkins and Wright indicating a higher acceptance rate among White Americans than among African Americans. Herbert and Martinez reported that both African Americans and Blacks Hispanics tended to be accepted less for VR services than White Americans and White Hispanics. Finally, other studies followed to support the assertion that racial and ethnic minorities tend to be accepted less for VR services (Dziekan & Okocha, 1993; Wilson, 2002). Hence, it is increasingly important for rehabilitation counselors to be culturally competent. This means counselors are aware of their own assumptions, values, and biases. By doing so, counselors are able to effectively operationalize Advocacy Competencies that benefit consumers/clients with disabilities.

CORE and CACREP Standards for Multicultural Competency

Accreditation standards related to multicultural competencies for counselors enrolled in counselor education programs come from two sources: the Council on Rehabilitation Education (CORE) and the Council for Accreditation of Counseling and Related Educational Programs (CACREP). These two sources identify attention to diversity as an important area of competence, yet there is a need for more consistent implementation and explicit guidelines that could be articulated through the adoption of the Multicultural Rehabilitation Competencies. Advocacy at a systems level for the multicultural competencies and the implementation of diversity-related accreditation standards helps address disparity issues identified by research.

The mission of CORE is the accreditation of rehabilitation counselor education (RCE) programs to promote the effective delivery of rehabilitation services to individuals with disabilities by promoting and fostering continuing review and improvement of master's-degree-level RCE programs. CORE also serves to assist and advise in the development and refinement of university-based programs related to the education of students for professional endeavors associated with the rehabilitation of people with disabilities (CORE, 2005). Current CORE requirements require graduate students in rehabilitation counseling programs to obtain essential knowledge, skills, and attitudes necessary to function effectively as professional rehabilitation counselors by responding to the culture and rights of people with disabilities. Section C.2: Social and Cultural Diversity addresses diversity issues, including cultural, disability, gender, sexual orientation, and aging issues (CORE, 2005).

The mission of CACREP is to promote the professional competence of counseling and related practitioners through the development of preparation standards, encouragement of excellence in program development, and accreditation of professional preparation programs (CACREP, 2009). CACREP standards were written to ensure that students develop a professional counselor identity and also master the knowledge and skills to practice effectively. Section II:2: Social and Cultural Diversity addresses multicultural issues, including an understanding of the cultural context of relationships, as well as issues and trends in a multicultural and diverse national and international society related to such factors as culture, ethnicity, nationality, age, gender, sexual orientation, mental and physical characteristics, education, family values, religious and spiritual values, socioeconomic status, and unique characteristics of individuals, couples, families, ethnic groups, and communities (CACREP, 2009). CACREP Section II contains the area of knowledge and skills associated with multiculturalism. Attention has been given to both the eight core areas relating the necessity of a sound knowledge in the area and the infusion of expected learning outcomes relating to applied multicultural competencies.

Practice standards are set nationally, statewide, and institutionally that, when adhered to properly, assist in increasing the competencies of students in training programs and counselors practicing in the field in efforts to encourage sound treatment of society. Dissonance between counselors and consumers/clients, as well as faculty and students, is created when counselor education programs do not take the lead to promote more advanced levels of training for counselors who will eventually become practitioners and ultimately be in a position to advocate for their consumers/clients. Lack of discussion on multicultural awareness perpetuates a lack of knowledge, rendering it inefficient to respond to the needs of the world in which we live. In order for cognitive and emotional awareness to occur in the therapeutic relationship, an unreserved and fundamental foundation of cultural awareness must be taught and practiced among all students in CORE- and CACREP-accredited programs in counselor education (Mu'min, Robinson, & Davis, 2008).

Expected Benefits of Implementing Advocacy Competencies in Practice

The Advocacy Competencies provide a common language and comprehensive set of minimum advocacy competencies that can serve as a framework for the various specialty groups in the counseling profession (Lewis et al., 2002). Within the larger profession of counseling in general, there has been a lack of training and coherent agreement about philosophy, definitions, and methods of implementation of advocacy. The Advocacy Competencies help to eliminate uncertainty about the appropriate role and impact that counselors can have on responding to and eliminating the sociopolitical challenges present in our society when those challenges impede the psychosocial development of the client. If counseling professionals are engaged in professional development based on a common core or set of standards for advocacy, interventions and treatments can be expanded and shaped in a way that focuses on the elimination of external barriers. The target of change includes not only the individual (as in traditional models of change) but also communities, schools, policies, and other agents and systems that impede consumers/clients from reaching their full potential in areas such as employment, independent living, and personal and social adjustment. Together, a fully exercised commitment to competency in multicultural rehabilitation counseling (Middleton et al., 2000) and advocacy (Lewis et al., 2002) can advance the profession, resulting in a reduction of (a) disagreements and biased conclusions regarding employment objectives; (b) biased judgments on where and what type of training should be pursued by the consumer/client; (c) contested, inaccurate, and incomplete evaluations; (d) denial of services or offering of less-than-adequate services to meet the consumers'/clients' needs; (e) narrowly focusing consumers/clients toward entry-level positions rather than a career; and (f) directing resources and advancements in technology away from cultural minorities and individuals with complex disabilities.

Conclusion

The professional identity of rehabilitation counseling is widely acknowledged in the field's historical ability to establish and maintain competency, advocacy, and ethical responsibility in practice and service delivery. Each of these distinctions promotes the ongoing and collective legacy of the counseling field and, more specifically, rehabilitation counseling. Advocacy at every intersection in the process of ongoing professional identity development has the ability to empower, enhance, and revolutionize the very nature of rehabilitation counseling. Through advocacy, individuals are being validated for who they are as consumers/clients and clinicians, empowered to act, and enhanced by their effortless duties, and they are bringing about needed change that is consumer-driven through the use of best practice.

CORE and CACREP are accrediting bodies of astute educational training and practice institutions that have successfully established a solid communal foundation of preparatory knowledge, skill, and excellence. Thus, to produce a multifaceted and diverse population of counselors, a multicultural perspective suggests that information and knowledge are not neutral but reflect the views of those who control the decision-making process (Hidalgo & Almeida, 1991). Rehabilitation counseling can be implemented across all curriculum, training, and practice in conjunction with the well-established Multicultural Rehabilitation Competencies (Middleton et al., 2000). These competencies parallel our belief that advocacy is not solely the responsibility of counselor educators but an additional critical element of the continued educational training for rehabilitation counselors everywhere. It is clear that the Multicultural Rehabilitation Competencies are urgently needed to ensure the ethical practice of rehabilitation counseling (Middleton et al., 2000). By infusing the creative operationalization of these multicultural competencies, rehabilitation counselors are agreeing to further acknowledgment of the field's professional identity and respect of individual differences and values, all of which require continuity and promote multiple levels of advocacy.

References

Age Discrimination in Employment Act of 1967, Pub. L. No. 90-202, 81 Stat. 602. Retrieved May 28, 2009, from http://www.eeoc.gov/policy/adea.html

Alston, R. J., & Bell, T. J. (1996). Cultural mistrust and the rehabilitation enigma for African Americans. *Journal of Rehabilitation, 62*(2), 16–20.

Alston, R. J., Harley, D. A., & Middleton, R. A. (2006). The role of rehabilitation in achieving social justice for minorities with disabilities. *Journal of Vocational Rehabilitation, 24,* 129–136.

Americans With Disabilities Act of 1990, Pub. L. No. 101-336, § 2, 104 Stat. 328 (1991). Retrieved May 28, 2009, from http://www.eeoc.gov/policy/ada.html

Atkins, B. J., & Wright, G. N. (1980). Three views: Vocational rehabilitation of Blacks: The statement. *Journal of Rehabilitation, 46*(2), 40, 42–46.

Bellini, J. (2002). Correlates of multicultural counseling competencies of vocational rehabilitation counselors. *Rehabilitation Counseling Bulletin, 45,* 66–75.

Bond, G. R., Drake, R. E., Becker, D. R., & Mueser, K. T. (1999). Effectiveness of psychiatric rehabilitation approaches for employment of people with severe mental illness. *Journal of Disability Studies, 10,* 18–52.

Capuzzi, D., & Gross, D. (2003). *Counseling and psychotherapy: Theories and interventions.* Upper Saddle River, NJ: Merrill Prentice Hall.

Conley, R. W. (1999). Severe mental illness and the continuing evolution of the federal–state vocational rehabilitation program. *Journal of Disability Policy Studies, 10,* 99–126.

Cook, J. A. (1999). Understanding the failure of vocational rehabilitation: What do we need to know and how can we learn? *Journal of Rehabilitation Administration, 18,* 6–21.

Council for Accreditation of Counseling and Related Educational Programs. (2009). *2009 standards.* Retrieved May 26, 2009, from http://www.cacrep.org/2009Standards.html

Council on Rehabilitation Education. (2005). *Accreditation manual.* Retrieved May 26, 2009, from http://www.core-rehab.org/accrman.html

D'Angelo, A. M., & Dixey, B. P. (2001). Using multicultural resources for teachers to combat racial prejudice in the classroom. *Early Childhood Education Journal, 29,* 83–87.

Dobren, A. A. (1994). An ecologically oriented conceptual model of vocational rehabilitation of people with acquired midcareer disabilities. *Rehabilitation Counseling Bulletin, 37,* 215–228.

Dunston-McLee, C. H. (2001). Rehabilitation counselors' attitudes toward persons with coexisting mental illness and substance abuse disorders (Doctoral dissertation, University of Maryland, College Park, 2001). *Dissertation Abstracts International,* 3035770.

Dziekan, K. I., & Okocha, A. G. (1993). Accessibility of rehabilitation services: Comparison by racial–ethnic status. *Rehabilitation Counseling Bulletin, 36,* 183–189.

Finch, J., & Robinson, M. (2003). Aging and late-onset disability: Addressing workplace accommodation. *Journal of Rehabilitation, 69*(2), 38–42.

Granello, D. H., & Wheaton, J. (1998). Self-perceived multicultural competencies of African American and European American vocational rehabilitation counselors. *Rehabilitation Counseling Bulletin, 42,* 2–15.

Harley, D. A., Feist-Price, S., & Alston, R. J. (1996). Ethics and culture: A need for diversity in the rehabilitation counselor code of ethics. *Rehabilitation Education, 10,* 201–210.

Herbert, J. T., & Martinez, M. Y. (1992). Client ethnicity and vocational rehabilitation case service outcome. *Journal of Job Placement, 8,* 10–16.

Hidalgo, N., & Almeida, C. (1991). Multiculturalism sparks tense debate. *New Voices, 1*(2).

Leahy, M. J., & Szymanski, E. M. (1995). Rehabilitation counseling: Evolution and current status. *Journal of Counseling & Development, 74,* 163–166.

Lewis, J. A., Arnold, M. S., House, R., & Toporek, R. L. (2002). *ACA Advocacy Competencies.* Retrieved July 17, 2008, from http://www.counseling.org/Publications/

Lewis, J. A., Lewis, M. D., Daniels, J. A., & D'Andrea, M. J. (1998). *Community counseling: Empowerment strategies for a diverse society.* Pacific Grove, CA: Brooks/Cole.

Locke, D. C. (1993). *Multicultural counseling.* Ann Arbor, MI: ERIC Clearinghouse on Counseling and Personnel Services. Retrieved May 3, 2007, from http://www.ericfacility.net/databases/ERIC_Digests/ed357316.html

Matrone, K. F., & Leahy, M. J. (2005). The relationship between vocational rehabilitation client outcomes and rehabilitation counselor multicultural counseling competencies. *Rehabilitation Counseling Bulletin, 48,* 233–244.

Middleton, R. A., Rollins, C., Sanderson, P., Leung, P., Harley, D., & Leal-Idrogo, A. (2000). Endorsement of professional multicultural rehabilitation competencies and standards: A call to action. *Rehabilitation Counseling Bulletin, 43,* 219–240.

Mpofu, E., & Harley, D. A. (2006). Racial and disability identity: Implications for the career counseling of African Americans with disabilities. *Rehabilitation Counseling Bulletin, 50,* 14–23.

Mu'min, A., Robinson, M., & Davis, T. (2008). Racial identity and multicultural issues in counselor education: Assessing models to create culturally competent counselors. *Rehabilitation Counselors and Educators Association Journal 2,* 35–43.

Noble, J. H., Jr., Honberg, R. S., Hall, L. L., & Flynn, L. M. (1999). NAMI executive summary. *Journal of Disability Policy Studies, 10,* 5–9.

Ohio Rehabilitation Services Commission. (2001). *Transition guidelines and best practices* (2nd ed.). Columbus, OH: Author.

Parker, R., Szymanski, E., & Patterson, J. (2005). *Rehabilitation counseling: Basics and beyond* (4th ed.). Austin, TX: Pro-Ed.

Paugh, C. (2003). Vocational rehabilitation for persons with dual diagnosis: Specific service patterns that enhance earnings at the time of case closure (Doctoral dissertation, Ohio State University, Columbus, 2003). *Dissertation Abstracts International,* 3088878.

Rehabilitation Act of 1973, Pub. L. 93-112.

Rehabilitation Act, Section 21. (2003). *Rehabilitation Act preamble.* Retrieved April 1, 2004, from http://www.rcep7.org/links/rehabact/Preamble/preamble.html#Sec.3

Rehabilitation Services Administration. (1993). *Rehabilitation Act of 1973 as amended by the Rehabilitation Act of 1992.* Washington, DC: U.S. Department of Education.

Robinson, H. (2005). Vocational rehabilitation for persons with dual diagnosis: An examination of outcomes for minority and non-minority clients (Doctoral dissertation, Ohio State University, Columbus, 2005). *Dissertation Abstracts International,* 3176431.

Robinson, M. (2007). Diversity and vocational rehabilitation: Implications for persons with dual diagnosis. *Rehabilitation Counselors and Educators Association Journal, 1*(2), 32–39.

Robinson, T. L. (1999). The intersections of dominant discourse across race, gender, and other identities. *Journal of Counseling & Development, 77,* 73–79.

Smart, J. F., & Smart, D. W. (1997). The racial/ethnic demography of disability. *Journal of Rehabilitation, 63*(4), 9–15.

Strohl, D., Robinson, M., & Wilson, K. B. (2008). RSA service delivery for underrepresented groups: Where are we and where are we going? *Proceedings of the National Association of Multicultural Rehabilitation Concerns.* Alexandria, VA: National Association of Multicultural Rehabilitation Concerns.

Sue, D. W., Arredondo, P., & McDavis, R. J. (1992). Multicultural competencies and standards: A call to the profession. *Journal of Counseling & Development, 70,* 477–486.

Sue, D. W., Bernier, J. E., Durran, A., Feinberg, L., Pedersen, P., Smith, E. J., & Vasquez-Nutall, E. (1982). Position paper: Cross-cultural counseling competencies. *The Counseling Psychologist, 10,* 45–52.

Sue, D. W., & Sue, D. (2003). *Counseling the culturally different: Theory and practice.* New York: Wiley.

Szymanski, E. (1985). Rehabilitation counseling: A profession with a vision, an identity, and a future. *Rehabilitation Counseling Bulletin, 29,* 2–5.

Toporek, R. L., Lewis, J. A., & Crethar, H. C. (2009). Promoting systemic change through the Advocacy Competencies. *Journal of Counseling & Development, 87,* 260–268.

Toporek, R. L., & Liu, W. M. (2001). Advocacy in counseling: Addressing race, class, and gender oppression. In D. B. Pope-Davis & H. L. K. Coleman (Eds.), *The intersection of race, class, and gender in multicultural counseling* (pp. 285–413). Thousand Oaks, CA: Sage.

Vash, C. (1987). Fighting another's battles: When is it helpful? Professional? Ethical? *Journal of Applied Rehabilitation Counseling, 18,* 15–16.

Vontress, C., & Epp, L. (1997). Historical hostility in the African American client: Implications for counseling. *Journal of Multicultural Counseling and Development, 25,* 170–184.

Watson, A. L., & Collins, R. (1993). Culturally sensitive training for professional. *Journal of Vocational Rehabilitation, 3*(1), 1.

Wheaton, J. E., Wilson, K. B., & Brown, S. M. (1996). The relationship between vocational rehabilitation services and the consumer's sex, race, and closure status. *Rehabilitation Counseling Bulletin, 40,* 116–133.

Wilson, K. B. (2002). The exploration of vocational rehabilitation acceptance and ethnicity: A national investigation. *Rehabilitation Counseling Bulletin, 45,* 168–176.

Wilson, K. B., Jackson, R. L., & Doughty, J. (1999). What a difference a race makes: Reasons for unsuccessful closures within the vocational rehabilitation system. *American Rehabilitation, 25,* 16–24.

Chapter 18

ACA Advocacy Competencies in Family Counseling

Bret Hendricks, Loretta J. Bradley, and Judith A. Lewis

At the heart of competent advocacy lies the belief that individuals are deeply affected by their environments. With this undeniable fact in mind, advocacy-oriented counselors know that their ability to provide truly effective help to individuals depends to a great extent on their capacity for intervening at broader levels. Family counseling, like advocacy, has historically had systemic thinking at its heart.

> Early family pioneers took the focus of pathology (problems) out of the individual and situated it in interactions between couples and family members. Problems were generated through the faulty interaction and communication patterns formed in families. Individuals were no longer seen as being the locus of the problem, and hence the focus of intervention shifted as well. Interventions quickly spread to encompass the entire system of the family or the couple. This shift of thinking, from the individual to the system, represents what may be the greatest leap in the treatment of family problems. (West, Bubenzer, & Bitter, 1998, p. 12)

The systemic thinking that characterizes the family counselor would seem, at first glance, to mean that a natural kinship exists between family work and advocacy. What has prevented this affinity from being fully realized, however, lies in the size of the system being addressed. Yes, family counselors do recognize that the individual's well-being is inextricably tied to the family. What they have not always noted as clearly is that the family itself exists within a powerful social, political, economic, and cultural milieu. McGoldrick and Hardy (2008) went so far as to say that "we continually turn a blind eye to the pervasive impact of oppression on the poor, the racially oppressed, and other marginalized groups" (pp. 6–7).

Moving the "locus of the problem" from the individual to the family was an important first step. Now, it is time for family counselors to take a second step: moving toward the use of an even wider lens as they examine the systems affecting—even oppressing—their clients.

Markowitz's (1997) multicontextual approach to working with couples highlights the importance of the wide lens:

> From this new perspective, the couple is no longer just two individuals wrestling in an interpersonal bubble or acting out their extended family dramas. . . . The couple's struggles suddenly make a

different kind of sense, as it becomes possible to see how their personal lives are entangled with the large, public forces of economics, politics, culture and history. . . . From that perspective, they can begin to notice how much of their conflict stems from pervasive social influence that they may never have seen so clearly before, like bleak economic prospects, political systems that discriminate against them, a culture that devalues them, societal messages that attack their self-esteem. (p. 53)

A family counselor who studies multiple contexts is unlikely to turn a blind eye toward the reality that oppression is the thread that connects many of the most damaging external factors affecting family life. As Carlson, Sperry, and Lewis (2005) noted, "The process of oppression is insidious because targeted people must face a lethal combination of overt bigotry, covert discrimination, and a socialization process that encourages internalization of negative self-views. How could this process fail to affect the dynamics of family interactions?" (p. 126). Once the multiple contexts of family behavior and the impact of oppression are recognized, both the therapeutic process itself and the potential for environmental intervention become clear.

Oppression, of course, has many targets, and it would be a rare counselor whose practice somehow sidestepped oppressed families. Consider, for example, the impact of racism.

The family has been contested ground for people of color in the United States since their initial contact with the West through conquest, enslavement, forced labor, colonization, and second-class citizenship. Societal protection and the idea of family as sacrosanct were benefits that were never afforded families of color. In fact, just the opposite is true. Families of color, historically, have been victims of legal and social measures that undermined their ability to nurture and provide economically for their members. Against the forces of institutionalized racism, sexism, and classism, people of color have had to fashion families that supported their physical as well as spiritual survival in a social context that ranged from benign neglect to open hostility. (Arnold, 2001, p. 15)

It is important to discern that connections among racism and other forms of oppression might come to the fore in working with families. Now, in a time of economic crisis, the impact of poverty must also claim the counselor's attention.

The gap between rich and poor continues to increase. Violence, including acts perpetrated by hate groups, perseveres. A backlash against equality shows itself in English-only movements, discrimination against immigrants, and attacks on affirmative action. The goal of universal coverage for health care seems to become more distant each year. Punitiveness toward the poor is disguised as welfare reform. Treatment for addiction is more likely to occur in prisons than in the health care system. Schools are failing to meet the needs of the children that need them most. (Arredondo & Lewis, 2001, p. 266)

It is not unusual for multiple, oppression-related issues to affect one family, as the example we will follow in this chapter makes clear. Given this dose of reality, any family counselor would be drawn to the concept of advocacy. As McGoldrick and Hardy (2008) pointed out, "It is impossible to understand or treat poor families without a comprehensive understanding of how stigma and limited access to resources affect (them)" (p. 6).

Operationalizing the Advocacy Competencies

In this chapter, we present as an ongoing illustration the case of a family that is affected by multiple oppressions. Using the Soto/Torres family as the base of discussion, we lay out a plan for using the American Counseling Association (ACA) Advocacy Competencies (Lewis, Arnold, House, & Toporek, 2002) at several levels and encompassing varied systems. The advocacy action plans described illustrate that, in order for family counseling to be successful, systems traditionally seen as "outside the family" must be viewed as inexorably connected to the family. Neighborhood, community, state, national, and international systems all influence each family and have direct impact on the success or failure of counseling interventions.

The Soto/Torres Family

The Soto/Torres family became the clients of a family counselor largely because of a crisis affecting one child: Carlos. Carlos, the oldest of the family's three children, was 14 years old and in the seventh grade, 1 year behind grade level. He had already had numerous encounters with the law, many of which were drug related. This time he was booked with a "minor in possession" charge, for which he was sentenced either to go to a youth corrections center for 6 months or to attend at least 3 months of court-ordered drug treatment offered through a juvenile-detention-sponsored drug treatment center. He chose drug treatment because it was 3 months instead of 6.

Carlos lived with his mother, Margareta, and his stepfather, Alberto Torres. Carlos's younger brother, Tomas, was also caught up in the juvenile justice system. The youngest child, Marisa, was in third grade and doing well. Carlos's mother, Margareta, had a part-time job earning minimum wage. Alberto was unemployed at this time but worked in-season at an agriculture processing facility. This year, though, he was not sure that he could afford the gasoline to get to work, and there was no public transportation available. Some child support money did come from Margareta's first husband, Carlos's father, but his financial position was also shaky.

The Soto/Torres family lived in a small house in a West Texas town. In their neighborhood, the crime rate was high and conveniences were few. The nearest grocery store was 3 miles away, the nearest post office 2 miles away. The street signs in the neighborhood were very old and difficult to read, so mail was often simply left at the post office. If fire or medical assistance was requested, it rarely arrived in time. The few small shops in the neighborhood sold incidentals to those with no transportation, but the wares were of dubious quality and high cost. There was a church across the street from the Soto/Torres house and schools were reasonably close. Medical care was available at a large hospital 6 miles away, and the nearest pharmacy was at the previously mentioned grocery store 3 miles away. For most in the neighborhood, medical care was accessed only in cases of extreme emergency. The Soto/Torres family, like many others, did not seek any preventive medical care because they did not have Medicaid or any other assistance. Margareta had been unable to get an appointment to meet with a case worker. Appointments were to be made 30 days in advance, and Margareta could never plan that far ahead because her work schedule would not allow it. Margareta was worried because she knew this was very important, but she could not risk the little income that the family had by being absent from work. The worry about the need for medical care was underscored for Margareta when she recently had the flu and pneumonia. She had to go to the emergency room at the hospital for care because she had no insurance. When she left the hospital, she had four prescriptions and a bill for nearly $3,000. She knew that she could afford neither the hospital bill nor the medicine. The letters and phone calls from the hospital said that she must start paying on the bill or they would give her name to a collection agency.

Given the combination between too many stressors and too few resources, the entire family was experiencing chaos. Between problems at school, problems with the law, problems with work, and seemingly insurmountable problems with finances, the family was constantly in turmoil. Adding to the chaos was the fact that all of the outside entities involved demanded time from the family. Probation meetings, parenting meetings, school progress meetings, and counseling all take time. The family constantly felt that they were about to implode.

The Referral

Laura Henry is a family counselor who has a contract to provide services to the juvenile justice system when family interventions are deemed necessary. In this situation, Carlos was the identified patient in a family that was seen as dysfunctional. Laura was not surprised at the attitude displayed by the detention officer who handed her the referral.

"We've got another one for you," he said. "Tomas, the kid who's over in short-term—that's his brother. He got himself caught with a bag of weed and a six pack."

The officer went on to tell Laura that, although he had to make the referral because of program protocols, he did not expect the family counseling to be very successful.

"Don't expect much from his mom or dad. Neither one of them does anything to discipline these kids, and they can't ever get anywhere on time for probation meetings or school. On top of this, they always make excuses; especially the mom who says that she can't get here because" he pauses dramatically and raises an eyebrow, "she 'can't get off work.'" He sighed, "These families are just a lost cause, and this one is really a mess. Stepdad just finished his time for a DUI and both kids are with us. Good luck, like you can do anything with this one!"

Laura was accustomed to hearing families described in this way, with the family being blamed for the presenting problem and most of the culpability being laid at the feet of the mother. All too often, the mother would arrive at the counseling office defensive and guarded, internalizing blame and seeing herself as a failure for being unable to provide for the nurturing and material needs of the entire family. Laura knew how important it was to establish a collaborative and supportive relationship with a family in stress.

> The phrase 'relational stance' refers to the way in which we approach clients. We can choose how we position ourselves in relation to others. We can position ourselves in ways that strengthen respect, curiosity, and connection in the therapeutic relationship. We can also position ourselves in ways that inadvertently pull us toward judgment, disconnection, and disapproval. (Madsen, 1999, pp. 1–2)

Laura knew how easy it was even for a counselor to fall into the kind of pessimism exemplified by the detention officer. Instead, she would be what Madsen terms an *appreciative ally*. "The phrase 'appreciative ally' refers to an approach in which clients experience us as 'on their side.' This approach necessitates a continual search for elements of competence, connection, vision, and hope in our work with families" (Madsen, 1999, p. 2). The respectful stance of an ally, which is so in tune with the advocacy orientation, is exactly what this particular family needed.

The Family Level

At the client/student level, the Advocacy Competencies emphasize empowerment-based direct interventions along with environmental interventions that help clients and students overcome barriers and gain access to needed resources. For the family counselor, the center of attention moves from the client or student to the family, but the same competencies apply. Working with a family, especially a family that is subject to multiple oppressions, requires that the counselor knows how to move the family as a whole in the direction of self-advocacy while continuing to recognize that counselor action on behalf of the family may be needed as well.

Empowerment and the Soto/Torres Family

Laura, the family counselor, knew how important it was to use an empowerment-focused approach with this family. The referring agency, as we know, had given only negative and even pejorative information about every member of the family unit. Laura knew how easy it would be to become part of a system that had already promoted disrespect, lack of empathy, and bias. Because this issue was intrinsic in most of the referrals she received, Laura had always known that she would have to be rigorous in her own self-examination. She knew that many of the families she served had virtually no experience of positive interactions with people in the human service, health, and educational settings. Their interactions had been punitive, evaluative, and even, in their eyes, vindictive. If she were not self-aware, she could fall into this pattern as well.

One of the things that Laura had done when she first came to the West Texas town she now called home was to try to confront her bias and increase her self-awareness simply by going into the neighborhoods in which her clients lived. By seeing the neighborhood first hand, she gained insight into the daily functioning of community members. What are the houses like? How available are public transportation, grocery stores, and social service agencies? Is there a park nearby? Are there activities for children? Is there a place to play other than the streets? Is medical treatment available? Is there a pharmacy in the neighborhood? What complications make it difficult for clients to keep appointments with human service workers? Perhaps the most salient thing she learned was that clients' statements about the difficulties in their lives—seen by many helpers as excuses—were all too painfully true. The most important thing she could do as a family counselor was to help the family recognize these barriers and develop strategies for overcoming or going around them.

The Soto/Torres family had experienced outside systems as being punitive and judgmental. People who had the task of helping them had deemed the family system a failure. Laura, through her strengths-based approach, saw the family differently. Margareta, the mother, had a job that was very important to her. Rather than seeing this as something that merely got in the way of probation appointments, Laura saw that the acquisition and retention of this job was a point of pride for Margareta. Alberto, the stepfather, had recently completed the court-ordered requirements of probation for his DUI charge. He was proud of the fact that he had finished this task successfully and even more proud that he had maintained sobriety through attending AA. While others might have seen Alberto's struggle with addiction as a negative, Laura saw his hard work as an indication of an intense will to succeed. In the past, other helpers had berated the family for making excuses and not "following through." One example of this problem was that neither Margaret nor Alberto read English very well, but they had always been expected to complete complex paperwork related to Medicaid. The social services and health systems moved, in effect, from helper to oppressor when their representatives failed to notice that both Margareta and Alberto, despite the barriers they faced, were committed to doing whatever their family needed, including paperwork.

Part of Margareta's and Alberto's story is that they were able to overcome an obstacle because Laura, their counselor, helped them understand the Medicaid application process and then checked the application for completeness before it was submitted. This effort may seem minor on first reading, but it did not seem minor to this family. Laura did not do the application for them; she simply facilitated and encouraged a process that had tremendous practical value while also enhancing the family's sense of its own power. It should be noted that many families find the process of accessing social, educational, and health services daunting. Applications are usually available online, but many families lack home access to computers. Once families find their way around these barriers, they are faced with the difficulty of traveling to social service offices when their work hours are long and their transportation options limited. Families are often denied services because they have not been able to manage problems related to application or access. In these situations, it is the counselor's duty to provide the tools and encouragement that their clients need.

Family Advocacy

As families try to get their needs met through the systems that are responsible for helping them, the counselor's first choice is, of course, to assist them in learning self-advocacy. In Margareta's and Alberto's situation, their problems related to Medicaid provided a learning opportunity that could prove valuable in future challenges. Sometimes, of course, families still need someone else to speak up on their behalf. In this family's case, their counselor, Laura, knew that they had filled out their Medicaid application correctly and submitted it in a timely manner. After a sufficient amount of time had passed, she checked with them and found that they had still not heard whether they had been approved. Laura did a follow-up call herself, knowing that she was more likely to find a listening ear at the agency.

Laura also found it necessary, with the Soto/Torres family and many others in her practice, to advocate on behalf of young people like Carlos and Tomas who were caught up in the juvenile justice system. Parents always find it heartbreaking when their children are in trouble. They want to do whatever they can to advocate for their children, but they may find it grueling because the systems are so resistant to change, they lack the financial resources that could help them access legal assistance, and, most of all, they do not know what rights their children have. In this case, because Laura was knowledgeable about the justice system and sensitive to the family's needs, she was able to speak up for Carlos and Tomas, not to protect them from the consequences of their behaviors, but to make sure that their treatment was fair and equitable.

Laura routinely contacted agencies and institutions on behalf of the families she served, knowing that sometimes families' voices would not be heard. Through a combination of direct empowerment strategies and family advocacy, Laura was able to put into practice the Advocacy Competencies of identifying barriers to healthy family development, negotiating relevant services, and helping families gain access to needed resources.

The Community Level

The Advocacy Competencies state, "When counselors identify systemic factors that act as barriers to their students' or clients' development, they often wish that they could change the environment and prevent some of the problems that they see every day" (Lewis et al., 2002, p. 5). When counselors are confronted with families who desperately want to succeed but who are unable to care for their most vulnerable members, this wish becomes an imperative. Working with many such families, day after day, can convince even the most recalcitrant counselor that healthy families depend for their lifeblood on healthy communities.

In the West Texas town where the Soto/Torres family lived, the healthy development of children and youths was jeopardized by the lack of resources in the community and lack of opportunity in the educational system. Laura and other counselors realized that in order to prevent some of the problems being faced by families, they would have to take action by developing alliances with organizations in the community and by putting their own ingenuity to play in bringing about change. They began by focusing on simple, practical strategies that had the potential for generating larger changes.

Access

The Soto/Torres family was not the only one that had difficulties regarding access to health and human service assistance. Access problems were particularly problematic when the services being accessed involved the juvenile justice system. Families that failed to appear for their mandated contacts with their child's probation agent knew that they might be jeopardizing the child's future. The worry they felt on behalf of their children was very real, but that did not give them the power to change the location of the probation office, which was many miles away from their neighborhood.

The neighborhood church, in contrast, was an accessible source of support, providing Sunday lunches and afternoon activities for children and adolescents and acting as a regular meeting place for community activities. A meeting with families and concerned community members spawned an audacious idea: Why not ask the probation agents to meet with families in the church? Virtually no one actually believed that this idea would be accepted by a probation office that had seldom been involved in community outreach. Laura volunteered to bring the idea to the probation office administrator and was as surprised as anyone when he proved amenable to the idea. Probation meetings began to take place at the church building. The program was so successful in lessening the problem of no-shows that the juvenile justice system began offering parenting classes and anger management training at the church building instead of at the probation office where they were usually held. Attendance at meetings and trainings was increased by 50% with a simple change of location. This seemingly small change also led the way for other human services in the area to take a harder look at the question of accessibility.

Access to human service resources can be affected by changing the location of services, but there is also another option: improve the transportation itself. When counselors and community members see that public transportation is not readily available for a neighborhood, two choices arise: bemoan the problem or play a part in fixing it. In this community, counselors chose to play a part in change, even though the goal seemed daunting. A counselor, on behalf of the community, went to the local transportation provider to find out what would need to occur to bring increased public transportation to specific areas of town.

The answer: Prove that a need exists and that there is public demand.

The strategy: A door-to-door petition drive.

The short-term outcome: A new bus route to and from the target neighborhood.

The longer term outcome: A sense among community members that participation can bring results.

Some of the local school counselors also signed on to this advocacy effort. These counselors had been working hard within their own schools to build an environment conducive to academic success. In keeping with the concept of school–family–community partnerships (Bryan & Holcomb-McCoy, 2007), they could see the connection between the academic challenges faced by their students and the community pressures faced by these students' families. The participation of school counselors in these efforts led to an increased sense of community, with parents and other community members now able to see the school as a source of support that they had not trusted in the past.

Participation

These experiences of collaboration between community members and public agencies and institutions helped to lead in the direction of consumer memberships on the advisory boards of mental health and social service agencies in the area. Most service provider agencies have wisely added consumers to their advisory boards. When counselors become aware of situations where this is not taking place, the counselor might suggest that consumers be actively sought to provide feedback for the services that they receive. In some states, consumers serving on advisory boards for family services have themselves become outspoken advocates by providing testimony at local, state, and national venues. In essence, the empowerment of the individual family goes on to enhance the community, which in turn has impact on myriad systems at state and national levels.

The Larger Public Arena

According to the Advocacy Competencies, "Counselors regularly act as change agents in the systems that affect their own students and clients most directly. This experience leads toward the recognition that some of the concerns they have addressed affect people in a much larger arena" (Lewis et al., 2002, p. 6). When this happens, counselors use a combination of public information and social/political advocacy to bring about the change that is needed.

The Texas counselors whom we have been following in this chapter enlarged their focus from the family to the community and, finally, by necessity, to still larger systems. One potential crisis was averted in Texas in a year when Medicaid funding for adult mental health services failed to be reinstated, thus rendering hundreds of thousands of adults without any access to mental health services. Counselors, through the Texas Counseling Association (TCA), moved into action, calling upon not only counselors but also social workers, psychologists, nurses, and psychiatrists to coalesce and move as a single body to rally for the reinstatement of these services. They were successful in that year. In ensuing years, this collaboration has had to continue because Medicaid funding is not perpetually guaranteed, it is merely reapproved (or not) through each legislative session. TCA and its coalition partners not only continue to work with one another but also keep adding new members to the coalition. Included in this coalition now are representatives from affected groups and community and regional social service and mental health provider representatives.

Further emphasizing the idea that community advocacy has a ripple effect on larger systems, a counselor in a midsized city observed that few adolescents in her poverty-stricken community were realizing their dreams of higher education. Young people like Carlos and his siblings had little hope of the possibility of higher education. The counselor worked to organize a meeting of the administrators of colleges and universities in her area. The meeting, held in the neighborhood center and presented to an overflow crowd, was the first meeting ever held at which high-level administrators of all the area colleges and universities presented together on the same platform. The organizers made sure that the attendees were able to ask questions of the panel prior to the presentations. The panel members were so moved by the community pleas to increase the availability of higher education for their community that the administrators agreed to better align entrance requirements with community needs, to make financial aid more readily available, and to increase grant availability to include middle-income families. Now, one of the universities is making a national plea challenging other universities to increase access to higher education, stop increasing tuition rates, and generally make higher education more readily available to those who no longer can afford to go to college.

The Soto/Torres family, like many others, needs entree to good education; access to health care, including prevention programs; affordable housing; and responsive human service systems. Family counselors are in a good position to discern the impact of these interrelated systems and understand that advocacy on behalf of families must take place at every systemic level.

Multicultural and Diversity Issues

Advocacy-oriented counseling is inextricably connected with antioppression work, which means that it must have a multicultural perspective at its core. As Ivey and Ivey (2001) pointed out, "the failure to see cultural and contextual issues actually denies and oppresses those whom we seek to help" (p. 221). This fact becomes particularly salient when we consider the work of family counselors.

> Along with race and ethnicity, a family's culture can be affected by age, language, social class, income, geographical location, education, religion, gender, sexual orientation, and myriad other factors. Family members may also hold values and worldviews that differ from those of the therapist. In fact, cultural differences may even occur among family members themselves. The key to a multicultural perspective is to embrace the reality of cultural diversity, recognizing the impact of culture on family life and working with all clients in accordance with their own cultural meanings. (Carlson et al., 2005, p. 122)

When family counselors provide direct services to their clients, they always need to begin with a high degree of self-examination, making sure that their assumptions about what family life should be do not taint their approach with families whose worldviews may differ from their own. This step becomes especially important when client families are affected by multiple oppressions. The Soto/ Torres family and many of their fellow community members are adversely affected by a world that stereotypes and demeans people with low incomes, people for whom English is a second language, and people who are caught up in the criminal justice system. They may lack access to community resources while simultaneously being blamed for not making use of them. The adults are so blatantly criticized for their parenting skills that they begin to internalize the notion that they are somehow lacking. The children receive few messages of hope and optimism for their futures. The counselors who succeeded in carrying out advocacy work in their community were able to do so only because they, themselves, first went through an intensive process of cultural learning. According to Sanders (2000),

> Cultural Awareness is the first step. Advocates must know themselves. To advocate against endemic constructs, one must have a personal conviction grounded from self analysis. Notice instances when you collude with tripartite oppression. Make opportunities for your views to be challenged and expanded. Unlearning oppression may initially be frightening, but it is liberating as you challenge the essence of who you are. (pp. 18–19)

Challenges

Throughout this chapter, we focused primarily on what Madsen (1999) called *multistressed families*. Such families can also be described as families that bear the brunt of multiple oppressions. It should not be surprising to realize that these families often bear a strong sense of distrust for people who purport to be helpers. Lewis and Arnold (1998) wrote,

> People are frequently victimized by the very systems and institutions that have supposedly been set up to serve them. Impersonal bureaucracies such as welfare and child protective services may intrude in and constrict the lives of individuals through the imposition of dominant cultural values. Health care, educational, and legal systems often play abuse roles in the lives of people who should be able to receive help from them. . . . People suffer every day from oppression by health, education, and human service systems that should be ameliorating their pain instead of adding to it. (p. 57)

In the face of this barrier, family counselors are obliged to take action to build bonds of trust with their clients.

Of course, all counselors know that the relationships they forge within their office walls must be built on an expectation of trust. What they might not have realized, however, is that the assumption of trust is even more important in their advocacy work—and yet more difficult to engender. Advocacy involves a level of risk that can sometimes be worrisome for clients. Suppose the mother in our case, Margareta, takes seriously the self-advocacy skills she has learned in the context of family counseling. If she uses those skills to confront a juvenile justice officer who has power over her children, what might happen? Suppose her counselor, Laura, somehow fails in her effort to follow up on the family's Medicaid application. What might happen? Advocacy addresses delicate matters, matters that may be more treacherous than the intrapsychic processes that are seen as frightening by so many people. It is true that intrapsychic probing can expose wounds, but advocacy can also awaken the dangerous beasts of oppression. The challenge faced by counselors and clients is to make sure that the risks as well as the benefits of advocacy are carefully weighed. If counselors and clients carefully expose and address any potential threats to the client's well-being before action is taken, the benefits will surely outweigh the challenges.

Benefits

To say that competent advocacy is *beneficial* may be a vast understatement. It may be more accurate to say that, when it comes to good counseling, advocacy is *necessary*. An advocacy-oriented counselor brings to the counseling process an understanding that people's lives are lived in context. When counselors ignore context, they are not just making a choice between theories; they are wrong.

An advocacy-oriented approach to counseling provides a perspective that can help counselors and their clients recognize and overcome the "fundamental attribution error" (FAE). The FAE is a common error that skews the ways in which people explain the behaviors of others. Gladwell (2000) explained that people all tend to use a dispositional explanation of events as opposed to an explanation based on context. "When it comes to interpreting other people's behaviors, human beings invariably make the mistake of overestimating the importance of fundamental character traits and underestimating the importance of the situation and context" (Gladwell, 2000, p. 160).

Unfortunately, people in the helping professions are as prone to this misattribution as anyone else. Even family counselors, whose work depends on awareness of systems, often overlook the role of environmental factors. To the detriment of their clients, some family counselors still focus more attention on negative characteristics that are internal to the family than they do on the cultural, political, and economic factors that affect their clients' lives. All too often, the counseling spotlight stays on the clients' diagnoses rather than on their strengths and on their personal vulnerabilities rather than on their environments. The result is that families feel increasingly powerless.

When family counselors bring a focus on advocacy into their work, they can wipe away that feeling of powerlessness and help families see the possibility of change. What could possibly be better than that?

Conclusion

This chapter began by exploring what should be the natural affinity between family counseling and advocacy. Family counselors, by the very nature of their work, recognize that individuals are deeply affected by their family systems. An advocacy orientation helps them recognize that families, in turn, are affected just as deeply by their social, political, economic, and cultural milieus. The case of Soto/Torres, a West Texas family affected by multiple stresses, provided an example of advocacy-oriented counseling in action as their family counselor moved from family advocacy to community organizing and finally to social/political advocacy at the state level.

References

Arnold, M. S. (2001). Women of color and feminist family counseling: Caveats. In K. M. May (Ed.), *Feminist family therapy* (pp. 15–27). Alexandria, VA: American Counseling Association.

Arredondo, P., & Lewis, J. (2001). Counselor roles for the 21st century. In D. C. Locke, J. E. Myers, & E. L. Herr (Eds.), *The handbook of counseling* (pp. 257–268). Thousand Oaks, CA: Sage.

Bryan, J., & Holcomb-McCoy, C. (2007). An examination of school counselor involvement in school–family–community partnerships. *Professional School Counseling, 10,* 441–454.

Carlson, J., Sperry, L., & Lewis, J. A. (2005). *Family therapy techniques: Integrating and tailoring treatment.* New York: Routledge.

Gladwell, M. (2000). *The tipping point: How little things can make a big difference.* Boston: Little, Brown.

Ivey, A. E., & Ivey, M. B. (2001). Developmental counseling and therapy and multicultural counseling and therapy: Metatheory, contextual consciousness, and action. In D. C. Locke, J. E. Myers, & E. L. Herr (Eds.), *The handbook of counseling* (pp. 219–236). Thousand Oaks, CA: Sage.

Lewis, J. A., & Arnold, M. S. (1998). From multiculturalism to social action. In C. C. Lee & G. R. Walz (Eds.), *Social action: A mandate for counselors* (pp. 51–66). Alexandria, VA: American Counseling Association.

Lewis, J. A., Arnold, M. S., House, R., & Toporek, R. L. (2002). *ACA Advocacy Competencies.* Retrieved February 1, 2009, from http://www.counseling.org/Publications/

Madsen, W. C. (1999). *Collaborative therapy with multi-stressed families: From old problems to new futures.* New York: Guilford Press.

Markowitz, L. (1997). The cultural context of intimacy. *Family Therapy Networker, 21*(5), 51–58.

McGoldrick, M., & Hardy, K. V. (2008). Introduction: Re-visioning family therapy from a multicultural perspective. In M. McGoldrick & K. V. Hardy (Eds.), *Re-visioning family therapy: Race, culture, and gender in clinical practice* (2nd ed., pp. 3–24). New York: Guilford Press.

Sanders, J. L. (2000). Advocacy on behalf of African-American clients. In J. Lewis & L. Bradley (Eds.), *Advocacy in counseling: Counselors, clients, and community.* Greensboro, NC: ERIC/CAPS.

West, J. D., Bubenzer, D. L., & Bitter, J. R. (1998). *Social construction in couple and family counseling.* Alexandria, VA: American Counseling Association.

Chapter

19

Applying the ACA Advocacy Competencies to Group Work

Deborah J. Rubel and Jennifer Pepperell

Applying the American Counseling Association (ACA) Advocacy Competencies (Lewis, Arnold, House, & Toporek, 2002) to group work is essential. In this chapter, we provide a rationale for applying the Advocacy Competencies to group work, outline the unique properties of group work that affect application of the Advocacy Competencies, and then describe their application to group work using a case example. Finally, we summarize the diversity and multicultural issues, challenges, and benefits of applying the Advocacy Competencies to group work.

Rationale for Applying the Advocacy Competencies

Group work is used in prevention and treatment across many populations and encompasses task groups, psychoeducational groups, and counseling and therapy groups (Association for Specialists in Group Work [ASGW], 1998). The literature suggests that group work is particularly useful for work with culturally diverse people (Merta, 1995). Application of the Advocacy Competencies to group work is becoming increasingly important as attributions of client distress move from intrapsychic to ecological and sociopolitical causes and group workers are encouraged to look outside their groups to understand and intervene in the functioning of their groups and group members (Bemak & Conyne, 2004; Tropman, 2004). Additionally, the ASGW Diversity Competencies state that group workers should be aware of how oppression affects group and group member functioning and how institutional barriers restrict full participation of marginalized populations in the spectrum of helping groups (ASGW, 1999). The Diversity Competencies further state that group workers should have the skills to intervene at the institutional level to address inequalities resulting from biases, prejudices, oppression, and discriminatory practices (ASGW, 1999). These mandates to address the systemic causes of client distress speak directly to the necessity of applying the Advocacy Competencies to group work.

The nature of group interaction may also necessitate application of the Advocacy Competencies within the group as well as outside the group at the school/community and public arena levels of advocacy. Group work has been defined by the ASGW (2000) as "a broad professional practice involving the application of knowledge and skill in group facilitation to assist an interdependent collection of people to reach their mutual goals" (p. 329). Further, Kline (2003) asserted that the primary question answered during group work is, "How can we work together in a way that benefits us all?" (p. 7). This suggests the tension that results as the needs of individual members, subgroups, and the group as a whole are balanced in a way that, ideally, does not leave anyone behind. However, too often this balance is not achieved, particularly in groups with diverse or multicultural composition (Merta, 1995; Rubel, 2006). This potential for imbalance indicates that group workers must be able to apply the Advocacy Competencies within their groups.

Finally, the Advocacy Competencies focus on empowerment. The practices of empowerment and group work are inextricably linked in the historic counseling literature. Empowerment groups and consciousness-raising groups have allowed people who share common disempowering experiences to externalize their challenges, gain a sense of control over their lives, and change their environment (O'Brian, 2001). While some literature addresses empowerment through group work (Astramovich & Harris, 2007; Bemak, 2005; Fallot & Harris, 2002; O'Brian, 2001), very little literature specifically describes the facilitation of empowerment in groups. Applying the Advocacy Competencies to group work will encourage group workers to make empowerment a critical element of all groups.

Operationalizing the Advocacy Competencies for Group Work

Several differences critical to applying the Advocacy Competencies exist between individual work and group work. The multilevel environment of groups affects advocacy within groups in the following ways: (a) Advocacy interventions must be beneficial, or at least not harmful, to other group members and the group as a whole; (b) advocacy interventions must respect group members' increased vulnerability due to the group environment; (c) advocacy interventions may be necessary within the group to address inequalities within and outside of the group process; and (d) potential advocacy interventions must be included in the planning of groups for optimal group functioning.

Group work interventions affect the member they are directed at as well as other group members and the group as a whole. Group work can be conceptualized as a web of member-to-member and leader-to-member relationships that support a therapeutic group environment, which in turn supports individual and environmental change (Okech & Rubel, 2007). Ultimately, group leaders are responsible for creating this environment and for encouraging members to benefit from it (Yalom & Leszcz, 2005). To this end, effective group leadership can be characterized as the careful selection, application, and evaluation of interventions that simultaneously maintain a vital group environment and move individuals and the group toward agreed-upon goals (Rubel & Kline, 2008). Thus, group worker advocacy interventions must be selected, applied, and evaluated in terms of benefit to the individual, other group members, and the group environment. This suggests that advocacy interventions for individual group members that do not contribute to other group members and the overall group environment should be conducted outside the group, which in turn may also affect the group environment (Yalom & Leszcz, 2005).

The literature on ethics in the practice of group work outlines areas of increased vulnerability that affect application of the Advocacy Competencies (Corey, Williams, & Moline, 1995), including the following:

1. Confidentiality cannot be guaranteed within group work.
2. The potential for coercion due to group pressure is increased in group work.
3. The potential for psychological harm is increased.

Advocacy interventions within and outside of groups should be evaluated in terms of confidentiality risks, potential for coercion to participate, and potential for psychological harm related to self-disclosure and shaming. Because of issues of confidentiality and vulnerability, group leaders may decide to address an individual member's advocacy issues outside of the group. As with issues that are taken out of the group due to lack of relationship to group purpose and goals, group leaders need to consider how actions outside the group will affect interaction within the group (Yalom & Leszcz, 2005).

Another unique consideration related to advocacy applied to group work is that advocacy may be required on behalf of clients *during* group interaction. Fair and equitable treatment within the boundaries of the group's purpose and goals is the right of all group members (Corey et al., 1995). Recognizing that group member needs are not being met and responding constructively is part of normal group leader functioning. However, understanding these leadership actions as advocacy emphasizes the impact of the social system on the group, the potential impact of group interaction on the world outside the group, and the social responsibility of group workers.

Finally, the literature suggests that groups function best with a level of planning, member selection, and member preparation that may not be necessary for individual counseling (ASGW, 1998). Competent advocacy also requires a high level of planning and intentionality (Ezell, 2001). To achieve this level of intentionality, application of the Advocacy Competencies to group work ideally should begin before the group meets and requires group workers to have a high level of comfort with group work and advocacy principles.

Many of the issues that affect application of the Advocacy Competencies to group work tend to occur within the group and fall under the client/student domain. However, the influence of the macrosystemic level is crucial in the functioning of groups and falls under the collaboration/systems and public domains. To better illustrate the interplay of the three levels in the application of the Advocacy Competencies to group work, we use the following case throughout the discussion.

Case Study

You were recently hired by a women's shelter, and you lead a partner violence survivor's group that provides for both shelter residents and community referrals. The goals of the group are support for partner violence survivors and education about partner violence, but the group often functions as a place to process shelter issues and individual crises. This is the only group dedicated to partner violence survivors in your midsized town. No assessment is done beyond the shelter's intake, and screening is minimal. The group is open and frequently has new members. You are concerned because the executive director is unhappy with the low number of community referrals that remain in the group past their first session. More immediately on your mind is Amy, who has attended the group for 8 weeks and is the only community referral in the group. She has made some positive changes outside the group, but her self-disclosures are brief, careful, and indirect. When encouraged to speak, she reported that she might quit attending because school, work, child care, and other obligations make her schedule difficult. The stress has her feeling that another relationship may be the only way out, although she knows she is not ready to make healthy relationship choices. The normally supportive group is silent after she shares.

Applying the Advocacy Competencies in the Client/Student Domain

The client/student domain of the Advocacy Competencies describes counselor action, either empowerment or client advocacy, focused on an individual case (Toporek, Lewis, & Crethar, 2009). The first step is to become aware that a group member's needs are not being met either in the group or in the environment. This is challenging in an individual setting but becomes more so in the more complex environment of groups. Group leaders must be sensitive to cues about group members' experiences in the group and outside the group.

Group Work and the Client/Student Empowerment Domain

While group work and empowerment seem a natural fit, the multilayered environment of the group may make translating empowerment from one-on-one counseling to group counseling challenging. Lee (1994) suggested that group workers must have the skills to plan empowerment into groups, see group interaction in terms of opportunities for and barriers to empowerment, and encourage empowering interaction not only between leaders and members but also between members. Ideally, before the group begins, group workers should plan for empowerment by evaluating the group goals, group composition, group structure, and pregroup preparation.

While not every group is an empowerment group, group leaders should decide how empowerment fits with client goals, group goals, and agency structure. The client/student empowerment domain can provide outcome goals when planning empowerment strategies in groups. To encourage empowerment, group goals should be clear enough to be communicated effectively to group members so that they can make informed decisions about participation but should be flexible so that group members have a degree of self-determination (McWhirter, 1991). Additionally, empowerment in groups should be thought of in terms of not only outcome goals but also process goals. Empowering process goals encourage self-determination in group, egalitarian relationships between members and with the leader, and supportive and empowering interaction between members.

Group composition is important to group success (Kline, 2003) and becomes especially significant for empowerment in groups. In addition to members sharing a common purpose for being in the group, group member identity factors such as gender, race, ethnicity, sexual orientation, age, acculturation level, ability status, and religion may be significant to group functioning (Rubel, 2006). Because empowerment in groups depends on members' ability to connect with each other, homogeneity, or similarity, may be desirable. Homogeneity may become more important if connection must occur quickly, for instance, in open or short-term groups (Merta, 1995). However, heterogeneity, or difference, may benefit members who have developed sufficient skills to cope with the increased stress of mixed composition (Merta, 1995). For example, a woman who has been recently victimized by male intimate partners may not be empowered in a mixed-gender group but may be empowered by successful interactions with men in a safe group environment after gaining self-worth and assertiveness skills.

Group structure should support empowerment and includes such factors as group length, session length, amount of structured activity, nature of content, and flexibility of agenda. Empowerment is maximized if, as their empowerment and skills increase, members have increasing control over the structure of the group rather than external forces imposing the structure (Roy, 2007). Responsive, empowering groups have strong democratic norms, group leaders who embody a mostly democratic leadership style, and an adequate amount of time and focus on process to develop cohesion and interpersonal feedback. If groups contain psychoeducational material, the material should not represent oppressive discourses about the causes of client distress (McWhirter, 1994) but embody the client/student empowerment domain by providing sociopolitical context and self-advocacy skills. For instance, psychoeducational material for an intimate partner violence survivor group should not pathologize group members' actions but should provide information about how societal expectations enable these actions as well as provide positive, empowering alternatives.

Pregroup preparation refers to providing information and orientation to group members before the start of the group and has been shown to positively influence group outcomes (Burlingame, Fuhriman, & Johnson, 2004). Because providing context and skill-building are empowering (McWhirter, 1991), pregroup preparation should be considered imperative to empowerment in groups. However, balancing the benefits of thorough pregroup preparation with a sense that group members still have control over the group is essential to empowerment. If pregroup preparation time is spent one on one with clients, group workers will have time to assess their experiences, skill levels, cultural identity, and potential need for advocacy before the member enters the group. This allows group workers to further screen, if necessary, and may assist group members in feeling more capable as they enter the group. Additionally, if advocacy may be included as part of the group, then members should be informed how this may happen (Ezell, 2001).

How do these guidelines apply to the case above? This partner violence survivor group is the only one offered in the community, so its operation should be critically evaluated. Shelter administration is aware that the group's impact is limited, but tight budgets and the chaotic environment of the shelter have made it easy to allow the group to continue unchanged. The group has a mix of purposes, processing shelter relationships, support, psychoeducation, and therapy, and you suspect that this mix may keep group member and community needs from being met. Ideally, the purpose and goals of the group should be clarified, and if shelter and community needs cannot be accommodated, then more groups should be created. Adequate rationale exists for the creation of at least one other group. While having an open group may be necessary in the shelter environment, women who want greater support, empowerment, and change may not be well served by the format.

Availability of a variety of groups may encourage empowerment by allowing better screening, placement based on needs, and opportunities to offer a closed group. It is clear that the conflicting purposes of the group are not conducive to informed consent and pregroup preparation that are essential to empowerment. Also, the psychoeducational material that is meant to provide the sociopolitical context of partner violence and develop communication skills often takes the backseat to crises. Nor is there time to fully process member relationships to build trust and increase feedback. You wonder how these things have contributed to Amy's recent interaction. Amy clearly does not feel safe in the group, and you wonder if she is disempowered because of gender and violence, if her status as the only "outsider" is playing a part in her behavior and the group's response, or if the issue is something else. It is important that, as a group leader, you process Amy's and the group's interaction, but you wonder if this will seem dangerous to the group because time has normally been spent on support to one another and somewhat on the psychoeducational material. However, you decide to proceed because opening up more about what is keeping them from connecting may serve everyone better.

Group Work and the Client/Student Advocacy Domain

Sometimes empowerment alone does not meet the advocacy needs of group members. Group leaders may need to take action in and out of the group on behalf of a group member when that member does not have the skills or is not psychologically able to advocate for himself or herself. The client/student advocacy domain can inform these actions. In addition, group leaders must determine several things. First, the group leader must revisit the purpose of the group to determine if the potential advocacy/self-advocacy is within the group's scope and if other group members can benefit from its exploration. Second, group leaders should determine if the elements of empowerment, such as self-advocacy skills training, have been covered sufficiently in the group and if more support from the leader or the group may help. Third, group leaders should determine if the affected group member wants advocacy on his or her behalf and in what parts the member wants the group involved.

Intragroup advocacy includes actions taken within the group on behalf of the client/student and is called for when that group member is not benefiting from the group process because of the inability to identify or express needs; differences in identity, culture, values, life experiences, or communication style; or shame over differences that interfere with connection between the group, group members, and leader (Rubel, 2006). Group leaders must assess the potential for constructive connection between the group member and group, and if the potential is low, referral may be the best option (Rubel, 2006). Intragroup advocacy should include assessment of how to best empower the group member and balance individual attention with the needs of the group and other group members. Though processing in the group may be desirable, the limits of confidentiality and potential for increased psychological vulnerability make it important to determine if consent, information gathering, and support for self-advocacy efforts should occur in the group or individually, outside the group. Intragroup advocacy often functions to help other group members understand the isolated group member's perspective and facilitates connection, but leaders must not disclose information learned outside of group without the member's consent. Additionally, the group leader should consider how advocacy in the group may affect relationships within the group, for instance, by creating perceptions that the group leader has taken sides (Yalom & Leszcz, 2005).

Intragroup advocacy might be warranted after Amy shares in the group and is met by silence. You've been aware that Amy has not shared much in the group despite encouragement from you and other group members. After you ask the group members to support Amy, they still seem reluctant to reach out to her. You ask Amy if she would like support at this time and she admits that she does. Because support has been the primary function of the group, you are hesitant to confront, but you do bring up the discrepancy between what you are observing and the group's usually supportive environment and ask for ideas to explain it. When a couple of members mention that Amy has been very reserved while most members have shared very emotionally, you have the group clarify what that means to them. Several of the members agree that this, combined with Amy's declaration that she may quit, indicates to them that the group doesn't mean much to Amy and they don't feel justified in extending themselves to her. In addition, another group member shares the perception that since Amy has not had to live at the shelter and seems to be "getting on" with life, she doesn't need the group as much as those who have lived at the shelter. With this sharing, you are confident that the lack of support is due to a lack of connection and trust felt by the rest of the group.

To maintain confidentiality connected to your individual relationship with Amy, you do not disclose that she is in recovery, which you became aware of during her intake for the group. However, as you encourage and help her to clarify her feelings during the group, Amy shares that she has been afraid to talk about her addiction and recovery to the group and that she seems unable to talk about relationship violence without talking about her struggles with substance abuse. As part of your advocacy for Amy, you add that anywhere from 33% to 85% of women receiving services for partner violence also may struggle with addiction issues (Fowler, 2007) and then explore the group's reaction to this. You also draw out a general theme of shame that may prevent sharing and use this theme to help the group connect with Amy. In future groups, Amy shares more and the group responds more empathically. Also, more women in the group begin to discuss their own issues with drug and alcohol use.

Extragroup advocacy is an advocacy action taken on behalf of individual or collective group members outside the context of the group. During group work, the group leader may become aware of external factors that impinge on group member development or barriers that limit access to needed resources. Most of the issues that are relevant to intragroup advocacy are relevant to extragroup advocacy as well. For example, it is still relevant to consider if exploring the advocacy issue with the group is useful to the group as a whole or is respectful of the group member's privacy and wishes. Additionally, group leaders should consider if there are benefits to involving other group members not only in the exploration and planning of advocacy but also in the implementation of advocacy.

Amy is now better connected to the group but still feels quite stressed about school, work, recovery, and child care. You believe that processing these issues in the group may be beneficial to all because other group members experience similar stressors. With the group's support, Amy has advocated for herself in several ways. However, one of Amy's primary stressors remains. She is working 20 hours a week for a temp agency, and although her employers work with other employees to accommodate everything from doctor appointments to child care, Amy is afraid to ask for time to attend Alcoholics Anonymous (AA) meetings and this group. So far she has only missed a couple meetings, but she is afraid this will increase if she doesn't speak up.

Because the issue of stigma related to their challenges is a common theme for this group, you decide to process this in the group rather than alone with Amy. To ensure that Amy is comfortable, you ask her permission to continue to focus on this issue in the group. She agrees, and you lead the group to explore her feelings about her recovery and history of partner violence. With the group's help, Amy decides that she is mostly proud of her recovery but sees evidence that her employer may have negative feelings about people who have abused substances. With the group's support, Amy comes up with a self-advocacy plan outlining her strengths and needs and the benefits to the employer if she continues her employment and group attendance. You provide Amy with information about the Americans With Disabilities Act of 1990 that may offer her protection from employment discrimination (Hennen, 1997). Throughout the process, you encourage all group members to connect and apply this to their own life situations.

Despite the support she has received in the group, Amy is still uncertain of her ability to communicate clearly when she is stressed and wants someone to go with her in case she gets flustered. You wonder if it might be more empowering for Amy to do this herself but respect her desire to have someone with her for support. You also consider the impact of extragroup contact between members and assess that it is not detrimental in this case. You explain to the group that you could go with her but believe that helping each other might be more powerful. After some discussion, Deanna, a long-standing member who no longer lives at the shelter, agrees that she is probably in the best position to support Amy. Amy seems comfortable and excited that Deanna will go with her, as does the group. The next week Amy reports that she was successful in asking that her group schedule be respected, and though Deanna did not have to intervene directly, her presence allowed Amy to present herself calmly to her employer. You process this with the group, and they seem genuinely happy for Amy and excited that they may be able to do similar things for themselves. When several members express concern that they haven't received as much support as Amy, you use the group process to help them check their perceptions and focus on how to get their needs met.

Applying the Advocacy Competencies at the School/Community Level

Although exploring the application of the Advocacy Competencies to group work at the client/student level is important both to serve clients and to protect and enhance the experience of others in the group, exploration of its application at the school/community level is also critical. Given that group work holds an important place in prevention and provision of culturally appropriate services (Merta, 1995), access to high-quality groups is essential. However, group work also is logistically more challenging to provide than individual services. As such, group workers often need to collaborate and advocate within their agencies, communities, and mental health systems to provide accessible and effective groups.

Group Work and the Community Collaboration Domain

Groups offered in schools and mental health agencies often rely on collaboration with other entities for funding, staffing, and referrals (ASGW, 1998; Bemak & Conyne, 2004; Tropman, 2004). This means that development of groups to address inequalities and unmet needs often requires connection and communication within a community (Lewis, Lewis, Daniels, & D'Andrea, 2003). The community collaboration domain provides group workers with a useful framework for guiding their actions to form these collaborations. The community collaboration domain focuses on understanding and clarifying group goals, respecting resources and strengths, and making use of counselor skills, and it fits well with the process that group workers may engage in to support the creation and operation of high-quality groups.

You've become increasingly aware of how the needs of all within the group are not being met. For example, it has become apparent since Amy's disclosure that substance abuse issues may affect approximately half of the group. With your director's support, you set up a meeting with supervisors, clinicians, and caseworkers who work with women with addictions in your community to gain their perspective on partner violence survivors and substance abuse. At the first meeting, you are careful to listen and validate what each attendee and agency has to offer. Consensus quickly builds that a need exists for services for women affected by substance abuse and partner violence. While the drug and alcohol treatment programs in the community are well respected, there are no dedicated resources for women who experience both issues. Several participants indicate that they often refer women to your group. A case manager relates that she has had numerous clients comment on the lack of a women's-only 12-Step meeting. The group decides that a formal community needs assessment is necessary to clarify next steps and to access potential grant-funding in the future. The group brainstorms potential stakeholders and decides to invite 12-Step representatives, community college counselors, and public health and counseling interns with an interest to the next meeting.

Group Work and the Systems Advocacy Domain

Systems interventions specific to advocacy for group work clients most often address issues of access to quality group work. The systems advocacy domain provides a useful framework for planning group workers' potential actions to meet client needs through addressing systemic issues. For implementing groups to meet client needs, this may involve quantifying the impact of having inadequate groups, providing research that supports proposed group structures, identifying barriers to the creation of groups such as funding, determining who has the power to make the necessary decisions, and creating a plan to influence decision makers.

The need to restructure and add groups in the case example can be used to illustrate application of the systems advocacy domain. To advocate within the shelter system for additional groups, counselors would do well to collect information including observations of group process, input from women in the group and those who have quit the group, research about factors that influence group work effectiveness, and treatment guidelines for partner violence survivors. Presenting the data and discussing the relevance of groups with administrators would be the next critical step. This discussion could include proposals to form three groups: (a) an open group to resolve shelter issues, (b) an open group to help support and stabilize women in crisis, and (c) a closed group that will focus on process, skills acquisition, and empowerment. Although all the groups are relevant, it may be important to prioritize them in case not all can be approved. Because cost may be an issue, it may be important to also explore using master's-level students from a local counseling program to run some of the groups.

Applying the Advocacy Competencies at the Public Arena Level

Although the public arena level of the Advocacy Competencies is the most difficult to conceptualize specifically for group work, group workers should always consider how applying the Advocacy Competencies can positively influence the quality and accessibility of group services provided to vulnerable populations. Despite the lack of conclusive literature regarding public attitudes toward group work and public policy affecting group work, there are some indications that issues of access to quality group work may need attention. Groups have been shown to be as effective as individual counseling for many issues (Burlingame et al., 2004) and are the modality of choice for prevention work (Conyne, 2004). Theory indicates that groups are a natural way to empower individuals and that they have huge potential for benefiting marginalized populations. However, there is a need for more research regarding group work effectiveness with these populations (Merta, 1995), and there is evidence that group workers are often operating with less group-specific education and group-specific supervision than they receive for individual work (ASGW, 2000; Barlow, 2004; Council for Accreditation of Counseling and Related Educational Programs, 2009). The juxtaposition of group work's potential contribution with its less-than-ideal implementation indicates that both the public information and social/political advocacy domains can assist group workers in identifying ways to promote quality group work and better serve populations that will benefit from it.

Group Work and the Public Information Domain

The public information domain can inform group work in several ways. First, the Advocacy Competencies may help promote group work as a means of prevention and treatment for vulnerable populations by highlighting the need to understand public perceptions of group work and how these perceptions affect willingness to attend, refer to, and support groups. Little has been written about the stigma of participating in group treatment or prevention. Some authors suggest that groups may be considered "second-rate" treatment by the public (Yalom & Leszcz, 2005), whereas others indicate that the stigma may be lower for groups than for individual treatment for some culturally diverse clients (Merta, 1995). Applying the public information domain to group work can include researching public perceptions of group work to assess whether it is viewed as second rate (Yalom & Leszcz, 2005) or oppressive (Roy, 2007) and whether perceptions such as these affect use, access, or provision.

Second, the Advocacy Competencies emphasize the need for sound information in the form of process and efficacy research groups used in prevention and intervention with marginalized populations, facilitation of advocacy efforts, and promotion of public awareness of social justice issues. Group workers utilizing the public information domain may identify and contribute to sound research and program evaluation that provide useful information about the suitability of groups for prevention and treatment and then disseminate this information to both the public and professionals. Important research and dissemination of information may also address the role of groups within advocacy efforts, for instance, task group facilitation, and in changing oppressive attitude and beliefs at all systemic levels.

Third, applying the Advocacy Competencies to group work reveals group work's potential as a means of disseminating public information for the purpose of social justice advocacy. It is well known that while knowledge is an important component of individual, organizational, community, and societal change that benefits marginalized groups, attitudes and beliefs can be a significant barrier. Information regarding how oppressive conditions affect the life experiences and development of people within marginalized groups and how systems may need to change to rectify these conditions can be easily discounted by those who are threatened. Small groups can be an ideal format to process the emotional reactions and explore the attitudes and beliefs that affect openness to this crucial information.

Group Work and the Social/Political Advocacy Domain

The social/political advocacy domain can inform and challenge group workers in several ways. First, the Advocacy Competencies challenge those who do group work to be vigilant of instances in which public policy and the factors that influence public policy affect accessibility to quality group work services, especially those aimed at populations marginalized through mental illness or other target identity status. Although there is no documentation of legislative or social issues that directly affect provision of group work services to marginalized populations, it would be surprising if these issues did not exist. Most likely, issues specific to group work are eclipsed by other issues that affect access to prevention, mental health services, and basic resources. This implies the importance of group workers becoming involved in non-group-work-related advocacy issues at the social and political level. Social/political advocacy that increases access to helping professionals, supports training of clinicians at all levels, and increases mental health prevention and treatment funding will tend to help all those who benefit from group work.

The Advocacy Competencies and the social/political advocacy domain also challenge group workers to collaborate across professional boundaries for the purpose of facilitating advocacy for marginalized populations. Professional infighting can only further disadvantage the vulnerable people who are served by these professions, and policy actions that limit access of clients in need to qualified mental health professionals are unethical. Group workers can use their facilitation skills to help build vision between professional groups for the common purpose of providing better services to disadvantaged groups and advocating for macrosystemic changes.

Finally, the social/political advocacy domain illuminates the potential of clients and students being empowered through groups to lead or participate in social/political advocacy on their own behalf or for others. Historically, empowerment and consciousness-raising groups were often connected with external efforts to influence public policy. The opportunity to connect with others with similar life experiences, to gain power through working together, and to influence attitudes and policy benefits not only the group members but many others. Group workers can use the Advocacy Competencies to help guide group members toward involvement in effective social/political advocacy.

After successful collaboration with other helping agencies in the community to create a unique system of referral and provision of groups for survivors of intimate partner violence with substance abuse issues, analysis of your team's carefully collected program evaluation data indicates that the numbers of female clients with co-occurring substance abuse and partner violence issues identified and receiving appropriate treatment in your community have increased. Additionally, dropout rates of groups provided by the shelter have decreased, and there are slight improvements in relapse rates for participants. Your team, including several women who have participated in the program, present the data and personal experiences of creating and participating in the program at a state conference on intimate partner violence and later at a national conference. You have received inquiries from attendees at these presentations for more information about how to advocate for similar programs in their communities. The director of county mental health has also asked your team to speak about the success of the program to state legislators who are deliberating on funding for group-work-based addictions programs across the state.

Multicultural and Diversity Issues in Applying the
Advocacy Competencies

Multicultural and diversity issues are inextricable from the process of applying the Advocacy Competencies to group work. As with any helping relationship, diversity and multicultural issues affect relationship formation, goals, conceptualization of problems, and appropriateness of interventions during advocacy (Ezell, 2001). With the added layers of interaction that occur during group work, diversity and multicultural issues become even more significant.

As stated earlier, oppressive environments may be replicated within the group process (Yalom & Leszcz, 2005), and often the most different and most vulnerable in society, those of target identity, receive the least benefit. To correct these inequities, group leaders must recognize typical manifestations, which include the following:

- Leaders who are not self-aware may instill their own biases in the group.
- Norms will conform to agent standards, and topics will be more relevant to agent members.
- Members may hide their invisible, target identities and may experience a sense of invisibility that parallels their experience in society.
- Members may be unwilling, due to shame or fear, to discuss experiences related to their target status and may be criticized by agent members if they do share.
- Agent members and leaders may scapegoat target members for resisting agent norms or for expressing oppression-related anger, mistrust, or pain.
- Target group members may be pressured to represent their identity group or educate agent members and leaders (Griffin, 1997; Han & Vasquez, 2000; Helms & Cook, 1999; Kline, 2003; Rubel, 2006; Sue & Sue, 2008).

Another issue in applying the Advocacy Competencies to group work related to diversity and multiculturalism is the role of communication. In the group environment, group leaders must be cognizant not only of their ability to communicate respectfully and effectively with group members but also of group members' abilities to communicate with each other. Group leaders must be aware of the cultural basis of their own communication style and be willing and able to adapt so that group and advocacy interventions are understandable and respectful. Communication differences may also be the source of disconnection between group members and may require advocacy on the part of the leader to correct.

Subgrouping may also occur within the group because of differences in identity, differences in culture, or historical conflict within the community. If this subgrouping is destructive to individuals or the group process, it may require or affect advocacy efforts. Use of culturally sensitive processing and conflict mediation techniques may be appropriate to resolve issues such as these (Camacho, 2001).

Perceptions of the power of the leader may also affect advocacy in the group environment. Perceptions of power can be affected by clients' and leaders' cultural identity (Sue & Sue, 2008). Advocacy should only be undertaken when agreed to by the client (Ezell, 2001), and perceptions of power over the client may result in coercion of the client to accept advocacy or for other group members to participate in advocacy.

Finally, group workers must look beyond the obvious issues of their groups. For example, our case looked primarily at the group issues of heterosexual women. However, partner violence does not belong only to this population, and the issues related to providing adequate group treatment to survivors of partner violence of all ages, races, cultures, religions, ability statuses, genders, and sexual orientations should be considered. Group leaders must challenge themselves to consider not only how well are they treating group members but also whom they assume they are treating and whom they are not treating at all.

Challenges to Applying the Advocacy Competencies to Group Work

The challenges of implementing the Advocacy Competencies in a group work environment are related to the inherent complexity of group work. Conceptualization of group work issues requires understanding how leader actions affect each level of the group, individual, interpersonal, and group as a whole. Advocacy ethics dictate that advocates should analyze the impact of advocacy efforts on other clients and client populations to determine if advocacy for one is a detriment to others. The complexity of this analysis in a counseling group can be daunting and provides a challenge to implementing the Advocacy Competencies at the client/student, community/school, and public arena levels. For instance, empowerment strategies that encourage connection between group members outside of group for the purpose of community/school and public arena level self-advocacy, while common in consciousness raising, mutual aid, and support groups, contradict the traditional structure of counseling and therapy groups. Group workers who choose to use empowerment strategies that involve outside connection should weigh benefits of empowerment versus the perceived benefits of firm group boundaries. Also, due to the potential for client vulnerability and pressure in the group, caution must be taken in gathering information, deciding to advocate, and implementing the advocacy. These factors may complicate implementation of all levels of the Advocacy Competencies in group counseling settings because decisions must be made regarding whether they should be implemented individually with group members or as part of the group process.

Benefits of Applying the Advocacy Competencies to Group Work

The benefits to applying the Advocacy Competencies to group work settings far outweigh the challenges. A focus on creating empowerment can benefit any group by allowing members self-determination. Additionally, the therapeutic factors of group work emphasize learning through inter-personal action and cohesion (Yalom & Leszcz, 2005), and intragroup advocacy to increase members' connection with one another will promote these conditions. For group members who feel powerless and struggle to connect, intragroup advocacy can provide a powerful corrective emotional experience of understanding, relationship repair, and fairness. The benefits to individuals of extragroup advocacy are increased access to resources for the individual, but other group members and those outside the group may also benefit. If they are involved in advocacy efforts or if advocacy is processed in the group, group members have an opportunity to help and support each other with the process and thereby experience beneficial altruism. By applying the Advocacy Competencies, group workers and group members and those with whom they collaborate can potentially effect systemic changes that allow greater access to groups for prevention and treatment, generation of research that promotes best practices, and better training for group workers. Ultimately, these efforts can add incrementally to greater societal changes toward social justice. Finally, applying the Advocacy Competencies to group work offers group workers the opportunity to use their skills to facilitate task groups as part of community collaboration and advocacy at the systems, public information, and social/political levels. Work groups can be challenging, and group dynamics are often cited as barriers to effective advocacy. Group workers can become empowered, help empower other professionals, and effect greater change by using their group work skills in these situations.

Conclusion

Application of the Advocacy Competencies to group work is both challenging and exciting. Ethical application of the Advocacy Competencies requires group workers to evaluate and balance the benefits to the individual with the benefits to the group and other group members, consider group members' potentially increased vulnerability, and mindfully apply the Advocacy Competencies early in group planning if possible. Additionally, diversity and multicultural issues cannot be separated from application of Advocacy Competencies to group work. Although the conceptual complexity of group work complicates the application of the Advocacy Competencies, it is our hope that group workers will not be daunted. The intentional application of empowerment principles to the planning and process of groups has the potential to raise group work to another level, and intragroup advocacy is a means of promoting fairness and group functioning for all group members. Potential benefits extend not only to individuals but also to other group members and group workers themselves.

References

Association for Specialists in Group Work. (1998). ASGW best practice guidelines. *Journal for Specialists in Group Work, 23*, 237–244.

Association for Specialists in Group Work. (1999). ASGW principles for diversity-competent group workers. *Journal for Specialists in Group Work, 24*, 7–14.

Association for Specialists in Group Work. (2000). ASGW professional standards for the training of group workers. *Journal for Specialists in Group Work, 25*, 327–342.

Astramovich, R. L., & Harris, K. R. (2007). Promoting self-advocacy among minority students in school counseling. *Journal of Counseling & Development, 85*, 269–276.

Barlow, S. H. (2004). A strategic three-year plan to teach beginning, intermediate, and advanced group skills. *Journal for Specialists in Group Work, 29*, 113–126.

Bemak, F. (2005). Reflections on multiculturalism, social justice, and empowerment groups for academic success: A critical discourse for contemporary schools. *Professional School Counseling, 8*, 401–406.

Bemak, F., & Conyne, R. K. (2004). Ecological group work. In R. K. Conyne & E. P. Cook (Eds.), *Ecological counseling: An innovative approach to conceptualizing person–environment interaction* (pp. 195–218). Alexandria, VA: American Counseling Association.

Burlingame, G. M., Fuhriman, A., & Johnson, J. E. (2004). Process and outcome in group counseling and psychotherapy: A perspective. In J. L. DeLucia-Waack, D. A. Gerrity, C. R. Kalodner, & M. T. Riva (Eds.), *Handbook of group counseling and psychotherapy* (pp. 49–62). Thousand Oaks, CA: Sage.

Camacho, S. (2001). Addressing conflict rooted in diversity: The role of the facilitator. *Social Work With Groups, 24*, 135–153.

Conyne, R. K. (2004). Prevention groups. In J. L. DeLucia-Waack, D. A. Gerrity, C. R. Kalodner, & M. T. Riva (Eds.), *Handbook of group counseling and psychotherapy* (pp. 621–629). Thousand Oaks, CA: Sage.

Corey, G., Williams, G. T., & Moline, M. E. (1995). Ethical and legal issues in group counseling. *Ethics and Behavior, 5*, 161–183.

Council for Accreditation of Counseling and Related Educational Programs. (2009). *2009 standards*. Retrieved May 15, 2009, from http://www.cacrep.org/2009standards.html

Ezell, M. (2001). *Advocacy in the human services*. Belmont, CA: Brooks/Cole.

Fallot, R. D., & Harris, M. (2002). The trauma recovery and empowerment model (TREM): Conceptual and practical issues in a group intervention for women. *Community Mental Health Journal, 38*, 475–485.

Fowler, D. (2007). The extent of substance use problems among women partner abuse survivors residing in a domestic violence shelter. *Family and Community Health, 30*, 106–108.

Griffin, P. (1997). Facilitating social justice education courses. In M. Adams, L. Bell, & P. Griffin (Eds.), *Teaching for diversity and social justice* (pp. 279–298). New York: Routledge.

Han, A., & Vasquez, M. (2000). Group intervention and treatment with ethnic minorities. In J. Aponte & J. Wold (Eds.), *Psychological intervention and cultural diversity* (2nd ed., pp. 110–130). Needham Heights, MA: Allyn & Bacon.

Helms, J., & Cook, D. (1999). *Using race and culture in counseling and psychotherapy: Theory and process*. Needham Heights, MA: Allyn & Bacon.

Hennen, A. (1997). Protecting addicts in the employment arena: Charting a course towards tolerance. *Law and Inequality, 157,* 172–173.

Kline, W. (2003). *Interactive group counseling and therapy.* Upper Saddle River, NJ: Prentice Hall.

Lee, J. (1994). *The empowerment approach to social work practice.* New York: Columbia University Press.

Lewis, J. A., Arnold, M. S., House, R., & Toporek, R. L. (2002). *ACA Advocacy Competencies.* Retrieved May 15, 2009, from http://www.counseling.org/Publications/

Lewis, J. A., Lewis, M. D., Daniels, J. A., & D'Andrea, M. J. (2003). *Community counseling: Empowerment strategies for a diverse society.* Pacific Grove, CA: Brooks/Cole.

McWhirter, E. H. (1991). Empowerment in counseling. *Journal of Counseling & Development, 69,* 22–27.

McWhirter, E. H. (1994). *Counseling for empowerment.* Alexandria, VA: American Counseling Association.

Merta, R. (1995). Group work: Multicultural perspectives. In J. Ponterotto, J. M. Casas, L. Suzuki, & C. Alexander (Eds.), *Handbook of multicultural counseling* (pp. 567–585). Thousand Oaks, CA: Sage.

O'Brian, P. (2001). Claiming our soul: An empowerment group for African-American women in prison. *Journal of Progressive Human Services, 12,* 35–52.

Okech, J., & Rubel, D. (2007). Diversity competent group work supervision: An application of the supervision of group work model (SGW). *Journal for Specialists in Group Work, 32,* 245–266.

Roy, B. (2007). Radical psychiatry: An approach to personal and political change. In E. Aldarondo (Ed.), *Advancing social justice through clinical practice* (pp. 65–90). Mahwah, NJ: Erlbaum.

Rubel, D. (2006). Diversity issues in group work. In D. Capuzzi, D. Gross, & M. Stauffer (Eds.), *Introduction to group work* (4th ed., pp. 213–238). Denver, CO: Love Publishing.

Rubel, D., & Kline, W. B. (2008). An exploratory study of expert group leadership. *Journal for Specialists in Group Work, 33,* 138–160.

Sue, D. W., & Sue, D. (2008). *Counseling the culturally diverse: Theory and practice* (5th ed.). New York: Wiley.

Toporek, R. L., Lewis, J. A., & Crethar, H. C. (2009). Promoting systemic change through the Advocacy Competencies. *Journal of Counseling & Development, 87,* 260–268.

Tropman, J. (2004). An ecological systems perspective. In C. D. Garvin, L. M. Gutierrez, & M. J. Galinsky (Eds.), *Handbook of social work in groups* (pp. 32–44). New York: Guilford Press.

Yalom, I., & Leszcz, M. (2005). *The theory and practice of group psychotherapy* (5th ed.). New York: Basic Books

Chapter 20

Using the ACA Advocacy Competencies in Career Counseling

Mark Pope and Joseph S. Pangelinan

The development of the American Counseling Association (ACA) Advocacy Competencies (Lewis, Arnold, House, & Toporek, 2002) was a milestone in the profession of counseling. Advocacy as central to the professional identity of counselors was only beginning to reemerge in the 1990s and early 2000s. Leaders of the ACA, including Loretta Bradley, Courtland Lee, Judy Lewis, Jane Goodman, David Kaplan, and Mark Pope, along with a host of other leaders of the profession were instrumental in laying the foundation for these Advocacy Competencies and in helping to institutionalize them within the profession.

Advocacy competencies applied to career counseling were an easy marriage because of the history of career counseling.

> Career counseling was born in the USA in the early 1900s out of societal upheaval, transition, and change. This new profession was described by historians of that time as a "progressive social reform movement aimed at eradicating poverty and substandard living conditions spawned by the rapid industrialization and consequent migration of people to major urban centers at the turn of the 20th century" (Whiteley, 1984, p. 2). Participants in the early days of the "vocational guidance" movement describe it as a "calling," they had a passion to help people who were being ground up in this transition, a transition characterized by the loss of jobs in the agricultural sector, increasing demands for workers in heavy industry, loss of "permanent" jobs on the family farm to new emerging technologies such as tractors, increasing urbanization of the USA, and the concomitant calls for services to meet this internal migration pattern, all in order to retool for this new industrial economy. Returning veterans from World War I and those new workers, who had taken the soldiers' places in the factories and were now being displaced by their return, only heightened the need for career counseling. (Pope, 2000, pp. 195–196)

Such advocacy discussions were, however, absent in the career counseling literature for some time but have become a more important topic in recent years (Arthur, 2000, 2005; Herr & Niles, 1998; Pope, 1995, 2003, in press). Pope (1995) found that advocacy was one of the most important and most consistently recommended interventions in the literature on providing career counseling to lesbian and gay clients. Herr and Niles (1998) identified a key debate within the career counseling profession as to the appropriate role of the career counselor in providing counseling and noted that there has been a historic shift from the traditional focus on just individual differences to a larger systemic focus that also addresses the social and institutional influences on an individual's career development. Arthur (2005) proposed advancing international standards for career counselors by revising them to include "advocacy and social change practices" (p. 137).

With this reinvigorated discussion has also come recognition that both advocating for clients within the broader society and understanding the role of diversity in providing career counseling are important competencies for all career counselors. In the United States, the National Career Development Association (1997) has included diversity as a touchstone in their promulgated competencies. In Canada, cultural competencies are part of the core content of the *Canadian Standards and Guidelines for Career Development Practitioners* (National Steering Committee for Career Development Guidelines and Standards, 2004). Australia has also included such competencies in their standards of practice for career counselors (McMahon, 2004). Finally, the International Association for Educational and Vocational Guidance has included advocacy as one of the competencies in their document, *International Competencies for Educational and Vocational Guidance Practitioners* (Repetto, Malik, Ferrer, Manzano, & Hiebert, 2003).

This chapter is organized to address the issues of career counselors' self-preparation for advocating for their clients as well as specific career counseling interventions that address the Advocacy Competencies' themes of client/student empowerment, client/student advocacy, community collaboration, systems advocacy, public information, and social/political advocacy.

Career Counselor Self-Preparation

A career counselor's self-preparation is a precursor to implementing any advocacy strategy (Pope, 1995). The first step for career counselors who want to be effective advocates for their clients is to take a personal inventory of the ways that their often subtle or unconscious biases may influence the career counseling process. Bias toward a particular culture, system, or individual will affect interventions that the individual career counselor chooses to use as well as how that intervention is used (Bowman, 1993).

Even well-meaning career counselors can sometimes cause harm. For example, Pope (1992) used the example of how heterosexually oriented counselors may have the idea that, if they can help a young man become more masculine in his behaviors, he can change his sexual orientation and will not have to deal with all of the problems that being gay might bring for him. Such counselors are simply trying to help, but these interventions are not research based, and although they may seem intuitively appropriate to some counselors, there is no research literature that suggests (a) that training in gender-appropriate behavior is a determinant of sexual orientation nor (b) that a same-sex sexual orientation is subject to change any more than an opposite-sex orientation is. In fact, there is a growing body of literature to suggest that attempts to deny and to change one's sexual orientation can bring about "significant long-term (psychological) damage from the conversion therapy" (Shidlo & Schroeder, 2002, p. 254).

If one lives in communities that routinely discriminate against culturally diverse individuals, it is virtually impossible to avoid internalizing negative stereotypes or attitudes about "other" cultures. Misinformation or misunderstanding will quickly be evident to clients from these "other" cultures and may cause them to seek help elsewhere or not to get help at all. Career counselors, however, must be familiar with the various cultures of their communities so they are credible and congruent in their attitudes. Attending workshops, reading the literature, and participating in the diverse cultures in one's community are effective ways to acquire knowledge about those cultures. Friends and former clients who come from culturally diverse groups will be an invaluable source of information, too. In particular, career counselors must understand the process of developing a cultural identity because this is a critical component in successful career counseling (Ponterotto & Park-Taylor, 2007).

The process of cultural identity development is critical in the lives of culturally diverse adults, and career counselors need to be aware of their clients' stage of cultural identity development as well as their other development issues to provide effective career counseling. Career counselors must also be aware of their own culture and cultural identity development as unawareness can have disastrous effects on career counseling outcomes.

Bowman (1995) provided an example of what might happen even when both the counselor and client were African American:

> African American career counselors in the conformity stage (Stage 1) may not perceive certain occupations to be open to, or appropriate for, African Americans, so they may subtly dissuade clients from certain career paths. Clients in racial identity stages that are incongruent with the career counselor's stage . . . may be less likely to pay heed to the counselor's suggestions or recommendations. (p. 140)

Further, issues of multiple identities are complex and challenging. Martinez and Sullivan (1998) examined the complexity of identity development in African American gay men and lesbian women. They identified three specific issues as adding the most complexity and as differentiating their identity development from most African American and gay/lesbian identity development models: racial prejudice, limited acceptance by the African American community, and a lack of integration into the larger White gay community.

A career counselor's self-preparation is a precursor to implementing any advocacy strategy. Career counselors who want be effective advocates for their clients must begin with a personal inventory of the ways that their often subtle or unconscious biases may influence the career counseling process.

Client/Student Empowerment and Advocacy

Client/student empowerment is a critical advocacy competency for career counselors because such interventions lay the groundwork for self-advocacy of the client/student. Many career counseling recommendations that address this competency have appeared in the published literature. In the following recommendations, some are generally appropriate, whereas others are more culture specific (these are identified below in parentheses after reference citations as generally appropriate for individualist/collectivist cultures or as specifically appropriate for an identified culture):

1. Address occupational discrimination issues directly (Bowman, 1995).
2. Identify the level of acculturation into the dominant culture (Bowman, 1995; Fouad, 1995; Leong & Gim-Chung, 1995; Martin, 1991) (collectivist).
3. Identify the level of occupational knowledge the client has (Bowman, 1995; Fouad, 1995; Rivera, Chen, Flores, Blumberg, & Ponterotto, 2007).
4. Involve the family in the career counseling process (Bowman, 1995; Fouad, 1995; Leong & Gim-Chung, 1995; Pope, 1999) (collectivist).
5. Help the person cope with the consequences of his or her decisions (if they go against the wishes of their support system) (Fouad, 1995) (collectivist).
6. Evaluate English language proficiency for purposes of both testing and job search (Casas & Vasquez, 1996; Leong & Gim-Chung, 1995) (nonnative English speakers).
7. Provide assertiveness and communication training (Bowman, 1995).
8. Use group career counseling for individuals from collectivist cultures (Bowman, 1995; Leong & Gim-Chung, 1995; Pope, 1999).
9. Explore, especially with more traditional Hispanic females, a wide variety of careers and make particular efforts to increase their awareness of nontraditional careers (Fouad, 1995).
10. Normalize the client's anxiety of not having a clear idea of what career to pursue and help the client understand the various stages of career development (Leong & Gim-Chung, 1995) (Asian and Pacific Islander).
11. Explore issues of gender and the encouragement to strive for high-status and high-income careers along with expectations to maintain traditional gender roles as wife and mother (Leong & Gim-Chung, 1995) (Asian).

12. Train clients in asking and responding to informational interview and job interview questions such as "Are you married?" and "How many children do you have?" and "What is your religion?" and others (Hetherington & Orzek, 1989) (especially gay, lesbian, bisexual, and transgender clients).

13. Offer special programming to meet the career development needs of diverse adults (D'Augelli, 1993; Evans & D'Augelli, 1996), including special programming on:
    a. resume writing (what to include and what to not include) and
    b. job interviewing.

14. For ethnic and racial minorities for whom English is not their first language, a more specific issue is the role of English language proficiency in limiting career choices and as a factor in the actual process of career counseling (Casas & Vasquez, 1996; Leong & Gim-Chung, 1995).

The following client/student empowerment interventions include a more detailed explanation as the issues appear often in the literature:

1. Provide career counseling with dual-career couples (Gilbert, 1993; Stoltz-Loike, 1992). The issue of dual-career couples has been explored more in the women's and sexual minority career development literatures than in the ethnic and racial minority literature, in which the focus has been more on the special role of the family in career decisions.

It is important to work with both individuals in a relationship on dual-career couple issues (Pope, 1995). The issues are especially important for same-sex couples with no experience and only few "out" dual-career couple role models. Special issues for same-sex couples include differences in socioeconomic status between the partners, partner relocation, how to present the relationship, how to introduce one's partner, whether to openly acknowledge the love relationship, how to deal with social events, lifestyle that one partner would want to maintain while employed, problems that one partner's job may cause for a partner who may not want to be as open about this orientation, when to tell people at work, and how to handle situations that may arise at work for which the partner must be involved.

2. Recognize the role of the family in collectivist cultures. Defined as broad and extended, the family is exceptionally important in the provision of career counseling services to individuals from collectivist cultures (Bowman, 1995; Fouad, 1995; Leong, 1992; Leong & Gim-Chung, 1995; Martin, 1991; Pope, 1999; Pope, Cheng, & Leong, 1998; Rivera et al., 2007). In almost all important decisions in a person's life, both family and community are involved. In traditional Asian cultures, for example, when an individual wants to get married, the marriage most likely has been arranged between the two families in consultation with community elders. Although the modern custom in Asian families is that the bride and groom select each other, parents and older relatives often have much input into this matter, especially if the young people still live with their respective parents (Fernandez, 1988; Yu & Gregg, 1993). Such issues, although moderated by increased levels of acculturation into the dominant U.S. culture, remain important to consider in providing career counseling services to individuals from collectivist cultures.

Similarly, career decisions for clients from collectivist cultures are also rarely made without both family and community consultation (Leong, 1992; Pope et al., 1998). When clients first present for career counseling, it is important that counselors assess how much involvement of both extended family and community is needed by the clients in their decision-making process. This assessment of family influence should take into account such factors as the level of modernity of the family; the birth order of clients in their family of origin; clients' income in relation to the socioeconomic status of their family; and clients' educational level, occupational status, and age.

All or selected family and community members may attend each of the group counseling sessions or only selected sessions. Prior to family attendance, it is especially important to discuss with the client the roles of each of his or her family and community members and to identify who is the most important person in the group decision-making process. This person will need the most information and most deference when the client is ready to choose an occupation (Pope, 1999). Among some Pacific Islanders, the client may give in to the wisdom of the community elders to make career selections. This practice may become problematic when the client's interests, values, and abilities do not match the occupation or college major selected by the parent or community elder. The counselor's sensitivity to this cultural practice and skill in advocating for the client will be critical in reconciling these differences.

3. Understand the special procedures that have been recommended for using psychological tests with individuals from various cultural communities. Career counselors need to know what special procedures are required to get accurate results or to make accurate interpretations. Because the use of career interest inventories, other personality tests, and card sorts are all important interventions in the repertoire of career counselors, how these items are used with culturally diverse adults is an important issue (Hartung et al., 1998).

Some researchers have reported problems in the development of career interest inventories. Carter and Swanson (1990) found problems with the development of the Strong Interest Inventory (1984 version). They reported that the validity studies used small samples that included few individuals from diverse ethnic and racial groups and that those who were included from such groups were usually male. They questioned the validity of that version of the Strong with culturally diverse adults. Later, in the 1994 renorming of the Strong, those issues were directly addressed and were reported prominently in the new technical manual (Harmon, Hansen, Borgen, & Hammer, 1994). Further, the 2004 revision built upon and expanded the work begun in 1994 with a particularly ethnically robust national sample (38% Caucasian, 32% African American, 13% Hispanic, 17% Asian; Schaubhut, Donnay, Gasser, & Borgen, 2004). Fouad (1993) discussed the issues of bias in the construction of career interest inventories, including linguistic differences as well as the problems with functional and conceptual equivalence across vocational instruments.

4. Help clients overcome internalized negative stereotypes or internalized oppression (Bowman, 1995; Y. B. Chung & Harmon, 1994; Hetherington & Orzek, 1989; Morgan & Brown, 1991; Pope et al., 2004). It is important for the professional career counselor to understand the concept of internalized oppression because this may affect the client's life and occupational choices. Oppression oppresses even the mentally healthy and well-adjusted people in cultural minorities. Societal messages repeated over and over again about "evil, sick, lazy, oversexed, stupid" people and so on may be believed and accepted at some conscious or unconscious level, and these messages permeate the U.S. dominant culture. Internalized oppression, when it occurs, cannot be overcome easily. It is important that career counselors understand and appreciate the effect that these messages can and do have on all cultural minorities in the United States. For example, an academically gifted African American female client with an educational diagnosis of emotional disability does not consider postsecondary education because she has internalized that nobody from her neighborhood, family, and especially with a "crazy" diagnosis makes it in college. When the client is a sexual minority, a gender minority, and a racial/ethnic minority, these issues are intensified (Y. B. Chung & Katayama, 1998; Keeton, 2002; Pope & Chung, 2000). Culturally appropriate self-esteem interventions (e.g., positive self-talk, reframing, forgiveness) can be used here to overcome these internalized negative stereotypes.

5. Understand the special issue of whether to disclose one's culture to others. This is particularly important with clients whose cultural membership is not obvious, such as gay/lesbian/bisexual/transgender, multiple race/ethnicity, political affiliation, religion, some (dis)abilities, and others. In the sexual minority counseling literature, this is termed *coming out*. In the sexual minority career development literature, the issue of coming out has been central for gay men and lesbian women who are seeking career counseling (Pope, 1995). Even if unstated, it is important for the counselor who knows the cultural membership to recommend this topic for discussion as part of the career counseling process. Career counselors can provide clients with opportunities for behavioral rehearsals directed toward developing and training strategies for informing others. The first step in this process—coming out to self—is many times followed by coming out to family and friends. The final step in this process for many is coming out in the workplace.

Anderson, Croteau, Chung, and DiStefano (2001) reported on the initial development of the Workplace Sexual Identity Management Measure (WSIMM). Psychometric properties of the WSIMM were successfully assessed a continuum of strategies for coming out in the workplace. Such measures as this are important to aid lesbian and gay workers in assessing their work environment and exploring appropriate strategies for sexual orientation disclosure.

Special attention also must be paid to the issue of coming out in families from cultures that do not readily accept same-sex sexual orientations. "There is not much qualitative difference between Asian and United States cultures in terms of traditional attitudes toward homosexuality, but the intensity of heterosexism and homophobia is much stronger in Asian cultures than in U.S. culture" (Y. B. Chung & Katayama, 1998, p. 22). The coming-out strategies that are used in more collectivist cultures such as Asian cultures are different from those used in more individualist cultures such as the mainstream U.S. culture (Han, 2001; Pope, 1999; Pope et al., 1998; Pope & Chung, 2000). Newman and Muzzonigro (1993) studied differences between gay males in general who were raised in more traditional families and those raised in less traditional families. They reported that gay males from more traditional families felt more disapproval of their sexual orientation than gay males from less traditional families. Wooden, Kawasaki, and Mayeda (1983) addressed the issue of sexual identity development (coming out to self) in a sample of Japanese men and found that, although almost the entire sample had come out to their friends, only about half had disclosed their sexual orientation to their families. These issues must be addressed when providing career counseling to lesbian women or gay men from such cultures, and strategies must be revised accordingly. Other authors have similarly addressed these issues for African Americans (Maguen, Floyd, Bakeman, & Armistead, 2002; Martinez & Sullivan, 1998; McLean, Marini, & Pope, 2003), Hispanic Americans (Fimbres, 2001; Merighi & Grimes, 2000), and Native Americans (Morris & Rothblum, 1999; Piedmont, 1996).

Finally, other career counseling interventions that have been recommended in the published literature include the special issues of multiple cultural identities and special oppression such as that of lesbian/gay Native Americans (Pope & Chung, 2000; Van Puymbroeck, 2002). Career counselors must develop with their clients special interventions that take into account these important cultural issues, such as collectivist versus individual decision making, coming out to family, and other issues that are culture specific (Y. B. Chung & Katayama, 1998; Pope, 1999).

Client/student advocacy flows from the career counselor's awareness of external factors that act as barriers to an individual's development and includes specific counselor actions that advocate for the client. This is especially important when individuals or vulnerable groups lack access to needed services. Each of these advocacy efforts identified here is preceded by the empowerment strategies identified in the previous section. These career counseling interventions include the following:

1. Help clients to identify barriers to their career success and teach them ways to overcome such barriers. Such barriers can be subjective and constructed by a client, but they can also be objective and imposed on a client by a social environment. Discrimination in hiring is one such social barrier. Discrimination against individuals on the basis of their race, ethnic origin, gender, disability, religion, political affiliation, age, or sexual orientation is a fact of life in U.S. society. Professional career counselors who fail to recognize this and do not assist their clients in coping with this reality do a disservice to their clients.

Issues of dual and multiple discriminations also must be addressed when providing career counseling services. For example, lesbian women face at least two virulent forms of discrimination in U.S. society: sexism and heterosexism. If individuals are a member of an ethnic or racial minority, older, gay or lesbian, and physically challenged, they face daunting barriers to achieving their career goals. Bowman (1995), identifying the potential individual outcomes of such discrimination, found that past experience (direct or vicarious) with discrimination may result in anxiety about one's options and lowered self-esteem, including loss of hope, foreclosed horizons, and a tendency to set one's sights lower than necessary.

Openly addressing these issues and preparing clients to cope with the more overt manifestations of racism, sexism, heterosexism, ableism, ageism, and other forms of discrimination are important and primary roles of the career counselor (Y. B. Chung, 2001). As simple as it may seem, talking openly with clients about issues of employment discrimination is very important. Even if clients are not the first to broach the subject, the issues ought to be discussed so that the client is aware of the career counselor's sensitivity and knowledge in this area. When these issues are openly and fully discussed, such discussions lead to both improved decision making on the part of the client and an even better-informed advocacy on the part of the career counselor.

2. Train clients in culturally appropriate assertiveness skills. This will enable clients to differentiate between appropriate assertiveness in their families, their cultures, and other cultures, including the dominant cultures. For example, in the dominant U.S. cultures, it is many times appropriate to ask directly for what one wants, such as a salary raise, but it might be done differently in an Asian-owned business or setting in which high-context, indirect messages are more acceptable (Bowman, 1995). Helping clients to learn different assertiveness strategies and then helping them choose the best assertiveness strategy based on the situation are important counselor actions that lead to improved and appropriate assertiveness on the part of the client. This intervention will also lead to improved advocacy on the part of the career counselor to be better able to support clients in defining their actual needs and successfully getting them met.

3. Intervene on behalf of clients when the clients' own self-advocacy has been ineffective. For example, the counselor can help an immigrant worker explain to an employer the importance of missing work to attend an Individual Education Program (IEP) planning meeting for the worker's child. In another example, clients who are confronting large government bureaucracies, such as one-stop career centers, may need a counselor's help in navigating the maze of rules and regulations. Also, when the clients/students are children or early adolescents, they may not be able to do effective self-advocacy and may require the school counselor to intervene on their behalf (Schultheiss, 2005, 2008).

4. Identify potential client allies for confronting the barriers. For example, in the case of the one-stop career center identified above, a client may also need a counselor's help to identify a helpful person at that agency who can give some more individualized attention to the client's career development needs. A career counselor's knowledge of career resources in the community and ability to develop relationships with such resources are invaluable tools in helping clients.

5. Develop career exploration, job search, and other career groups for clients. Do this with the express agenda of discussing the barriers clients are confronting in their career, devising ways to surmount those barriers, and practicing those strategies in the group prior to implementing them. Further, group career counseling has a strong appeal to many racial and ethnic minority clients (Bowman, 1995; Pope, 1999; Shea, Ma, & Yeh, 2007). Several characteristics of group-oriented or collectivist cultures—including primacy of group survival over individual survival, interdependency, and connectedness—make them especially suited to group career counseling techniques. For example, Asian clients' preferences for a more directive and authoritarian style of leadership along with structured situations and practical solutions (Leong, 1986; Tsui & Schultz, 1988; Yu & Gregg, 1993) strongly coincide with the characteristics of career counseling groups in general (Garfield & Nelson, 1983).

Brammer (1978), Blustein (1982), Sue and Sue (1990), and R. C. Y. Chung and Okazaki (1991) have noted that the primary way that most people in "non-Western" countries receive psychological help is through systems of informal groups. Such informal groups arise from the individual's community and are composed of individuals who have chosen to be a part of the group (Blustein, 1982). Examples of informal groups are peer groups, book discussion groups, self-help groups, religious groups, and school groups. Further, Banawi and Stockton (1993) noted the role of groups in Islamic societies including Indonesia, Malaysia, and parts of the Philippines. In these Islamic countries, there is an inherent group orientation that allows group counseling to "be seen as an optimal setting and a way for Muslims to experience personal growth" (p. 152). Salvador, Omizo, and Kim (1997) specifically recommended the use of group counseling, peer counseling, and family interventions as important when working with clients from the Philippines because of the special attributes of Filipino culture, which include *amor propio* (love of self), *pakikisama* (group solidarity), *kapwa* (recognition of shared identity), and *compadrazgo* (extending the family with godparents), to name a few.

6. Negotiate the proper use of psychological tests, including career interest or personnel selection testing for clients who must use institutional resources. Career counselors can advocate for their clients who use or are required to use institutional testing resources for a variety of reasons (financial, required by a college for admission into a graduate program, required by a potential employer for selection for a job, etc.). Special procedures have been recommended for using psychological tests with individuals from various cultural communities (Carter & Swanson, 1990; Y. B. Chung, 2003; Y. B. Chung & Harmon, 1994; Fouad, 1993, 1995; Hartung et al., 1998; Leong & Gim-Chung, 1995; Leong & Gupta, 2007; Mobley & Slaney, 1996; Pope, 1992; Pope et al., 2004; Porfeli, Hartung, & Voncracek, 2008; Prince, 1997a, 1997b; Tracey & Sodano, 2008). Career counselors need to know what special procedures are required to get accurate results or to make accurate interpretations. Armed with such knowledge, the career counselor can be a proper advocate prior to and after the testing to be sure that the inventories are administered properly and the results are not misused. For example, the career counselor could go with the client to challenge the incorrect use of such inventories that led to the client not receiving a job offer. Because career interest inventories, other personality tests, and card sorts are all important interventions in the repertoire of career counselors, how these items are used with culturally diverse adults, adolescents, and children is an important issue (Hartung et al., 1998; Tracey & Sodano, 2008).

Community Collaboration

Career counselors' role in community collaboration is one of ally and supporter, to alert existing organizations that are already working for change and that might have an interest in the specific issues that are relevant for an individual or a cultural group. This is about change at the community and organizational levels, not individual or family.

Such community career counseling interventions include the following:

1. Identify environmental factors that are supportive of students' and clients' development and inform the community of these factors. The career counseling literature is filled with research on career barriers and career assessment instruments designed to identify such barriers to successful career development (Krumboltz, 1994; Luzzo & McWhirter, 2001; Swanson, Daniels, & Tokar, 1996). Career counselors can use this information when designing or helping to design career development programs in the community, including in schools and in both government and nonprofit community-based agencies.

2. Alert community or school groups with common concerns related to the issue. Career counselors can provide expert testimony at the local level regarding such research as communities begin to design career counseling programs in the schools or for the broader community focused on adults as clients in one-stop career centers.

3. Develop alliances with groups working for change. It is not enough to play the role of expert and inform groups of the issue. Career counselors must also play an active role in community organizations working for change.

Career counselors, and really all counselors, are experts in developing interpersonal relationships. This competency extends that expertise to developing relationships at the community level to effect change there. That process includes (a) using effective listening skills to gain understanding of the group's goals; (b) identifying the strengths and resources that the group members bring to the process of systemic change; (c) communicating recognition of and respect for these strengths and resources; (d) identifying and offering the skills that the counselor can bring to the collaboration; and (e) assessing the effect of counselor's interaction with the community

Systems Advocacy

There are systemic factors that act as barriers to clients' career development and require that the system be changed to remove such barriers (Pope, 1995). Career counselors can take the lead in advocating for such systemic change. For example, the lack of school counselors in many elementary schools limits the career exploration interventions that are implemented as well as the basic career knowledge that is so important for students as they move toward adulthood and career decisions. Advocating for changes in the staffing patterns of school counselors and decreasing student-to-counselor ratios would help students be more ready for their eventual career choices (McMahon & Watson, 2008; Schultheiss, 2005, 2008; Watson & McMahon, 2008).

To implement such a systemic change may include (a) identifying the systemic factors that are impinging on clients' career development; (b) designing research studies to collect appropriate data on the need for such systemic change; (c) working with other school stakeholders to develop a shared vision to guide the change; (d) analyzing the sources of political power and social influence with the school system; (e) developing a step-by-step plan to implement the change process, including how to deal with probable responses to change and how to recognize and deal with resistance to change; and (f) assessing the career counselor's advocacy efforts on the system and constituents.

Such career counseling interventions include the following:

1. Implement workplace mentoring programs, diversity workshops, and culturally affirmative policies such as nondiscrimination policies and domestic partners benefits.

2. Understand the important role that occupational stereotypes and role models play in career choice for special populations that have historically been limited in their occupational choices by some type of societal stereotyping (Bowman, 1995; Fouad, 1995; Hetherington & Orzek, 1989; Leong & Gim-Chung, 1995; Rivera et al., 2007). For example, Chinese have been stereotyped as computer programmers, research scientists, and owners of restaurants or laundries. Filipinos are supposed to work in health care or as hotel housekeepers. Gay men have been stereotyped as hairdressers, florists, dancers, actors, secretaries, nurses, flight attendants, and other occupations traditionally held by women. Lesbian women have been stereotyped as truck drivers, athletes, mechanics, and other occupations traditionally held by men. These very narrow stereotypes serve as "safe" occupations, in which these culturally diverse adults may feel more accepted and more able to truly be themselves; however, these occupations can also limit these individuals' occupational vision and choices. For some individuals, however, they are seen as the only possible choices. Career counselors could advocate for and develop programs that break down such stereotypes, for example, having regular panel presentations of workers in nonstereotypical occupations, such as Chinese counselors or gay male truck drivers.

3. Create a supportive atmosphere in your workplace. This is one way to get the word out that you are supportive of the struggles of culturally diverse persons who are seeking career counseling (Pope, 1995). It can be as simple as having a selection of culturally appropriate books in the library or placed strategically in the principal's, company president's, and counselor's office right beside other professional literature. This will help some clients realize that the school and company are prepared to acknowledge the existence of individuals from diverse cultures. Placing such literature in the various offices and waiting rooms will send a clear and overt signal that this school or company is culturally affirming. Popular magazines and newspapers focused on various cultural communities send obvious signals to all clients and may help clients in general gain more information about their culturally diverse coworkers.

4. Implement a model career guidance program into the K–12 curriculum that focuses specifically on issues of cultural diversity and that identifies students who need special assistance (McMahon & Watson, 2008; Schultheiss, 2005, 2008; Watson & McMahon, 2008).

Public Information

Counselors who specialize in career counseling have special expertise that other counselors may not have (Pope, 2003). Because careers are ubiquitous in every society, and because of the special expertise that career counselors may have in workforce development, career choice, employment discrimination, personnel selection, career interest testing, and other career development issues, career counselors may be more likely to experience situations in which they can share this expertise with the public. Such situations are opportunities to awaken the general public to macrosystemic issues regarding human worth and dignity.

The interventions might include the following:

1. Recognize the impact of oppression, discrimination, and other barriers to an individual's healthy human and career development. Career counselors are trained in the developmental theories of careers. Being able to speak to public audiences on the role of such barriers in deforming individual career development is an important societal contribution, because such education may help people in the audience reexamine their own conscious or unconscious behaviors that contribute to hurting others. Further, collaborating with the community that is affected to develop appropriate materials to combat these barriers allows for direct advocacy with the community.

2. Be familiar with environmental factors that are protective of healthy human and career development. It is important to be able to communicate with the general public, as opportunities arise, about such protective factors and what one can do to initiate and enhance social environments in the development of these factors. For example, career counselors understand the developmental research on career interest patterns and design school programs that focus on career exploration prior to age 15 when career interest patterns begin to be more crystallized and that focus on career choice only after that. Again, collaborating with the community that is affected to develop appropriate materials to explain these factors to the larger community allows for direct advocacy.

3. Disseminate career information in a variety of formats using knowledge of learning styles and culture to design appropriate materials and delivery systems. For example, students with emotional or learning (dis)abilities may benefit from a career exploration program that involves lecture, video, and experiential components. Job shadowing and community service are also career-related activities that expose students to different occupations. Such collaborations with the community that is affected to develop appropriate materials allow for direct advocacy with the community as well.

Social/Political Advocacy

Social/political advocacy includes interventions that are focused on the external, social environment of the client (Herr & Niles, 1998; Pope, 1995). Positive social advocacy for clients could include lobbying for the inclusion of their cultural group in the nondiscrimination policies of local employers. An example would be to talk to employers about including sexual orientation in company and organization nondiscriminatory clauses. Another positive social advocacy for clients could include picketing a speech made by an "ex-gay" who claims to have become a happy, fully functioning heterosexual. Some clients will need basic information on their cultural community as well as the facts on employment, housing, and other discrimination.

These social/political interventions might include the following:

1. Know and provide clients with information on the geographic location and the size of the cultural communities in their area, information on the employment policies and EEO statements of local businesses, information on local and federal antidiscrimination laws, assistance on clients' avoiding arrest, and assistance to clients about constructing affirming work environments; and work to change employer-related statements or policies that discriminate.

2. Be affirming and go beyond the "do no harm" admonition to encompass a positive advocacy for clients and their rights. Examples of such a positive advocacy include working to change employer-related statements or policies that discriminate, working to change the laws that criminalize certain sexual acts between two consenting adults, working to changing housing laws that do not allow two "unrelated" persons to live together, or working to stop police harassment and entrapment. Such laws are often used to prevent a person or family from renting a house or apartment or to deny employment to teachers, counselors, police officers, and other professionals.

Even if some laws are rescinded, people who have had such laws used against them are subject to continued problems because certain kinds of violations may remain on computerized police records for years. A professional who faces a background investigation as a routine part of employment may fear that exposure of such a police record will lead to renewed public humiliation. Clients may decide to take the risk that previous histories may not be discovered or to not continue to pursue a particular job. Whatever the course of action selected, the career counselor can expect the client to experience significant anxiety and anger that this injustice may continue to be a limitation. While not routine, situations like this may lead some clients to choose to remain in unsatisfying or limited careers. Career counselors have an opportunity to lobby law enforcement officials to stop entrapments as well as the unequal enforcement of laws. Career counselors must take an active, advocacy approach to working with all cultural minorities.

Conclusion

This chapter was developed to apply the Advocacy Competencies to career counseling and organized to address the issues of career counselors' self-preparation for advocating for their clients as well as specific career counseling interventions that address the Advocacy Competencies' themes of client/student empowerment, client/student advocacy, community collaboration, systems advocacy, public information, and social/political advocacy.

The marriage of career counseling to advocacy is an easy one that has been facilitated by the history of career counseling as it developed in the early 1900s out of progressive social reform movements aimed at instituting child labor laws. Today, career counselors bring special expertise in workforce development, career choice, employment discrimination, personnel selection, career interest testing, and other career development issues that can be used to advocate for their clients at the school, community, state, and federal levels.

References

Anderson, M. Z., Croteau, J. M., Chung, Y. B., & DiStefano, T. M. (2001). Developing an assessment of sexual identity management for lesbian and gay workers. *Journal of Career Assessment, 9,* 243–260.

Arthur, N. (2000). Career competencies for managing cross-cultural transitions. *Canadian Journal of Counselling, 34,* 204–217.

Arthur, N. (2005). Building from diversity to social justice competencies in international standards for career development practitioners. *International Journal for Educational and Vocational Guidance, 5,* 137–148.

Banawi, R., & Stockton, R. (1993). Islamic values relevant to group work, with practical applications for the group leader. *Journal for Specialists in Group Work, 18,* 151–160.

Blustein, D. L. (1982). Using informal groups in cross-cultural counseling. *Journal for Specialists in Group Work, 7,* 260–265.

Bowman, S. L. (1993). Career intervention strategies for ethnic minorities. *The Career Development Quarterly, 42,* 14–25.

Bowman, S. L. (1995). Career intervention strategies and assessment issues for African Americans. In F. T. L. Leong (Ed.), *Career development and vocational behavior of racial and ethnic minorities* (pp. 137–164). Mahwah, NJ: Erlbaum.

Brammer, L. M. (1978). Informal helping systems in selected subcultures. *Personnel and Guidance Journal, 56,* 476–479.

Carter, R. T., & Swanson, J. L. (1990). The validity of the Strong Interest Inventory with Black Americans: A review of the literature. *Journal of Vocational Behavior, 36,* 195–209.

Casas, J. M., & Vasquez, M. J. T. (1996). Counseling the Hispanic: A guiding framework for a diverse population. In P. B. Pedersen, J. G. Draguns, W. J. Lonner, & J. E. Trimble (Eds.), *Counseling across cultures* (4th ed., pp. 146–176). Thousand Oaks, CA: Sage.

Chung, R. C. Y., & Okazaki, S. (1991). Counseling Americans of Southeast Asian descent. In C. C. Lee & B. L. Richardson (Eds.), *Multicultural issues in counseling* (pp. 107–126). Alexandria, VA: American Counseling Association

Chung, Y. B. (2001). Work discrimination and coping strategies: Conceptual frameworks for counseling lesbian, gay, and bisexual clients. *The Career Development Quarterly, 50,* 33–44.

Chung, Y. B. (2003). Ethical and professional issues in career assessment with lesbian, gay, and bisexual persons. *Journal of Career Assessment, 11,* 96–112.

Chung, Y. B., & Harmon, L. W. (1994). The career interests and aspirations of gay men: How sex-role orientation is related. *Journal of Vocational Behavior, 45,* 223–239.

Chung, Y. B., & Katayama, M. (1998). Ethnic and sexual identity development of Asian-American lesbian and gay adolescents. *Professional School Counseling, 1*(3), 21–25.

D'Augelli, A. R. (1993). Preventing mental health problems among lesbian and gay college students. *Journal of Primary Prevention, 13,* 245–261.

Evans, N. J., & D'Augelli, A. R. (1996). Lesbians, gay men, and bisexual people in college. In R. C. Savin-Williams & K. M. Cohen (Eds.), *The lives of lesbians, gays, and bisexuals: Children to adults* (pp. 201–226). Fort Worth, TX: Harcourt Brace College.

Fernandez, M. S. (1988). Issues in counseling Southeast Asian students. *Journal of Multicultural Counseling and Development, 16,* 157–166.

Fimbres, M. F. (2001). Case study of a gay Mexican American. *Journal of Gay and Lesbian Social Services, 12,* 93–101.

Fouad, N. A. (1993). Cross-cultural vocational assessment. *The Career Development Quarterly, 42,* 4–13.

Fouad, N. A. (1995). Career behavior of Hispanics: Assessment and career intervention. In F. T. L. Leong (Ed.), *Career development and vocational behavior of racial and ethnic minorities* (pp. 165–191). Mahwah, NJ: Erlbaum.

Garfield, N. J., & Nelson, R. E. (1983). *Career exploration groups: A facilitator's guide.* Palo Alto, CA: Consulting Psychologists Press.

Gilbert, L. A. (1993). *Two careers/one family: The promise of gender equality.* Thousand Oaks, CA: Sage.

Han, S.-H. (2001). Gay identity disclosure to parents by Asian American gay men. *Dissertation Abstracts International, 62*(1-A), 329. (UMI No. AAI3000394)

Harmon, L. W., Hansen, J. C., Borgen, F. H., & Hammer, A. L. (1994). *Strong Interest Inventory: Applications and technical guide.* Palo Alto, CA: Consulting Psychologists Press.

Hartung, P. J., Vandiver, B. J., Leong, F. T. L., Pope, M., Niles, S. G., & Farrow, B. (1998). Appraising cultural identity in Career-Development Assessment and Counseling. *The Career Development Quarterly, 46,* 276–293.

Herr, E., & Niles, S. (1998). Career: Social action in behalf of purpose, productivity, and hope. In C. C. Lee & G. R. Walz (Eds.), *Social action: A mandate for counselors* (pp. 117–136). Alexandria, VA: American Counseling Association.

Hetherington, D., & Orzek, A. M. (1989). Career counseling and life planning with lesbian women. *Journal of Counseling & Development, 68,* 52–57.

Keeton, M. D. (2002). Perceptions of career-related barriers among gay, lesbian, and bisexual individuals. *Dissertation Abstracts International, 63*(2-B), 1075.

Krumboltz, J. D. (1994). The Career Beliefs Inventory. *Journal of Counseling & Development, 72,* 424–428.

Leong, F. T. L. (1986). Counseling and psychotherapy with Asian-Americans: Review of the literature. *Journal of Counseling Psychology, 33,* 196–206.

Leong, F. T. L. (1992). Guidelines for minimizing premature termination among Asian American clients in group counseling. *Journal for Specialists in Group Work, 17,* 218–228.

Leong, F. T. L., & Gim-Chung, R. H. (1995). Career assessment and intervention with Asian Americans. In F. T. L. Leong (Ed.), *Career development and vocational behavior of racial and ethnic minorities* (pp. 193–226). Mahwah, NJ: Erlbaum.

Leong, F. T. L., & Gupta, A. (2007). Career development and vocational behaviors of Asian Americans. In F. T. L. Leong, A. Ebreo, L. Kinoshita, A. Inman, & L. H. Yang (Eds.), *Handbook of Asian American psychology* (2nd ed., pp. 159–178). Thousand Oaks, CA: Sage.

Lewis, J. A., Arnold, M. S., House, R., & Toporek, R. L. (2002). *ACA Advocacy Competencies.* Retrieved March 11, 2009, from http://www.counseling.org/Publications/

Luzzo, D. A., & McWhirter, E. H. (2001). Sex and ethnic differences in the perception of educational and career-related barriers and levels of coping efficacy. *Journal of Counseling & Development, 79,* 61–67.

Maguen, S., Floyd, F. J., Bakeman, R., & Armistead, L. (2002). Developmental milestones and disclosure of sexual orientation among gay, lesbian, and bisexual youths. *Journal of Applied Developmental Psychology, 23,* 219–233.

Martin, W. E. (1991). Career development and American Indians living on reservations: Cross-cultural factors to consider. *The Career Development Quarterly, 39,* 273–283.

Martinez, D. G., & Sullivan, S. C. (1998). African American gay men and lesbians: Examining the complexity of gay identity development. *Journal of Human Behavior in the Social Environment, 1,* 243–264.

McLean, R., Marini, I., & Pope, M. (2003). Racial identity and relationship satisfaction in African American gay men. *Family Journal, 11,* 13–22.

McMahon, M. (2004, August). *Shaping a career development culture: Quality standards, quality practice, quality outcomes.* Paper presented at the National Forum for Career Practitioners, Sydney, Australia.

McMahon, M., & Watson, M. (2008). Children's career development: Status quo and future directions. *The Career Development Quarterly, 57,* 4–83.

Merighi, J. R., & Grimes, M. D. (2000). Coming out to families in a multicultural context. *Families in Society, 81,* 32–41.

Mobley, M., & Slaney, R. B. (1996). Holland's theory: Its relevance for lesbian women and gay men. *Journal of Vocational Behavior, 48,* 125–135.

Morgan, K. S., & Brown, L. S. (1991). Lesbian career development, work behavior, and vocational counseling. *The Counseling Psychologist, 19,* 273–291.

Morris, J. F., & Rothblum, E. D. (1999). Who fills out a "lesbian" questionnaire? The interrelationship of sexual orientation, years "out," disclosure of sexual orientation, sexual experience with women, and participation in the lesbian community. *Psychology of Women Quarterly, 23,* 537–557.

National Career Development Association. (1997). *Career counseling competencies.* Retrieved August 28, 2008, from http://www.ncda.org/pdf/counselingcompetencies.pdf

National Steering Committee for Career Development Guidelines and Standards. (2004). *Canadian standards and guidelines for career development practitioners.* Retrieved August 31, 2008, from http://www.career-dev-guidelines.org

Newman, B. S., & Muzzonigro, P. G. (1993). The effects of traditional family values on the coming out process of gay male adolescents. *Adolescence, 28,* 213–226.

Piedmont, O. (1996). The veils of Arjuna: Androgyny in gay spirituality, east and west. *Dissertation Abstracts International, 57*(6-B), 4076. (UMI No. AAM9633907)

Ponterotto, J. G., & Park-Taylor, J. (2007). Racial and ethnic identity theory, measurement, and research in counseling psychology: Present status and future directions. *Journal of Counseling Psychology, 54,* 282–294.

Pope, M. (1992). Bias in the interpretation of psychological tests. In S. Dworkin & F. Gutierrez (Eds.), *Counseling gay men and lesbians: Journey to the end of the rainbow* (pp. 277–292). Alexandria, VA: American Counseling Association.

Pope, M. (1995). Career interventions for gay and lesbian clients: A synopsis of practice knowledge and research needs. *The Career Development Quarterly, 44,* 191–203.

Pope, M. (1999). Applications of group career counseling techniques in Asian cultures. *Journal of Multicultural Counseling and Development, 27,* 18–30.

Pope, M. (2000). A brief history of career counseling in the United States. *The Career Development Quarterly, 48,* 194–211.

Pope, M. (2003). Career counseling in the twenty-first century: Beyond cultural encapsulation. *The Career Development Quarterly, 52,* 54–61.

Pope, M. (in press). Career counseling with diverse adults. In J. G. Ponterotto, J. M. Casas, L. A. Suzuki, & C. Alexander (Eds.), *Handbook of multicultural counseling* (3rd ed.). Thousand Oaks, CA: Sage.

Pope, M., Barret, B., Szymanski, D. M, Chung, Y. B., Singaravelu, H., McLean, R., & Sanabria, S. (2004). Culturally appropriate career counseling with gay and lesbian clients. *The Career Development Quarterly, 53,* 158–177.

Pope, M., Cheng, W. D., & Leong, F. T. L. (1998). The case of Chou: The inextricability of career to personal/social issues. *Journal of Career Development, 25,* 53–64.

Pope, M., & Chung, Y. B. (2000). From bakla to tongzhi: Counseling and psychotherapy issues for gay and lesbian Asian and Pacific Islander Americans. In D. S. Sandhu (Ed.), *Asian and Pacific Islander Americans: Issues and concerns for counseling and psychotherapy.* Commack, NY: Nova Science.

Porfeli, E. J., Hartung, P. J., & Voncracek, F. W. (2008). Children's vocational development: A research rationale. *The Career Development Quarterly, 57,* 25–37.

Prince, J. P. (1997a). Assessment bias affecting lesbian, gay male and bisexual individuals. *Measurement and Evaluation in Counseling and Development, 30,* 82–87.

Prince, J. P. (1997b). Career assessment with lesbian, gay and bisexual individuals. *Journal of Career Assessment, 5,* 225–238.

Repetto, E., Malik, B., Ferrer, P., Manzano N., & Hiebert, B. (2003). *International competencies for educational and vocational guidance practitioners.* Retrieved August 26, 2008, from http://www.iaevg.org/iaevg/index.cfm?lang=2

Rivera, L. M., Chen, E. C., Flores, L. Y., Blumberg, F., & Ponterotto, J. G. (2007). The effects of perceived barriers, role models, and acculturation on the career self-efficacy and career considerations of Hispanic women. *The Career Development Quarterly, 56,* 47–61.

Salvador, D. S., Omizo, M. M., & Kim, B. S. K. (1997). Bayanihan: Providing effective counseling strategies with children of Filipino ancestry. *Journal of Multicultural Counseling and Development, 25,* 201–209.

Schaubhut, N. A., Donnay, D. A. C., Gasser, C. E., & Borgen, F. H. (2004, July). *Validity of the 2004 SII: Gender and ethnicity effects.* Paper presented at the annual meeting of the American Psychological Association, Honolulu, HI.

Schultheiss, D. E. P. (2005). Elementary career intervention programs: Social action initiatives. *Journal of Career Development, 31,* 185–194.

Schultheiss, D. E. P. (2008). Current status and future agenda for the theory, research, and practice of childhood career development. *The Career Development Quarterly, 57,* 7–24.

Shea, M., Ma, P. W. W., & Yeh, C. J. (2007). Development of a culturally specific career exploration group for urban Chinese immigrant youth. *The Career Development Quarterly, 56,* 62–73.

Shidlo, A., & Schroeder, M. (2002). Changing sexual orientation: A consumers' report. *Professional Psychology: Research and Practice, 33,* 249–259.

Stoltz-Loike, M. (1992). *Dual career couples: New perspectives in counseling.* Alexandria, VA: American Counseling Association.

Sue, D. W., & Sue, S. (1990). *Counseling the culturally different* (2nd ed.). New York: Wiley.

Swanson, J. L., Daniels, K. K., & Tokar, D. M. (1996). Assessing perceptions of career-related barriers: The Career Barriers Inventory. *Journal of Career Assessment, 4,* 219–244.

Tracey, T. J. G., & Sodano, S. M. (2008). Issues of stability and change in interest development. *The Career Development Quarterly, 57,* 51–62.

Tsui, P., & Schultz, G. L. (1988). Ethnic factors in group process: Cultural dynamics in multi-ethnic therapy groups. *American Journal of Orthopsychiatry, 58,* 136–142.

Van Puymbroeck, C. M. (2002). Career development of lesbian, gay, and bisexual undergraduates: An exploratory study. *Dissertation Abstracts International, 62*(12-B), 5982. (UMI No. AAI335159)

Watson, M., & McMahon, M. (2008). Children's career development: Metaphorical images of theory, research, and practice. *The Career Development Quarterly, 57,* 75–83.

Wooden, W. S., Kawasaki, S., & Mayeda, R. (1983). Lifestyles and identity maintenance among gay Japanese-American males. *Alternative Lifestyles, 5,* 236–243.

Yu, A., & Gregg, C. H. (1993). Asians in groups: More than a matter of cultural awareness. *Journal for Specialists in Group Work, 18,* 86–93.

Chapter 21

Applying the ACA Advocacy Competencies in Employment Counseling

Robert C. Chope

Social justice means moving towards a society where all hungry are fed,
all sick are cared for, the environment is treasured, and we treat each
other with love and compassion. Not an easy goal, for sure, but
certainly one worth giving our lives for!

—Medea Benjamin, cofounder
of Global Exchange and Code Pink, as cited in Kikuchi, 2005

The purpose of this chapter is to provide a rationale for employment counselors for not only empowering but also advocating for clients who face emotionally demanding experiences in entering and gaining tenure in the work world. The challenges in this enterprise include articulating and choosing a career path; applying for, securing, and adjusting to new work or a new job; and making decisions about whether, when, and how to transition upward in the workplace.

For some clients these activities will take place while they must concurrently address issues of isolation, discrimination, and potential harassment. Pointing out some of these issues should assist employment counselors to become more sensitive to these challenges. Sensitivity, knowledge, and awareness can also allow employment counselors to develop a shared worldview with their clients that will empower them and eventually lead to successful employment and productive careers.

Employment counselors work in the private and public sectors, but unlike career counselors, their primary goal is to assist individuals in securing jobs and managing their careers. The work of the employment counselor may take place in state and local unemployment offices, private industry council offices, rehabilitation settings, Veterans' Administration facilities, community centers, and social service agencies such as Goodwill, the Salvation Army, and the Society of St. Vincent DePaul. Employment counselors are also prevalent in city centers that focus on homeless individuals; occasionally, some work in community colleges and vocational technical schools. Regardless of the setting, employment counselors need to be competent in more than simply their counseling skills. They also need to be equipped with an understanding of local, state, and federal economics, labor market conditions, public and private institutional hiring practices, workplace discrimination, workplace harassment, and the myriad needs of those clients who may be among the most disenfranchised.

Although social justice ideals are embraced by many working in the employment counseling field, it is a truism that employment counselors, perhaps more than many other types of counselors, are exposed to issues of inequity and injustice. They are often invested in the position of protecting those who are least able to advocate and protect for themselves. While the field of counseling is a product of social policy, employment counselors are exposed to the vast inequities of the resources of the United States regardless of social initiatives and remedies.

A Brief Historical Perspective

Employment counselors have a historical model of effective individual client empowerment, individual social advocacy, and social and political systems advocacy in Frank Parsons. Often credited as the founder of career counseling, Parsons was a socially responsible practitioner of the new field of vocational counseling, and he was highlighted by Hartung and Blustein (2002) as a counselor, theoretician, mentor, and teacher.

Parsons has been characterized as the original career counselor, but his efforts also established the roots of employment counseling. Parsons was a pragmatist, establishing the first vocational counseling center in the United States over a century ago, the Boston Vocation Bureau in Massachusetts (Pope, 2000). Trained as an engineer, Parsons developed an approach to service delivery with a socialist perspective, hoping that government intervention would assist in the creation of an egalitarian society and work would be an entitlement, especially for the poor and disenfranchised (Hartung & Blustein, 2002). Davis (1969) stated what many know: The date of Parsons's posthumously published *Choosing a Vocation* (Parsons, 1909) is characterized as the beginning of the field of career counseling.

Employment Counseling and Economic Context

In discussing the early 21st-century employment climate in the United States, Chope and Johnson (2008) described circumstances that in many ways can be compared with the context that Parsons experienced. They portrayed a housing market of the new millennium filled with tribulations, a United States dollar that has fallen to new lows against most world currencies, petroleum products that are at all-time highs, and the globalization of work that has led to increasing unemployment, underemployment, and the rise of the service sector in which most of the jobs are dead end and minimum wage. In addition to the destabilizing effects of the U.S. and allied wars in Iraq and Afghanistan, there is an enormous disparity in earning potential between different multicultural groups due to diminished employment opportunities, discrimination, and the denial of equal educational opportunities. Moreover, the low-paying sectors of the service industry offer employment but often without job protections or anything more than meager benefits.

Unemployment is the crux of the work of employment counselors, so they need to understand its causes and effects. Economic Policy Institute President Lawrence Mishel (2003) explained that unemployment is affected by continued slow growth in the economy along with increased productivity in the workplace. To generate enough jobs to significantly lower the unemployment rate, the economy will need to grow more than 3.5%, possibly 4.5%. Mishel noted that real wages (wages adjusted for inflation) for full-time workers were falling for the first time since 1990, and declining real weekly wages will continue to hinder overall wage and income growth. This will affect consumption, which will contribute to impeding an economic recovery.

The current economy is riddled with uncertainty, even more so since the election of 2008. Today large companies can be sold overnight on the floor of any of the major international stock exchanges and may not exist the next day. They can also go bankrupt, giving their employees 1-day's notice as was the case in 2008 with two U.S. airlines, ATA and Aloha Airlines. In the fall of 2008, the United States Treasury was called upon by the Bush administration and the United States Congress to deliver $700 billion to rescue companies like Bear Sterns and AIG, which were on the verge of collapsing, and General Motors and the Ford Motor Company, which were in dire need of cash infusions. Meanwhile, other large companies like Lehman Brothers were not given government bailout protection.

The large mortgage funders Fanny Mae and Freddie Mac relinquished control to the U.S. government to purportedly be run as government entities.

Stettner and Wenger (2003) pointed out earlier that many highly educated, high-functioning workers are affected by economic downturns, with the numbers concentrated among mid-career workers, college graduates, and executive, professional, and managerial workers. However, the instability of companies most often affects workers who are less well educated and less well prepared for the work world. Zakaria (2006) underscored that people born into privileged circumstances can weather the economic and unemployment storms. They have the opportunities to attend schools that will educate them and network them to others, thus stimulating them to flourish. Those born into impoverished communities with significant ecological barriers do not have many options, resulting in a lack of personal, economic, and vocational maneuverability.

Beyond the economic downturn of 2008–2009, all employment counselors know that there are daunting mountains and valleys for everyone over the course of their life spans. This is particularly true for people from very low incomes, those who are underserved and lacking in privilege, and those who are poorly educated or simply forgotten about. Too often, unfortunately, a pool of bright and creative children are not pushed or motivated by family members, teachers, or other relationships to be the best that they can be. They are lost in the cracks; a life with encouragement and positive family influences is unavailable.

Moreover, parents with spotty employment histories and unstable incomes influence the trust that their offspring have about their futures in the work world. Those parents who, by necessity, move from their communities and support systems to secure employment may adversely influence both the educational direction and social networking of their children.

The abovementioned factors all point to the importance of the current contextual intersection between the larger social and economic picture and the individual client. Traditionally, employment counseling has focused on working toward alleviating clients' feelings of distress or dysfunction by helping clients to find employment without necessarily identifying or addressing external problem sources. The continuing development of disparities in income among individuals seeking employment services should be in the consciousness of employment counselors everywhere.

Balancing Empowerment and Advocacy

All of these considerations lead to fear and uncertainty about the current and future standards of living in the United States along with the future of work as the citizens know it. In times like these, employment counselors need to serve not only as counselors and coaches but also as advocates for those who may be the most affected and marginalized. In some circumstances, employment counselors may need to serve primarily as advocates, intervening with different social service and political systems to best serve individual clients and those who come after them with similar issues. What is most clear is that their work is heavily influenced by economic context. Employment counselors must be aware of those contextual variables at the local, state, and national levels that affect their clients.

Clients depend more heavily on employment counselors to be their advocates because they are currently missing the traditional advocacy groups—strong progressive labor unions, legislators, and social movement leaders who championed them before. Johnson (2008) reminded us that over 40 years ago, these advocacy changes began with the transformation of the United States from an industrial-based to a service-based economy. This resulted in the progressive elimination of traditional assembly-line arrangements in factories inhabited by well-paid workers who were almost always protected by union membership. Within the old industrial-based society, secure jobs were the norm for both college and noncollege graduates alike. That is no longer the case. Along with the unions' decline has come the decline in influence and numbers of progressive civic and government leaders. Like corporations, neither government nor advocacy groups have the financial resources to serve a population of people seeking work at levels not seen since the beginning of the new millennium.

The Importance of Work and the Place of Advocacy

Employment counseling is not just finding a job for a client. To be able to work means much more. Blustein (2006) showed that work is a primary factor in people's well-being; the context of work shapes the lives of people. Employment is an indicator of how people live and begs the question as to whether they are getting ahead. Blustein argued that work is a means of survival and power; it provides social connections and serves as a means of self-determination.

Chope (2000) wrote that the loss of work affects the identity that a person has developed. It also changes a person's role within a family unit, so a shift in financial power and decision making takes place. Job loss elicits stress on the family unit, insecurity among the children, a change in status among peers, and quite possibly an extreme lifestyle change.

Meyer, Chope, Weisblatt, and Knudson (2003) pointed out that those who are unemployed for extended periods of time engage in comparative labeling and estimate their self-worth to be low. This is true whether they have been prisoners, homeless, drug dependent, or simply unable to find work. These people are also overwhelmed and helpless, believing that they cannot change their situation easily. It is crucial for them to feel empowered because their tendency is to undervalue their accomplishments. Meyer et al. also pointed out that highly discouraged job seekers are often emotionally exhausted, cynical, lacking in a sense of personal accomplishment, and numb to other people's suggestions.

To be sure, employment counselors can help the unemployed gain a sense of empowerment by having them prioritize their activities, break up tasks into smaller components, be willing to compromise, and stay focused. They can also advise these clients to get away from the job search for a day or find other ways to gain a sense of control.

With this in mind, it is clear that employment counselors are potentially pivotal players in the process of taking social action and affecting social change by empowering and advocating for their clients. Counselors have been viewed for years as agents of change (Kiselica & Robinson, 2001; Lee, 1998; Lewis & Bradley, 2000).

Employment counselors can heartily use the American Counseling Association (ACA) Advocacy Competencies (Lewis, Arnold, House, & Toporek, 2002) to strike a balance between client empowerment and client advocacy for many of the clients they serve. They can also move on to create social justice advocacy that gives them the opportunity to expand their services to a larger arena in a manner similar to the work of Parsons. Toporek and Liu (2001) described a range of counseling roles and goals on a continuum from empowerment (individual and small scale) to social action (systemic and large scale). This continuum reflects the potential complexity of the roles of the employment counselor. Many will need flexibility in their provider roles to address both empowerment and advocacy and between the individual, situational, contextual, and multicultural issues of their clients and the larger needs of society.

The Working Alliance

To be connected and to work effectively, counselors form a working alliance with their clients that serves as a framework for the establishment of trust and rapport. Bordin (1979) pointed out that three ingredients are necessary in creating the working alliance: agreement between the counselor and client on their goals, agreement on the tasks of the counseling process, and the experience of a bond that reflects care and trust. Counselors assist their clients with appropriate active listening, exploration, and assessment that create a foundation for a plan of action for a client to consider. However, other factors, including a shared worldview and positive client expectations, are also elements that strengthen the alliance (Fischer, Jome, & Atkinson, 1998). Together, the client and the employment counselor view many troubling outside social patterns, for example, inequality, discrimination, and injustice. Advocacy-competent employment counselors will know how to implement empowerment strategies as they help their clients understand their lives in context.

According to Evans (2008), those who are involved in the process of working with people who are seeking work have the opportunity of intervening and working toward the elimination of discrimination against oppressed groups whether it is in hiring, training, or promotions. Evans suggested that there are opportunities for employment counselors to address the inequities. There are also chances for employment counselors to assist in breaking the glass ceiling for women and men of color, among others. And there are chances to use civil rights protections to improve opportunities for gay, lesbian, bisexual, and transgender individuals.

How Employment Counselors Can Use the Advocacy Competencies With Clients, Students, and the Public at Large

Not only can employment counselors assist their clients with finding work, but they can also serve as advocates for clients who are faced with situations such as employment and educational discrimination, sexual harassment, and workplace violence or trauma. They can also advise clients who observe wrongdoing in their workplace and are trying to decide whether to "blow the whistle" on their employers. The following examples serve to illustrate the contextual variables that employment counselors must contend with. These include the effect of income disparity, prejudices toward particular jobs, past history with the criminal courts, and weight-related discrimination. Counselors must be aware of contextual issues in the career and employment counseling process, especially when working with a disenfranchised or marginalized clientele (Niles & Harris-Bowlsbey, 2002).

Examples of Contextual Variables

Income disparities among racially diverse students in urban settings often lead to disparities in educational and career attainment, according to Kenny et al. (2007). The authors identified categories and subcategories of the students' perceptions of both barriers and supports. Similarly, Noonan, Hall, and Blustein (2007), using urban adolescents in a school-to-work program, showed how perceived differences in social class are experienced. They identified four thematic categories: (a) navigation of identity; (b) perceptions of similarity, difference, and being understood; (c) receipt of mobility encouragement; and (d) awareness of stratification.

Bergman and Chalkley (2007) noted work-related stigmas that can lead to prejudice against individual workers even if they have left the occupation. "Dirty work" is the title used to illustrate their point. "Dirty work" roles such as exotic dancers lead to continued devaluation. Even after employees have left these industries, the stigmas remain. Likewise, probationers, parolees, and ex-offenders make up a significant population of individuals who are often underserved by employment counselors. Shivy et al. (2007) reported that incarceration rates are climbing, with close to 2.2 million people currently being jailed. Approximately 650,000 inmates are released from prison each year and face immense challenges: returning to their communities and homes, keeping straight, finding work, or continuing their education. Many try to work under continuing court-related supervision. Substance abuse often also affects their reentry and employment progress.

Roehling, Roehling, and Pichler (2007) studied employment discrimination related to a person's body weight and perceived weight. With a survey of 2,838 American adults, their data showed that women were over 16 times more likely than men to perceive employment-related discrimination and to identify weight as a basis for their own discriminatory experience. Overweight respondents were 12 times more likely than normal-weight respondents to report discrimination. Those who were obese were 37 times more likely and those who were severely obese 100 times more likely to report discrimination.

These examples speak to the demanding contextual issues that are a part of employment counseling. Fortunately, the Advocacy Competencies allow employment counselors to determine the level and the domain of their work. They can counsel the client toward empowerment, and they can act on behalf of the client as an advocate. They can also advocate on behalf of a particular marginalized community, or they can act within that community. And they can work on behalf of the public by advocating in the public arena or with the public to provide public information about unfortunate employment challenges.

To illustrate the role of an employment counselor with a particular population, an example is provided with transgender clients that demonstrates the process of acting with and on behalf of the client, the community, and the public arena.

Transgender Employees: One Underrepresented Group in Need of Empowerment, Client Advocacy, and Social Justice Advocacy

Transgender people raise a rich variety of issues when they are clients of employment counselors. A wide range of contextual concerns come into play that must be addressed through empowerment and advocacy.

Consider the following. There are an estimated 19,000 transgender people in San Francisco (Vega, 2007) and between 750,000 and 3 million nationwide (Chope & Strom, 2008). While their work experience may be reflected in many different occupational titles, they are often severely underemployed or unemployed and, of course, discriminated against.

Transgender employees have rarely been studied in the workplace. Until recently, they have been absent from the employment counseling literature (Kirk & Belovics, 2008). Instead, transgender people have been described as the "canaries for the other sexual minorities" by Doan (2001), referencing the age-old practice by coal miners of transporting a canary into a mine shaft to determine whether the air was safe to breathe. Transgender people are known to elicit public feelings of condemnation, and this has sometimes been used as a warning to the larger gay, lesbian, and bisexual community. Transgender people have been less willing to "come out" in part because they often risk high levels of discrimination and physical harm.

Only nine states plus Washington, DC, have antidiscrimination laws that protect transgender people, although three other states had legislation pending in 2008. Recently the U.S. House of Representatives enacted a hate crimes prevention bill that included gender identity (Rosenberg, 2007). Employment counselors could work as change agents by working with federal legislators to increase the number of states with antidiscrimination laws.

It is important to note that Title VII of the Civil Rights Act of 1964 prohibits discrimination in employment because of sex. Until recently, federal courts have not afforded workplace discrimination protection that included gender identity, so transgender employees did not have equal protection under the act. However, the U.S. Court of Appeals for the Sixth Circuit has recently decided two discrimination suits in favor of transgender plaintiffs (Ilona, 2007). Clients who believe that they have been discriminated against may wish to pursue remedies through the federal court system. Employment counselors can act on a client's behalf by keeping a referral list of labor attorneys well versed in transgender employment discrimination.

Clinical and Social Justice Issues in Working With Transgender Clients

Individual Interventions

As Blustein (2006) suggested, the worldview of the transgender client regarding the culture of work must be taken into consideration in employment counseling. Work can be a fearful place, and especially so for transgender employees. Cecilia Chung, deputy director of the Transgender Law Center in San Francisco, says that transgender people are discriminated against and judged by almost everyone (Vega, 2007). This discrimination can lead to feelings of low self-esteem, depression, self-medication with alcohol and other substances, and the inability to properly perform in the workplace (Denny & Green, 1996).

Pernicious discrimination such as this demands that employment counselors develop empowerment strategies in direct counseling. These include focusing on the different stressors that the client experiences, including the biological and physical stressors that are a part of the transgender experience; attending to the psychological stress and sense of belonging that change when employees change their gender; and addressing the family stress and social stress that the client experiences when there is disparate contact with former friends and family members and truly vast changes in employment opportunities. Employment counselors will need to be sensitive to the tendency for their transgender clients to feel emotionally depleted and undervalued, even when they have been successfully performing in the jobs for years.

Chope and Strom (2008) pointed out that the work world is a place where everyone owns attitudes about earning potential, achievement, independence, and vocational competence. Workers also bring family attitudes about money, savings, comparative assets, and salaries of others, along with occupational prestige. These evaluative attitudes and criteria are especially oppressive to transgender employees who know that their capacity to be employed at the level to which they once expected will probably not occur. In a world in which employees move up the employment ladder by making their presence known, transgender employees typically refrain from drawing attention to themselves.

One's appearance or changing appearance will most assuredly elicit reactions in the workplace, and some of these can be hostile, harassing, or career jeopardizing. Rosenberg (2007) reported on three cases, all with different outcomes. When a male Baptist minister began preparing for sexual reassignment surgery, he was taking hormones and using the name Julie. Her employer of 15 years barred her from dressing as a woman or wearing earrings. Her workload and pay were cut, prompting her to file a discrimination suit.

On the other hand, a woman kept her job as a high school teacher in Illinois after she shaved her beard and transitioned from being a man. And when a Prudential Financial vice president came to work as Margaret in 2002, her colleagues adjusted to her change with humor, partially alleviating their discomfort before getting back to work. Employment counselors can empower their clients by discussing and preparing them for differential reactions in the workplace. Some colleagues may be accommodating, many will be discriminatory.

The best advocacy will come about with new ways of thinking about work with marginalized clients. The following are several suggestions that should be a part of training and practice of the employment counselor (Meyer et al., 2003).

1. Clients can become empowered by considering new income streams, and they might be encouraged to consider several different part-time jobs rather than a full-time job in what is commonly called a portfolio career. Instead of looking for job security, clients might look for work that may only last a few months, taking advantage of each project as an opportunity to learn new skills and develop new professional contacts before moving on to something else.

2. Clients can be empowered through apprenticeships. For years, people obtained many skilled jobs through apprenticeships. These can provide an organized format for training and mentoring. Accordingly, employment counselors might work as advocates as they encourage the companies that they have contact with to create apprenticeship opportunities. They can also work with human resources departments to advocate for health and dental benefits for those engaged in apprenticeships. Employment counselors can also work with local and state policymakers and chambers of commerce to provide benefits to apprentices.

3. Employment counselors can also urge volunteering and advocate for health benefits for those who partake of volunteer opportunities. What the difficult-to-employ need most is a network base, and there is no better way of developing a new network than in volunteer work in a specialty area related to the worker's career choice.

4. Employment counselors could assist skilled clients to work as consultants to organizations, and they might work to find a coterie of companies that would be willing to hire their clients as consultants for 5 to 10 hours a week on projects that may not require full-time employment. Moreover, clients might be encouraged to turn their hobbies into moneymaking ventures, creating their own new opportunities.

5. If clients have time available, they could pursue further education. This activity can help to establish feelings of goal attainment while providing a context to build a new network of contacts. Education can also serve as a distraction from the demands of everyday living without work. Suggesting activities like these to appropriate clients can increase a sense of self-esteem and empowerment.

6. Employment counselors should attend to their clients' description of barriers to their success. They should understand the unique needs of their clients and the way that these needs interface with a successful pursuit of a job.

Community Interventions

Perhaps to be the best of advocates, employment counselors need to realize that they cannot always focus on individual issues. Instead they work as advocates for their entire class of clients by ensuring that their communities are taking advantage of all of the resources in programs such as the federal Carl Perkins III and Workforce Investment Acts. These programs provide for career counseling services that can be used for job development, skill development, job seeking, and job-keeping activities. They also provide for increases in postsecondary education services in vocational and technical programs. Employment counselors can work with their federal regional offices to be aware of services that their clients might be entitled to and to advocate for service and educational programs when these are warranted under the acts.

Continuing with the example of working with the transgender community, there are clear circumstances in which employment counselors will need to negotiate relevant community services on behalf of their transgender clients. These will not only include referrals to legal services or supportive facilities like the Transgender Law Center but also necessitate providing valuable information to the personnel in these facilities.

Employment counselors know that most employment applications ask for a check as to whether a person is male or female. While a potential employee may feel that this poses no problem, for a transgender person, it can be an awkward experience when an applicant is clearly of the opposite gender from that being checked on the employment application. This experience could give an employer the wherewithal to later terminate an employee for falsifying information on an application. The applicant can, of course, face other discrimination in the personnel office. Employment counselors can provide clinical case examples and training information to community resources so that their personnel have the knowledge, awareness, and skills to address the evolving issues that occur as transgender clients become increasingly open.

Employment counselors should be aware that employers are required to provide reasonable access to restroom facilities. They can advocate organizationally with institutions to ensure that there are unisex restrooms in the workplace. With transgender employees, corporate bathroom issues have been addressed with the "Principle of Least Astonishment," suggesting that a person who presents as a woman will be less astonishing using the women's bathroom. If a concern evolves, the employer must provide alternative solutions (Beth, 2005). Further, in *Cruzan v. Davis* the federal appeals court in Minnesota ruled in 2002 that an employer is within its rights to instruct a transgender employee to use the bathroom matching the employee's presentation (Rosenberg, 2007).

To some extent, advocating for transgender clients reminds counselors of the history of advocating for disabled clients in the early days of the Americans With Disabilities Act of 1990. Sometimes the advocacy results in changes that benefit everyone even though the focus was on only one group. Recently the public has been made aware of the increasing prevalence of unisex bathroom facilities. The creation of unisex bathrooms not only benefits transgender people but also parents who wish to assist their youngsters and adult partners who wish to help each other.

Employment counselors can advocate for their clients by informing personnel and human resources managers along with the local chambers of commerce that matching names with gender is the primary area in which transgender people have a difficult time keeping their professional and private lives at a distance. For example, changing the gender marker on any health records will almost always elicit a response from insurance carriers and might threaten certain benefits.

Public Information Interventions

Public information in the Advocacy Competencies refers to advocacy in collaboration with a community on a systems level. As employment counselors work as advocates on behalf of their clients, they will need to avail themselves of the most current legal information. Carroll, Gilroy, and Ryan (2002) advised counselors working with transgender clients to have adequate knowledge of local, regional, and national support networks for the transgender community. Information on these networks can be found on organizational websites exemplified by the following: National Center for Transgender Equality (www.nctequality.org), Equality California (www.eqca.org), Transgender Law Center (www.transgenderlawcenter.org), and National Center for Lesbian Rights (www.nclrights.org).

Employment counselors should add to their advocacy roles by increasing their awareness of, and advocacy for, transgender-friendly companies. More than 230 major companies now protect transgender employees from employment discrimination. Gender identity and expression have been added to their nondiscrimination policies according to the Gender Public Advocacy Coalition (2007). The coalition reports further that 149 colleges and universities have added the gender-based protections to their nondiscrimination policies to prevent unequal treatment and harassment of those who do not fit traditional gender expectations. Counselors can assist clients in exploring companies that have transgender-friendly policies on the website Transgender at Work (www.tgender.net). Further, counselors can assist employers in understanding and changing practices so that they become more transgender friendly.

Employment counselors can engage in needed advocacy at legislative and policy levels. For instance, transgender clients often face identification issues (Herman, 2006). Name change orders can be made for Social Security cards, drivers' licenses, and birth certificates, but gender changes cannot be made without proof of surgery. Furthermore, the Department of Homeland Security may examine gender mismatches with the Social Security number verification system. With this knowledge, employment counselors can work toward greater equity in these identification issues.

In addition to the above, there are recent examples of transgender people being left out of important work-related legislation, such as the Employment Non-Discrimination Act of 2009 (ENDA). For those counselors interested in playing a role in creating public policy changes, there may be ample opportunities. Some of the work can be controversial. For example, House Speaker Nancy Pelosi and Congressman Barney Frank, while expressing personal support for transgender people, worked to remove gender identity from the ENDA legislation, suggesting that it would not be passed if transgender people were covered (Lochhead, 2007). Both thought that including transgender people in the legislation would result in its failure.

This example of one group in need of employment services allows us to consider a social justice perspective in employment counseling as counselors not only empower but also advocate. The example demonstrates how social justice principles can be formally integrated into employment counseling. It calls for a greater degree of awareness of client advocacy and the advocacy of social justice issues and offers suggestions on ways that employment counselors might be inspired to consider changing social structures and policies, not simply individuals.

Training

Employment counselors assist clients in clarifying employment objectives and work experiences. Working with those who may be marginalized requires special consideration and training. Special attention will be needed for counselors working with those clients who have inconsistent employment records, difficulty with verbal communication, court records, problems with rudimentary hygiene, and perhaps limited English. Employment counselors not only need to be able to identify a client's unique strengths but also need to understand the social, political, economic, and cultural factors that affect the client while seeking work.

Moreover, newcomers and students in the field who wish to play advocacy roles will need the skills necessary for consulting with organizations and engaging in social action at organizational and legislative levels. Their training should include consultation regarding fairness in hiring practices, preventing workplace violence, confronting discrimination, facilitating institutional "whistleblowers," and finding new methods to create systemic change. Interdisciplinary skills and knowledge will help new professionals and students learn to build bridges between various types of service providers and expertise, including business, law, social work, public health, and others. Finally, training in ethics should facilitate new employment counselors to examine their work and their roles as change agents with social justice concerns.

Other authors have described ways of integrating advocacy into human service work (e.g., Lewis, Lewis, Daniels, & D'Andrea, 1998; Toporek & Liu, 2001). It is a truism that the working alliance between the employment counselors and the client needs to be especially strong when a client brings an issue, such as workplace discrimination, to the session. That issue may transcend those typically experienced in employment counseling, and the employment counselor will need training to know how to address the client's needs while also referring the client to other service interventions. When the client is making a charge against another employee or employees in an organization, the employment counselor may need to spend much more time engaging in questioning and fact finding to fully understand the situation and assess the credibility of the client's perception. The counselor's role becomes complex, especially when working within that same organization or advocating on behalf of the client. With this type of investigative inquiring, the employment counselor will want to ensure that the client continues to feel supported even in the face of demanding scrutiny, while at the same time gathering sufficient information to be able to advocate appropriately. Training can help the employment counselor with this type of questioning while working to have a shared worldview of the work, politics, and the behavior of a particular organization.

Conclusion

Through the employment counseling process, clients gain a sense of power along with self-knowledge that can inculcate them with the necessary confidence they need to more easily communicate their needs, skills, and talents to a current boss or potential employer. For unemployed individuals, it is particularly important that they hold onto their personal power to persevere in a protracted job search and comfortably communicate their strengths and skills, despite disappointments. For clients who are employed, Meyer et al. (2003) pointed out that being able to move laterally or vertically upward in an organization promotes a sense of personal power. Employees who believe in their own power will more likely make direct and sustained contributions in the workplace and increase the probability of gaining job tenure. Individual advocacy helps to positively affect the client's sense of personal power.

As employment counselors look to the world of work to determine career options for their clients, they can encourage clients to become advocates and to consider the issues or problems that they believe to be important in the world at large and apply their talents to helping to resolve these problems. Working in the green industries is one example of this. This is an approach that might emerge during a discussion of the client's values or interests or the client's own predicament. Considering solving large-scale problems (whether they are global, local, or national) can help clients retain their sense of individual power in the world and perhaps have an impact where they want to work. It is another frame with which to look at career choices. In addition, as we look to the future, Meyer et al. (2003) pointed out that other views of the work world will derive from new alliances forming between different industries. An example is the Apollo Project, an alliance of 10 labor unions along with environmentalists with a plan to back a 10-year, $300 billion research project to promote energy efficiency and reduce dependence on foreign oil. It is expected to preserve manufacturing and construction jobs, improve the public infrastructure, and be good for the environment by promoting sound energy technology (Greenhouse, 2003). Employment counselors can provide information to clients about these alliances, and they can advocate for the alliances in the legislative and policy arenas.

Finally, changing demographics and technology will also promote new career opportunities for clients. Longer living seniors, aging baby boomers, and future generations will need new and different services. The reality that the United States is, indeed, a multicultural, multiethnic, and multiracial society presents trends that will provide new career opportunities.

It is clear that with a slow economic recovery, changes in work have begun. Employment counselors need to remain open to look for new ways to empower and advocate for clients as they find engaging and satisfying work where they can feel some sense of stability and security in uncertain times.

References

Beth. (2005). *Transgender/transsexual bathroom references.* Retrieved October 16, 2007, from http:etransgender.com/viewtopic.php

Bergman, M. E., & Chalkley, K. M. (2007). "Ex" marks a spot: The stickiness of dirty work and other removed stigmas. *Journal of Occupational Psychology, 12,* 251–265.

Blustein, D. L. (2006). *The psychology of working: A new perspective for career development, counseling, and public policy.* Mahwah, NJ: Erlbaum.

Bordin, E. S. (1979). The generalizability of the working alliance. *Psychotherapy: Theory, Research and Practice, 16,* 252–260.

Carroll, L., Gilroy, P., & Ryan, J. (2002). Counseling transgendered, transsexual, and gender-variant clients. *Journal of Counseling & Development, 80,* 131–138.

Chope, R. C. (2000). *Dancing naked: Breaking through the emotional limits that keep you from the job you want.* Oakland, CA: New Harbinger.

Chope, R. C., & Johnson, R. A. (2008). Career identity in a turbulent world. *Perspectives in Education, 26,* 1–10.

Chope, R. C., & Strom, L. S. (2008). Critical considerations in career and employment counseling with transgender clients. In G. R. Walz, J. C. Bleuer, & R. K. Yep (Eds.), *Compelling counseling interventions: Celebrating Vistas fifth anniversary* (pp. 125–135). Ann Arbor, MI: Counseling Outfitters.

Davis, H. V. (1969). *Frank Parsons: Prophet, innovator, counselor.* Carbondale: Southern Illinois University Press.

Denny, D., & Green, J. (1996). Gender identity and bisexuality. In B. Firestein (Ed.), *Bisexuality: The psychology and politics of an invisible minority* (pp. 84–102). Thousand Oaks, CA: Sage.

Doan, P. (2001). *Are the transgendered the mine shaft canaries of urban areas?* Retrieved October 10, 2007, from http://www.plannersnetwork.org/publications/2001_146/Doan.html

Evans, K. (2008). *Gaining cultural competence in career counseling.* Boston: Lahaska Press.

Fischer, A. R., Jome, L. M., & Atkinson, D. R. (1998). Reconceptualizing multicultural counseling: Universal healing conditions in a culturally specific context. *Counseling Psychologist, 26,* 525–588.

Gender Public Advocacy Coalition. (2007). *230 major corporations adopt gender protections.* Retrieved October 17, 2007, from http://www.gpac.org/workplace

Greenhouse, S. (2003, June 6). *Unions back research plan for energy.* San Francisco: Apollo Alliance. Retrieved from http://www.apolloalliance.org/apollo_in_the_news/nyt060603.cfm

Hartung, P. J., & Blustein, D. L. (2002). Reason, intuition, and social justice: Elaborating on Parsons's career decision-making model. *Journal of Counseling & Development, 80,* 41–47.

Herman, J. (2006). *Forced out: A real ID problem for trans people.* Retrieved October 29, 2008, from http://www.advocate.com/print_article_ekid36069.asp

Ilona, M. T. (2007). Sex stereotyping per se: Transgender employees and Title VII. *California Law Review, 95,* 561.

Johnson, R. A. (2008, March 31). African Americans and homelessness: Moving through history. *Journal of Black Studies OnlineFirst,* 1–23.

Kenny, M. E., Gualdron, L., Scanlon, D., Sparks, E., Blustein, D. L., & Jernigan, M. (2007). Urban adolescents' constructions of supports and barriers to educational and career attainment. *Journal of Counseling Psychology, 54,* 336–343.

Kikuchi, D. (2005, October 26). *What is social justice?: A collection of definitions.* Daly City, CA: Reach and Teach. Retrieved November 15, 2005, from http://www.reachandteach.com/content/article.php?story=2004

Kirk, J., & Belovics, R. (2008). Understanding and counseling transgender clients. *Journal of Employment Counseling, 45,* 29–39.

Kiselica, M. S., & Robinson, M. (2001). Bringing advocacy counseling to life: The history, issues, and human drama of social justice work in counseling. *Journal of Counseling & Development, 79,* 387–397.

Lee, C. C. (1998). Counselors as agents of social change. In C. C. Lee & G. R. Walz (Eds.), *Social action: A mandate for change* (pp. 8–14). Alexandria, VA: American Counseling Association.

Lewis, J. A., Arnold, M. S., House, R., & Toporek, R. L. (2002). *ACA Advocacy Competencies.* Retrieved August 28, 2008, from http://www.counseling.org/Publications/

Lewis, J., & Bradley, L. (Eds.). (2000). *Advocacy in counseling: Counselors, clients, and community.* Greensboro, NC: ERIC Counseling and Student Services Clearinghouse.

Lewis, J. A., Lewis, M. D., Daniels, J. A., & D'Andrea, M. J. (1998). *Community counseling: Empowerment strategies for a diverse society* (2nd ed.). Pacific Grove, CA: Brooks/Cole.

Lochhead, C. (2007, October 2). Gays angered by scaled-back rights bill. *San Francisco Chronicle,* pp. A1, A7.

Meyer, D. M., Chope, R. C., Weisblatt, S. E., & Knudson, K. (2003). Counseling the long term unemployed. In G. R. Walz & R. L. Knowdell (Eds.), *Global realities* (pp. 127–137). Greensboro, NC: CAPS Press.

Mishel, L. (2003). *The economy, the war and choosing our future.* Washington, DC: Economic Policy Institute. Retrieved April 27, 2003, from http://www.epinet.org/content.cfm/ webfeatures_viewpoints_war_economy_future

Niles, S. G., & Harris-Bowlsbey, J. H. (2002). *Career development in the 21st century.* Upper Saddle River, NJ: Merrill Prentice Hall.

Noonan, A. E., Hall, G., & Blustein, D. L. (2007). Urban adolescents' experience of social class in relationships at work. *Journal of Vocational Behavior, 70,* 542–560.

Parsons, F. (1909). *Choosing a vocation.* Boston: Houghton-Mifflin.

Pope, M. (2000). A brief history of career counseling in the United States. *The Career Development Quarterly, 48,* 194–211.

Roehling, M. V., Roehling, P. V., & Pichler, S. (2007). The relationship between body weight and perceived weight-related employment discrimination: The role of sex and race. *Journal of Vocational Behavior, 71,* 300–318.

Rosenberg, D. (2007, May 21). Rethinking gender. *Newsweek Magazine, 50–57.*

Shivy, V. A., Wu, J. J., Moon, A. E., Mann, S. C., Holland, J. G., & Eacho, C. (2007). Ex-offenders reentering the workforce. *Journal of Counseling Psychology, 54,* 466–473.

Stettner, A., & Wenger, J. (2003). The broad reach of long-term unemployment. *EPI Issue Brief #194.* Washington, DC: Economic Policy Institute. Retrieved May 15, 2003, http://www.epinet. org/ content.cfm/issuebriefs_ib194

Toporek, R. L., & Liu, W. M. (2001). Advocacy in counseling: Addressing race, class, and gender oppression. In D. B. Pope-Davis & H. L. K. Coleman (Eds.), *The intersection of race, class, and gender in multicultural counseling* (pp. 285–413). Thousand Oaks, CA: Sage.

Vega, C. M. (2007, May 12). Transgender pioneer rises to powerful spot. *San Francisco Chronicle,* pp. A1, A6.

Zakaria, F. (2006, January 9). We all have a lot to learn. *Newsweek,* p. 37.

Section

III

20/20: The Future of the Counseling Profession

Chapter

22

Advocacy and Social Justice:
Entering the Mainstream of the Counseling Profession

Judith A. Lewis, Rebecca L. Toporek, and Manivong J. Ratts

Every chapter in this volume reflects the ideas and practices of counselors who are at the top of their game. They give their students and clients the best that they can offer, but they know that sometimes an individual's well-being depends on systemic change as well as personal transformation. These counselors have found a professional balance that combines the empathy of the counselor with the courage of the advocate.

- In a Southwestern border state, a young man explains to his counselor that he needs treatment for depression and anxiety. His career is at a standstill, with jobs hard to come by for a gay man with less-than-perfect English and limited job skills. He is afraid to enroll in college and afraid to seek health care because of his fear of being sent back to Mexico, where he was born. His counselor helps him recognize that his emotional state may be a healthy response to real systemic pressures. But the counselor also goes beyond the limits of the office to engage in legislative advocacy, confronting unjust laws affecting undocumented workers and fighting for human rights across the spectrum.
- In a West Texas town, a counselor works with a family that is dealing with multiple stressors and the lack of access to health care and human services that the family needs. The counselor helps the parents develop self-advocacy skills, but she knows that many of the families she sees everyday are forced to cope with the same kinds of problems, especially with regard to transportation to required appointments. She takes part in a successful community advocacy effort to establish accessible services in the neighborhood and even bring new bus routes to the area.
- In a large, Midwestern city, an intravenous drug user finds the help she needs by stopping in at a van where she can get clean needles, nonjudgmental counseling, and, if necessary, crisis intervention. Her counselor knows that these kinds of services depend on public policies that support them, so she plays an active role in disseminating information about the validity of harm reduction models. She also joins with community members and advocacy groups to carry out legislative lobbying efforts at the state and national levels.

- In an suburban high school, an African American honors student attends a school dance and is confronted by a teacher who accuses him of drinking but ignores the White students who were also part of the group. The school counselor is able to advocate on the student's behalf, but only because she has been successful in bringing about changes to a zero-tolerance disciplinary policy that ignored individual differences but tended to target students of color.
- In a suburb of Chicago, the school counselor sees a fifth-grade student who has been identified as having "behavior problems." The counselor realizes that the problem lies not with the student's behavior but with the school itself. The student's primary language is Spanish, and this school has very few Latino students. Recognizing that systemic barriers exist for students whose primary language is not English, the counselor becomes involved in advocacy for change first at the level of the school, then the district, and finally the state.
- In city after city, day after day, something new is happening. A family with young children finds itself suddenly joining the ranks of people who are grappling with poverty and homelessness. The counselor is able to help the parents move from blaming themselves for this traumatic experience to framing poverty and homelessness as a situational event. Although this way of framing the issue is important for empowering clients, the counselor realizes that it is just as important to address the attitudinal dimension throughout the community. An organizing effort brings together community leaders, donors, shelter residents, and representatives of the helping network to find common cause.

These particular stories have all been drawn from the chapters in this book, but similar incidents take place in real life across every counseling setting and every specialization. Counseling and advocacy have always fit well together, but the awareness of this fact was sometimes buried just below the surface of our professional identity. Advocacy and social justice have finally begun to enter the mainstream of thought in the counseling profession because counselors have learned that they can be both good counselors and good advocates. All of the examples cited above demonstrate that master counselors move in the direction of advocacy largely because of what they have learned from their individual clients and students.

Choosing the Counseling Profession

Counselors tend to be drawn to the helping profession because it affords the opportunity to make real, human connections with people who need their help. Counselors hope that these connections will be characterized by the kind of mutuality that engenders growth both in their clients and in themselves.

> As a counseling practitioner, I learn from each of my clients. . . . My role as a counselor is to walk with my clients along their paths and explore the world that they know. My frequent questions include: What is your life about? What do you want your life to be about? What are you willing to do to change? How are you going to manifest the changes you wish to make? These are starting places for the journey. In exploring such questions with my clients, I continually have the opportunity to examine those questions myself. (Hutchins, 2005, p. 109)

When counselors' facilitative qualities are at their best, they can take pride in their work, knowing that they have helped their clients, one by one, transform their lives. But then, as counselors work with client after client or student after student, they begin to notice that personal transformation is not necessarily in the hands of the individual. Counselors see common issues arise among many members of the population they serve and realize that these ubiquitous problems result not from the clients' personal characteristics but from their attempts to adapt to discouraging—even oppressive— environments. If counselors are to avoid blaming the victims of oppression, they must find ways to address the oppression itself before more people are victimized.

> As counselors attempt to respond to the needs of all community members, particularly the most vulnerable people, the need to negotiate environmental changes becomes apparent. Their work brings counselors face to face with the victims of poverty, racism, sexism, and stigmatization; of political, economic, and social systems that leave individuals feeling powerless; of governing bodies that deny their responsibility to respond; of social norms that encourage isolation. In the face of these realities, counselors have no choice but to promote positive changes in those systems that directly impact the psychological well-being of their clients. (Lewis, Lewis, Daniels, & D'Andrea, 1998, p. 24)

Although some counselors still believe that they can meet all of their clients' needs through direct intervention, most have accepted the fact that advocating on behalf of clients and students is an integral part of a counselor's role. Toporek, Lewis, and Crethar (2009) wrote,

> Through the years that the profession has existed, there have always been career and employment counselors who fought against racism and sexism in the work place, family counselors who brought hidden violence and abuse into the open, school counselors who sought to eliminate school-based barriers to learning, and community counselors who participated in social action on behalf of their clients. (p. 260)

Yes, counselors do move out of their offices to carry out advocacy in the broader public arena. And yes, counselors do stay in their offices sometimes to use their talents for person-to-person interactions. As we consider this situation, the question always arises: Must counselors choose between helping their clients directly and helping their clients through systemic advocacy? Can they, instead, find a way toward a seamless connection between what they do in the counseling office and what they do in the Capitol Building?

A Seamless Connection

As the chapters in this book make clear, there is a natural connection between the counseling role and the advocacy role. This connection arises in part because what counselors do helps to make them successful advocates as well. In their work with students and clients, counselors see firsthand the impact of detrimental environments on vulnerable individuals. Counselors are often the first to notice a systemic problem because they see its effects. Once counselors do take note of a problem, they have human development knowledge to share with the public and human relations skills to work with others toward common solutions.

Counselors must remember, however, that the seamless connection goes not just from the office to the public arena but also from the public arena back to the office. This connection necessitates an empowerment orientation in the way counselors work with clients. There needs to be an unbroken line between counseling and advocacy strategies. That line abruptly breaks when a therapeutic approach involves diagnosing deficits and focusing attention solely on intrapsychic phenomena. Counselors can find a sense of wholeness in their work only if the theoretical perspectives that inform their direct counseling are broad enough to encompass a variety of roles. An empowerment approach meets this criterion.

The Individual Student or Client: Empowerment and Advocacy

Counselors who view their clients from a broad perspective that recognizes the impact of social, political, economic, and cultural forces are of course able to see the connection between counseling and advocacy. Moreover, the way they work directly with their clients is strongly affected. They realize that it is not only important for them but just as important for the client to see the impact of environmental factors on the client's well-being. When clients and students are pressed to look only within themselves for the cause of their concerns, they become mired in self-blame. When clients are given ample opportunity to explore the impact of oppression on their lives, they actually become more able to see what they, themselves, can do to overcome externally imposed obstacles to their own development. As strong as these clients may become, however, they still need advocates who can try to break down barriers and build constructive environments.

Members of oppressed and marginalized groups reap benefits when their counselors are willing to recognize both their strengths and their environmentally rooted vulnerabilities. The connections between empowerment strategies and advocacy show up across all of the chapters in the section *Advocacy Across Populations,* with the authors emphasizing both the strengths of the group members affected and the limitations inherent in using direct services alone. In Chapter 4, for instance, Singh suggests that counselors should "take an active role in both addressing systemic discrimination and prejudice toward queer people and valuing the resilience of this community." Liu and Estrada-Hernández (Chapter 5), in discussing their work with clients in poverty, point out that while it is important to help clients learn about what services are available to them, "advocacy-oriented counselors need to constantly think systemically how agencies and other help services may better work with clients in poverty." In Chapter 6, West-Olatunji's discussion of culturally diverse clients includes the recognition that the theoretical perspectives used by counselors and other helping professionals must, themselves, change, moving "beyond adapting conventional Eurocentric counseling theories of personality to developing therapeutic frameworks that centralize cultural values and worldviews as the basis for normalcy." To West-Olatunji, the involvement of the community provides an empowering environment within which individual solutions can be found. Kenney and Kenney (Chapter 7) emphasize the fact that environmental support can serve as a vehicle for empowerment, suggesting that documents like the Multiracial Bill of Rights and the Transracially Adopted Child's Bill of Rights are "powerful sources of empowerment." In addressing the needs of women in Chapter 9, Evans raises the interesting point that "some counselors believe that acting on behalf of the client takes away that client's power, but there are situations when the opposite is true," since lessening external stressors can actually facilitate the client's empowerment. Running through all of these chapters is the notion that a seamless connection between direct services and advocacy is not only possible but even necessary for clients who face societal barriers.

The School and Community: Collaboration and Systems Advocacy

The connection between counseling and advocacy remains watertight even when the area of emphasis moves beyond the individual to the school or community. Through all of the chapters in this book, authors describe a similar process: (a) recognizing an issue that affects a client or student, (b) becoming conscious of the fact that many clients or students are affected by the same problem, (c) developing an awareness that the source of the problem is plainly systemic, and (d) realizing that other people might be willing to collaborate in an effort to bring about change. This process shows up especially clearly in the chapters that address specific settings.

Crethar, in his review of advocacy in the school counseling milieu in Chapter 11, describes an example of one child's dilemma but moves from what might have been seen as a unique case to lay bare a systemic deficit within the school environment. Once that systemic barrier has been identified, the counselor is able to move on to the establishment of a group of allies prepared to take action. In Chapter 12, Diemer and Duffy depict the conditions addressed by a university-based counselor who has become intensely aware of "a rising tide of covert and overt acts of racism against students of color" at his university. Students of color have come to the counseling center to talk about their discomfort with the racial climate on campus. The counselor addresses the counseling needs of these students but recognizes the urgency of targeting the environment. His advocacy efforts are responsive to the students of color who have sought his help but focus on White students, who unquestionably have greater power to affect the racial climate for better or worse.

In Chapter 13, which is devoted to the work of the private practice mental health counselor, Hutchins highlights some of the challenges that are unique to that setting. The client Hutchins describes is affected by multiple oppressions that require multiple advocacy efforts. On behalf of this one client alone, the counselor needed a list of resources including but not limited to "career specialists, English as a Second Language programs, immigration and discrimination law specialists, employment law resources, health care professionals, social service resources in the LGBT community, community college and university resources, group work opportunities, and resources throughout the Spanish-speaking community." As Hutchins points out, a private practice counselor, unlike a school or college counselor, is not embedded within a system that is shared by all of his or her clients. Counselors in private practice must consider the entire community their system and become so entwined with the network of local resources that they can always find advocates and allies when their clients need them. With a solid network of community resources on hand, a counselor in private practice can maintain a seamless connection between direct service and systemic advocacy.

The Public Arena

Some counselors might see the macrolevel public arena as the one most distant from their personal connections with their students or clients. In fact, however, even a brief overview of the material presented in this book shows clearly that virtually every counseling specialty connects with a public agenda. As Middleton, Robinson, and Mu'min note in Chapter 17, rehabilitation counselors have always provided a strong voice on behalf of the people they serve, knowing that "the facilitation of independence, integration, and inclusion of persons with disabilities" depends on public policy at the broadest possible level. Family counselors know that the quality of family life depends on the degree to which policies attack or defend it. Substance abuse counselors understand that punitive regulations at the local, state, or national level often revictimize people who have been put at risk by drug use. Across all specialties, counselors who are committed to an advocacy orientation learn from their clients, gaining a deep perspective on human needs that few others can attain.

> Counselors who are oriented to a social justice perspective always eschew the microscope in favor of the wide-angle lens. Instead of using the psychological equivalent of a microscope to magnify and define the deficits within their clients, they seek the widest possible view of the context within which their clients' development takes place. (Lewis, 2007, p. 95)

Counselors who have this wide-angle lens know that their responsibilities as helpers extend from their clients to the community and the broader public arena. They are most likely to act on that knowledge when they remind themselves to do so. "The influence of oppression from the larger social, political, and economic context must be kept in the foreground so that the counseling process is not detoured down a dead-end road" (Arnold, 2001, p. 26).

Conclusion

More and more counselors have begun to use the wide-angle lens in their work. The counseling profession has come to accept the idea that advocacy strategies and a social justice perspective belong at the center of good practice. Undoubtedly, however, these changes are easier to think and write about than they are to practice in real life. Like any new paradigm, the advocacy orientation calls on practitioners, educators, and scholars to alter the assumptions that guide their work. Transformational change is always difficult. As then Senator Obama pointed out on February 10, 2007, however, "in the face of impossible odds people who love their country can change it." This idea holds true for the counseling profession as well. People with a deep and abiding commitment to their profession can bring about the kind of change that their students, their clients, and their communities require.

References

Arnold, M. S. (2001). Women of color and feminist family counseling: Caveats. In K. M. May (Ed.), *Feminist family therapy* (pp. 16–27). Alexandria, VA: American Counseling Association.

Hutchins, A. M. (2005). There is an eagle in me: Touching the spirit. In R. K. Conyne & F. Bemak (Eds.), *Journeys to professional excellence: Lessons from leading counselor educators and practitioners* (pp. 101–116). Alexandria, VA: American Counseling Association.

Lewis, J. A. (2007). Challenging sexism: Promoting the rights of women in contemporary society. In C. C. Lee (Ed.), *Counseling for social justice* (2nd ed., pp. 95–110). Alexandria, VA: American Counseling Association.

Lewis, J. A., Lewis, M. D., Daniels, J. A., & D'Andrea, M. J. (1998). *Community counseling* (2nd ed.). Pacific Grove, CA: Brooks/Cole Thomson.

Obama, B. (2007, February 10, 2007). *Senator Barack Obama's announcement for president.* Retrieved March 13, 2009, from http://www.gwu.edu/~action/2008/obama/obama021007sp.html

Toporek, R. L., Lewis, J. A., & Crethar, H. C. (2009). Promoting systemic change through the ACA Advocacy Competencies. *Journal of Counseling & Development, 87,* 260–268.

Appendix
A

American Counseling Association (ACA)
Advocacy Competencies

Commissioned by Dr. Jane Goodman, 2000 ACA President

Advocacy Competencies Taskforce: Dr. Judith A. Lewis, Governors State University (Retired), Dr. Mary Smith Arnold, Governors State University, Dr. Reese M. House, The Education Trust, and Dr. Rebecca L. Toporek, San Francisco State University

Adopted by the ACA Governing Council in March 2003

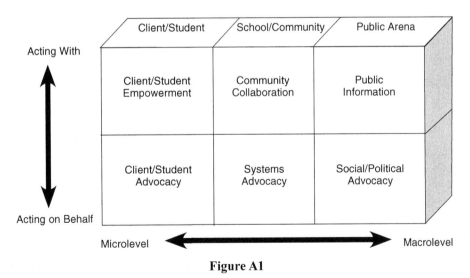

Figure A1

ACA Advocacy Competency Domains

Note. The ACA (American Counseling Association) Advocacy Competencies were endorsed by the ACA Governing Council, March 20–22, 2003. From ACA Advocacy Competencies, by J. A. Lewis, M. S. Arnold, R. House, and R. L. Toporek, 2002. Available at http://www.counseling.org/Publications/. Copyright 2002 by the American Counseling Association. Reprinted with permission.

Advocacy-Related Competencies at the Client/Student Level

Client/Student Empowerment

Conceptualization

An advocacy orientation in counseling involves not only systems change interventions but also the implementation of empowerment strategies in direct counseling with individuals, families, and groups. Advocacy-oriented counselors recognize the impact of social, political, economic, and cultural factors on human development. They also help their clients and students understand their own lives in context. This understanding helps to lay the groundwork for effective self-advocacy.

Counselor Competencies

In direct interventions with clients and students, the advocacy-oriented counselor is able to:

- Identify the strengths and resources that clients/students bring to the counseling process.
- Identify the social, political, economic, and cultural factors that affect the client/student.
- Recognize the signs indicating that an individual's behaviors and concerns reflect responses to systemic or internalized oppression.
- At an appropriate developmental level, help the individual identify the external barriers that affect his or her development.
- Train clients and students in self-advocacy skills.
- Help clients and students develop self-advocacy action plans.
- Assist clients and students in carrying out self-advocacy action plans.

Client/Student Advocacy

Conceptualization

Advocacy is integral to the counseling process. When counselors become aware of external factors that act as barriers to an individual's development, they may choose to respond through advocacy. The client/student advocate role is especially significant when individuals or vulnerable groups lack access to sorely needed services.

Counselor Competencies

In environmental interventions on behalf of clients and students, the advocacy-oriented counselor is able to:

- Negotiate relevant service and education systems on behalf of clients and students.
- Help clients and students gain access to needed resources.
- Identify barriers to the well-being of individuals and vulnerable groups.
- Develop an initial plan of action for confronting these barriers.
- Identify potential allies for confronting the barriers.
- Carry out the plan of action.

Advocacy-Related Competencies at the School/Community Level

Community Collaboration

Conceptualization

Counselors' ongoing work with people gives them a unique awareness of recurring themes. Counselors are often among the first to become aware of specific difficulties in the environment. Advocacy-oriented counselors often choose to respond to such challenges by alerting existing organizations that are already working for change and that might have an interest in the issue at hand. In these situations, the counselor's primary role is as an ally. Counselors can also be helpful to organizations by making their particular skills available to them: interpersonal relations, communications, training, and research.

Counselor Competencies

In support of groups working toward systemic change at the school or community level, the advocacy-oriented counselor is able to:

- Identify environmental factors that impinge on students' and clients' development.
- Alert community or school groups with common concerns related to the issue.
- Develop alliances with groups working for change.
- Use effective listening skills to gain understanding of the group's goals.
- Identify the strengths and resources that the group members bring to the process of systemic change.
- Communicate recognition of and respect for these strengths and resources.
- Identify and offer the skills that the counselor can bring to the collaboration.

Systems Advocacy

Conceptualization

When counselors identify systemic factors that act as barriers to their students' or clients' development, they often wish that they could change the environment and prevent some of the problems that they see every day. Counselors who view themselves as change agents and who understand systemic change principles are able to make this wish a reality. Regardless of the specific target of change, the processes for altering the status quo have common qualities. Change is a process that requires vision, persistence, leadership, collaboration, systems analysis, and strong data. In many situations, a counselor is the right person to take leadership.

Counselor Competencies

In exerting systems-change leadership at the school or community level, the advocacy-oriented counselor is able to:

- Identify environmental factors impinging on students' or clients' development.
- Provide data to show the urgency for change.
- Develop a vision to guide change in collaboration with other stakeholders.
- Analyze the sources of political power and social influence within the system.
- Develop a step-by-step plan for implementing the change process.
- Develop a plan for dealing with probable responses to change.
- Recognize and deal with resistance.

Advocacy-Related Competencies in the Larger Public Arena

Public Information

Conceptualization

Across settings, specialties, and theoretical perspectives, professional counselors share knowledge of human development and expertise in communication. These qualities make it possible for advocacy-oriented counselors to awaken the general public to macrosystemic issues regarding human dignity.

Counselor Competencies

In informing the public about the role of environmental factors in human development, the advocacy-oriented counselor is able to:

- Recognize the impact of oppression and other barriers to healthy development.
- Identify environmental factors that are protective of healthy development.
- Prepare written and multimedia materials that provide clear explanations of the role of specific environmental factors in human development.
- Disseminate information through a variety of media.

Social/Political Advocacy

Conceptualization

Counselors regularly act as change agents in the systems that affect their own students and clients most directly. This experience often leads toward the recognition that some of the concerns they have addressed affect people in a much larger arena. When this happens, counselors use their skills to carry out social/political advocacy.

Counselor Competencies

In influencing public policy in a large, public arena, the advocacy-oriented counselor is able to:

- Distinguish those problems that can best be resolved through social/political action.
- Identify the appropriate mechanisms and avenues for addressing these problems.
- Seek out and join with potential allies.
- Support existing alliances for change.
- With allies, prepare convincing data and rationales for change.
- With allies, lobby legislators and other policymakers.

 **Appendix**

B

Advocacy Competencies Self-Assessment (ACSA) Survey©

Directions: To assess your own competence and effectiveness as a social justice change agent, respond to the following statements as honestly and accurately as possible.

Statements	Almost Always	Sometimes	Almost Never
1. It is difficult for me to identify clients' strengths and resources.			
2. I am comfortable with negotiating for relevant services on behalf of clients/students.			
3. I alert community or school groups with concerns that I become aware of through my work with clients/students.			
4. I use data to demonstrate urgency for systemic change.			
5. I prepare written and multi-media materials that demonstrate how environmental barriers contribute to client/student development.			
6. I distinguish when problems need to be resolved through social advocacy.			
7. It is difficult for me to identify whether social, political, and economic conditions affect client/student development.			
8. I am skilled at helping clients/students gain access to needed resources.			
9. I develop alliances with groups working for social change.			
10. I am able to analyze the sources of political power and social systems that influence client/student development.			
11. I am able to communicate in ways that are ethical and appropriate when publicly taking on issues of oppression.			
12. I seek out and join with potential allies to confront oppression.			
13. I find it difficult to recognize when client/student concerns reflect responses to systemic oppression.			
14. I am able to identify barriers that impede the well-being of individuals and vulnerable groups.			

Statements	Almost Always	Sometimes	Almost Never
15. I identify strengths and resources that community members bring to the process of systems change.			
16. I am comfortable developing an action plan to make systems changes.			
17. I disseminate information about oppression to media outlets.			
18. I support existing alliances and movements for social change.			
19. I help clients/students identify external barriers that affect their development.			
20. I am comfortable with developing a plan of action to confront barriers that impact clients/ students.			
21. I assess my effectiveness when interacting with community and school groups.			
22. I am able to recognize and deal with resistance when involved with systems advocacy.			
23. I am able to identify and collaborate with other professionals who are involved with disseminating public information.			
24. I collaborate with allies in using data to promote social change.			
25. I assist clients/students with developing self-advocacy skills.			
26. I am able to identify allies who can help confront barriers that impact client/student development.			
27. I am comfortable collaborating with groups of varying size and backgrounds to make systems change.			
28. I assess the effectiveness of my advocacy efforts on systems and its constituents.			
29. I assess the influence of my efforts to awaken the general public about oppressive barriers that impact clients/students.			
30. I lobby legislators and policymakers to create social change.			

Directions for scoring: Score numbers 1, 7, and 13 first, and then record the score next to the corresponding number below:

> *Almost Never* = 4 points
> *Sometimes* = 2 points
> *Almost Always* = 0 points

Then score the remaining items by recording the score next to the appropriate number.

> *Almost Always* = 4 points
> *Sometimes* = 2 points
> *Almost Never* = 0 points

Total the number of points earned for each domain. Then add the total scored earned for the 6 domains to find out your advocacy rating scale.

Client/Student Empowerment	Community Collaboration	Public Information
1. _____	3. _____	5. _____
7. _____	9. _____	11. _____
13. _____	15. _____	17. _____
19. _____	21. _____	23. _____
25. _____	27. _____	29. _____
Total _____	Total _____	Total _____

Client/Student Advocacy	Systems Advocacy	Social/Political Advocacy
2. _____	4. _____	6. _____
8. _____	10. _____	12. _____
14. _____	16. _____	18. _____
20. _____	22. _____	24. _____
26. _____	28. _____	30. _____
Total _____	Total _____	Total _____

Advocacy Rating Scale

100–120   You're on the way to becoming a strong and effective social change agent.

70–99   You've got some of the pieces in place. However, you need to do some work to develop your competence in specific advocacy areas in order to be an effective social change agent.

69 & below   If you earn low scores in certain advocacy domains (e.g., client/student empowerment, systems advocacy), obtaining training in these areas can greatly improve your effectiveness as a social justice counseling advocate. If being an advocate at the client/student level is a low area, you can expand your repertoire by familiarizing yourself with feminist counseling principles and multicultural counseling competencies. If, however, low scores are in a majority of domains, you may want to reconsider your commitment to being a social justice advocate.

Note. Advocacy Competencies Self-Assessment Survey, by Manivong J. Ratts and Amy Ford. Reprinted with permission of the authors. Material may not be reproduced for publication purposes without the express permission of the authors.

Index